Date Due

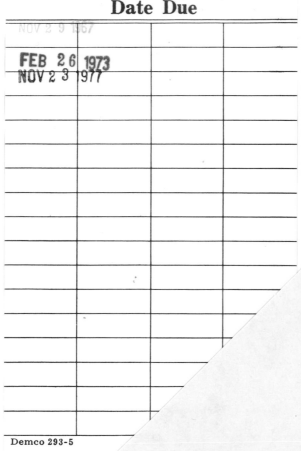

THE SPIRIT OF THE LETTER

Renato Poggioli

THE SPIRIT OF THE LETTER

ESSAYS IN EUROPEAN LITERATURE

HARVARD UNIVERSITY PRESS

Cambridge, Massachusetts

1 9 6 5

CONTENTS

OTHER LITERARY PAPERS

PREFACE

Not one but two distinguished literary careers were cut off in their prime by that brutal highway accident, near the Oregon border of California, which took the life of Renato Poggioli on May 3, 1963, at the beginning of his fifty-seventh year. For his last twenty-five years, he had played a role of increasing prominence as an American scholar-teacher at Smith College, Brown University, and — for nearly seventeen years — Harvard University. During the whole of that period he had continued his previous career as an Italian man of letters: as a translator, chiefly from Russian poetry but also from prose fiction and from numerous other languages, and as a critic, contributing many of his reviews and articles to *Inventario*, the international quarterly that he co-edited with his lifelong friend, Luigi Berti, who survived him by less than ten months. A native of Florence and a doctor of its university, he had rounded out his Slavic studies in Czechoslovakia and had taught Romance Languages at two Polish universities. An outspoken social democrat, who had found it less and less possible to live under Mussolini's Fascism, he ultimately gravitated to the United States, where he served in the army during the war and was naturalized as a citizen in 1950. At Harvard he particularly valued his renewed association with his old teacher, Gaetano Salvemini, the political conscience of the Italian expatriation. Keeping up close European contacts, Poggioli served as visiting professor at the University of Rome and at the Sorbonne, but he remained unshakeable in his commitment to the country of his adoption.

Thus his own wide circuit joined that intellectual diaspora which has so enriched American culture out of Europe's tragedies in our time. In more academic terms, it was his presence, along with that of such friends and fellow emigrés as Leo Spitzer, Erich Auerbach, Pedro Salinas, and René Wellek, which shifted the center of gravity in the field of Comparative Literature. Indeed Poggioli seemed to embody the length and breadth of that field within his person, as a townsman of Dante's whose Latin roots went deep into the Etruscan past, and whose professional interests extended across Europe to new worlds in both directions. The present volume attests this unique perspective by ranging from the *Commedia* to Perse's *Anabase*, and from the medieval epic to the Bolshevik Revolution. The two books published by Poggioli in English during his lifetime dealt respectively with certain modern Russian prose writers (*The Phoenix and the Spider*) and with *The Poets of Russia: 1890–1930*. It was a *tour de force* for him to write so effectively, in another language than his own, about the masterpieces of still a third language; and it is a permanent boon for us to have these solid and penetrating interpretations of a literature too often obscured by foreign ignorance or native prejudice. Moreover, the experience of crossing so many boundaries, national, cultural, and linguistic, gave him a special insight into the dynamic principles of artistic change, experimentation, and development. These principles he sought to formulate in his last book, his major work in Italian, now being translated into English, French, and Spanish, *Teoria dell'arte d'avanguardia*.

Poggioli's increasing concern with world literature and with critical theory would have reached its fruition in a number of projects on which he was working when he died. Some of them were near enough to completion so that they may be published in some form: notably a monumental treatment of the pastoral as a genre and a mode of thought, *The Oaten Flute*; a monograph on the concept of decadence, *The Autumn of Ideas*; and possibly additional manuscripts, all reflecting the scope of his knowledge and the energy of his talents. He had also planned to collect those essays which he had written in English for various occasions and published here and there. He had fully discussed that project with his publisher and had tentatively drawn up several tables of contents. This collection includes all items which, at one time or other, he had seriously considered; in addition, it reprints what may be his latest article, "The Artist in the Modern World," and rescues one of the earliest from the files, "The Death of the Sense of Tragedy." It should be added that he first suggested and then rejected the title of the present volume, presumably remembering that Ortega y Gasset had already used it in Spanish. We found ourselves coming back to it, in spite of Poggioli's compunction, since it seemed to typify both his expression and his approach, without involving a

serious risk of confusion. The Johannine phrase, with its Augus-
tinian gloss, is one of the interpretative keys in his essay on Dante.
It sums up his mastery in extracting the universal from the technical, poetics from metrics, the history of ideas at many periods from
the *explication des textes* in many languages.

Though the draft he left for a prefatory note is incomplete, the
following sentences from it should be transcribed, since they are
still relevant:

> It is apparent that there is no rationale in this volume, or even a pattern:
> in one sense the book is but a collection of random pieces. Yet, except for
> the presence of the opening essay, which appears here for the first time as
> translated from its Italian original, I might perhaps say that I have gathered
> between these covers most of the occasional writings I have composed or
> reworked within an American environment. Whatever their pretext or their
> source, these writings reflect some of the lines of work I have been pursuing
> since the time I chose America as my home, and English as my vehicle.
> This, by the way, is the reason why, despite some revision in matters of de-
> tail and the addition of a few postscripts, none of these pieces has been
> updated.

The grouping and the sequence of these pieces, slightly modified to
fit the enlargement, follow the author's original plan. It may well
have more rationale than, in his modesty, he was ready to claim. For
his colleagues and students a pattern may be implicit in its very
diversity: in the impress of the brilliant pedagogue, the range of
the well-stored mind, the role of scholar's critic and critic's scholar.
Literature was his element, and he viewed it as a continuum. His
subtitle for his first three "readings" frankly presents them as pedagogical demonstrations. It should be noted that he had some hesita-
tion about republishing the opening essay. Recent arguments from
Soviet Russia have again called into question the authenticity of
the Igor Tale. Poggioli's reading, though it accepts the work at face
value, stresses its exceptional character as an epic to an extent which
might undermine its position, if its challengers manage to shift the
burden of evidence. The experts can be trusted to carry on the controversy. Poggioli's commentary on one of the most famous passages
in Dante, the episode of Paolo and Francesca from the *Inferno*,
makes us wish there had been more opportunities for him to comment upon his great compatriot. Yet this is the crucial canto for
readers concerned with the problem of how literature gains its
effects, and the outcome of his philological explication is an im-

portant distinction between two genres. Here, and even more in his discursive reading of Pascal's *Pensées*, we may watch the modern imagination reconstructing a historic viewpoint, while   in the latter instance — demonstrating how there can be a classical style in religion as well as art.

What he envisaged as a "profile" of Tolstoy, perhaps the best-rounded of Poggioli's many returns to a favorite author, he placed at the intersection between his classics and his moderns, the second and largest group. Though the Russians always figure refreshingly in his frame of reference, the emphasis falls upon the Italians in these critiques. Into a popular article explaining the wave of the Neo-Realists, he all but condenses a cultural history of Italy since De Sanctis. His appraisals revive the spirit of the latter, rather than continuing the tradition of Croce, and it is not surprising that he prefers the irony of Svevo to the afflatus of D'Annunzio. Of the gifted and short-lived Leo Ferrero and his anti-Fascist dramatic satire, *Angelica*, Poggioli speaks in a prize-winning essay, written with the admiring affection of a friend and contemporary. On the other hand, though he once acted as Pirandello's guide on a visit to Prague, it is with an appropriate detachment that he appraises that master of the problematic. Yet it is through his personal recollections of the German-Jewish-Bohemian capital that he vividly conjures up the restless shade of Kafka. And he brings a poignant awareness to bear upon the spiritual exile of writers who have been caught between cultures, as it were: Kafka, Svevo, Perse. This is particularly evident in his capacity for scanning the remote horizons opened up by the exploratory French poet. The consideration of Trotsky departs, as its subject does, from the terrain of letters altogether; but, in following the intellectual into the sphere of action, it applies social and moral criteria which are never far beneath the surface of Poggioli's criticism; and an earlier paper rounds the cycle by proposing Trotsky's fall as a tragic theme.

The essay on the death of tragedy is virtually the outline for a book, and that may be why Poggioli did not plan to reprint it. Yet it deserves a second hearing, if only because its notions have lately been in the air. More rigorous is the later attempt to derive a critical method from a given sociological doctrine, that of Pareto, with sidelights on Taine, Marx, and Freud. More characteristically, Poggioli is his own sociologist when he considers the status of the artist, with that comprehension of masks and movements which informs his book on the avant-garde. These five papers, making up the last section, are addressed to theoretical problems; but theory is never divorced from practice; and "unwritten poetics" are generated from a discussion of prosody. Finally we hear Poggioli discussing, with the authority of his accomplishment, "that most vexing of all literary questions," as he construed it, "what a translator does, or a translation is." We hear him, I have said; for despite its rhetorical suspensions and dialectical qualifications, his discourse has the tone of a natural speaker, an eloquent teacher, a memorable conversationalist. English was perhaps the tenth of his languages, and he was over thirty when it became his principal medium. He wrote it, as he spoke it, with polyglot verve and epigrammatic flair, using learned allusion as freely as casual slang, and tempering his formulations with humor. Though he had received and acknowledged help, he gradually achieved a style that was too much his own to be tamed by copyediting. We should have had to apologize for trying to reduce it to conformity; for letting it stand — except for routine corrections — and bespeak the man, we make no apology.

HARRY LEVIN

Cambridge, Massachusetts
21 September 1964

NEW READINGS OF OLD TEXTS

THE IGOR TALE

1. History of the text. Fortunes of the work

In 1185 Prince Igor, a descendant of Rurik the Norman conqueror, and lord of the little Russian principality of Novgorod-Seversk, led a small band of warriors in a rash expedition against an old enemy of Kievan Russia, the nomadic nation of the Kumans.[1] Defeated on the field of battle, he fell into the hands of the enemy, but succeeded in escaping from captivity and returning safely to his own people. This is the story as told in the ancient Russian Chronicle that takes its name from the monastery of Saint Hipatius (*Ipatievskaya Letopis*). The Chronicle relates also that Igor signed a peace treaty after the rout, and that he sealed the peace by marrying his heir, Vladimir, to the daughter of one of the enemy leaders. It was possibly on the occasion of such a wedding that an anonymous poet, probably a layman of Igor's court, obviously endowed with great literary learning and inspired by strong patriotic feelings, composed an epic in rhythmical prose which the later tradition entitled (in modernized form) *Slovo o polku Igoreve*, and which we know in English as the Igor Tale.[2]

This work is the greatest poetic monument Kievan Russia has handed on to us through the ages, and it is a magnificent testimony to the splendor of its culture. But the civilization of Kievan Russia was destined to vanish with the Tatar invasion, bequeathing its legacy to a Russia less splendid and less cultured, that of Moscow. It was in Muscovite Russia that an unknown sixteenth-century scribe, perhaps connected with one of the Pskov monasteries, transcribed the Igor Tale in a manuscript that contained other secular writings, including a Russian version of the ancient Byzantine epic, *Digenis Akritas*. In 1795, in what we might call the Russia of Petersburg, the manuscript fell into the hands of Count A. Musin-Pushkin, a lover of Russian antiquities. The *Slovo* was published for the first time in 1800 in an edition prepared by Musin-Pushkin, A. F. Malinovski, and N. Bantysh-Kamenski. Count Musin-Pushkin's library was lost in the fire of Moscow and the manuscript perished in the flames. The first edition, very few copies of which have been preserved, would have remained our only authority for the text of the Igor Tale had not another copy of the manuscript, made in 1796 by order of Catherine the Great, been unearthed in the imperial archives toward the middle of the past century.

The short-lived history of the manuscript, from its belated appearance in a single codex to the early destruction of the same, two events which coincided by chance with the Ossianic vogue, was bound to suggest sooner or later that the *Slovo* might be a spurious work like that of MacPherson. Such a suspicion was unintentionally implied by an anonymous note that appeared in 1797 in *Le Spectateur du Nord*, issued in Hamburg. The note was penned by N. K. Karamzin. After announcing to the scholarly world the discovery of the manuscript, the future historian remarked that this "fragment," as he called it, was worthy of being placed "à côté des plus beaux morceaux d'Ossian." Inasmuch as Karamzin never doubted either the worth or the antiquity of the Ossianic poems, the hypothesis that the Igor Tale was a literary mystification was to be made only later, and by others: it was advanced for the first time in 1812, with great emphasis but with little authority, by two Russian erudites now forgotten, Kachenovski and Rumyantsev. But with the passing of time, the notion of the spuriousness of the *Slovo* became less convincing, especially since 1839, after the recovery and publication in that year of another ancient epic composition in prose. That composition, the *Zadonshchina*, or Tale from Beyond the Don, which celebrated the victory of the Russians over the Tatars in the battle of Kulikovo (1380), could be dated back only as far as the late fourteenth century: yet modern criticism interprets it as deliberate palinode to the *Slovo*, as a triumphal reply, uttered more than two centuries later, to the defeat sung in the Igor Tale, which the unknown author of the *Zadonshchina* had seemingly taken as the precedent of his own work and as its model.

In any event, what became immediately evident was that the *Zadonshchina* was at least in part a verbal imitation of the Igor Tale. It was on the basis of this evidence, which seemed to settle the matter, that the Russian philological school was able, especially during the second half of the nineteenth century, to devote itself freely to the scientific study of the *Slovo*, and to produce among other things an extensive series of editions and commentaries which have continued almost without interruption up to the present day. The constant progress of this research, which had been helped also by the contributions of many scholars outside Russia, was unexpectedly halted when the French specialist André Mazon, professor at the Collège de France, brought back the theory that the *Slovo* was a literary mystification, a theory that seemed discredited and rejected forever. From 1938 to 1944 Professor Mazon produced a series of studies which he reprinted together in a volume entitled *Le Slovo d'Igor* (Paris 1940), with the professed intent of demonstrating without a trace of doubt that the Igor Tale was a forgery of the late eighteenth century. Mazon maintained in his writings that the would-be forger (whom he went so far as to identify as the archivist Bantysh-Kamenski, one of the compilers of the *editio princeps*), had made use not only of such a belated production as the *Russian History* of the seventeenth-century writer Tatishchev but also of that very Hipathian Chronicle which up to that time scholarship had considered, if not a source of the *Slovo*, certainly a parallel historical document. As for the style of the forgery, Mazon claimed that the author of the false Igor Tale had modeled his work at one side on the Ossianic poems, and, at the other, on the *Zadonshchina* itself, thus reversing the theory according to which the latter had been written on the pattern of the *Slovo*.

Mazon's assertions immediately provoked a lively and angry controversy, which succeeded in weakening the French scholar's position and in placing many of his arguments in doubt. But the tide was to be turned only a few years later. A group of European scholars, working in the United States under the leadership of the Russian emigré philologist Roman Jakobson, prepared an imposing volume, *La Geste du Prince Igor*, which they issued in New York in 1948.[3] This work immediately won the enthusiastic approval of the specialists. The main contributions were made by Jakobson himself, who published in that volume a new text of the *Slovo*, the only one which now seems almost definitive.[4] Jakobson's critical edition is full of brilliant readings and luminous emendations, and resolves for the first time the most vexing questions still left open by the textual tradition of the Igor Tale. The same scholar provided a long and exhaustive study in which he demolished Mazon's theses one by one and triumphantly reaffirmed the authenticity of the *Slovo*, which at least for a while the French scholar had put in doubt. Jakobson proved his point on linguistic and literary grounds, as well as on archeological, historical, ethnographic, and mythological ones. Here and there he used effectively also arguments *ad absurdum* and *ad hominem*. By suggesting that no modern philologist would have been able to produce such a forgery, Jakobson demonstrated *a fortiori* that no Russian erudite could have even tried to accomplish such a feat in the late eighteenth century, when the science of Slavic philology was still in its infancy.

The pioneering labors of Jakobson produced a rich and varied crop of writings about and around the *Slovo*, including a new series of translations,[5] and it is on the foundations of these studies that any critical reinterpretation of the Igor Tale (like the one attempted in the pages that follow) has been made feasible, or at least possible.

II. *Epos versus history. The contrast with Boyan*

The first question to be asked by any student of the *Slovo* is how to place its anonymous author within history and time. Actually the question quite simply answers itself: there is enough internal evidence to prove that the work was undoubtedly composed by an eyewitness, if not by one of the actors of the events it retells. As for the external evidence, it comes to us from the Hipatian Chronicle, which gives historical authority to the narrative, the more so since it seems to have been written shortly afterward, but without apparent knowledge of the *Slovo*'s report of the same facts. The comparison between these two reports, one poetic, the other historical, confirms the authenticity and the validity of the *Slovo*'s testimony also in matters of detail, to a point which leads one to infer that the author must have actually taken part, at least as a follower, in Igor's campaign. It would not be an exaggeration even to reverse the usual argument, and to maintain that it is the *Slovo* which confirms the historical report of Igor's exploit in the Chronicle version: and that it does so not merely because of its temporal precedence, but also because of the effect of authenticity produced by the poet's account. There is, for instance, no better proof of the *Slovo*'s exactitude than the perfect chronological sequence whereby the various phases of the campaign are marked by datings which are often indirect but always precise, starting with the first of the three decisive days, identified by its name within the week: "early on Friday" (37).[6]

The first paradox of this epic is the evocation of a historic fact belonging to a past which is recent rather than remote. And if it is true, as it has been claimed, that the *Slovo* was written and recited two years after the event, on the occasion of the marriage of the son of Igor, which coincided with the latter's return from captivity, as the happy outcome of an unhappy undertaking, then we may say without fear of error that the past events which are the *Slovo's* subject belong to the historical present. Such contemporaneity of historical experience and of poetic inspiration is exceptional in the history of epic literature, or at least in most of its surviving monuments. It is only met with in the heroic poetry of the Serbs or in some of the later Russian *byliny*, where, however, the historical experience becomes almost unrecognizable. As for the great epic poems of the classical world, there is no doubt that the heroic events they celebrate are centuries distant in time, while for the medieval epics the interval must be measured at least by several generations. Thus, for example, the *Chanson de Roland*, which was composed less than a hundred years before the *Slovo*, is more than three centuries removed from the defeat at Roncevaux, and the *Poema de mio Cid*, which precedes the *Slovo* by more than half a century, is separated from the death of the Campeador by the same lapse of time.

If Mnemosyne is the true muse of epic poetry, then it must be said that the *Slovo* was dictated by a memory which was individual and direct, whereas most of the other epics were dictated by a memory which was indirect and collective. In other words, what occurs in the *Slovo* is that a historical recollection, immediate and still alive, transmits at once the legendary traditions of times gone by. Yet history, refusing to be turned into a mere fable, re-emerges almost unchanged while transcending itself into epic representation and heroic vision. The extraordinary quality of all this will become even more evident if we recall that the story was known in all its particulars not only to the poet, but also to his listeners, who must have taken part, either as actors or as spectators, in Igor's undertaking.

What is even more extraordinary is that the poet is clearly aware of this particular feature of his own work. He thus establishes from the very opening a distinction between himself as a poet "of these times" (2) and the legendary Boyan, "nightingale of the times of old" (14). Such an opposition may be understood not as a contrast between two historical epochs different in spirit and temper, but as an antithesis between a legendary era and a historical one. Since the antithesis is made in terms of two kinds of poets and poetry, it may be translated on the plane of aesthetic psychology into a contrast between imagination and memory or, as the poet himself says, between the actual events ("happenings of these times") he reports and the artful fancies ("contriving") of Boyan (2). Thus, at least in intention, the poet would seem to deny himself that fabulous evocation and legendary transfiguration of the narrated events which is the aim of every genuine epic inspiration. But in reality such is not the effect of the work, much less its intention.

The complex and apparently contradictory attitude of the author toward his mythical predecessor and his own creation by no means implies that he intended to compose a historical work, while Boyan had intended to compose a purely poetic one. What such an attitude implies is rather the awareness on the part of the author of the *Slovo* that the time has finally come for a new kind of epic poetry: for a kind of epic poetry more suitable to an epoch which could be defined, in terms of Vico's cyclical theory, as more of an "age of man" than an "age of the gods." It is such a view that, notwithstanding the poet's sharp distinction between past and present or between history and legend, ultimately helps the author of the *Slovo* in bringing together the various contrasting elements to form a harmonious and organic creation. This means that he succeeded in evoking, with the proper poetic distance, a chronicle of current events.

It is in this, and in no other sense, that the poet seems to be conscious of the originality of his own work, a consciousness which is neither negated nor impaired by the fact that the opposition between his own method and the manner of Boyan is essentially a literary device, a formal convention, a poetic reminiscence. In fact, as Roman Jakobson has shown, the entire proem of the *Slovo* is an imitation, not only in the general phraseology, but even *in ipsis verbis*, of the preamble to an account of the Trojan War which can be read in the Chronicle by Constantine Manasses, a Byzantine writer of the first half of the twelfth century. The author of that preamble contrasts his own "true" stories to the poetic fables of Homer, whereas the poet of the *Slovo* substitutes the wizard ("vatic") Boyan for the Homer of his model (3). And to Boyan he attributes the very gifts of prophecy and magic that the Byzantine and medieval Latin traditions attributed respectively to Homer and Virgil.

The poet of the *Slovo* seems to realize the diversity of his own work not only from the standpoint of the novelty of its attitude and content, but also, paradoxically, from the standpoint of its stylistic archaism. In this respect he knows himself to be indebted to the tradition established by the ancient Boyan, even though he hardly mentions this fact. It is only by keeping this in mind that the reader can understand the rhetorical question that opens the *Slovo*, the aim of which is to anticipate and offset the objections of anyone wanting to call into question the appropriateness or the convenience of an archaic style ("the diction of yore") for a work of this kind: or of the very fact that it resumes and revives the ancient manner of speech marking the heroic songs which had preceded it. In the lines that follow the opening question (2–6) the poet seems, however, to react against some of the surviving conventions of the archaic heroic style, as if the metaphorical and mythical idiom had lost all prestige for him. It is the obvious duty of any critical inquiry to find the rationale of all these contradictions, and to reconcile them.

III. *Written and oral tradition. Verse or prose?*

Such contradictions are due to the complicated relationship of the *Slovo* to the main traditions of its poet's culture, which are on one side heroic poetry, which coincides with oral literature (*slovesnost, ustnaya slovesnost*), and on the other historical or religious prose, which coincides with written literature (*pismennost*). The *Slovo* differs from the first of these traditions through the radical antithesis of the technique of written composition and the methods of oral creation. There is no doubt that the *Slovo* is not only a written work, but that it is exquisitely literary. This is indirectly and partially proven by the fact that it was handed down in written form, even though it reached us only through single and rather late manuscript; and that no parts or fragments of it have come to us through oral transmission. Even from this standpoint, the *Slovo* must be considered a product of *Kunstdichtung* in the simple as well as in the complex sense of this expression. This is not to say that oral poetry, to which the *Slovo* is both related and opposed, and which by taking other forms will even survive it, was in its time, despite its ethnographic roots, a product of *Volksdichtung* in the narrow sense of the term. Almost all recent scholars think that the oral poetry which preceded the *Slovo* must have been the slow and mature fruit of a secular tradition handed down from master to disciple through generations of professional singers. The essential difference, then, is that the *Slovo* is the expression of a cultural situation more advanced and complex, as well as subtler and richer: one that differs more in degree than in essence from the poetic culture that preceded it.

This is why, notwithstanding all his declarations to the contrary, the poet of the *Slovo* ends by taking toward the old heroic poetry represented by Boyan the attitude of an unavowed disciple. One of the paradoxes of the *Slovo* is indeed that of being a written work that up to a point was led to follow the methods of oral poetry, as may be seen for example in the constant use of the vocative "brothers," by which the poet means the comrades at arms of his *druzhina* or guard, which is proper only if addressed to an audience of listeners rather than to a reading public (1, 5, 6, 56, 84). The fitness of the example cannot be denied even by considering that the spoken tone of the work might partly derive from the oratorical conventions of any sermon or *slovo*. At any rate, only a deliberate repatterning after the models of oral poetry can explain why the poet feels obliged to cite Boyan and to evoke in the climaxes of the story the proverbs and oracles attributed to his fabulous predecessor (146, 163, 201); or why he imitates the magniloquent, metaphorical, and imaginative language of the latter. To prove this point it may suffice to mention the passage where the poet feigns to feel defeated in a kind of ideal competition with the forgotten master (14), introducing two preludes which he pretends are not his own, the one supposed to represent the manner of Boyan (17–18), and the other that of a presumed disciple (15–16).

But the *Slovo*, though very literary, is distinguished even more sharply from the written literature of its age. Whereas *slovesnost*

was secular and profane in inspiration, cultivating as its only genres
the epic and the lyrical, and making use of popular speech, or at
least of a language which was neither erudite nor learned, the
pismennost, moralistic and religious in inspiration, developed
preferably the edifying genres of the sermon and the treatise, using
as its unique vehicle a prose overburdened by the artificial diction
of the liturgical tongue. Yet, while his work seems far more alien
to this tradition than to the folk poetry of the former heroic culture,
the poet of the *Slovo*, who was certainly a man of letters, under-
went in his turn the influence of a bookish culture.

The very fact that it was the product of written composition,
affected in other ways by its relationship with a bookish culture,
resolves the problem of whether the structure of the *Slovo* is metrical or not. Being a *slovo*, it belongs to *pismennost*: it could not
have been composed except in *sermo solutus*. This is now the opinion of most scholars, who consider all the metrical reconstructions
tried up to now as groundless. We do not know, however, whether
the *Slovo* was intended to be sung from its written text, with or
without the accompaniment of music. What seems certain is that
it was meant to be recited, in a scanned and modulated reading
voice, as if it were a "prose" in the medieval sense of the term. The
individual units or phrases may sound to the ear of the modern
reader like Biblical versicles, even though endowed with a clearer
rhythmical ring. During moments of epic emphasis or of lyrical
ecstasy, the *Slovo* gives the illusion of song. There is no doubt that
such passages re-echo Russian popular poetry, which, in the later
forms we are acquainted with, follow the accentuative system, in
patterns that seem to anticipate some of the more melodic variants
of modern free verse.

It is perhaps because of this wavering between the opposite
poles of the *cursus* of prose and the rhythm of verse that the poet
gives his own work the different names of *povest* or "tale" (1, 6)
and of *pesn* or "song" (2, 15). It is probably also in the terms of
this ambiguity or polyvalence that he opposes his own conception
of poetry to that of Boyan. As the etymological tie between the
Latin *carmen* and the French *charme* easily shows, all ancient and
primitive cultures consider poetry an incantation, and view the
vehicle of such magic power in the main poetic instrument, which

is rhythm itself. The author of the *Slovo* is obviously acquainted with this notion, which, however, he attributes to Boyan and treats not without an indulgent irony. Thus, for example, in the famous opening passage he pretends to take seriously the legendary wonderworking of Boyan (3–4), only to reduce it afterwards to purely verbal and magic portents. But these in their turn are literally described, in a most beautiful image, as that specialized witchcraft which consists of the dominion of the spirit over the technique and the instruments of art, by themselves deaf and dumb: hence the pathetic metaphor of the live strings that "twanged out by themselves" a praise to the princes (5). In this regard the author of the *Slovo* seems to be acquainted with the ancient fable of Orpheus, which attributes to the poet the power of taming and soothing the brutes, as shown by his comparison between poetry and the art of falconry (4), as well as the power to give life and the faculty of speech to inanimate things, as shown in the image of the quivering and singing strings. But the author reveals an understanding of the Orphic myth in a sense quite different from the literal. As a man no longer primitive, he knows that poetic sorcery is an incantation not of things but of words: yet he seems to imply that this makes it not a lesser but a greater wonder.

All this suggests that the *Slovo* operates at once both within and outside the framework of tradition. This is not rare in great poetry. What this means in the case at hand is that the difference between an oral and a literary epic is cultural and technical, rather than aesthetic and formal: and that the interval between a spontaneous epic and a literary one can be overcome by a smooth transition. In other terms, it shows that in moments of particularly creative bliss it is not impossible to reconcile in a new synthesis these opposing extremes, in the recurring cycles of the history of poetry, which are conventionally called primitivistic and Alexandrian. Such reconciliations, though always rare, took place frequently in the very age which Vico designated as *barbarie ricorsa*, that is, the Middle Ages. It is perhaps more than a mere coincidence, as has already been observed, that the plant of the *Slovo* grew in the Byzantine garden of Kievan Russia just when the arts and the letters of the West were blooming anew: at the very moment to which an American historian gave the glorious name of "the Renaissance of the Twelfth Century."

IV. *Heroic poetry and the feudal order. Epics and the theme of love. The national spirit and the epos of reconquest*

Like all heroic poetry, of any age or land, the *Slovo* is based on an aristocratic conception of the social order and of life itself. Though the author takes a stand of opposition toward the figure of his legendary forerunner, he still acts as a court bard, no less than Boyan or the type that Boyan represents, as we see in the work's valediction (215–218). He thus plays the same role as any member of the school of professional singers who preceded him, and whose traditions he must have embodied, at least in part. That such a school did really exist is no longer seriously doubted. And since the Russian princes were of Scandinavian origin, descending from the Norman stock of the Varangians, that school of singers must have been related to the poetry of the Scalds, as can be proved by the stylistic archaisms of the *Slovo*, in which we encounter in petrified form those stereotyped formulae or metaphorical periphrases replacing the names of the objects they refer to, and which in Scaldic poetry are given the name of *kenningar* (*kenning* in the singular).

Rich as it is with a broad and deep sense of real life, the *Slovo*, like Scaldic poetry, shows no interest or liking but for the moral and social values of the military caste, which was after all the ruling and dominant class. Thus, for example, the work abounds in references to valuable objects and rare commodities, like that booty of "gold, and brocades, and precious samites" which the Russians seize in the tents abandoned by the Kumans (37); or in frequent allusions to gold in the form not only of ingots or jewelry but of coins as well: yet, in spite of all this wealth, there never appears the figure of a single merchant. Likewise the poet often speaks of the various objects produced by the skilled and laborious hands of armorers (135) and goldsmiths (147), but without ever once mentioning the trade of a single artisan. We meet frequent allusions to country life and agriculture, as well as to sowing and reaping (157): yet we do not see any peasant, except in the collective vision of the plowmen stunned by the fratricidal wars that since the time of Oleg have turned Russia into a wasteland (65). In brief, all the *Slovo*'s characters, even the minor and nameless ones, are princes, boyars (XIV), and knights, all belonging to the nobility by right of blood or office, because they wield the sword and own the land. From this standpoint the *Slovo* differs considerably from the popular *byliny* that celebrate the merchant and the sailor in *Sadko*, and raise to heroic stature the peasant Mikula Selyaninovich.

The warrior class is not only the ideal object or subject, but also the natural audience of this kind of poetry. As in the case of the Scandinavian Scalds, this anonymous Russian poet of the twelfth century addresses himself to a public as limited as it is compact, since it coincides with the retinue of his own lord: a retinue made more of warriors than of courtiers, practically identical with the *druzhina* of the prince, with the men who are his table-companions, his blood-brothers in hunt and war, as the poet often directly hints (110, 218). In such a circle the prince is little more than *primus inter pares*, according to the rule of the Round Table; yet this does not mean that in the case of the Russian and Scandinavian lords the tie should be understood as chivalric in the Western sense of the word. The old aristocracy of Kievan Russia was a society of the heroic type, if not barbaric, intent upon conquest and plunder, inclined to raids and adventures, and as such they were aliens to the ethical ideas of medieval Western nobility, from vassalage to courtesy.

To prove this it will suffice to show how the poet of the *Slovo* treats the theme of love. He treats this theme in a manner totally different from that of the romances of chivalry, and also from that of the epic poems of France and Spain. In the latter, love appears only as a family tie or conjugal bond, as in the *Poema de mio Cid*, in which the only female characters are the wife and the daughters of the protagonist. In the *Chanson de Roland* there are only two women, and we see them all too briefly. One is the hero's chaste fiancée, Aude the Beautiful, who appears only to lament for the untimely end of Roland, in a complaint uttered in a scene of some thirty lines, which stands in sharp contrast to the far longer lamentation of Yaroslavna in the much shorter *Slovo* (XXVI). The other female figure, also the only wife to appear in the *Chanson de Roland*, is the pagan queen Bramimonde, widow of the Saracen king Marsilius, whose destiny is not the shameful and painful slavery of an Andromache, but peace of the soul, since she is converted to the religion of the victors and takes the veil of a nun.

Thus the *Slovo* does not seem to share that Christian ethos which marks the *Poema de mio Cid* and the *Chanson de Roland*, and contrasts them with the barbaric epics of the Germanic world. The attitude of the *Slovo* toward woman and love reminds us more of the Homeric poems, where there is place for the slave and the concubine beside the young bride and the loyal wife. To prove this point it will suffice to recall on the one hand that cynical and vividly realistic scene in the *Slovo* where the Kuman maidens are abducted as booty, just like the precious goods seized from the enemy (37), in a scene which has no parallel except perhaps in *Digenis Akritas*; and on the other, the tender passages by which the poet evokes the fidelity and devotion of the spouses of the warring princes, the wives of Vsevolod (56) and Igor (XXVI).

If the *Slovo* seems unaffected by the moderating influence of the Christian ethos, it seems equally indifferent to Christian-national pathos in its conception of war. Yet, like the Byzantine *Digenis Akritas* (in which the very surname of the hero indicates the duty of guardian of the border); like the *Poema de mio Cid*; or better still, like those epic-lyric compositions which in English and Spanish take on the names of *border ballads* and *romances fronterizos*, the *Slovo* is an epic of reconquest. This is easily proved from internal evidence, since Igor repeatedly declares to his companions from the very beginning of the *Slovo* that the aim of their undertaking is to "take a look at the blue Don" (11) or to "drink a helmetful of the Don" (13). This means, as George Vernadsky has remarked, that the political and military intent of Igor's enterprise was to reopen the great river route to the South, as far as the Black Sea. In another passage, precisely in the boyars' speech, the campaign and its objectives, one a major and the other a minor one, are likened to the unsuccessful flight of two falcons who had set off "in quest of the town of Tmutorokan — or at least to drink a helmetful of the Don" (102). The maximum limit of Igor's ambition was then to include in his domains this remote city, which formerly had been part of his ancestors' domain up to the time when Oleg abandoned that outpost, or, as the poet says, "he set foot in the golden stirrup in the town of Tmutorokan" (59) to go back to the North, where he "forged feuds with the sword" (58) in an attempt to conquer the central principalities and to seize the hegemony of all the Russian lands. This implies that Igor's war of reconquest is conceived not only as a patriotic duty, but also as a dynastic necessity. When Igor starts to retrace in the opposite direction his grandfather's footsteps, he seeks to redeem a fief as well as a marque. The spirit of his enterprise is, then, not that of a national and religious undertaking, of a crusade or holy war, of *gesta Dei per Russos*.

It is true that the Kumans, like the Saracens of the Carolingian cycle, are here constantly called "pagans" in the sense of unbelievers. It is also true that the poet once addresses the "pagan Kuman" with the formula "black raven" (41), which recalls the similar formula, "infidel dogs," by which the paladins refer to the Moorish warriors, when challenging them to personal duels, in the Italian chivalric romances. Actually the *Slovo's* appellation for the enemy differs little from the Greek designations of all aliens as barbarians. It is evident that the author of the *Slovo* considers the Kumans barbarians in a similar sense, as shown by the way in which he continuously compares and contrasts the martial behavior of the Russians with the military conduct of the nomads. So, for instance, while the former await the attack in silence, the latter move in to assault them with stentorian cries (52), a custom which the poet attributes also to the Turkish mercenaries in the Russians' service (115). In other words, "pagan" is in the *Slovo* little more than a synonym for "foreigner" or "enemy": its poet opposes the Kumans with the "sons of Russia" rather than with the "Christians." As a matter of fact, the word "Christian" never appears in the text. From this standpoint the Lithuanians (who up to that time had not yet been converted to Christianity) do not differ in any sense from the other enemies of the South and East, except that they threaten Russia from another side and that at this moment they are inactive. Whereas the Kumans are once called "fiends," or "Fiend's sons" (52), the Russians on the other hand are never treated as chosen children of the one and true God, but rather as the "sons of Dazhbog (64, 76), that is, as the offspring of an ancient god of the pagan Slavs. But it would be wrong to attach excessive importance to a formula such as this, since it is merely a conventional metaphor, a traditional *kenning*.

In conclusion, the relationship between believers and infidels which obtains in the *Slovo* differs little from that between Christians and Turks as treated in Serbian epics, especially in the Marko Kraljević cycle, or from that between Arabs and Byzantines in

Digenis Akritas. The contest is between two neighboring peoples rather than between two opposing creeds. The proximity of two populations determines two equal and contrary necessities, now hostility, now coexistence. The enemy may even be viewed as a neighbor and relative to whom one is bound by ties of blood, in peace as well as in war. As in the case of the Greek hero Digenis, whose name means "of two races," enemy or infidel blood runs through the veins of the Christian warriors. We learn that Igor was born of a Kuman mother, and that the Kuman Vlur, who delivers him from captivity, is the son of a Russian mother. The poet of the *Slovo* does not emphasize these facts; yet in a famous passage he designates the enemy with the epithet "in-laws," which can also have the meaning of "wedding guests" (73), an expression that would have sounded false and blasphemous to the ears of a Western contemporary of the author's, even if understood merely as a figurative term.

Yet that very term may well allude to the frequent matrimonial alliances which bound the families of the Russian princes to the Kuman khans. As a matter of fact, it is with just such a reference to another of these alliances that the *Slovo* ends. The reference itself enhances the uniqueness of the *Slovo's* finale, which, as we shall see, has no equivalent in the epic literature of medieval Christianity. In this finale, the marriage between the son of Igor and the daughter of Konchak, the foremost of the enemy leaders, is announced, or rather, hinted at, as a future event, which will follow at some distance in time the outcome of the tale, that is, the return of Igor. It is possible that the poet and his audience looked at the wedding between the Igorevich and the Konchakovna as the result of abduction or as the fruit of an act of seduction — an erotic motive exploited in the nineteenth-century opera which Borodin composed after the *Slovo*, entitled *Prince Igor*. Such a circumstance might explain how and why the allusions to such a wedding, the celebration of which was seemingly the very occasion of the composition, are so rare and brief, so evasive and elusive. It is perhaps the silent suggestion of such a fact that makes even more comic the dialogue between the father of the girl and the other Kuman leader (XXIV), especially Gza's anticlimactic remark, "if we entoil him by means of a fair maiden" (208), which seems to confirm the hypothesis suggested above.

It is from this view of the enemy as a close relative that the author of the *Slovo* looks at war, an outlook that finds magnificent expression in the epic metaphors by which the poet compares the battle to a banquet (72–73) and to a wedding (144). The image of the bloody encounter of war as a wedding seems to confirm the conjecture that the word *druzhina* also had the meaning of "wife," "companion," and "friend," as it seems suggested in one of Boyan's oracles (146). On the other hand, the singular duels between heroes and knights which abound in the chivalric romances are replaced by the slaughter of anonymous victims, by mass murders and merciless exterminations (54, 127, 144); hence the vision of the battlefield as a plowed ground "sown with bones and irrigated with gore" (67); hence the splendid simile likening martial operations to the work of threshing and winnowing (157).

v . *The epos of defeat and the romance of flight. Christianity, paganism, and the treatment of myth*

If the *Slovo* is an epos of reconquest, like the *Poema de mio Cid*, it is also, like the *Chanson de Roland*, an epos of defeat, which it contemplates in a spirit of serenity, free from any rancor or fanaticism. The poet does not feel the need to evoke in its turn, like the author of the *Chanson*, the *revanche* which will follow the rout. Such a serenity was possible only to a heroic, rather than purely epic, inspiration, though even here the theme of defeat is dictated not so much by a sense of patient suffering of the destinies of war as by the muse of pride and hope, certain of a not too distant upturn. For this very reason the poet was naturally led to exaggerate the importance of the undertaking and the gravity of the rout, which after all involved only a handful of men, even though, probably because it was a historic event still fresh and alive in everyone's memory, he avoided magnifying it out of all proportion as did the author of the *Chanson de Roland* in regard to the engagement lost by Charlemagne's rear guard at Roncevaux.

The similarities and differences between the *Chanson de Roland* and the *Slovo* are not limited, however, to the common theme of defeat. Another similarity is that the heroes of both epics are in part responsible for the defeat itself. Roland refuses to listen to the voice of reason when the cautious Olivier tells him to blow the horn and call for help from the main body of the Franks, so as to avoid being cut to pieces by the Saracen army in the pass of Ronce-vaux. In a similar manner, Igor launches his expedition without adequate preparations or proper aid, and refuses to withdraw, not only in the face of evil omens, but even when seeing himself assaulted by overwhelming forces, simply because he and his brother want to "be heroes on their own" and to win for themselves an unrivaled glory, even at the cost of their lives (116). But the similarities end here, for, whereas Igor acts like Roland, Vsevolod, who is ready to sacrifice himself like Olivier, not only fails to dissuade his brother from a hopeless enterprise; he even incites him with foolhardy audacity to adventure and risk (IV).

Several critics have compared the *Chanson de Roland* to a Greek tragedy. The protagonist, just like a tragic hero, is the victim of a weakness or folly (*desmesure*) acting as the nemesis of his character, and thus becoming his destiny. In Christian terms one could say that he commits a sin of pride and is punished for it. But the hero of the *Slovo* escapes all retribution in spite of his *hubris* or *hamartia*: Igor does not pay the penalty for his own crime or suffer the consequences of his own error. This very fact deprives the *Slovo* of tragic pathos; and it may even check the heroic sweep of its inspiration. The return home of the embattled and defeated warrior is an ending less than heroic, especially when we consider that he returns as a fugitive, if not from the field of battle, at least from the enemy camp.

Whereas the *Chanson de Roland* ends in the death of the hero and of all his companions in a hecatomb that is also a deliberate self-sacrifice, the *Slovo* ends with the flight of the protagonist, who survives not only the public shame of defeat but also the private shame of imprisonment, even though he had in the beginning declared to his men that "it is better . . . to be slain than to be enslaved" (10). The *Slovo* is perhaps the only epic in which the hero is not only defeated but made a prisoner, and wins praise for acting more like a fox than like a lion, outsmarting the enemy whom he had failed to conquer. The poet actually celebrates the escape of Igor as though it were a victory, as he does in the words which he has the river Donets say: "not small is your triumph" (193), as well as in the triumphal song which closes the work (XXX).

A case of this kind is indeed more unique than rare in the annals of epic poetry. In *Rabinal*, a heroic drama of the Quiché, a tribe of Guatemala Indians, the hero is conquered and made prisoner. But the protagonist represents the enemy tribe of Rabinal, while the Quiché are represented in the person of the antagonist. The drama ends at any rate with a feigned duel, which is in reality an execution, and with the immolation of the captured prince on the sacrificial altar. A hero who escapes or evades, then, is inconceivable in epic and tragic terms: yet the situation becomes acceptable and possible when heroic deeds turn into chivalric adventures or knightly feats. Cervantes could afford to have Don Quixote so often defeated, or even made prisoner, only because he found precedents for this in the very chivalric romances of which he wrote the parody. In brief, the routed and fugitive hero belongs primarily to the realm of fiction, to that fiction which triumphs so easily in the epic narratives fashioned by the flowery fantasy of the Near and Far East, as, for example, in the *Knight of the Leopard Skin*, a work of the great Georgian poet Shota Rustaveli, who is almost contemporaneous with the author of the *Slovo*. The inspiration of fiction, as well as the theme of the fugitive hero, appears fleetingly even in such a poem as the *Odyssey*, where Ulysses, like Igor, and indeed after longer and harder sufferings, returns to his home and his country without any of his companions. Like Igor, too, Ulysses saves himself by flight and cunning; rather than fighting men and heroes like himself, he confronts gods and monsters who represent the same natural elements which challenge Igor on his flight, and which the poet of the *Slovo* portrays by means of direct personifications rather than mythical metamorphoses.

The romanesque quality of the story, while failing to turn the *Slovo* into a courtly or a sentimental work, supplies it with a modicum of pathetic interest, exemplified in the tender solicitude the poet feels for the person of the protagonist, for the sake not only of his ultimate safety, but even of his health or well-being. The concern of the poet for the anxiety and the pain of the hero reflects itself in the praise which the poet has Igor himself address to the river Donets for having given him care and shelter (195–196). Yet, despite such pathetic concern, the *Slovo* recalls the romances of late Greek antiquity rather than the Western romances of the Middle Ages. The very quality of the romanesque elements, as well as of the epic or heroic ones, shows once again the absence of a truly Christian spirit within the *Slovo*. This does not mean that the poet was a pagan, as some have thought; or that after baptism he remained a false convert, like a Spanish *marrano*. Either alternative is a historical and cultural impossibility, as well as a psychological absurdity. There is no doubt that, if only to be a man of letters, the poet of the *Slovo* must have actually been in form and substance a Christian. To prove this it may suffice to recall that he has the services for the dead celebrated in the sanctuaries of the new creed, and not in the ruins of pagan temples, as when the body of Izyaslav is borne to the cathedral of Saint Sophia (63), or that he closes the final song with the vision of Igor going up to another church in Kiev to give thanks to the Lord (213).

Yet notwithstanding this final thanksgiving, neither the hero, nor Igor's wife, nor the poet himself had till that moment implored the help of Providence and called on the God of the Christians, who, for his part, seems to remain as indifferent to the trials of the hero as he is remote, or even absent, from the ordeal of the faithful. Such indifference and remoteness are, however, not absolute. For instance, there is at least a simple, literal intervention of God's hand, and that is when the Lord points to Igor the way of salvation and escape, though the hero had not even deigned to call on him for help (184). On the other hand, one could maintain that the final thanksgiving is merely an edifying but incongruous interpolation, rather than the natural ending of such a work; and that it may seem as alien to its spirit as the Amen which traditionally closes all old Russian *slova* and which was tacked onto the text of the Igor Tale by the scribe of the only manuscript in which it was ever known.

The princes fallen on the field of battle may be buried in consecrated ground according to Christian rituals, while prayers are being said for the rest of their souls: yet despite this, and without fear of contradiction, the poet of the *Slovo* insists on referring at the same time to religious ceremonies and funeral rites pagan by origin or nature (82, XIII). This fact attests the survival of the ambiguous phenomenon known under the name of *dvoeverie* or double faith, or of the persistence within the cultural life of Kievan Russia of pre-Christian traditions and beliefs side by side with the liturgy and doctrine of the new creed. A negative proof of such a persistence may be seen also in the demonology of the *Slovo*, which is both Christian and pagan. The first, to be sure, limits itself to the verbal image of the Kumans as "fiends" or "Fiend's sons," while the second unfolds itself a little more fully in the appearance of the inhuman monster, Div (29, 108).

Yet it is not this religious parallelism or cultural syncretism that explains the frequent allusions in the *Slovo* to the deities of the Slavic pantheon. The gods of the ancient national mythology perform here a high literary function: they act as local equivalents of the classical divinities of the Homeric poems, probably known to our poet second hand through the Byzantine tradition, as shown by the proem and by such an allusion as that to the "Troyan affrays" (57). In this respect the *Slovo* is just the opposite of *Beowulf*, which is a genuine pagan epic coated over with a late and thin Christian varnish. In the use of myth the *Slovo* is much closer to the *Inferno* of Dante, where, however, a total and absolute faith makes it possible on the one hand to call the God of the Christians "Great Jove," and to treat on the other the "false and lying gods" of the pagans as imaginary monsters or creatures of fancy. The difference is that the *Slovo*, though the work of a Christian hand, is neither religious nor edifying: the secular and heroic character of its inspiration renders the use of mythology at once more symbolic and more literal.

This is to say that the poet of the *Slovo*, while employing myth in a manner which is not too different from that of the author of a literary epic, is yet able to do so with a sense of temporal and spiritual proximity to an earlier mythmaking age, which was impossible to such poets as Virgil, Camoens, Tasso, and the like. That is why the appearance of such divinities of the pagan pantheon as Dazhbog (64, 76) and Stribog (48), Veles (17) and Chors (159), never gives the impression of a *deus ex machina*; even though one should remember that such apparitions take place on a metaphorical plane, a fact which prevents those gods from becoming personnages and from taking part in the action. They act only within the framework of an emblematic imagery. Yet, by a new wonder, they do not play merely a decorative or ornamental role: even though they never act, so to speak, on the stage, we feel their poetic if not their mystical presence.

VI. *The account of Igor's exploits. The scene with Svyatoslav*

The critical examination of the *Slovo* must be based upon a structural analysis, and this in its turn must be grounded upon a correct reconstruction of the text. The cornerstone which supports this interpretation is the critical edition of Roman Jakobson, which is not only technically and linguistically the most valid from the scholarly standpoint, but also the most moderate and prudent in the reordering of all the parts of the whole. As Joseph Bédier found it wiser to follow the authority of a single manuscript, that of Oxford, in the manuscript tradition of the *Chanson de Roland*, so Roman Jakobson also felt that rearranging the *Slovo* on such a wild conjecture as that of gross mistakes by the scribe, or of a wrong pagination of the codex, was an arbitrary solution to be studiously avoided in the case of a text based on the authority of a single manuscript now lost and known to us only by means of modern copies of doubtful value.

Well aware that there was no place for *chorizontes* and *drascevastes*, for dividers and discriminators, among the students of this text, convinced that the first duty of its editor was to act merely as a scholiast, Jakobson undertook first to resolve satisfactorily many obscure questions of detail. Unable to loose the Gordian knots of the text, many of the previous editors had simply cut them by the sword, and broke down the *Slovo* into parts. Since some of these parts no longer seemed to fit together, they had rejected them, and then reassembled the remaining ones into a sequence of their own. Jakobson put a remedy to the harmful effects of such arbitrary manipulations by re-establishing the text of the *Slovo* in its pristine integrity, without interpolations or mutilations and, above all, without violating the originary and natural order of its parts.

The work so restored reveals to the attentive and sensitive reader the perfect proportions of the parts, and the full harmony of the whole. Even at first sight we see that it is naturally divided into three parts, symmetrically related to one another. The first part, which includes, according to my division, twelve sections and some ninety odd versicles (1–92), comprising one third of the work, begins with a proem rather long and complex (I–III, 1–18).

This proem opens with an appeal to the audience and closes with the apostrophe to Boyan. The opening and the closing section of the proem are separated by a brief account of the preparations for the campaign, as well as of the appearance of a distressing sign, that eclipse of the sun to which Igor refuses to attach any importance (II). The following sections (IV–VI, 19–29), which describe the progress of the campaign, open with the martial appeal of Vsevolod (IV) and the rapid advance of the Russians (V): their climax is an ephemeral military success, which the poet greets with a hymn of victory, his joy not lessened by other signs of impending misfortune (VI).

The poet opens the following section (VII–XII, 40–92) with newer and direct forebodings, so as to prepare the reader for the ordeal of the hero, for that peripateia or reversal of fortune that Igor is about to undergo. After announcing that the Kumans have rallied and are striking back, the poet proceeds to narrate the encirclement of the Russian camp and the rout in the making (VII). This narration is repeatedly interrupted by allusions to the fratricidal wars of the Russian princes in the past and in the present (IX–X), unfolding into a series of reproofs and complaints which contrast with the hymn of glory closing the preceding part. To that hymn the lamentation of Russia (XI) responds here, followed by the reproach which the poet addresses to Igor himself, caught in the sad and dishonorable act of surrendering into enemy hands (XII). The closing digressions of the poet serve as transition to the second part; yet their rhetorical character does detract from the prevailing mood of the first, which is naturally and profoundly epic, rising to a supreme poetic height in the almost Homeric scene describing the prowess of Vsevolod (53–56) who, more than an Olivier, seems to have become an Ajax.

The following part, the most difficult and complex, is not so much narrative and epic in nature as dramatic and oratorical. It is almost equal in size to the part preceding it. It is made up of thirteen sections, (XII–XXV), including a smaller number of versicles (93–167), but of greater average length. This part is divided into two sequences, the first of which (XIII–XVI) can truly be called dramatic. As the first part opened with the evil sign of the eclipse, so the central part begins with the ominous dream of Svyatoslav (XIII), which the dreamer retells in the first person. The narrative continues with an account of the quarrels of the boyars (XIV), which they retell in the first-person plural, and finally ends, always in the form of direct discourse, with the reproach of the lord of Kiev to the two young princes, Igor and Vsevolod (XV).

The scene, in reality, consists of three monologues instead of a single dialogue, giving the impression of a Byzantine mosaic from the background of which seem to stand out, all of them motionless, in separate positions and symmetrical attitudes, on the one side the ruler of Kiev and, on the other, the nobles of his court. Nevertheless, in spite of the stylized and static nature of the vision, which would seem to make any genuine communication between the characters impossible, this episode in the form of a triptych constitutes an authentically tragic scene, in which the monodic lament of the main personage sounds like a solo accompanied by the complaint of a full-voiced choir (93–122). There is no doubt that Svyatoslav plays in the *Slovo* a role similar to that of Charlemagne in the Carolingian cycle. The poet even exaggerates his age, portraying him as an old man, and accentuates his senile grief (114). Yet just at the moment when he condemns the imprudence of the two young princes, the elderly sovereign feels himself become a youth once more while thinking of their boldness (117). Thus, in this episode, Svyatoslav reminds us also of the *buon Re Carlone* of the Italian popular versions of the Carolingian cycle, whereas his similarity to the Charlemagne of the *Chanson de Roland* is apparent in that passage of the first part where the poet recalls the campaign which the Lord of Kiev had successfully led a few years earlier against the same Kumans (89).

VII. *Political inspiration and historical background.* *Eloquence in the Slovo*

Such extreme tension as that obtaining in the scene with Svyatoslav could not be maintained very long. Thus at the proper point the poet intervenes in person, devoting the second of the two central sequences to his own political passion, expressed with magnificent eloquence (XVII–XXIII, 123–152). After alluding to the fate of Prince Volodimir, the innocent victim of defeat (XVI), the poet, using as a start the sighing words of Svyatoslav in one of the preceding versets ("of no help are the princes to me," 119), directs a series of appeals to the Russian princes who have been remiss in their duties, namely of giving assistance to Igor or of participating in his undertaking. This sequel of apostrophes, which unfold in warnings and admonitions, proceeds according to a rigid pattern determined by criteria of dynastic rank. The reader cannot understand the motivations of this scheme, or the inner consistence of the poet's catalogue of princes, without recalling the political history of Kievan Russia: above all without referring to that state of permanent discord which existed among its princely families.

For more than a whole century, the Russian state and nation had been convulsed by an uninterrupted and interminable series of dynastic feuds, of bloody succession disputes, brought about by the fact that the hereditary principle prevailing in the dominions of Rurik's descendants followed a horizontal rather than a vertical line. Kievan Russia consisted, so to speak, of a hierarchy of principalities, culminating in the grand duchy, or better grand principality, of Kiev. At the death of the grand duke or grand prince, the legitimate power over the metropolis and its territory passed directly to the nearest relative. For example, it passed to the oldest of the brothers or cousins rather than to the oldest son. The new grand prince ceded in his turn to another blood relative the domain of which he had been lord up to that time, producing similar dynastic displacements along the whole chain of principalities. This circumstance justifies the interest the poet shows in heraldry and especially in genealogy, as well as his justified concern, and well-founded fear, that under the combined pressures of internal and external dissent, the disorders created by hereditary controversies might in the long run lead to the downfall of Russia.

It is the poet's political vision and wisdom that dictate his nostalgic regrets for the age of Vladimir the Saint or the Ancient and of his son Yaroslav the Wise (5, 6, 60, 164–165). These two sovereigns were in fact able to establish and maintain an equilibrium which was to last until it was destroyed by their descendant Oleg. Oleg broke forever the political balance of Russia, fighting ceaselessly against many rivals, and especially against Vladimir Monomach, Prince of Chernigov. In order to hold his own he was frequently obliged to call for Kuman help. The poet describes particularly the deleterious state of anarchy produced by Oleg's ambition (62–65), and accuses him of having forged feuds (58). For this reason he refers to him suggestively and sorrowfully as the "child of Malglory" (64). And it is worth remarking that, while remaining deeply loyal to the lords of Chernigov and to Oleg's descendants, the poet places squarely on the shoulders of their ancestor the prime and supreme responsibility for the century-old fratricidal wars which are devastating and bleeding the Russian land.

In fact, at the time of the composition of the *Slovo* the struggle for dynastic hegemony had brought again to the fore the descendants of Vladimir Monomach (the Monomahovichi) and those of Oleg (the Olgovichi). And the principal bone of contention was as usual the throne of Kiev. The leading contender among the members of the first branch was Vsevolod Yurievich, the lord of Vladimir in the land of Suzdal, to whom was legitimately due the title of grand prince, which the poet gladly grants him (123). The principal contender on the rival side was Svyatoslav Vsevolodovich, better known as Svyatoslav III and the first Russian monarch to be in fact the sovereign of Kiev. The latter should not be confused with Svyatoslav Olgovich, father of the two heroes of the *Slovo*, even though the poet treats Igor and Vsevolod as sons and spiritual heirs of the youngest and most powerful of the two Svyatoslavs, who in reality was only their natural cousin. The poet in fact calls him their father (102) and godfather (112), in the double role of lord of Kiev and the head of their family. The personal and family rivalry between Svyatoslav of Kiev and Vsevolod of Suzdal was complicated by other secondary rivalries; hence the poet's accusation to all Russian princes that they had served paltry interests (77) and "forged discord" (77, 86). The principal among all such lesser feuds was that between Yaroslav of Chernigov, descendant of Oleg, and another branch of Rurik's offspring, the princes of Polock, who in the *Slovo* are referred to as the "grandsons of Vseslav" (149: Vseslavichi).

The political or oratorical part of the *Slovo* consists then of a series of exhortations for a reciprocal reconciliation, first addressed to the descendants of Vladimir Monomach (XVII–XXII), who are admonished to make peace with the stock of Oleg; and then to Yaroslav of Chernigov and the heirs of Vseslav (XXI–XXIII), who are summoned to call a truce. The poet would have all Russia unite to chase away the Kuman menace, to sustain the progeny of Oleg

(40) and to save the lives of the princes in danger. The Olgovichi, in spite of their faults, have a merit which sets them apart from all the other irresolute Russian princes: they are "ready for battle" with external enemies (139). So the poet's exhortations take on the form of a direct and personal call to avenge the "wounds of turbulent Igor" (129, 142) and to shoot the enemy leader Konchak, the "vile infidel" (132). The appeals to the Monomahovichi open naturally with the apostrophe to Vsevolod of Suzdal (XVII), then proceed from his own family to the princes of the central domains and then to those of the peripheral areas (XIX–XX). When at length the poet returns to the Vseslavichi, lords of the western and northern marches (XXI), the poet takes the occasion to commemorate the noble sacrifice of their prince Izyaslav, who fell on the field of battle, not spilling Russian blood but fighting off the Lithuanians, the other external enemy of Kievan Russia (XXII).

As may be seen, the poet establishes a constant antithesis between the honor and glory of war against the enemies of the native land, even if it ends in defeat, and the dishonor and infamy of internecine war, even though it may be crowned with victory. It is perhaps to avoid the sense of horror and pity which death in battle, even when for the sake of a just cause, always arouses that the Igor Tale never presents in personal terms the killing of a single warrior, evoking only, besides and beyond the fierce and bloody encounters, the merciless slaughter, by Russian hands, of an endless number of obscure Kuman fighters (54–55). As if to compensate for this, the political and historical passages recall with abundant detail the pitiful and cruel ends of famous personages, such as those of the young princes Bryachislav (62) and Rostislav (197–198), finally opposing dramatically to each other the equal and diverse deaths of the first and the second Izyaslav. The latter is portrayed in the instant of the supreme struggle, and his fall by a Lithuanian sword is compared to the gesture of the bridegroom lying down on the nuptial bed. His death is thus celebrated in the triumphal tone of a epithalamium (144). In contrast with this, the first Izyaslav, who fought to spill the blood of his brothers, is evoked by the poet not in the last moment of his life, but in the peace of death, at the moment of mourning and burial, as though he were not a hero but a victim (63).

In this long oratorical excursus, as in the passages anticipating it in the preceding part, the poet mingles the past and the present, and even projects the present into the future (6, 14). With consummate artistry, he employs all the instruments which the arsenal of rhetoric may supply. He persuades and cajoles, perorates and exhorts, deplores and curses, shifting from irony to sarcasm, alternating praise with blame, mixing panegyrics with invectives. The variety of the treatment of each historical figure results in a gallery of lively portraits, among whom the most skillful are those of Vsevolod of Suzdal (XVII), Yaroslav of Chernigov (115), and Yaroslav of Galicia (XIX). Some of the profiles are drawn with a caustic wit, like the cutting caricatural vignette of Vladimir Monomach who, at Chernigov, every morning would stop his ears in fear (61). But satire never degenerates into insolence. The poet's wrath never descends to the level of vituperation: his discourse avoids all unseemliness, maintaining always an austere dignity, as though the poet were aware that he speaks as a prophet or judge.

The ringing and solemn accents of Byzantine religious eloquence sound a new and different note, more human and secular; and in its highest moment this florid, yet moving oratory seems almost to become patriotic poetry in the modern sense of the word. The *Slovo* contains, however, all the contradictions typical of that kind of poetry, combining into a single feeling the hatred and love it feels for the object of its passion. This consideration may help to solve the problem of the contrasting attitudes of the poet toward the hero and his brother Vsevolod, who plays the part of deuteragonist in the work. It is on such sentimental ambiguities that some critics have based the hypothesis that the political part of the *Slovo* is the later reworking of an unknown compiler. The premise is false since it does not take into account that such changes of heart and mind belong to the daily reality of life and poetry. Thus, while the poet praises Igor in the beginning of the work for having "steeled his mind with fortitude, whetted his heart with manliness" (6), later he curses him for having let the flame of heroic passion darken his understanding (12). Elsewhere the poet blames the two princes for having imprudently aroused the anger of the enemy after Svyatoslav had calmed their fury (88). And he cites the opinions of foreign nations which mock the vainglory of Igor while exalting Svyatoslav (90). The boyars speak of disgrace in regard to the failure of Igor's raid (106), and Svyatoslav himself condemns Igor and Vsevolod for the sins of arrogance (112), insolence (113), pride (116): above all, for having shed Russian blood (112).

But in Svyatoslav's speech, as in the poet's judgments, there ring other feelings, such as fervid admiration and generous indulgence; and, at the very end of the *Slovo*, a Russia which would have lost its Igor is likened to a body without a head (210). And it is actually due to formulae such as this that the language of the poet, no less than that of his personages, becomes truly, from beginning to end, "a word of gold" (111). A new Chrysostom of political eloquence, the poet ends by proving, through the burning ardor of his passionate patriotism, that there is a moral intent behind every epic work, even the simplest one. Such intent, in this as in other cases, is to build an ideal bridge between the heroes of the past and the men of the present. The redreaming of myth and fable has no other function than to supply models and examples for future practical action, teaching the lessons of both ardor and patience, so that the tribe might be able to mold its own national image on the forge of history.

VIII.   *The closing section of the Slovo. Yaroslavna's lament*

Nothing differs more from this long rhetorical interlude at the center of the work than the third and final part, the shortest and perhaps the most beautiful of the *Slovo*, which should be defined as lyrical and romanesque. It occupies only five sections (XXVI–XXX) and is composed of some fifty odd versets (168–218). The exordium ties itself with the preceding parts by means of a new reference to the Kuman invasion, already threatening the very heart of the Russian land, as the poet means to say with the beautiful epic image of the lances that "hum on the Dunaj" (167). The opening fragment (as those of the other parts) is mournful in tone. It is in fact the celebrated threnos of Yaroslavna, a splendid overture to the entire finale, and perhaps the poetic climax of the work (XXVI, 168–183).

As if the direct result of the words of suplication of a loving wife, the threnos is immediately followed by the episode of her husband's flight (XXVII, XXVIII). If the complaint of Yaroslavna is the highest lyrical moment of the *Slovo*, the flight of Igor, as we have said, represents the intrusion of the romanesque element. The presence of this element, pervading the whole episode, manifests itself with special intensity in the details of the episode, which turn the story into an adventure. To cite a single example, consider the brief scene in which Vlur, the Kuman who is Igor's accomplice, gives him the signal that all is ready for the escape by whistling from across the river (186). But the same element is no less apparent in the most fantastic traits of the episode, such as the supernatural intervention of those creatures and elements which give help and comfort to the fugitive: elements and creatures always similar if not identical to those supreme beings to whom Yaroslavna had addressed her own prayer.

In order to underline the miracle of this supernatural assistance, no less effective than the complicity of Vlur, the human agent, the poet invents the marvelous dialogue in which the Donets greets and congratulates the prince, who, in turn, gives honor and thanks to the river for having favored his flight and saved his life. This dialogue, which is almost an amoebic song, unfolding in dual eulogy and reciprocal homage, sounds like a heightened conversation between a supreme lord and an eminent vassal, whereby the one graciously praises and rewards the other for having served his sovereign with generous loyalty in his hardships and darkness (XXVIII, 192–196). That is why this dialogue rings with triumphal accents, which the poet, however, suddenly softens when he contrasts the Donets with the ignoble deed of a wretched river that, at another time and during another campaign, had let perish a prince who had entrusted himself to its waves, instead of delivering him safe and sound to the other bank (197).

Having thus tempered the joyous tone of his account of Igor's happy flight, the poet inserts as a comic digression, almost as if to produce an effect of distension, a second dialogue, this time realistic rather than fantastic, but no less admirable than the preceding one. This dialogue consists of the exchanges between the two Kuman khans, who, realizing they had allowed to escape the falcon they had caught in the snare of war, decide to lure the young falcon, Igor's son, into the traps of matrimony and love (XXIX, 200–208). Whereas the two single long periods of the dialogue between the Donets and Igor take the shape of a formal and solemn discourse, the remarks in the dialogue between the two enemy chieftains are laconic and ironic. Their symmetrical and parallel replies give almost the effect of a comic stichomythia (204, 206,

208). No other interlude could have better prepared the last scene, the happy return of the prince (XXX). This is followed by the concluding farewell (215–218), which bursts into a last cry of joy, a song of joy (211–212) that sounds indeed like an ode and a hymn.

The tone of the ending of the *Slovo*, which is that of a triumphal song, seems thus to contrast with that of the threnos of Yaroslavna, which opens the final part. The poet had sealed the oratorical and central part with a public and collective lament (XXV) — which foreshadows the personal and private lament of Igor's wife. Many editors have been unable to grasp such skillful transition and deliberate parallelism, and have therefore placed elsewhere the versets that are a prelude to Yaroslavna's lament. In addition, they seem to have confused the Dunaj of the text with the great foreign river Danube, whereas that name seems to stand for some stream in the vicinity of Putivl, at least in the verset linking the lament of the poet to that of his character: "lances hum on the Dunaj" (167).

As for a few critics of ill will, they have vented their fury upon this fragment, which they have accused of all faults and sins. The upholders of the forgery theory have, for instance, denied the authenticity of a threnos uttered, as in Igor's case, for a person still alive. It is true that many of their opponents rejected this objection, on the authority of many similar complaints, openly or secretly pagan in spirit, which exist in Slavic popular poetry. But the most convincing testimony in this regard is a matter of internal evidence. In the *Slovo* Yaroslavna's lament is anticipated, so to speak, by the figurative complaint that the poet utters for the conquered army, treated as if it were a dead person (81), as may be seen also in the preceding verset, which sounds like a refrain: "but Igor's brave host cannot be brought back to life." This symbolic funeral lament is in turn followed by a literal one, by the choral complaint of the warriors' wives who, like Yaroslavna, cannot yet know whether or not they are widows, whether their husbands have fallen on the field of battle or are merely in the hands of the enemy (82–83). In brief, the special situation which dictates the complaint of Igor's princely wife is but an isolated instance in the *Slovo*, so that the threnos of Yaroslavna may be considered the supreme manifestation of a single leitmotiv.

The *Slovo* treats this leitmotiv, the complaint theme, in several ways, but prevalently in a popular mode. It is precisely because its components are mainly ethnographic and folkloristic in nature that the threnos of Yaroslavna is neither Christian nor classic but mythic and pagan in spirit. The lament begins by a series of supplications to the elements, which are personified: to the wind, who is blamed for not deflecting the arrows of the enemy from their human targets (174); to the river Dnieper, who is beseeched to flow upstream so as to bring back the body of Igor to his loving wife (180); to the sun, to whom Yaroslavna pays special homage, even though she reproves it for torturing the warriors of her spouse on the deserted steppe (183). Each of these three elements is treated as though it were a personage of high rank, as is seen by the threefold use of the vocative "Lord," (173, 180, 182) — by which Yaroslavna turns her appeals into pleas of clemency addressed to higher powers.

This may seem to suggest that in the lament of Yaroslavna, as in the dialogue between Igor and the Donets, the poet establishes a personal relationship of the feudal kind. Were it so, in this case the situation would be the same but with the parts reversed, since here the princess plays toward the elements the role of the person of humbler status, or of lower station. But here any social pattern or code is transcended: the situation is more universally human. Yaroslavna does not show her noble and regal quality; she speaks as a woman, rather than as a lady of high rank. There is the concern of love, rather than of gentility, in her woes: not only in her tears for the safety of her husband, whom she imagines pierced by a bloody wound that she might treat and heal (171), but also in her worries for the hardships of a loved one exposed to the inclemency of the elements. The voice of Yaroslavna issues forth from a heart that wants to touch other hearts, and rings in a song intended to reach the depth of all souls. The notes of her lament arouse charity and pity in all forms of being, even beyond human nature.

Just as she speaks of Igor as though she were merely a modest mother or simple sister, rather than his noble spouse, so it is in the language of a humble maidservant, naively believing in the brotherhood of things and creatures, that she speaks of the elements and addresses them. Hence the intimacy of her implorations, as we see in the tender familiarity of her invocation to the Dnieper, whom she calls not only by name but also by patronymic, thus recalling also the name of the being that begot the river (178). She extends her tender and merciful womanly compassion also to her husband's warriors. And in a most beautiful passage she attributes the power of life and the faculty of suffering even to inanimate objects, such as the things that soldiers hold most dear, the bows and quivers which seem to feel the torments of thirst no less than the warriors themselves (183). Her voice is a voice only of love, as shown by her failure to mention the human enemy, or by the mild reproaches she addresses to a nature which now seems to act as a malevolent stepmother.

This avoidance of any note of wrath or bitterness on the part of the lamenting or supplicating woman has given rise to the theory that the threnos of Yaroslavna is in effect a conjuration, which a superstitious soul utters with the intent of placating the mysterious fury of nature's elemental forces. But we do not hear in Yaroslavna's words the accents of an exorcism, even though we do hear those of a propitiation. This consideration proves the unique originality of the fragment which, as it is always the case with great works of poetry and art, consists first of all of the freedom and novelty by which the poet or artist reworks the motives handed down to him by his own tradition. The same principle also resolves the contradictions which seem to affect all those who still insist on considering the fragment a literal threnody. With the irrational logic of passion, Yaroslavna treats her own husband as if he were at the same time living and dead, now dreaming of washing and binding his wounds (171), now imagining him lifeless on the green grasses of the steppe (176), and still beseeching the Dnieper to lull and bring him to her on its waves. The sublime ambiguity of this passage makes it hard to determine whether the miracle she requests of the river is one of bringing back Igor's dead body against the flow of the current, or one of returning her husband home safe and sound (180).

As for the classic and popular metamorphosis of the lamenting woman into a plaintive bird par excellence, the cuckoo, it seems to suggest a series of psychic transformations, as if Yaroslavna were projecting her own body and soul in trembling expectation toward the place where the loved one and his men are suffering. The miracle for which she successfully prays is translated by the poet into the splendid union of the docile obedience of creatures similar rather than identical to those whom she implores — acting almost like brothers or sisters, realizing literally and immediately the supplications of Yaroslavna in all the phases of Igor's escape, each of which seems a tacit and magical reply to the litanies of her song.

IX. Tie between man and nature. The digression on Vseslav and the use of the supernatural

It is above all in the lament of Yaroslavna and in the scene of Igor's flight that we note the peculiar relationship that the poet of the *Slovo* establishes between the emotional climates of the story and what one might call the sympathy of nature. Such a relationship must not be understood in the sense of Ruskin's pathetic fallacy, which designates the eminently modern tendency to humanize animals and plants, or even nature itself, not by means of mythical metamorphoses but rather of psychological analogies, as if all things were but shadows or copies of human archetypes. The anthropomorphism of the *Slovo* is not anthropocentric, that is, sentimental: instead of considering the universe a reflection of the human situation, the poet seems to consider it a mirror wherein man contemplates a destiny greater than his own.

This special affinity between man and nature is a bond at once positive and negative, generating the polarities of attraction and repulsion, of sympathy and antipathy. Creatures and elements are now active and now passive, at one moment friendly and at another hostile. Yet they are never indifferent to the ordeals of the Russian warriors, especially to those of the epic hero. Their moral participation in reported happenings may often take the form of an evil omen, as in the classic example at the beginning of the campaign, when the sun envelops itself within its own eclipse as in a veil of mourning (8, 27). All manifestations that precede and follow Igor's disaster have the same prophetic or symbolic meaning, from the nocturnal awakening of the birds terrified in their nests by the storm and the wailing of the wild beasts (28), to their seeking a daytime hiding place under the clouds where they are threatened and frightened by rapacious animals, eagles, wolves, and foxes (31). And the same significance must be seen in the clouds' turning black in the sky (44), or in the sunrise horizon's taking on a blood-red glow (34, 43).

When the calamity strikes, the moral participation of nature's realms takes the form of pity and sorrow: the grieving grass and trees are likened to a human being kneeling and bowing his head (74, 136, 199). But just at the moment when the men are about to succumb to their fate, the forces of nature enter the scene as actors, to play the role that in the Homeric poems belongs to the pagan gods, who descend on the field to sustain this or that group of warriors or to help a beloved hero. It is, for instance, a series of marine cataclysms that assist Igor and make possible his escape (184). During the flight itself Igor is aided by personified elements, beginning with the river Donets, which, as we have seen, serves and protects the prince with the generous loyalty of a knight, and ending with all the flora and fauna living in the domain of which that river is lord (XXVIII). If the Donets bears Igor on its waves just as Yaroslavna had beseeched the Dnieper to do, so the trees and the grasses on its banks provide him with a friendly shade and a soft couch (195). And whereas the water birds keep watch like sentinels on the winds (196), the marshland fowl sacrifice themselves to sustain the exhausted body of the fugitive (190).

As already hinted before, it is perhaps in order to emphasize the exceptional quality of the favor which nature grants to Igor, through the help of the Donets, that the poet refers to the contrary action, once performed on a similar occasion by another river, the insidious and evil Stugna. This stream did the very opposite of the majestic Donets, playing the role of a traitorous vassal or, like Scamander of old, acting as an ally of the enemy, when he vilely drowned another ardent and young prince in a huge, sudden flood of its otherwise shallow waters (197). As has already been pointed out, the reference to this long past incident softens the adventurous and romanesque temper of the flight episode, and acts as a kind of tragic warning. The hero's good fortune persists notwithstanding: Igor is able to count on the faithful allegiance of those things and beings, which help him even more than the companion of his flight. Thus, for instance, the woodpeckers show him the way to safety by beating their beaks on the tree trunks (202): this help the poet considers far from useless, even though the same aid has been given him by God's pointing finger (184).

The vivid woodpecker scene shows once more that the poet of the *Slovo* depicts such things with picturesque realism, or even with a keen zoological eye. The poet's observation is not static or descriptive, but suggestive and dynamic. His ear distinguishes with great precision the voices and calls of almost all the living creatures, who always speak "in their own tongue" (65). He reveals an exact knowledge of the daily activities of many animal species, and makes use of this knowledge to determine the time of day (98, 201, 202). That he knows how to portray the animal life in motion and action is proven by the wonderful simile likening Vlur to a wolf running about to shake off the cold dew (191). This fresh perception of the animal world is the more significant in that here and there the bestiary of the *Slovo* assumes the abstract and stylized character of a totemic, heraldic, or emblematic symbolism.

The anthropomorphism with which the poet treats animate or inanimate nature stands in a relationship of both parallelism and contrast to the zoomorphism of the famous digression on Vseslav, where the supernatural works as a magical agent not within the outer world of nature but the inner world of man. The metamorphosis of that prince, who is both wonderworker and adventurer, into a werewolf expresses what the German Romantics used to call the "night side" of nature and life. Vseslav actually assumes animal forms not only to subdue his own enemies but also to abolish space and time, stopping the very course of the sun, not like the hero Joshua but like an evil spirit (159). The superstitious anguish of popular fancy plays a no more striking part in this passage than in Yaroslavna's lament or in Svyatoslav's dream. That anguish is in the first case nothing but a prescient sense of suffering and pain; in the second, the insight of misfortune and death. What dictates the lament of Yaroslavna is then simply the superstition of the heart, while what inspires the dream of Svyatoslav is the prophetic fear of the soul. In contrast to them, the Vseslav episode is dominated by the blind and soulless superstition of matter, which reveals itself in nocturnal witchcraft and bestial transformations.

The Vseslav fragment helps to prove that the world of nature and the animal realm are the only spheres of experience supplying the *Slovo* with its fantastic element. The marvelous, which in this work stands out more prominently than in the *Poema de mio Cid*, but much less than in the *Chanson de Roland*, takes first of all the form of prophetic dream (XIII); then of intervention in the action of natural forces, now friendly, now hostile. The marvelous is here an immediate projection of either internal or external nature. It issues forth from the earth, not from heaven, neglecting or ignoring all the powers which are not of this world. It is worth repeating that in the Igor Tale we never encounter angels or demons in the roles of actors or agents. Even Div, the birdlike monster, has only a symbolic function, signaling the impending disaster. In other words, in the *Slovo* the marvelous is never ghostly. The supernatural acts there within the limits of the terrestrial and the human. There is neither the superhuman nor the otherworldly: even the subterranean world appears only for a flash, as a reflection of the brief presence of the wizard prince. This is why the whole work is pervaded throughout by a sense of serenity, by a joyful wisdom which contrasts sharply with that sense of inexorability oppressing the *Niebelungenlied*.

x. *Composition and structure of the work*

Many interpreters and readers have wrongly felt that the *Slovo* is a heterogeneous work. The critic who feels otherwise must therefore first probe carefully its components to see whether or where they fit within the whole. This may be done by re-examining the relationship between the three parts, reassessed in terms of the literary nomenclature of old Russian. The relationship itself may be stated by remembering that, whereas an ancient and yet belated tradition assigned to the whole work the general descriptive title of *Slovo*, some of its main components may be better defined by other terms, directly provided by the text, such as those of *povest* and *pesn*, by which the poet designates his own work in two series of contiguous passages (1, 6; 2, 15). Such terms have already served here as useful points of reference in determining the connection between the poetic core and the prose shell of the work.

Going further, we now may say that the *Slovo* begins as a *povest* or "tale," expressing in its first part an inspiration primarily narrative and epic; that it unfolds as a *slovo* in the sense of "oration" or "discourse," or of a composition designed to be recited or read, up to the point of reducing a considerable section of the central part to something like a long formal sermon, political rather than religious in content, a didactic excursus homiletic in tone and profane in subject; that it finally ends as a *pesn* or "song," in a closing lyrical outburst. In such a triptych (or rather, polyptych), the passages which often look extravagant or even interpolated are not the exceptional, romanesque episode of Igor's flight, the historicity of which has never aroused any suspicion, but rather the dramatic pause centered on the figure of Svyatoslav and the fabulous interlude recalling the adventures and portents of Vseslav.

The effect of contrast (really an effect of relief) which these two fragments produce on those who look at them against the compositional background of the whole has given rise to such conjectures as that the first is the work of another hand, the second the work of another period. For similar or different reasons, some critics have doubted the authenticity of the oratorical part itself, the very presence of which justifies the labeling of the Igor Tale, belatedly but not entirely arbitrarily, as a *slovo*. The same critics went so far as to suppose that the *Slovo* as we know it is but the reworking of a compiler, who had to make an earlier narrative into a sort of political tract. Such a notion is basically anachronistic because it predicates the conscious compliance on the part of the original poet with a poetics quasi-identical with the neoclassical doctrine of *genres tranchés*; it is also naive, since it implies the inability to admit that what looks like a compiler's interpolation might well be an extrapolation of the creator.

One thing is certain: the *Slovo*, far from being a simple work, is a work of extraordinary complexity. But this does not mean that we have to do with a creation devoid of unity. The *Slovo* is not the product of patchwork, or a laborious mosaic of fragments that do not match. By using more natural and dynamic images, one could say that its mainstream never stagnates, but flows freely throughout the composition, now running into the middle of the river bed, now stealing into subterranean streams, now rushing up like a flood. The lesser currents are here and there more apparent, yet they never change the course of the principal one. Thus discursive and lyric passages frequently emerge from the main body, that of the epic and narrative part, while the polemic vein breaks out in sudden oratorical whirls. Thus every part of the *Slovo* is at the same time a counterpart, and the interplay of the themes unfolds itself in a kind of contrapuntal technique.

This is no less true of the fragments that some critics consider interpolations, which, despite all appearance to the contrary, easily fit into the total scheme of the work. Thus, for instance, Svyatoslav's complaint is but a masculine and austere variation of Yaroslavna's lament, while both of them are but only enlarged echoes of the lamentations of the poet himself. The peculiar traits which mark the story of Igor's flight and the account of Vseslav's witchcraft are in the same manner related and opposed to each other, as it is the case with the romance and the fairy tale. And whereas both of these elements seem equally to contrast with the epic spirit, in the end they are reconciled to that spirit through a common concern for the mythical and the fabulous.

The lyrical element, which rules alone in the most exalted fragments, pervades all the phases of the story, as well as the many solos of the poet. Such solos partake primarily of the form and spirit of choral poetry and are patterned on the style of the ode and the hymn, while the complaints of Svyatoslav and Yaroslavna are shaped according to the mode of the elegy, and the dialogue between Igor and the Donets after the mode of the idyll. Nor should it be said that the lyricism of the *Slovo* is less intense because it is not always *melos*, or *melos* alone. The notes it issues are not musical signs; its songs are not operatic arias. This is another way of saying that the lyrical heights of the *Slovo* are reached even through nonlyrical paths: thus the lovely "word of gold" of Svyatoslav can be conceived not only as a lyrical utterance, but also in terms of eloquence and considered a perfect *prosopopoeia*.

Nevertheless, just because he always avoids the *cantabile* as well as the recitative, the poet changes into poetry even his own rhetoric, thus transcending that propaganda element which is part of the work. It is the lyrical essence, rather than the lyrical form, that remolds the materials and solders all the joints, enlivening the transitional or neutral passages, transforming the sudden shifts from one theme to another into truly Pindaric flights. Such "flights" appear more frequently at the moments when the poet adopts not only the postures but even the gestures of the oral poet: when the narrator performs as if he were an actor or a witness of the action of which he sings, captivating the attention of his lesteners or readers, making them participants in what he relives both with the senses and with the soul. Thus, when he comes to the crucial moment of the decisive battle, the poet conveys that fatal hour as if it were an immediate experience, by using the forms of the historical present and such temporal adverbs as "the morning" and "today" (69), whereas in a passage of the oratorical excursus, in which he apostrophizes an absent prince, he describes the battle-field by means of a locative adverb, as if the poet were seeing it with his eyes: "had you been here . . ." (125). In the same man-ner, before evoking the disaster about to befall the Russian army, he pretends to hear from afar the ringing noises of the arms of the enemy, who break in from all sides onto the vast plain (68). And, before beginning the lament of Yaroslavna, he also pretends that his ear is perceiving, as a distant echo, the cuckoo — like the voice of the wailing woman (168). Some of these acts or gestures have the sense or value of prophetic insights, as when the poet feigns to look at the sky to read there, as in an open book, the signs of the imminent storm: a storm which will consist of a rain of arrows, of a lightning of lances, of a thunder of dashing swords (44–46).

This sense of immediate vision, along with the clear and direct tone of the song, gives a lively quality even to the transitional pas-sages, preventing the story from being reduced to a series of still pictures or isolated scenes. Thus the intermezzi between the main episodes act as preludes or interludes rather than as discursive links. For this, as well as for its relative brevity, the story of the *Slovo* reminds us, rather than of the Homeric poems and their ancient and modern imitations, or of the huge Romance and Ger-manic epics, of that epic-lyric mode which marks Scottish ballads and Spanish romances.

xi. *Allegory and parabolic-figurative style. Chromatic and acoustic effects*

An element of special importance in the composition of the *Slovo* is the use of allegory, which performs a formal function as well as a structural one, determining what has been called its "para-bolic-figurative style." The functions hinted at by these two epithets derive equally from the eschatological allegory of Byzantine liter-ature, where allegory is not only a vehicle of mystic vision but also of trope or figure. If we may use two terms Bernard Berenson intro-duced into the criticism of the visual arts, we may say that allegory works in the *Slovo* as both "decoration" and "illustration." It thus often takes the form of personified abstractions, always and only of the female sex and the feminine gender, without however destroying the reality of the object, acting as a parallel or synthetic image, which accompanies the action as a mute sign or silent comment.

Sometimes allegory anticipates the course of the story, as prophetic vision or divinatory dream. Thus the defeat and capture of the two princes, first foreshadowed by a literal and real eclipse (8, 27), are then symbolized by an ideal or figurative one (103), which in a sort of sympathetic magic produces similar natural phenomena in the surrounding landscape (104). In the same way, the allegorical figure of the lamenting woman and the abstract personification of the lament immediately precede (81), as already remarked, the actual complaint of the warrior's wives (82–83), and act as a distant prelude to the threnos of Yaroslavna (XXVI). That such visions and prefigurations become an integral part of the work's structure and texture is proved by the rhetorical excursus, in which every phrase is an augury or auspice, every sentence an annunciation.

Allegory and the parabolic-figurative style have a compositional task which tends to create linear and geometric effects. The formal and imaginative originality of the work is, however, evident not only in the simplicity of the design but also in the richness of the coloring. The chromatism of the *Slovo*'s imagery is without precedent in other epics. This aspect, as a matter of fact, has already been the subject of a long and detailed comparative study on the part of the Spanish translators of the *Slovo*, in their prefatory essay to the work.

The Homeric poems give the impression of clear sunlight, of a pure and serene air, of lively and transparent colors. The Nordic epics are dominated by a gloomy darkness foreshadowing the northern mists of the Ossianic mystifications. Menéndez y Pidal was forced to admit the grayness of the *Poema de mio Cid*. As for the *Chanson de Roland*, it seems painted by an austere Gothic hand, shunning the temptations of the picturesque: its atmosphere is opaque, and seems to know no other hue than that of burnished iron. But the *Slovo* gives the impression of a dazzling and vivid painting, enameled and shining, striking the eye by the variety and the opulence of its polychromy. The dominant color is the yellow of gold, in which are forged numberless objects, great and small, from the roof of the royal palace of Kiev (97) to the thrones of princes (56, 102, 123, 130, 131, 154, 184); from the helmets

(54, 127, 141), stirrups (26, 59, 129), and saddles of the warriors (91) to the necklace of the grand prince (147) and the bracelets that the maiden of the Goths makes clink in cadence (109). The same precious metal also appears in the pure and lively splendor of its mass (37, 83), or sinks in solid ingots, like the gold of the Niebelungen, as a token of defeat, in the beds of the Kuman rivers (90).

Almost as frequently the color red appears in the *Slovo*, the color of wine (72), which turns blue in one famous passage (95), and the color of blood, which stains the grass or earth of all the battle-fields (67, 127, 144, 158). The very color of human life, it affects even nature, of which it conveys the wrath in the glows of sunrise (34, 43) and sunset (185). In the famous image of the "red pillars of light," it clothes the entire Russian army (103), gives shine to their "vermilion shields" (31, 36, 52, 144), flows through their banners and pennons (39). The landscapes sparkle with emerald green, the prime color of nature, from the blades of the steppes (62, 176) to Igor's rustic couch of grass (195), from the banks of the peaceful Donets (190) to the tree with its shady and gentle branches (195). Blue triumphs in the mists (155), in the waves of the Don (11), and in the vast spaces of the sea (76, 99, 175), whereas the waters of the Sula vanish in shades of silver (143). The color of the sky reappears in the smoky eagle (3), while the wolf is always gray (3, 25, 42).

If the *Chanson de Roland* is dominated by dark glimmers of burnished iron, the *Slovo* is pervaded by the dazzling glitter of steel (53, 66, 89, 135, 157), which once flashes as "blue lightning" in the enemy lances (44). Whereas silver appears but rarely (39, 83, 143), white is always present, taking on an almost blinding purity in the immaculate mantles of such animals as ermines (188), geese (190), and swans (4, 5, 190), or in the splendid spot of the "white-footed" wolf (189). And like red, white triumphs in banners and standards (39). The gray of dust (49) and the mud of stormy rivers (143) stand in opposition to this purity. As a more obvious contrast to white we have black, the color of mourning and death (94), properly clothing the raven, a bird of ill omen (41, 98); and it suddenly dyes stormclouds (44), the sod marked with horses' hooves (67), the riverbank where Rostislav was trapped (197), and other and greater phenomena of nature.

This emphatic and hyperbolic chromatism, often used conventionally, is ornamental without being decorative. Its real function is often symbolic: a fact which, along with the already observed predominance of the color of gold, suggests a fitting parallel with the mosaics or icons of Byzantine art. Nothing proves the Byzantine quality of the *Slovo*'s chromatic symbolism more than the role played by the colors representing darkness and shadow, which transcend the normal sphere of night and obscurity to invade the dream world of the spirit. Think, for instance, of a storm which is at once literal and figurative (103–104), or of that real eclipse (8, 27) haunting the whole campaign, thus outlasting its physical duration as an astronomical phenomenon (136).

In other words, the polychromy of the *Slovo* acts not merely as decor, but also as dramatic imagery, as we see by the very absence of sunlight: hence that effect of an airless background, which recalls certain kinds of oriental painting. The radiant serenity of the sun is missing also in the Vseslav passage, thus confirming that it belongs naturally to the work, of which it is an integral part. Nothing is more fitting in this regard than the vision of the wizard prince transformed into a werewolf in the act of checking at night the course of the sun (159). Yet the darkness cast over the work almost up to the end is neither absolute nor total: the sun is only hiding, or standing still, so that it will be able to appear again to illuminate and to crown him with a triumphant halo (211).

The acoustical effects are nearly as rich and varied. The *Slovo* rings with all kinds of sounds and noises, beginning with the clamors of war, conveyed as inarticulate cries, as the shrieks of the victims (121), and the barbaric howls of the enemy (52, 115). But more often we hear the clang of weapons, the hum of lances (167) and the crash of swords against helmets and armor (46, 55, 66, 68, 144). Then from time to time we hear the sound of other metals, such as the blare of trumpets (148) and the tinkling of golden bracelets (109). The earth re-echoes with the vibration of feet and hooves (49, 187); the uproar of battle deafens the ear like a clashing storm (45). In quiet moments we hear the cries of animals, each one speaking its own idiom which no one else can understand: the cawing of crows and ravens (35, 65, 98, 200–201), the trilling of nightingales (35, 202), the growls of wild beasts (28), the howls of wolves and foxes (31), and finally the song of a cuckoo (168). The call of Div (29) is like the wailing of a wild beast, while the outcry of the harassed warriors sounds like the bellowing of wounded bulls (128).

The sound in the *Slovo* should be studied as stylistic instrument rather than as acoustic material. Any inquiry into the phonetic structure of the *Slovo* could only be made by constant returns to the original language. Suffice it to say here that onomatopoeia and alliteration occur with great frequency, even if at irregular and intermittent intervals, in accord with the nature of the medium, which is prose. Since the sonority of the diction is not subordinated to the pre-established harmony of a metric scheme, the effect is that of a modulation at once spontaneous and deliberate. This shows that, even in the matter of verbal music, the *Slovo* is ruled by a unique fitness of form and content. Just as color does not have merely a decorative function, so sound fulfills more than a purely suggestive task. They are both equally compositional, joining together the visual and musical elements in the same images, as in that which turns into blue lightning the enemy lances flashing and resounding from afar (44).

XII. *Heroic formulae and epic imagery. Poetic and literary features of the* Slovo

This very example brings us to examine the problem of epic formulary, which plays an important part in the *Slovo*'s diction and imagery. The *Slovo* abounds in traditional heroic metaphors, fully unfolded, as in the elaborate sequence by which Vsevolod praises his Kursk warriors: "swaddled under the war-horn, nursed under the helmet, fed from the tip of the spear" (23); or briefly hinted, as in the fixed metaphor in which banners stand for whole armies (50, 166). We frequently encounter epithets or appositions in the heroic manner: such as the formula of "bold aurochs" often accompanying Vsevolod's name (19, 53), a formula to which a few scholars attribute totemic origins and in which they see remote traces of the cult of Thor. It is easy to find the deliberate use of epic exaggeration in all the passages that exalt warlike deeds, from the daring of Vsevolod (53–56) to the bravery of his homonym, the prince of Suzdal (XVII); from the feats of Svyatoslav (89) to the adventures of Vseslav (XXIV); from the martial fervor (7) that animates the auxiliary troops fighting for Yaroslav of Chernigov

(115) to the military power of Yaroslav of Galicia (130–131); from
the triumphs of Roman and Mstislav (135) to the slaughters of
Rurik and David (XVIII). Such exaltation of war culminates in the
hyperbolic metaphors of the warriors navigating a sea of blood
(127), and of the grand prince Vsevolod scattering in drops with
his oars, and drinking with his helmet, the waters of the Volga and
the Don, the great rivers of Russia (124).

Some of the stylistic formulae are analogous to those of the
popular epos, especially those following the universal model: "it is
not this (which is seen, felt, or believed), but it is that." Such a
model was made universally known by the famous beginning of
the Serbian song of Hasan Aga, so much admired by Goethe. It is
significant that such a formula, which the poet of the *Slovo* uses
in two places, appears first in the prelude in which the author pretends to imitate the manner of a Boyan disciple — "this is no storm
sweeping falcons" (16); and later in the passage immediately preceding the dialogue between the two Kuman khans — "no chatter-
ing magpies are these" (200). Since the prelude is meant as a parody, and the dialogue of the khans is the only comic situation in
the work, it seems as if the poet uses the formula with a caricatural
intent, as if to distinguish his own work in this respect from oral
epic.

Yet, as in popular poetry, the *Slovo* abounds in repetitions never
quite identical, which produce the effect of thematic variations, as
we can see by comparing certain couples of versets (36 and 52, 78
and 87, 80 and 137). The only exception is the nostalgic lament
for the distant homeland (32 and 47), which is the genuine refrain
to be found in the nonlyrical parts. A series of exact refrains runs
through the whole threnos of Yaroslavna, the greatest and largest
melic effusion in the *Slovo*, and the one most clearly patterned
after the forms of popular poetry. The lament is in fact broken
thrice by the verset describing the woman wailing and waiting on
the ramparts of the town, in a refrain which seems to echo her
plaintive song (172, 177, 181).

Repetitions and refrains, being devoid of any metrical scheme,
fulfill in the *Slovo* a task quite different from that of those fixed
phrases or of those metrical and verbal formulae which, according
to Milman Parry and Albert Lord, prove without doubt that a
composition is the product of oral creation.[6] A more direct proof

that the *Slovo* is a written work is offered by the internal evidence of its language and diction. The *Slovo*'s language is ecclesiastical, or rather bookish, as it happens so often in the medieval literature of Christendom: meaning that it was composed by a man of letters, or by a man of clerical education, which is the same thing (one is reminded of that kind of writing which in old Spanish literature took the name of *mester de clerecía*). It is just because of this tie with the religious tradition of the written word that the *Slovo* abounds in Biblical images, such as that of times which have turned inside out (120) or that of the grieving walls (84, 92). If not taken from the Bible, the mystical and eschatological images come from other edifying writings, thus showing on the part of the poet a direct or indirect knowledge of Byzantine literature, a knowledge producing the splendid spiritual metaphors of the "pearl-like soul" (147) and the "trees of thought" (14), as well as the tautological formulae (83) and the abstractions or personifications already mentioned (85, 106, 107). To these we may add other examples, such as the allegory of violence (76, 152) and the maidenly figure which stands for the metropolis and the crown of Kiev (153).

This religious and spiritual imagery, applied to secular themes, proves again the complexity of the *Slovo*'s stylistic and symbolic structure. Despite this complexity, the Igor Tale is far from being an eclectic product: it is rather the creation of a talented poet who was at once sophisticated and naive, Hellenized in taste and yet medieval in temper. This unique combination is evident chiefly in the rapport in both harmony and tension between the ornamental style and the oracular tone. The reader will ultimately realize that the *Slovo*'s inspiration, though solemn, is not hieratic; that its attitude, though ritualistic, is not liturgical; that its tone is not that of a sacred hymn, but of a secular song.

The nobility of the material and the symmetry of the design, far from oppressing the narrative, help to throw the action into sharper relief. Likewise, the suggestive obscurity of the evocation gives the drama greater intensity and significance. The *Slovo* indeed may be recondite, but it is not hermetic. Thus, although related to Scaldic poetry, it avoids the pitfalls of that school, which makes one sometimes think of Provençal *trobar alus*. The *Slovo* is full of meanders, but not of ambiguities. Though an aristocratic and courtly production, it speaks to princes and of princes with a voice which is public and civic. Thus there is little reason to compare the *Slovo* with modern poetry, except with regard to its verbal sorcery. Nothing proves this point better than such a poem as the *Anabase* of St.–John Perse, in which even the heroic becomes an almost private concern. It is not only to an elite, either of our time or of his, that the poet of the *Slovo* appeals, but to all men able to understand poetry as a song of the tribe as well as a song of man.

NOTES

1. The Kumans were a people of Turanic invaders, who had settled between the Don and the Dnieper. (In Russian they are called Polovtsy, which is the name used in the Igor Tale.) The Kumans and their land were to be visited, not too many years after Igor's ill-fated raid, by the most famous of all great Western travelers of the Middle Ages. This is how Marco Polo speaks of them in his *Milion*: "They have many cities and castles, and make plenty of cloth of silk and gold, which is the loveliest of the world; they have the loveliest and best falcons in the world, and abundance of everything that sustains life."

2. This is the most common and conventional way of rendering the title into English, even though it hardly does justice to the Russian *Slovo o polku Igoreve*. While we could easily replace "tale" with "discourse," which is a far better equivalent of *slovo,* we must on the other hand recognize that any attempt at a literal translation would fail at the second noun of the Russian title. Whereas modern Russian *polk* means merely "regiment," old Russian *p'lk'* means both "armed band" and "armed raid." The stated subject of the Igor Tale is then either Igor's "campaign" or Igor's "host": more probably, both. To my knowledge only the old French *geste* shared the same double meaning. Dante was aware of this fact, as shown by a passage alluding to the rout of Roncevaux (*Inferno,* XXXI.16–17), where the Italian *gesta* is used in the rarer sense of "host": "quando / Carlo Magno perdè la santa gesta" (when Charlemagne lost his sacred host). It was on Dante's authority and example that I employed the same word, with the same double meaning, in the title of my Italian translation of the Igor Tale, published in the volume *Cantare della Gesta di Igor* (for bibliographical data, consult the note at the end of this volume).

3. This book, the complete title of which is *La Geste du Prince Igor. Epopée russe du douzième siècle,* was edited by Henri Grégoire, Roman Jakobson, and Marc Szeftel, and appeared as issue number 8 of the *Annuaire de l'Institut de Philologie et Histoire Orientales et Slaves,* published by the Ecole Libre de Hautes Etudes à New York and the Université Libre de Bruxelles, which were part of the so-called "University in Exile."

4. Roman Jakobson supplied a few significant revisions when he authorized the reprinting of his own text beside my Italian translation of the *Slovo*. One could then say that the Italian edition contains the most up-to-date textual reading of the Igor Tale.

5. Such at least is the case of a translation into English from the pen of that outstanding writer in Russian and English, Vladimir Nabokov. When I wrote this essay, the author had made available a mimeographed reproduction of his translation to his friends, students, and colleagues, who recognized it immediately as a brilliant achievement. With Mr. Nabokov's permission, I used its renderings in all my various quotations from the Igor Tale. (One must not forget that the original version of this essay was written as a preface to my own translation into Italian, and this is the reason why my quotations from the Igor Tale were then, and are still now, limited to phrases of a few words each, failing to cover, even in a single case, a whole versicle.) Since then, however, to the great benefit of all those readers of English who love poetry in general, and Russian literature in particular, this splendid translation has finally appeared in print under the title of *Song of Igor's Campaign* (London, 1961); and with this publication all men of taste will realize how worthily the name of Vladimir Nabokov closes the roster of the illustrious men of letters who have translated the Igor Tale. The Russian authors who have reworded the *Slovo* into modern speech include such poets as Vasili Zhukovski and Apollon Maykov; even Pushkin thought of trying his hand at this task, as shown by the notes he prepared for a version which he never put on paper. As for the list of foreign translators, it includes the names of Rainer Maria Rilke, of Philippe Soupault, of the eminent Polish poet Julian Tuwim. We must mention along with them also a few of the distinguished scholars who accomplished the same task, such as the German Alfred Luther, the Belgian Henri Grégoire, the late Harvard professor of Slavic Samuel Cross, and the Argentinian María Rosa Lida, who worked in collaboration with her American husband, Yakov Malkiel.

6. All Arabic numerals in parentheses refer my quotations from the *Slovo* to its versicles according to the numeration adopted by Roman Jakobson in his critical edition as published in *La Geste du Prince Igor* (see note 3). Roman numerals refer instead to my own division of the *Slovo* into thematic sections, as applied in *Cantare della Gesta di Igor* (see note 2).

7. Heraldry and genealogy are a frequent concern of all heroic poets, but are treated with particular emphasis in the poetry of the Scalds and in the Scandinavian epic. The same can be said of the Igor Tale, a fact which may throw some light on the richness and complexity of the mixed tradition which made possible the creation of this masterpiece in a Russian court dominated by princes and warriors of Norman origin.

8. The late Milman Parry, Professor of Classics at Harvard, tried to prove that the *Iliad* had been originally a product of oral creation by a comparative analysis of the Homeric poems, on one side, and of Serbian poetry as it is practiced today on the other. Milman Parry's research has been developed and completed by his disciple Albert Lord, now Professor of Slavic and Comparative Literature at Harvard, who has eloquently expounded the practical and theoretical results of such investigations in *The Singer of Tales* (Cambridge, Mass., 1960), a book which is now revolutionizing classical and medieval studies in the field of epic poetry.

TRAGEDY OR ROMANCE?

A Reading of the Paolo and Francesca Episode in Dante's *Inferno*

As every schoolboy knows, Dante classified the sins punished in the *Inferno* in descending order, going from transgressions caused by the abuse of our normal instincts down to the graver violations involving perfidy and malice, which both deface the nobility of the human soul and sever us from our fellow men. So, even before crossing the passage from the first to the second circle, we know that there we shall find damned souls worthy still of tears of pity. The damned of the second circle, carnal sinners, are men and women who have subjected their nobler impulses to the animal urges of the flesh. Foremost in the ranks of these stand Paolo and Francesca, and their story is in a certain sense the first truly infernal episode.

The scene is one of tender pity, but not of forgiveness or indulgence. Dante does not absolve those whom God has condemned for eternity. Here Dante the protagonist of his own poem is just beginning his "pilgrim's progress." Only gradually will he learn and accept the stern lesson of the wages of sin. Dante the author and narrator of his own metaphysical experience sees already with perfect fullness the absolute harmony between God's justice and God's will. Thus what to the heart of Dante the pilgrim may still appear as the "tragedy" of human life, for the mind of Dante the poet has become but a minor interlude in the sublime "comedy" of the divine order. The author is morally detached, but artistically involved, and produces therefore one of the most moving episodes in the poem. One could say that the entire Paolo and Francesca story is based on a continuous tension between the ethos of contemplation and the pathos of experience. The artistic achievement lies in the fact that the poem reconciles within itself Dante the witness of the wretched misery of man, and Dante the beholder of the awful majesty of God.

I

The very opening of the episode rings with a sharply pathetic accent:

> Ora incomincian le dolenti note
> a farmisi sentire; or son venuto
> là dove molto pianto mi percuote.[1]

The verb by which Dante suggests the impression made on him by the vocal grief of the sinners (smites me, *mi percuote*) is the same by which he will later describe the torments inflicted on the damned by the storm preying on them; and this parallelism indicates that pity itself acts on man as a kind of blow.

After this prelude, the poet represents in stark outlines the place which in the meantime he has finally reached:

> Io venni in luogo d'ogni luce muto,
> che mugghia come fa mar per tempesta,
> se da contrari venti è combattuto.

The place is devoid of light, but full of the sound and fury of a formidable hurricane. The expression *d'ogni luce muto*, mute of all light, combining as it does optical and acoustic impressions, is powerfully suggestive, since the absolute absence of light, its "silence," as the poet says, parallels and balances the deafening roar of the elements. That hurricane, after all, is not a normal or natural one: and Dante tries to approximate its supernatural power by comparing it to a sea storm, battled by opposing blasts and streams. The similitude is quite proper since the ravaging force of the convulsed air mass carries along on the crest of its invisible waves the floating souls of the damned, tossing them around like victims of a shipwreck:

> La bufera infernal, che mai non resta,
> mena li spirti con la sua rapina:
> voltando e percotendo li molesta.

Unlike the tempests raging over our earth, the infernal hurricane knows neither interruption nor end, so that the sinners can expect neither that their ordeal will cease nor that the implacable wind whirling and smiting them will grant respite:

> Quando giungon davanti a la ruina,
> quivi le strida, il compianto, il lamento;
> bestemmian quivi la virtù divina.

The suffering of the damned is made worse by the awareness that any time the rotating hurricane rejoins a given point within the walls of the second circle, their torture will rise again to a pitch of intolerable acuteness. This happens when the surge of the storm breaks against what Dante calls *la ruina* or the landslide: perhaps a breach in the rocky side of the infernal abyss, which suddenly changes the gale into an aerial maelstrom. It is here that the shrieks of the sinners, up to now hardly audible over the noise of the blast, resound even higher than the crash of the storm. Dante evokes this shouting and crying with a threefold series of words, forming, by a varied gradation of intensity and meaning, a kind of musical diminuendo. The first to wound our ears are the *strida*, or loud cries, of the sinners; then the *compianto*, or their choral plaint; finally, the *lamento*, or faint groan. The line built around these three words ends by giving, paradoxically, also a crescendo effect: its slow rhythm, prolonged in a waning and softening trail of sounds, conveys powerfully the sinners' total powerlessness and exhaustion, and the merciless cruelty of the wind. Yet any further insistence on the plight of the damned would provoke a sense of insufferable anguish: so, to avoid a new excess of pathos, the poet hastens to remind us that that shouting and crying is also a "gnashing of teeth," something lower and viler than an articulate expression of human grief. Those souls are not guileless martyrs, but victims of their own guilt; and they show their everlasting wickedness by still rebelling in thoughts and words against the "divine virtue," by cursing the hand that chastizes them for their sins. Dante acknowledges all this, and recognizes them for what they are:

> Intesi ch' a così fatto tormento
> enno dannati i peccator carnali,
> che la ragion sommettono al talento.

Without explanation from Virgil, Dante has immediately guessed they are men and women who submitted the high claims of human reason to the yearnings of the brute. This recognition is based on the law of *contrappasso*, or retribution, wherein the punishment fits the crime, by a parallel or contrasting analogy with the very nature of the sin. Since the tempestuous violence of their lust led them astray, they are punished by being dragged by a wind which, unlike the storms of our flesh and blood, will never pause or rest. The internal hurricane is thus to be understood as a reality both physical and metaphysical, operating on the literal as well as on the figurative plane. The immediacy of Dante's realization is meaningful also in another subtler and more private sense. It may suggest a discreet autobiographical hint, and act as an implied confession that the poet as a man knew all too well the temptations of concupiscence and all too often yielded to them. Such are the manifold allusions contained in the simple opening verb, in the little word *intesi*, I understood.

II

Up to now Dante has devoted his almost undivided attention to the massive, anonymous, elemental violence of the storm, as shown by the frequency of such words as *tempesta*, gale; *bufera*, hurricane; *rapina*, rapine; and *ruina*, landslide. Now he is looking instead at the human prey of that violence: and he describes the crowd of the sinners as if they were a flock of birds, flying along with the wind. The main part of the canto's imagery will be based on a recurring bird motif, developed in three successive, and almost contiguous, similitudes, each one of which compares the sinners with a different species of birds. Since the souls hover forever in the air, so the birds are always described in a similar state of suspension — not as they appear when at rest, or when they stay on the ground. In this first simile the spirits are likened to a flock of starlings; and in order to make the likeness even more striking, the poet emphasizes the size of the flock, thus anticipating further statements as to the swarming multitude of the souls:

> E come li stornei ne portan l'ali
> nel freddo tempo a schiera larga e piena,
> così quel fiato li spiriti mali.[2]

One of the new things we learn from the image is that Dante and Virgil, who in the meanwhile must have come to a standstill, are now staring at the sinners from a particular point of view. The epithets by which Dante gives the first visual impression of the "troop" are "large and full" (*schiera larga e piena*). They indicate that the crowd of the damned is now facing the travelers in a sort of front formation, unfolding itself in the dimension of breadth, so that the eyes of the two pilgrims are now perceiving only the wide and thick first line of the troop, while they may only glimpse or guess the rows or files arrayed behind it. But the simile also contains references to things we already know. So the allusion to the bleakness of the season, to the *freddo tempo* in which the flight of the starlings is taking place, suggests a similarity between that climatic condition and the darkness of the air of the second circle, a detail to which Dante attracts the reader's attention in several passages of the episode. The poet completes this series of correspondences between the scene and the image by developing the most important of all their common traits; and he does so by describing the motion of the birds in terms identical with the motion of the shades, or as a passive rather than as an active process. Since the sinners do not move on their own power, but are pushed and pulled by the wind, so likewise the movement of the starlings is seen as caused not by their will, but by the automatic action of their wings, which are treated as organs different from and independent of the birds themselves. Yet this willful and arbitrary equivalence is deliberately misleading, since it distracts our attention from the devastating power of the hurricane, thus attenuating the impression of its irresistible force. This new, implicit diminuendo is made evident by the use of the term *fiato* (breath) to indicate, by way of understatement, the action of the wind.[3]

Such a softening of the elemental brutality of the punishing and torturing storm betrays a new undercurrent of pathos in the poet's mood: but Dante reverses that trend immediately by breaking the equivalence between the vision and its metaphorical vehicle, and by recalling to himself and his readers that those men and women are evil spirits (*spiriti mali*), not innocent birds. So, quite naturally, the opening line of the following terzina, with its merciless beat, evokes again the inexorability of the hurricane, hurling the souls in all directions, as if they were senseless things, while the remainder of the terzina conveys again the hopelessness of damnation, the absolute despair of a condition which admits neither end nor relief:

> di qua, di là, di giù, di su li mena;
> nulla speranza li conforta mai,
> non che di posa, ma di minor pena.

Having restrained the string of pathos, Dante slightly relaxes it again. As we have already noticed, the mainstream of this canto wavers and shifts between the opposite poles of the stern acceptance of the designs of God's justice and a feeling of compassion for the objects of God's wrath. The spectacle of the sinners' fate brings in, in the usual alternation, another wave of pity, and along with it a new comparison with another troop of birds. This time the damned are likened to a flight of cranes:

> E come i gru van cantando lor lai,
>   faccendo in aere di sè lunga riga,
>   così vidi venir, traendo guai,
> ombre portate da la detta briga:

Since Dante's sensitive attention is now attuned to the lamenting voices of the tormented, the detail standing out from this second simile concerns the singing of those birds and the sadness of their song. Such is the suggestion contained in the word *lai*, lays, which Dante uses both in its general sense of complaint and in a more special and technical meaning, designating a particular kind of medieval poetry, which in Provençal verse takes the form of the lyrical and melancholic re-evocation of an adventure of love. This all too significant allusion is but the first among the frequent literary references of the episode: and like almost all of them it reiterates the underlying pathos of the story. So the poet checks again the natural tendency of both the simile and the literary reference to idealize the situation; and he achieves such a controlling effect by introducing a qualifying parallel between the singing of the cranes and the lamenting of the sinners, by degrading the lays of the former to the level of the latter's *guai* or wails. Despite the shift to a lower key, even in this case the comparison obtains an absolute equivalence between the referential tenor and the emblematic vehicle. Such a harmony between trope and object is made even more evident by the metrical symmetry of the first and third lines, the one evoking the singing of the birds and the other suggesting, as a confused and trailing echo, the less musical, and yet equally rhythmical, human plaint. Like the preceding bird simile, also, the crane image has a dynamic function besides the metaphorical one: it helps us to visualize the positions successively taken by the crowd of sinners, and to localize them in space and time. From the comparison with the starlings we learned that at the moment the shades were moving toward Dante and Virgil in frontal formation; from the new comparison we learn that after a long wide turn the wind is now driving them in such a way that the two travelers, still standing motionless, see the troop through a longitudinal perspective rather than a transverse one. Now the army of the spirits is deployed in the sense of length, as we realize from the phrase *faccendo in aere di sè lunga riga* (making in air a long line of themselves): and the extension of the formation, as well as the duration of the passage, are suggested by the lingering effect of the rhythm, by the dragging quality of the sounds, and, even more, by the overflow of the metrical and syntactical phrase beyond the stanzaic structure, while normally each terzina is divided from the next by a long and clear-cut strophic caesura.

III

At this point the two pilgrims are able to see clearly enough at least some of the individual shades. The descriptive phase of the canto thereupon comes to an abrupt end. And now Dante the character, a man curious like ourselves, asks of his master the very question we would ask:

> per ch' i' dissi: "Maestro, chi son quelle
> genti che l'aura nera sì gastiga?"

Dante now wants personal identifications, not abstract examples of the divine vengeance, and betrays his desire in an indirect manner: in his question to Virgil he avoids calling those men and women sinners or shades, and uses instead the simple and human term *quelle genti*, those people.

Virgil understands the questioner's intent and answers straightforwardly by singling out among the sinners those whose memory is still alive and who will serve the edifying purpose of teaching an exemplary moral lesson to all of us, both high and low. He successively identifies, almost in chronological order, a few outstanding figures, giving us a typical medieval catalogue of famous persons, which, although of no great interest in itself, performs an important function in the economy of the canto, and acts as a kind of break in its narrative structure. As a matter of fact, the catalogue is meaningful also in the context of the Paolo and Francesca episode, and a re-examination of the former will at the proper time throw a significant light on the latter.

The first among the catalogue's figures, as they are listed by

Virgil, is Semiramis, who is dealt with at greater length than any other character and whose name, to create an effect of suspense, or to offer the learned reader the opportunity of recognizing by himself the Queen of Assyria, appears only in the opening line of the last of the three terzinas devoted to her. Virgil notes at the beginning and at the end of his treatment of that figure that she ruled an empire of many nations and tongues, and that she reigned not only over Babylon but also over Egypt, which is now one of the Sultan's domains. The widow of King Ninus, she succeeded him on his throne; and she was so dissolute (in the poet's drastic words, *A vizio di lussuria fu sì rotta,* to the vice of lust was so broken) as to marry her son. Thus Virgil accuses her of changing *libito* into *licito,* of making "the lustful lawful," or of legalizing incest:

> "La prima di color di cui novelle
> tu vuo' saper" mi disse quelli allotta,
> "fu imperadrice di molte favelle.
> A vizio di lussuria fu sì rotta
> che libito fe' licito in sua legge
> per torre il biasmo in che era condotta.
> Ell' è Semiramìs, di cui si legge
> che succedette a Nino e fu sua sposa;
> tenne la terra che 'l Soldan corregge.

The second figure is Dido, whom Dante's master had sung yet fails to mention by name, perhaps out of a sense of modesty. Yet she is easily identifiable through the brief periphrasis alluding to the passion that led her to suicide, after having led her to betray the promise made on the grave of her husband Sichaeus; and such a violation of the vows of widowhood is conveyed by the same verb, *rompere,* to break, by which Dante had already referred to the dissoluteness of Semiramis. After so devoting two thirds of the terzina to his own heroine, Virgil uses the last line to evoke Cleopatra, fully portrayed by the single and final epithet, meaning "lascivious," and stretched to the abnormal length of five syllables by a necessary diaeresis (*lussuri-o-sa*):

> L'altra è colei che s' ancise amorosa,
> e ruppe fede al cener di Sicheo;
> poi è Cleopatràs lussuriosa.

The closing lines of the catalogue open with the last woman on the list, Homer's Helen, briefly described as the cause of much grief and ill, and immediately followed by the first masculine character, Achilles. Achilles appears here because Dante follows not the Homeric tradition, but a later legend, according to which the hero of the *Iliad* ended his life while pursuing a love affair instead of fighting enemy hosts.[4] The catalogue terminates with the figures of Paris and Tristan, or rather with their mere names, the echo of which seems to linger for a while beyond the caesura of the line, where Virgil's speech, as directly reported, unexpectedly breaks in the middle, far before its end:

> Elena vedi, per cui tanto reo
>   tempo si volse, e vedi il grande Achille
>   che con amore al fine combatteo.
> Vedi Parìs, Tristano" . . .

The poet, with a perfect sense of both timing and balance, soon stops his review of the procession, shortly after it starts. This does not mean that the procession ends at this point, but merely that Dante chooses to reproduce only part of Virgil's speech. With great artistic economy he cuts that speech short, simply informing the reader that his guide went on showing to him one by one many other shades who, like Dido and Achilles, as well as Paolo and Francesca, died of love and by love:

> . . . e più di mille
> ombre mostrommi, e nominommi, a dito
> ch' amor di nostra vita dipartille.

Dante's statement that his guide identified for him more than a thousand (*più di mille*) souls is but a verbal exaggeration or poetic license, through which he conveys a sense of the immensity of their numbers, considering that most of them must have remained unrecognized and nameless. The hugeness of the figure stated by Dante, as well as the unknown total quantity it implies, will also suggest the unusual amount of time spent by the pilgrim in getting acquainted with the souls of the second circle, thus betraying the peculiar intensity of his interest. It is in this manner that the poet starts unveiling his own personal and psychological curiosity in matters of love, to be later more clearly and fully manifested by the question he dares to ask of Francesca, while revealing at the same time the deep admiration he feels for the passionate heroines and the pathetic heroes he now beholds. When at the beginning of his list, Virgil had referred to Dante's desire to have knowledge, *saper novelle*, of those spirits, he had shown his awareness that the information sought by his disciple was also purely factual, or historical, in character. In this sense, the catalogue is a tribute paid to the greatness and grandeur of a past forever gone. Such an intent is clearly intimated in the phrase by which Dante will define all the famous persons he has just seen: *le donne antiche e' cavalieri*, the ladies of old and the knights. The suggestion of the splendor and glamor which those figures still radiate among men makes even more poignant the spectacle of their plight, and the realization that their misery will never end. The contrasting impact of these opposite feelings provokes in the poet a new and stronger wave of pity, which bewilders and almost overwhelms him:

> Poscia ch' io ebbi il mio dottore udito
> nomar le donne antiche e' cavalieri,
> pietà mi giunse, e fui quasi smarrito.

This sudden spell of pity is so intense that Dante seems about to swoon: and the present bewilderment prepares us for the fainting fit of the pilgrim at the close of the episode, when he is unable to resist the surge of compassion stirred in his soul by Francesca's words. The parallelism between these two moments of emotional weakness is striking, because in this case also the poet abandons himself to the violence of his feelings only after having listened up to the end to what is being said to him. The heart has its reasons, and reason may well be unaware of them; but Dante acknowledges his heart's claims only when his mind has first asserted its demands. Now that his yearning for knowledge has been satisfied, he can give free rein to his emotional needs; now only may pathos prevail again.

IV

I have already stated that this procession of souls acts as a kind of break in the course of Dante's narrative. Later we must return to it, to see its function within the entire episode. Strictly speaking, the episode of Paolo and Francesca begins just after Virgil ends his list, and as Dante recovers from its painful impact. Now *in medias res*, the main section of the canto is fittingly opened by the poet's desire to speak to two shades. At this stage, Dante gives no hint whether he knows those two spirits. Further in the canto, he calls the woman by name, but only after she has told enough of her

story to be easily identified by anyone. Yet internal and external
evidence strongly indicates that the pilgrim recognizes them at first
sight. The external evidence is historical: we know, for instance,
that Paolo Malatesta spent some time in Florence as Capitano del
Popolo; and it is almost certain that Dante, who was then very
young, saw or met Paolo on that occasion. This took place in 1282
or 1283; shortly after, probably in 1285, he must have heard that
Paolo and Francesca had been killed by Gianciotto Malatesta, the
lord of Rimini, his brother and her husband: and this bloody event
undoubtedly left a lasting impression on Dante's mind. A long time
after completing the composition of the *Inferno*, when he was
already working on the *Paradiso*, the poet settled in Ravenna. His
generous and honored host was Guido Novello da Polenta (Francesca's nephew), but it seems that Dante had been in friendly contact with that family for a long time; and through such a contact
he may have learned very early the full story of Francesca, still
alive in the memory of her family and of all her father's descendants. As a matter of fact, his kind treatment of Francesca in this
canto of the *Inferno*, the only part of the *Commedia* then already
published, may have endeared him even more to her relatives. At
any rate, it is on a more convincing kind of evidence, internal and
poetic in character, that I base my assurance that Dante recognizes
at first sight not only Paolo but also Francesca: and that he immediately identifies in the two shades those whom only at the beginning of the following canto he will call the two in-laws (*i due
cognati*).[5]

Although decisive, the proof I have in mind is negative in character: Virgil, who has mentioned and described to his companion
"more than a thousand" among the souls of the second circle, significantly neglects to give "a local habitation and a name" solely to
Paolo and Francesca. This clearly means that any identification or
explanation was in this case totally unnecessary, at least for his own
disciple. At a later stage, any identification or explanation would
be almost equally superfluous for the reader, especially of Dante's
time. Even before reaching the point when in his question to
Francesca Dante utters her name (and her name alone), the medieval reader would have already silently uttered more than once
the same name. Dante presupposes so widespread a knowledge of
the story's background as to feel free to paint it in bold strokes

rather than in minute details. Yet it remains equally true that anyone reading the canto for the first time is able to recognize Paolo and Francesca only at second sight; and this adds an element of curiosity and suspense to the narrative:

> I' cominciai: "Poeta volontieri
> parlerei a quei due che 'nsieme vanno,
> e paion sì al vento esser leggieri."

With a powerful artistic synthesis Dante describes his sudden vision of Paolo and Francesca only through the words by which he will later convey to his master his desire to speak to the two he has just perceived and recognized. When he does so, he singles them out on the strength of two distinctive traits: first, that, unlike their fellow sinners, they go together; second, that they seem to yield to the violence of the wind more gracefully and willingly than the others. Since the poet adds no details, the reader at this stage has no ground to surmise that one of them is a man and the other a woman — although he will spontaneously guess that such is the case. In his words to Virgil, with tactful modesty Dante understates the intensity of his desire to talk with the two shades, and avoids referring to either their story or their names. Yet whether or not Virgil identifies them by name is irrelevant. Of the two poets, only one was a poet of love. Virgil, the heroic poet, sang *arma virumque*, and only in passing of the passion of Dido; but Dante, at least in his youth, had been a *fedele d'amore*, and a practitioner of the *dolce stil nuovo*. So it will be only fitting for Dante to address the two lovers, and Virgil willingly grants him this privilege. He merely advises him to wait until the wind brings the two spirits a little nearer, and then to turn to them with his request:

> Ed elli a me: "Vedrai quando saranno
> più presso a noi; e tu allor li prega
> per quello amor che i mena, ed ei verranno."

Virgil suggests that the request be made in the name of that love which still seems to lead the two shades, and foresees that they will come in response to such a request. Virgil's words, although addressed to Dante, are already words of entreaty and endearment, even of flattery; love may be the power that still binds the two souls together, but it is the vengeance of God that spurs them in their ordeal. The first force operates in accordance, and the second in contrast, with their will. Virgil here seems to allude again to the impression they give of assisting, rather than resisting, the rush of the wind: yet he reveals that the impression is only illusory by using for the operation of love the same verb and the same form (*mena*, from *menare*, to lead) by which Dante had already indicated the action of the storm. Dante tacitly acknowledges the wisdom of his teacher's counsel, and follows his advice at least in part, imitating Virgil's delicacy in thought as well as in word. I say in part, because he fails to refer to love as Virgil had suggested to him. So as soon as the wind turns the spirits toward them, the pilgrim sends the two lovers a moved and moving call:

> Sì tosto come il vento a noi li piega,
>   mossi la voce: "O anime affannate,
>   venite a noi parlar, s' altri nol niega!"

Strangely enough, in his appeal the poet addresses the two in such a way as not to distinguish them from the other sinners. The apostrophe, *O anime affannate* (O wearied souls), could apply to all the spirits in the flying crowd, so that we may easily imagine that it was accompanied by an unmistakable, beckoning gesture. Or perhaps the plural was enough, because Paolo and Francesca are the only spirits of the second circle who are not exclusively absorbed in their individual plight, who suffer as two souls in one. To make his request even more respectful and courteous, Dante, who in his previous words to Virgil stated his wish in terms of *his* speaking to them, now that he addresses the two spirits restates that wish in terms of *their* speaking to his companion and himself. Finally, in the conditional sentence by which the poet avows fear that his request may not be agreeable to God, he expresses that thought in such a way as least to offend them. Even here the poet follows his steadfast rule according to which the name of God is never uttered in Hell, and chooses to replace that name by the vaguest possible term. Instead of saying "unless God forbids," he merely says, "if another deny it not" (*s' altri nol niega*). Clearly discretion cannot go further than this.

The souls immediately heed Dante's appeal, exactly because they immediately feel, more in its tone than in its words, the loving charity of that sudden call. So they leave the swarm of sinners — which Dante describes here with words to be understood not as a qualifying statement, but rather as a compliment to Virgil, as *la schiera ov' è Dido*, the troop where Dido is — so the two spirits move easily and slowly toward the two pilgrims, who are waiting for them on the same spot, to remain there up to the end of their talk. To suggest the action and movement of Paolo and Francesca, Dante introduces here the third and last bird simile of the canto, and compares them to a pair of doves who suddenly abandon the large flock of their kind to rejoin their little ones and to return to their nest:

> Quali colombe dal disio chiamate,
> con l'ali alzate e ferme al dolce nido
> vegnon per l'aere dal voler portate;
> cotali uscir de la schiera ov' è Dido,
> a noi venendo per l'aere maligno,
> sì forte fu l'affettuoso grido.

The doves are carried through the air not so much by the force of their wings, or even of the wind, but by the power of their *volere*, which means "wish" rather than "will." Thus, in harmony with the previous similitudes of the same kind, which had represented the birds in a state of passive motion, this one too describes the flight of the doves in terms of what the French call *vol plané*. Like Paolo and Francesca, descending toward Virgil and Dante through the wicked air of Hell, so the doves do not fly, but rather glide, toward their nest: and that gliding is clearly suggested by the beautiful detail of their raised and steady wings.[6] The pertinence of the metaphor becomes even more striking if we consider that doves are traditionally held as the most tenderly loving, and the most tenderly lovely, of all birds. The spontaneous ease of the image must not lead us to forget that what is happening in the meanwhile is nothing less than a miracle, even if Dante prefers to understate, even to ignore, the strangeness of the event. It is clear that God has granted Dante's wish, that he has allowed the two sinners to heed his friendly and tender call. For this very reason the action of Paolo and Francesca is described as the almost unconscious effect of a sympathetic and reciprocal attraction, as the operation of an "elective affinity," rather than as the unilateral decision of their will, which is no longer free. All this seems to be suggested by the repetition of the verb *venire*, which in Italian has often a strong affective undertone, meaning not merely "to come" or "to go," but to go where one's heart is.

The psychological and spiritual force of the poet's "passionate call" (or "cry," as the Italian *grido* also means), coincides with the longing of the two spirits without conflicting with God's will: thus it operates its wonder, and joins together the two visitors and the two souls. Dante neglects to say who is speaking, and to whom; yet the reader understands that the speaker is a woman, and that it is to Dante she turns. Her language is not only feminine, but ladylike, revealing delicacy of feeling, as well as refined tact. She behaves as a well-born gentlewoman even in Hell; nay, as a princess, or at least as someone accustomed to command. Notwithstanding her tenderness and benevolence, despite the fact that her misery and her love place her on a level with Dante, she still stands on ceremony; her courtesy remains courtly, and she impresses the poet and the reader with the consciousness of her exalted station, of the privileged position she once held among men. She treats Dante as an equal, even better, as a friend: yet her familiarity is never informal, and her attitude seems to be inspired by the graciousness and generosity of a great lady condescending to honor someone of a lower status or lineage than herself. All her acts, gestures, and words, even when they are most captivating, betray a controlled pride, a sense of feudal dignity. This may lead us to think that she acts in this way in order to play the role expected from a woman of her status and breeding in a society which was educated in the cult of the "eternal feminine," and which raised all noblewomen (especially if married, as was the case in Provençal culture [7]) on a kind of pedestal. There may be something in this: but perhaps it is simply because she recognizes at first sight that Dante is not her equal that she does not ask him who he is and where he comes from, and that she greets him with the acknowledgment, not of the nobility of his blood, but merely of the nobility of his soul. Such is the meaning of the apostrophe by which she designates Dante as a living creature full of benevolence and good will:

> "O animal grazioso e benigno
> che visitando vai per l'aere perso
> noi che tignemmo il mondo di sanguigno,

Francesca's native pride manifests itself in the long relative clause following the apostrophe, with its implication that the pilgrim's journey through Hell was meant as a visit not to the sinners of all circles, but only to Paolo and herself, whom she defines extravagantly, in terms of their own tragic end, as those who painted the world blood-red. The line reveals Francesca's total absorption in the event that dominated her life and brought her to her death. After all, not Paolo and Francesca alone, but all the shades of this circle saw their worldly existence cut short by jealousy, hatred, passion, or lust; while all the circles of Hell (without mentioning the abodes of purgation and bliss) are full of numberless spirits who suffered a violent death. Yet it seems to Francesca that the whole earth is still stained by the blood which once flowed in Paolo's veins, and in hers. This disproportion between the import of the event and the measure by which she estimates its effects is so great as to escape nobody's attention, excepting her own. The modern reader may assess that disproportion by employing a concept which T. S. Eliot introduced for the first time in modern criticism, and may conclude that there is no "objective correlative" [8] between Francesca's emotions and the remote experience which forever stirs those emotions in her memory and soul. Yet in this case psychological imbalance is easily corrected by artistic equilibrium: we must not forget that the metaphorical exaggeration of Francesca's words is a characterizing device, through which the poet projects the passion of his heroine rather than feelings of his own. Yet the moving emphasis of Francesca's words brings along a new flow of pathos, which for a while threatens to become a flood. An emotional outburst of that kind, which would look unseemly and improper if it were part of the poet's statement, becomes acceptable and forgivable as the effusive expression of the grief filling Francesca's heart.

The powerful impact of the heroine's allusion to the manner of her death is due not only to its rhetorical emphasis, but also to what the image tacitly implies or suggests. The metaphor of the world painted red by human blood appears also in Shakespeare's *Macbeth*. There the image always fulfills a tragic function, since it recurs in the protagonist's mind as the most obsessive detail of the murder he committed, which he continuously rehearses in his memory and relives in his remorse. But in Dante the same image produces a pathetic effect: the blood, of which Francesca says that it stained not only the sea but the whole world, was shed by no others than Paolo and herself. The blood reappearing in the nightmares of Macbeth is the blood of his victims; the blood still haunting the memory of Paolo and Francesca is but their own. In Aristotelian terms, one could say that in the Shakespearean version of the same trope terror overwhelms pity, while in Dante's variant the self-pity of the heroine and the poet's compassion triumph over terror itself.

Contrasting as it does with Francesca's previous reference to the *aere perso*, to the black air of Hell, that blood image strikes us with a lasting impression of vividness, as a bright spot, or a gush of color, suddenly lighting up the dark background of a landscape painted at dusk. Still both the metaphor and the line carrying it are but an incidental sentence and nothing more. Francesca does not insist on it, since she wishes to return to the task at hand, which is to thank Dante for his affectionate interest, for the pity he feels toward what she ambiguously calls *nostro mal perverso*, a phrase which may equally mean "our wicked evil" or "our wretched ill." Yet Francesca cannot express her gratitude except in words, since her damnation denies her the highest human right, which is to pray God for the eternal peace of both the living and the dead:

> se fosse amico il re de l'universo,
> noi pregheremmo lui de la tua pace,
> poi c' hai pietà del nostro mal perverso.

As the words quoted show, Francesca does not say merely "we would pray to God for you if we could." Like Dante she dares not utter the name of God, which would always be uttered in vain in Hell. But unlike Dante, who had previously alluded to God by the vague and anonymous pronoun, *altri*, she refers to Him in very concrete, although indirect, terms. So, quite simply and naturally, she introduces the noble periphrasis defining God as "the king of the universe." By describing God as the supreme sovereign she reveals again her aristocratic bent, her feudal frame of mind. By the very clause *se fosse amico*, if he were our friend, Francesca indicates that she conceives of God's blessing or God's curse in terms of courtly grace or disgrace, as honors or privileges which a crowned head may bestow on his subjects or withdraw from them. In the same way, she seems to consider Paolo and herself as if they were two vassals who, having lost their king's personal favor, have also lost the right to intercede with him in behalf of others. Thus, by two brief conditional sentences, she succeeds in projecting the hierarchical idea of the feudal order into God's universe. All this is stated, or rather suggested, in thoughts and words both spontaneous and restrained, regretful and respectful at the same time. But if Francesca has lost her standing with God, she has not lost, even in Hell, her standing with her fellow men; so, with perfect composure, with the self-mastery of an accomplished lady, she gracefully grants the two pilgrims license to converse with Paolo and her:

> Di quel che udire e che parlar vi piace,
> noi udiremo e parleremo a vui,
> mentre che 'l vento, come fa, ci tace.

Francesca continues to speak in the first-person plural, while shifting from the second singular to the second plural in her form of address. Thus she uses the pronouns "we" and "you": yet the first sounds rather like a *pluralis majestatis,* and the second applies more to Dante than to Virgil. And to respect good manners, she pretends to leave to the visitors the choice of the subject to be discussed: she seems to hold them on a footing of absolute equality. Although declaring her willingness to listen as well as talk, she will be in reality, at least for some time, the only speaker; so, without waiting for a word or even a nod, she speaks out on the only topic which interests her. There is no time to lose: the wind has just quieted, but the storm may rage again at any moment. With an eloquent understatement, hardly more than an expressive gesture, she acknowledges the minor miracle now taking place for their benefit. Let us talk, she says, as long as the wind, as it does, will keep silent for us (*mentre che 'l vento, come fa, ci tace*).[9] This discreet reference to the truce suddenly granted by the storm adds a charming detail to the scene: the personification of the wind seems to intrude for a while from one of the corners of the picture, playing the role of a willing and helpful partner, hushing his voice and bending his ear, so as not to disturb an elegant conversation in which he has no right to take part.

V

Now Francesca introduces herself in a manner which again shows the pride she feels in her ancestry. Posterity knows her as Francesca da Rimini, from the abode of her husband and lover, from the city where she died as well as sinned; but she still thinks of herself as Francesca da Ravenna, from the city where she was born, an offspring of renowned lineage. This is the aristocratic, feudal, royal way of naming oneself: the great historical or legendary figures in Shakespeare's plays are called by their princedoms, dukedoms, kingdoms, or realms. Thus, although extended for three lines, Francesca's statement amounts to: "I am Ravenna." As she avoids uttering her name, so she avoids mentioning directly her native city, but refers to it through a long periphrasis, placing her town (such is the meaning of the old Italian *terra*) on the map:

> Siede la terra dove nata fui
> su la marina dove 'l Po discende
> per aver pace co' seguaci sui.

What Francesca has just told is merely that her birthplace lies on the Adriatic coast, not far from the Po's mouth. Yet the connotations of this geographical reference are far richer and more complex than its denotative content. First of all, Ravenna does not lie on the seashore, but sits (*siede*) on it, and a lofty throne image seems to be implied in the choice of such a verb. Then, the purely physical phenomenon of the overflowing of the river into the wide expanse of the sea is evoked in terms of the pathetic fallacy: Francesca humanizes and spiritualizes that blind natural force by comparing its consummation to the wish fulfillment of our soul, longing for an eternal peace denied to the damned, which Francesca would beseech for Dante, if she could pray to God. Finally, the river marching to its own serene death, within a body of water far greater than itself, is seen as going to its peaceful end not alone but accompanied by its tributaries and affluents, thus likened to a retinue of loyal vassals following their lord to his destination.

After employing a full terzina to reveal her identity, Francesca now devotes almost three terzinas to tell what happened to her companion and herself. She re-evokes the most important event in their lives with a threefold statement, in terms of what love did first to each one and, later, to both of them. Each one of the three parts of her statement occupies a terzina, or part of it. The final part, as a matter of fact, is made of two parallel sentences, taking only two lines, as symmetrically related to each other as the preceding terzinas are. In the first of these Francesca describes how Paolo fell in love with her; and in the second, how she fell in love with him. In the two concluding lines, which act as the closing crescendo of her statement, she first simply asserts that their love led them to a joint death, and then she states the revengeful assurance that their killer, who is still alive, will be damned like them: he will suffer eternally in Caina, that section of the ninth circle where those whose murderous hand broke the sacred ties of blood are punished. At this point Francesca has no more to tell, and Dante rounds off the last of the three terzinas by saying that the words he has just reported were uttered by the two shades to Virgil and himself:

> Amor, ch' al cor gentil ratto s'apprende,
>   prese costui de la bella persona
>   che mi fu tolta; e 'l modo ancor m'offende.
> Amor, ch' a nullo amato amar perdona,
>   mi prese del costui piacer sì forte,
>   che, come vedi, ancor non m'abbandona.
> Amor condusse noi ad una morte:
>   Caina attende chi a vita ci spense."
> Queste parole da lor ci fur porte.

The opening line of each one of the first two stanzas begins with the word *Amor*, which we must always envision as being capitalized, and which is immediately followed, in the rest of the line, by a brief general definition of its modes of operation. The second line describes how passion suddenly mastered one or the other of the two lovers, while the third indicates, from Francesca's viewpoint, the present or lasting effects of their love. Each one of the two terzinas rises toward its climax in the middle, but at the end its tension relaxes somewhat. The action of love, as well as the consequences of that action, are always suggested by such violent verbs as "to catch," "to seize," and the like. The first stanza is dominated by Francesca's feeling of grief for the cruel and degrading way the feminine and youthful loveliness of her handsome body (*bella persona*) was defaced by the vengeful hand of her outraged husband and lay disfigured in death. The second is dominated instead by a feeling of possessive pride at the thought that her love survived life itself: that even Hell has been unable to destroy it and to separate her lover from her. In each stanza she refers to him by the pronoun *costui*, that one, which in Italian, when used in direct speech, indicates someone who is more obviously visible to the listener than to the speaker; and by the mere use of such a pronoun the poet helps us to visualize the scene. Thus our imagination realizes that, while speaking, Francesca looks steadily at Dante, without ever turning her gaze toward her companion, as if she could not even doubt that he is still at her side. Francesca's speech seems to increase gradually in emotional pitch, as may be easily shown by comparing the alternate lines alluding to Love. In the first, Love is described as a natural attraction for every noble and sensitive heart; [10] in the second, as a fatal necessity forcing its object to return the passion it has stirred in another soul; in the third, as a tragic consummation, which in their case brought both of them to a single death.

After this nothing further can be said, except, since we are in the all too human world of Hell, words of hatred and revenge against the man who, by giving them no time to repent, was also the unconscious instrument of their damnation, of their "second death." Yet those words of hatred and revenge sound so unexpected and sudden that many interpreters attribute them to Paolo, rather than to Francesca. They argue that the reference to Caina is more proper in the mouth of him who was the brother of the man he wronged, and who wronged him in his turn; and they find support for their claim in the plural forms which Dante uses at the end of this passage: *Queste parole da lor ci fur porte* (Such words were brought to us from them), and at the beginning of the following one: *Quand io intesi quell'anime offense* (When I heard those injured souls). But the great majority of the critics maintain, I believe rightly, that Dante merely means that Francesca and Paolo are two souls in one: and that the woman, even when she speaks in the first-person singular, speaks always for both of them.

VI

The passage following acts as an interlude between the two speeches of Francesca, serving to calm the heroine's rekindled emotions, as well as the reader's excited imagination. This braking pause, sounding like the andante of a concerto, gives the poet the opportunity to describe the effect which Francesca's talk has produced on him. While listening to her words Dante had held his eyes constantly fixed on her, as we realize from the statement that he lowered his gaze (*viso*) as soon as she ended ("she," and not "they," as the second of the two plurals mentioned above would literally mean). With his head bent down, the poet remains absorbed for such a long time in his broodings and musings that Virgil asks him what he is thinking about, not in order to get an answer, but merely to rouse Dante from his mood:

> Quand' io intesi quell'anime offense,
>   chinai 'l viso, e tanto il tenni basso,
>   fin che 'l poeta mi disse: "Che pense?"

Dante is so engrossed in his thoughts that he fails to take notice of Virgil's words, and still remains speechless and motionless. When he finally decides to break the spell, he speaks not to reply to his master, but to unburden himself of the sorrowful reflections still agitating his soul. The language and rhythm seem to express the effort by which Dante breaks away from his mood, and the difficulty which he feels in articulating his words, the first of which will be only the sad exclamation "alas":

> Quando rispuosi, cominciai: "Oh lasso,
>   quanti dolci pensier, quanto disio
>   menò costoro al doloroso passo!"

Dante's words sound like a melancholy acknowledgment of the decisive role that both imagination and instinct must have played in the moral crisis, the outcome of which was for the two lovers adultery and death: this is what the poet means by sweet thoughts (*dolci pensier*), or suggestive and self-indulgent visions of love, and by desire (*disio*), or the seductive power of a yearning still unconfessed to its object and perhaps unavowed by the subject itself. By referring to Paolo and Francesca as *costoro* (those ones, those two), the poet clearly shows that he still is looking down while uttering those words, which are thus addressed only to himself. But as soon as he wishes to speak to the two lovers, he lifts his eyes up and gazes intently at them, while slowly unfolding his thoughts:

> Poi mi rivolsi a loro e parla' io,
>   e cominciai:

Dante emphasizes that it is now his turn to speak. Here again, the plural "to them" (*a loro*) notwithstanding, it is only to Francesca that he addresses himself. Dante, who up to now has spoken as a tactful courtier, becomes again the moralist eager to know the how and why of man's fall. Thus now he wants to learn how two noble hearts like those could be brought to commit a sin made even more heinous by the betrayal of a brotherly bond. Hence the pilgrim does not hesitate to ask straightforwardly the question that has troubled his mind during his silent spell. He realizes that what he is doing is like probing an open wound, so he speaks with great delicacy and softens, as much as possible, his touch. He begins by stating his compassionate feelings for what he calls all too kindly Francesca's tortures (*martiri*), as if her torments were excessive, even unjust, or at least such as to deserve the tears they are stirring within his heart:

> . . . "Francesca, i tuoi martiri
> a lacrimar mi fanno tristo e pio.

Yet, without lingering further, boldly using an adversative particle and a concise imperative form, he enjoins her to tell when and how her criminal love began. He attenuates the crudity of his question by using the elegant and sophisticated language already used by Francesca, and by referring, like her, to Love as if it were a supernatural power or a superhuman being. Yet, although equally abstract, Dante's personification is less forceful: he attributes less responsibility to Love, whom he treats not as a despotic ruler but as a gentle lord, who does not constrain, but rather unbinds. Thus Dante asks Francesca how Love made it not necessary, but possible, for Paolo and her to realize that the longing troubling their souls was but the temptation of sin:

> Ma dimmi: al tempo de' dolci sospiri,
> a che e come concedette amore
> che conosceste i dubbiosi desiri?"

The parallel words closing the first and the last line of the terzina, sealing their similarities and differences in the ringing echo of the rhyme, reveal how distant and how near to each other are the innocent beginnings of love and its sinful consummation, first in thought and then in deed. Dante knows how fatally and easily sweet sighs (*dolci sospiri*) may be replaced by what he calls dubious desires (*dubbiosi desiri*), and with this marvelous expression fully reveals his genius as a searcher of the human soul. The adjective *dubbiosi* is certainly used in its etymological sense, meaning "ambiguous"; modern psychology would translate it with such terms as "subconscious" or "half-conscious." The very use of such an epithet shows that Dante needs to know everything about Francesca's fall: and such a need is dictated not by a vicarious or morbid curiosity, but by a deep urge for psychological and ethical knowledge. Dante the poet, through the simple and full answer Francesca is about to give, will satisfy this urge, which affects the reader as well.

To understand the meaning and value of all this, it may suffice to recall that even one of the greatest literary and moral figures of modern culture, Leo Tolstoy, did not dare to look so fearlessly into the obscure depths of temptation and sin. In *Anna Karenina* we have a complete report of what happened to the heroine before and after her fall: but, as for the fall itself, the writer passes it over, as if to say, "the rest is silence." Tolstoy avoids telling us about the when and the how of Vronsky's and Anna's sin, and replaces with a series of suspension points the omitted tale of the climax of their story, of the novel's crucial event.[11] By doing so, the great Russian master shows his reverence for the mysteries of the human soul; but Dante shows the same reverence in the opposite way, by probing that mystery and by laying it bare in front of us. Tolstoy refused to describe in detail Anna's fall to avoid either one of two alternatives. The first was to evoke that fall pathetically or, more simply, romantically: but this would have involved an attitude of indulgent forgiveness, and so destroyed the stern morality of the tale. The other was to represent Anna's fall realistically, in all its brutal ugliness, in the crudity of its naturalistic details: but this would have prevented both author and reader from feeling for the heroine all the sympathy she seems to deserve. Alessandro Manzoni was faced with the same dilemma, and, like Tolstoy, he solved it by omission and silence. Thus, in *The Betrothed*, he finally refused to include the pages he had already written about the psychological crisis which ends with the fall of the nun Gertrude, replacing them with only three words, summing up all her future sins and crimes with the mere statement that she failed to reject the first, apparently innocent, advances of her would-be seducer: "la sventurata rispose" (the unlucky woman replied).[12] Dante, no less a moralist than Manzoni or Tolstoy, accepted the challenge implied in their dilemma, and as a poet succeeded in giving us a direct and total report of Francesca's fall which avoids the pitfalls of moralism and sentimentalism. This he does dramatically by letting Francesca tell in her own words how and why she became an adulteress.

Thus Dante the character asks his fatal questions without any qualm, and Francesca answers with great candor, and without shame. That question has stirred in her soul a feeling of overwhelming self-pity, and that feeling alone — since, as she says, there is no greater sorrow than remembering a happy past in a time of wretchedness. The sorrow is made even greater in her case by the realization that her past happiness and her present misery are equally irrevocable. Francesca implies that Dante may be unable to understand such truth, which, however, is well known to his teacher. Like the spirits who have been damned for their sins, Dante's companion will always long, if not for the happiness he may have once enjoyed on earth, at least for that eternal bliss which God's grace has denied him. Francesca has already recognized Virgil, although she has not remarked upon his presence. Here she corrects her previous oversight, thus indirectly conveying to him her interest in his person and her sympathy for his plight:

> E quella a me: "Nessun maggior dolore
> che ricordarsi del tempo felice
> ne la miseria; e ciò sa 'l tuo dottore.

The entire terzina must be read at a rapid pace, almost without stopping at the end of the line. By the feverish agitation of her words Francesca indicates that she is uttering a truth directly experienced, and not merely a gnomic sentence; [13] or better, a general truth which she personalizes both within and without herself, extending it to that Virgil who is Dante's teacher and who has learned that lesson as sadly as she has. After this Francesca states her willingness, despite the pain it will cost her, to gratify the visitor's wish. So, she says, if you are so eager to know *la prima radice del nostro male*, "the first root of our ill (where the last word, as always in Italian, means not only "ill," but "evil"), I will comply with your request. But she warns him that by doing so she will speak and weep at the same time:

> Ma s' a conoscer la prima radice
> del nostro mal [amor] tu hai cotanto affetto,
> dirò come colui che piange e dice.

The first two lines of the terzina are an obvious reminiscence from the *Aeneid* (II.10–13) and seem to be meant as another courteous allusion, or flattering tribute, to the great poet who was once Virgil.[14] This charming trait, which could be defined as a compliment by quotation, indicates that Francesca never loses her feminine sophistication even under emotional stress. In a calm and quiet tone, before unveiling her most deeply buried memory, she announces the tears which she may shed during her speech, but which we shall never see.

VII

Francesca tells her story as if she were reminiscing aloud. One day, Paolo and she were reading together, for their own entertainment, the romance of Lancelot du Lac, and particularly that section of the romance describing how the protagonist was overpowered by his passion for the fair Guinevere. Francesca alludes to all this very succinctly, through the single phrase: *come amor lo strinse* (how love seized him), where she uses again a violent verb, *stringere*, "to grasp" or "to squeeze," to indicate the violence of the passion mastering the knight's soul. We imagine the two sitting beside each other: one listening, the other, probably Francesca, reading aloud. But the only thing we are told by Francesca is that they were alone, without the company of even the fear of their weakness, or the suspicion of their own selves. It would be impossible to state more concisely the perfidy of temptation, lying in wait to assail two unprepared and defenseless human hearts. The malice of sin threatens and ruins our souls when they yield to self-oblivion, when they abandon themselves, deceitfully, to their own innocence:

> Noi leggiavamo un giorno per diletto
> di Lancialotto come amor lo strinse:
> soli eravamo e sanza alcun sospetto.

Francesca's memory rehearses all the unforgettable instants of that fatal moment. They were looking down at the pages of their book, when the suggestive power of the story suddenly raised their gazes toward each other; or, as Francesca says, "that reading made us lift our eyes." This happened more than once; and Dante seems to lengthen the duration of each of those instants calling for a diaeresis on the word *fiate*, times. At every turn, each recognized the same paleness on the other's face. Yet the reading would have perhaps failed to seduce them into sin, if the climax of the tale had not finally broken down all restraints and overcome their resistance:

Per più fiate li occhi ci sospinse
quella lettura, e scolorocci il viso;
ma solo un punto fu quel che ci vinse.

The crucial point, the passage by which they were vanquished, is that famous scene in the romance where the noble Gallehaut begs Guinevere to reward the gentle knight Lancelot for loving her so loyally and faithfully, and the Queen complies and kisses Lancelot on his lips. The scene, and the electric effect of its reading, are recalled by Francesca with some of the loveliest lines of the canto:

Quando leggemmo il disiato riso
esser baciato da cotanto amante,
questi, che mai da me non fia diviso,
la bocca mi baciò tutto tremante.

The transition from a vicarious to a genuine consummation, from the first kiss of Lancelot and Guinevere, which belongs to the realm of fancy, to the first kiss of Paolo and Francesca, which took place in the realm of experience, is beautifully conveyed not only by the change of rhythmical pace, but also by the sudden transformation of Francesca's mode of expression, by the metamorphosis of her language. The lips of Guinevere, the heroine of the romance, are at first marvelously metaphorized as *disïato riso*, a longed-for smile. These words are made even more insistently caressing by the diaeresis lengthening the adjective and intensifying the radiance of the image. The select choice of words and sounds, as well as the trope itself, by which the curved lips of the loved and loving queen lose all physical reality, becoming as light and incorporeal as their inviting and wordless smile, tend to give a spiritualized and idealized vision of that imaginary embrace. The queen's inviting gesture is re-experienced from the viewpoint of Guinevere, as shown by the passive form of the verb *esser baciato* (being kissed), which suggests a feeling of feminine abandon, a gesture of self-offering. As for the complement agreeing with that passive form, *da cotanto amante* (by so great a lover), it reveals Francesca's own awareness of the personal merits of her partner in passion and sin, and tends to equate his qualities with Lancelot's aristocratic and chivalric virtues. All this implies a process of self-identification: if Francesca sees in her lover the peer of such a worthy as Lancelot, she may also see in herself the equal of his queen; and she may even think that she had a right to betray Gianciotto, if Guinevere betrayed King Arthur himself. But here the parallelism, and double impersonation, suddenly end. Up to now Francesca has evoked a vision of romantic love through both empathy and sympathy, through the alluring mirror of both sentiment and art. As soon as she deals, not with the fleshless kiss of two fictitious creatures, but with the real one of two living beings, she immediately realizes that she was no Guinevere and that Paolo was no Lancelot. This realization is evident in the line where she alludes, simply and directly, to her lover. Now she does not refer to him with the usual *costui*, that one, but with *questi*, this one, so as to indicate his physical and moral closeness to her. The relative clause following this pronoun (*questi, che mai da me non fia diviso*, this one, who will be never divided from me) is a cry of possession, where pride mingles with despair. That pronoun and that cry presuppose either a fleeting turn of her eyes or merely a blind gesture of her hand, as if to assure herself, as well as the two visitors, that her lover still is, and will forever remain, at her side. All this takes but a line, which separates, as a curtain or a barrier, the kiss she once read about from the kiss still alive in the memory of her flesh. Only after raising such a barrier will she be able to re-evoke, in its loneliness and singularity, their own kiss — which, however, she catches only in Paolo's gesture. Paolo is described as she saw him at that moment, moving toward her full of trembling and fear. The vision reveals him to us as a weaker and more human vessel than even the timid Lancelot. And we, the readers, see Francesca receiving that kiss not on curved but on closed and unsmiling lips, to which she refers by using a cruder, singular word. This is what I meant by the transformation of Francesca's language: and such a falling off from the spiritual to the physiological, from the smile (*riso*) of Guinevere to the mouth (*bocca*) of Francesca, is but the shift or descent from literature to life, from fiction to reality, from romanticism to realism; or more simply, from sentimental fancy to moral truth. Lust and adultery replace for a moment passion and love: a cry of nature breaks forever the mirror of illusion and the veil of self-deceit.

VIII

The proof of this is evident in the two statements by which Francesca concludes her tale, each being enclosed in a single line. The first is but an exclamation, ambiguous and significant at the same time. Its clear purport is the acknowledgment, on Francesca's part, of the role which the reading of that famous medieval romance played in their life, as well as the recognition that that role was identical with the one played by Gallehaut in the story they read not too wisely but too well. The ambiguity lies in the mixed tone of the phrase, conveying a double sense of regret for all the bliss and evil of which that hour was the seed: *Galeotto fu il libro e chi lo scrisse.*

By equating the effect of that reading with the action performed by Gallehaut, by identifying the unknown author of the romance with Gallehaut himself, who still preserves a graceful dignity despite the vileness of his services, Francesca treats the book and its author as if she would like to accuse and to absolve them at the same time. She cannot forget the beauty of the story and the glamor of the characters, since that beauty and that glamor still reflect a kind of redeeming light on the sin they committed at the example of Lancelot and Guinevere. While on one side Francesca tries to emphasize in her story all the aspects that may ennoble her experience, she has still too much sense of responsibility to lay more than part of their guilt on others than Paolo and herself. She knows that she has been more sinning than sinned against; hence she dares not call the romance and its writer by the ugly name of panderer. The reader feels nothing more need be added, yet Francesca has something more to say. Strangely enough, she feels it necessary to allude to what happened after the reading had aroused and bared to them their own "dubious desires." To be sure, the allusion is merely negative in character, and takes the form of another reference to the book which they forgot and discarded, as soon as it had led them to their first kiss: *quel giorno più non vi leggemmo avante.*

At first sight, the final words of Francesca (since these are her final words) seem to be superfluous and even to lack propriety: they may sound impudent, or at least too complacent, even more than merely unnecessary. What is Francesca's purpose in telling Dante that they did not read in that book any further? Why unveil so deviously, as well as so brutally, those intimate secrets which even a lost woman prefers to keep hidden? Only a harlot, devoid of the last shred not only of modesty, but even of self-respect, would go so far as to speak of her fall in such cynical terms. There is a difference between unchastity and impurity: a woman may be candid without being shameless. In all her behavior Francesca has consistently shown not only great delicacy of feeling, but also tactfulness and good taste. She has given proof of intellectual and moral courage by facing truth in all its nakedness; yet she has constantly avoided the pitfalls of vulgarity and coarseness. If such is the case, we are forced to conclude that her final words must mean something less plain and obvious than what they seem to suggest. I am unwilling to follow the example of some interpreters, who take these words at their face value. The clue we need is perhaps to be found in the very turn of the phrases by which Francesca opens and closes the story of her fall. The first and the last line of that story begin with almost identical words: *un giorno, quel giorno*. In the second case the temporal reference appears to be hardly useful or necessary. It would have been sufficient to say, "and then we read no further." Yet Francesca feels the need to emphasize that they did not read any further "that day." These two small words cannot be explained away as a mere pleonasm, as syllables that are there solely to fill the line. They become pertinent and relevant, and as such necessary, only if they are supposed to hint or imply that Paolo and Francesca took up again, on other occasions, the reading of the book which had been "the first root" of their sin. Why does Francesca wish to suggest these successive readings, after the one which was interrupted by their first kiss on the first day of their love? Such a question may not be answered, but it must be asked. The only thing we need to realize is that Francesca wants us to know that the two lovers returned on other days to the book which once and for all acted as their go-between. The reason for this, as for Francesca's indirect reference to such a fact, may be seen in a wish not so much to recapture the wild happiness of the first, fatal moment, as to recover, if only for an instant, the idealizing and sublimating illusions which literature creates around the realities of sex and lust. It was the worship of passion, the ideology of love, its idolatry and cult, which had hidden from their consciences the danger of damnation and the ugliness of sin; it was the written word, both harmless and harmful, that had spelled their doom. Yet they tasted the intoxicating sweetness of that worship or cult not only before, but even after, knowing the bitterness of sin.

Now that Francesca has ended her story, the canto goes rapidly toward its end. At this point, Dante has very little to tell us. He merely observes that while Francesca had been talking, Paolo had been unashamedly weeping, and implies that his tears did not stop even after she had ceased to speak. From Dante's manner of speaking, rather than from what he says, we realize that he must never have taken his eyes from Francesca's face all the while she had been talking to him: and this is perhaps the first time he has been able to look on the tearful countenance of her lover. The echoes of Francesca's words, which still fill and rend his heart, or perhaps, even more, the pitiful spectacle of Paolo's grief, are too much for Dante, who breaks down under the stress. The poet suddenly swoons, and falls down like a dead man:

> Mentre che l'uno spirto questo disse,
> l'altro piangea sì, che di pietade
> io venni men così com' io morisse;
> e caddi come corpo morto cade.

Dante loses his senses out of compassion, while Paolo and Francesca lost their senses out of passion alone: yet, although caused by sentimental participation rather than by moral complicity, his fall parallels their fall. The almost perfect iambic beat of the line seems to reproduce the thud of his body, which for a while will lie on the earth as a lifeless object, as a soulless thing.

IX

Now that we have completed the line-by-line commentary, we must undertake our final quest, trying to rediscover the unique and total mystery of this appealing page of poetry. Every great work of art, even the most lucid, is a kind of hieroglyphic. The key to decipher it lies hidden in the work itself. Close reading of the episode has already supplied several clues for unlocking the mystery of its power.

The first is to be found in Virgil's catalogue, to which we are now bound to return. If we re-examine that list, we shall notice among many remarkable details that it includes more women than men. The imbalance may seem slight if we content ourselves with a mere counting of heads: after all, the seven figures listed by Virgil fall into two groups not very different in size, respectively comprising four units and three. A more important distinction may be seen in the fact that the procession is led by the representatives of the female sex, following each other without break; while the masculine representatives, at least in Virgil's reported speech, close the pageant. This does not necessarily mean that the crowd of sinners is so divided in fact. It is true that such a division has been surmised by a few commentators through a too literal interpretation of Dante's further reference to *la schiera ov' è Dido* (the troop where Dido is); but the supposition seems to be denied by the consideration that it is to that very troop that not only Francesca but also Paolo belongs. This brings in another problem, whether Paolo and Francesca are the only lovers forming a couple even in death, a question which we think must be answered in the affirmative. At any rate, the separation of the sinners into two series according to sex may take place merely in Virgil's mind; and the only thing it proves is that the poet assigns a certain kind of supremacy and priority to the feminine over the masculine components of the entire band. That such is the case is proved by the disproportionate emphasis with which the catalogue deals with the great ladies of love, as contrasted with the cursory, and even curt, treatment of their partners in passion and guilt. The catalogue itself stretches for about seven stanzas; yet the women occupy four full terzinas, while the men take less than three lines and scarcely a greater number of words, since the remainder contains other matter, of more general interest or of indifferent purport. Another significant fact is that all of the women were famous queens, while the men belong to the less exalted status of princes.

All this is quite suggestive, and further study of the catalogue will show the possibility of classifying its figures into two different cultural groups. Of the seven characters mentioned, six belong to the classical tradition, with only Tristan, the last on the list, belonging to the lore of the Middle Ages. This classification is only implicit and, as such, highly misleading. The really significant point is that all the women represent, without exception, classical antiquity; that among them there is not a single modern heroine. As for the men, they include only one modern figure, Tristan, while the other two, Achilles and Paris, derive originally from the classical tradition. Yet, although representing the pagan past, Achilles and

Paris are not treated classically, but in the light of the medieval interpretation of their legends. In brief, they are conceived as if they were the moral peers or, so to say, the literary equals of Tristan. This classification, dividing the catalogue's figures into ancient and modern, and exemplifying the former with feminine and the latter with masculine characters, is the only valid one, and is stated explicitly in the phrase already referred to, one generally neglected by the commentators, by which Dante sums up his master's list: *le donne antiche e' cavalieri*. The ladies of old are Semiramis, Dido, Cleopatra, and Helen; the knights are Achilles, Paris, and Tristan.[15] The fact that in this list the women precede, outnumber, or more generally play a far more important role than the men serves again to emphasize the truth that love is the passion where woman, even when she is the seduced rather than the seducer, still remains the ruler and the leader, as Francesca proves so eloquently to us. In brief, in love women are far more interesting than men.

This is clear enough; what is less clear is my contention that here even Achilles and Tristan are conceived in medieval rather than in classical terms, as romantic figures rather than heroic ones. I may prove my point by recognizing that the classical tradition is primarily epic in character, and that its heroes may be conquered in battle but are never vanquished in love. Even Virgil's Aeneas abandons Dido in order to fulfill his undertaking, sacrificing her and his love to his task. For this very reason, classical antiquity is represented in this catalogue by loving women rather than by loving men. It is true that the list contains the names of Achilles and Paris, but, as I have already remarked, both of them are treated not according to Homer but to the various *romans de Troie*. It was indeed in a romance by that title that the French poet Benoît de Sainte More had taken up the Hellenistic legend I have mentioned before, which Virgil also had briefly treated (*Aeneid*, III.322). According to that legend, Achilles had died not as a victim of war, or even of fate, but of passion alone. Dante accepted this version of the hero's death, as shown by the words: *il grande Achille che con amore al fine combatteo* (the great Achilles who fought to the end with love). The adjective sounds here almost ironic, because the hero of the *Iliad* is now seen not in his prowess but in his weakness. Dante is well aware that the Achilles he describes is not the Achilles of Homer, but something and somebody else. Like Paris,

Achilles is here changed into a medieval knight, into a passionate and adventurous soul able to slay dragons and monsters, and yet liable to be defeated in the encounter of love. So his name resounds in this canto not with the lofty notes of the ancient epos, but with the lower tunes of medieval romance. The episode thus already approaches the most complex of all the allusions contained within its literary frame of reference — so obscure and complex as to have escaped the eye of even the most searching interpreters of this episode. That literature is playing a role within the catalogue itself may be easily proved by a passing statement in Virgil's portrait of Semiramis. Practically all details concerning the Queen of Assyria are borrowed from the *Historia* of Paulus Orosius; [16] and without citing his author, the poet, or Virgil for him, points out that all those notions derive from the written tradition, from literary sources. Such is certainly the aim and meaning of the relative clause following the name of Semiramis, *di cui si legge* (of whom one reads), by which Virgil seems to warn us that it is through books that we learn not only of great feats and noble deeds, but also of sinful passions and criminal acts. This brief incidental sentence anticipates the moral of the canto, with its implied claim that history and poetry, or literature in general, by preserving and transmitting through the written word the love stories of old, may lead us into sin, as Paolo and Francesca were led by the reading of their *libro galeotto*,[17] the romance of Lancelot du Lac. Literature is full of *falli scritti*, of faults written down, to employ an expression which Dante uses in another passage of the *Commedia*, where he refers again, this time incidentally, to the same romance (*Paradiso*, XVI.15).

X

The significance of this clue lies in its implications: if Virgil's catalogue is to be read in the key of medieval romance, why not read in the same key the scene of Francesca's fall or, more simply, the whole episode? The love story that Dante retells in his own way (which coincides, although only in part, with Francesca's way) is romantic in the old-fashioned meaning of that term: a meaning fully preserved in the French adjective *romanesque*, but partly surviving even in the epithet "romantic," to which modern usage has given such a broad semantic range. Medieval culture was full of trends which may be defined as romantic in the traditional sense; and it expressed those trends in literary forms which, being essentially anticlassical and new, took for their name the word from which both *romantic* and *romanesque* were to derive, that is, "romance." That the figures of Paolo and Francesca, as well as the story of their love, had been conceived by a poetic imagination fully aware of both those trends and those forms was recognized by no less an interpreter and judge than Dante's literary successor, Petrarch himself. It is well known that Petrarch undertook to write his *Trionfi* out of rivalry with his predecessor, to challenge the supreme achievement of the latter, and to prove to the world and himself that he was as great a master as Dante in all fields of vernacular poetry, in the epic as well as in the lyrical genre. It is equally well known that Petrarch failed in this attempt, which he was even unable to bring to completion, despite many years of hard toil. What is less well known is that in the first of the *Trionfi* he gave us in passing what seems to amount to an implied critique of the Paolo and Francesca episode; and it is with the purpose of analyzing such critique that we must first say something about the entire work.

Petrarch's poem tries to compete with the *Commedia* by both imitating and transcending it, and takes the shape of a symbolical and philosophical narrative where metaphysical vision is replaced by a series of mystical dreams. Each dream evokes a procession or pageant, representing, in medieval fashion, a personified abstraction, the allegory of a virtue or value, of an idea or concept. The intent, as in Dante, is didactic and moral: the poet aims at establishing a scale of perfection and at conveying, in all its successive steps, the gradual progression of man's religious and ethical insight. Petrarch does so by showing how each one of his abstractions vanquishes the preceding one: and this series of victories manifests itself, emblematically, in a series of "triumphs." The first of these is the "Triumph of Love," which conquers all other passions of man. Love, in its turn, is superseded by the "Triumph of Chastity," while the latter yields to the "Triumph of Death." Death seems to withdraw before the "Triumph of Fame," and this before the "Triumph of Time," which is finally annihilated, as are all human and earthly things, by the "Triumph of Eternity." In the first of the

Trionfi, the *Trionfo d'Amore*, Petrarch visibly tries to compete with *Inferno*, V; yet the only thing he succeeds in doing is merely to rewrite and to expand, out of all proportion, Virgil's, or rather Dante's, catalogue. The latter takes seven verses at the most, and mentions only an equal number of names, but Petrarch fails to follow Dante's example and his perfect lesson in artistic economy. Thus he extends his procession for four full cantos, each one of which is of greater length than Dante's, and includes hundreds of historical, mythological, and literary figures, in an almost endless list. Petrarch seems to derive the majority of his characters from the authority of Ovid, from both the *Heroides* and the *Metamorphoses*: at any rate, practically all of them belong to classical antiquity. Even here, the ladies of old far outnumber the men; and the latter include Achilles, whom Petrarch treats, on Dante's example, not as an epic or tragic hero but as a pathetic one:

> . . . e l'altro è Achille,
> ch' ebbe in suo amar assai dogliose sorte.[18]

The medieval heroes and heroines of love are, in Petrarch's list, very few, and quite significantly he cites Paolo and Francesca among them. In other terms, he equates the protagonists of this canto with the protagonists of the love romances. This is not merely implied but clearly stated, since Paolo and Francesca, no less than Lancelot and Guinevere, or Tristan and Iseult, are defined by him as "those who fill pages with dreams." The poet of the *Trionfi* seems to disapprove of the fact that such phantoms and their fancies are still haunting the imagination of man; and this disapproval, which apparently extends up to the story of Paolo and Francesca as reported by Dante, may also derive from Petrarch's strong humanistic bias against a form of vernacular writing which he finds devoid of formal decorum and of classical dignity, appealing more to the taste of the *profanum vulgus* than of the elite. Dante would have shared such a literary prejudice only in part, but he would certainly have accepted the moral judgment which derives from it. Even if Petrarch seems to feel otherwise, Dante wrote the episode of Paolo and Francesca in order to condemn the evil suggestive power that the reading of the romances did once exercise on the souls of the two protagonists of this canto, and may still exercise on the souls of too many living women and men. Even if he pretends not to have learned it from Dante, in this passage of the *Trionfo d'Amore* (I.25–26) Petrarch is teaching the same lesson:

> Ecco quei che le carte empion di sogni,
> Lancilotto, Tristano e gli altri erranti,
> ove conven che il vulgo errante agogni.
>
> Vedi Ginevra, Isolda e le altri amanti,
> e la coppia d'Arimino che 'nseme
> vanno facendo dolorosi pianti.

This passage contains many details of great interest. First, in this part of his list, Petrarch, as Virgil does in his catalogue, separates the men from the women (Lancelot and Tristan on one side and Guinevere and Iseult on the other); but, like Dante, he refuses to separate Paolo and Francesca, whom he seems to place together among the representatives of the weaker sex. Petrarch feels, like every reader, that Paolo and Francesca are the only couple of lovers whom Dante sees still joined, at least among the souls of the second circle. Of even more import, Petrarch identifies the "chivalric" and the "romantic," which he condemns together, as forms of feeling, and as literary themes as well. The identification is made by way of a simple pun, which attributes the same epithet to the masculine protagonists of the romances and to the readers of those stories of adventure and love. The former, exemplified by Lancelot and Tristan (and even by Paolo, who is their peer) are called *erranti*, in the sense of "wandering (knights)"; while the reading public seeking a vicarious experience in the fancies of the romances is the *vulgo*, or crowd, equally *errante*, in the sense of "erring," or deviating from the right path. By this identification of the chivalric with the romantic, Petrarch gives the best available proof of the validity of my assertion that Dante knows what he is doing when calling *cavalieri* all the heroes of love, whether modern or ancient. Thus Petrarch seems to realize as well as Dante that there is no glory, but only error, in the supreme adventure of love, which always ends, even for the most valiant knight, only in captivity and defeat: and also that there is more fallacy than beauty in a literature that panders to our passion, and paints as a victory our surrender to temptation and sin. Dante, of course, goes farther and deeper than Petrarch, who, after all, remained all his life a poet of love, even if he conceived of it in a spiritual way, even if he tried, at the approach of death, to repudiate it. What Petrarch says in the passage I have just quoted is edifying, but hardly more than a pious wish. The guide that points for him the victims of Love is Love itself; and even in the *Trionfi* Love is vanquished only allegorically, first by the "Triumph of Chastity" and later by the "Triumph of Eternity." But in Dante's canto Love is vanquished by the nemesis it carries within itself. As the four cantos of Petrarch's pageant easily show, the latter's scorn for romantic love was more apparent than real; and his detachment is due to the fear that a deeper contemplation would entail more self-involvement than he cares to confess. But Dante probes the innermost secrets of both passion and lust: and this is why, instead of contemplating "romantic love" from without, he dares to reconstruct the sinful story of Paolo and Francesca from inside, within the framework of the "romance" itself. Yet, as we shall see later, that framework is used not to re-evoke romantic love, but to exorcise it.

XI

To the hints contained in Dante's catalogue, as well as to the external ones provided by Petrarch's imitation of it, we must add other clues, such as the most relevant document which Dante left imbedded in the canto itself: namely, Francesca's manner of speaking, the language and diction she employs in telling her story of passion and death. The heroine makes abundant use of the medieval casuistry of love, and her discourse, far from being spontaneous, is rather deliberately constructed. Her words are, and are meant to be, highly conventional, even rhetorical, in character. This conventionalism is so intentional, and so intense, that we cannot certainly apply to her, and to her speech, the definition that Dante gives elsewhere (*Purgatorio*, XXIV.52–54) of himself and of his own poetry of love:

> . . . "I' mi son un, che quando
> Amor mi spira, noto, e a quel modo
> ch' e' ditta dentro vo significando."

By these words Dante means that when a genuine feeling of love truly inspires a poet's heart, it immediately determines the forms of expression best suited to itself. To do so, that feeling must have some purity and innocence; that love must be a matter of the soul, rather than of the senses. The feeling dictating Francesca's fashionable diction is of a very different sort; at any rate, the love of which she speaks in conventional terms is not necessarily identical with the love which bursts forth through the shell of that diction and often breaks it. When she is less self-conscious, Francesca's passion overflows beyond the barriers of convention, and even of convenance; but generally she tries to keep within the limits of a studied elegance, of a stylized modulation of both thought and speech. And this amounts to saying that one of the outstanding critical hypotheses, the one maintaining that Francesca speaks according to the tenets of the *dolce stil nuovo*, is completely wrong. The point may be proved in many ways: for instance, by arguing that no woman was ever a member of Dante's "circle," or that no feminine character ever speaks in the first person in any of the poems written by the poets of that school. It is true that Francesca's speech is full of literary mannerisms, but it is easier to find among them a few peculiar Provençal traits than to find any characteristic features of the "sweet new style." The most typical Provençalism to be found in Francesca's speech is *piacer*, nearer, even linguistically, to the original *plazer* than to its equivalent *piacenza*, normally used before Dante's time by the Italian imitators of the troubadours. As a matter of fact, Francesca uses the term *piacer* or *plazer* in a novel way, by applying it to masculine, rather than feminine, beauty; and this reference to the good looks of her lover contributes to the almost womanly, or at least unmanly, impression that Paolo seems to produce.

Even so we must still recognize that the first line of Francesca's confession sounds not merely as a reminiscence, but as a repetition of the main belief of the "sweet new style" school, according to which there is an affinity, nay an identity, between love and a noble heart. That line, *Amor ch' al cor gentil ratto s'apprende*, seems to be an echo, or rather a replica, of the opening words of the famous canzone by Guido Guinicelli, *Al cor gentil ripara sempre amore*, which the young Dante had paraphrased in the beginning of a famous sonnet of the *Vita nuova*: *Amor e 'l cor gentil sono una cosa*.

Yet, if my reading of the episode is right, I feel that despite their verbal identities Francesca's statement and the passages just quoted have different, even opposite, meanings. As used by Francesca, *amore* and *cor gentile* signify an experience and a reality that cannot be compared, except in contrast, with the ideals and values those two formulae designate in the language of Guinicelli and the Dante of the *Vita*. When these two poets connect the two concepts, they intend to say that the spiritual power of love finds its natural abode in a heart made noble by its own merits and virtues. But when Francesca makes the same connection, she means instead that passional love is the calling and destiny of every heart which is noble in this world's literal sense, that is, made such by the gentility of its blood. This is the way Francesca feels, as is proved by the manner in which she speaks about herself and of her own passion and person, or alludes to Paolo, whom she implicitly defines as *cotanto amante*, so great a lover, by so defining Lancelot. One must not forget that the notary Guinicelli and Dante, who was officially a member of the medical guild, were respectively citizens of Bologna and Florence, or of two free communes, of two democratic commonwealths. Their very conception of love, despite its aristocratic origins, reflects already the cultural awareness of the new burghers' class. The "sweet new style" reacts against the feudal ideology of the troubadours and their disciples, who believed literally in the doctrine of courtly love, and considered it a privilege of the highly placed and the well born. But Francesca was the member of a family that tried to reduce the city of Ravenna into its own fief, and the pride of her birth and station induces her to prefer the Provençal view. That view had survived the decline of Provençal poetry and culture, and had found new expression in the prose fiction of northern France, where an equally refined, but less spiritual, sort of love was still considered the exclusive privilege of knights and ladies, of men and women of high breeding and lineage. For Dante and his group, love will always remain a matter of election and grace, based on the reciprocal sympathy of two lofty souls; and the poet rephrases this doctrine in a famous passage in the *Purgatorio* (XXII.10–12), through the following words attributed to Virgil:

> . . . Amore,
> acceso di virtù, sempre altro accese,
> pur che la fiamma sua paresse fuore.

It has been suggested that these lines are meant as a kind of retractation of the principle embodied in the line where Francesca speaks of the fatality of love, of its refusal to absolve any person being loved from loving in return (*Amor, ch' a nullo amato amar perdona*); but the hypothesis seems to be groundless. Through the words just quoted, Dante qualifies in a higher ethical sense the doctrine of his youth, his own belief in the reciprocity of spiritual love. As for Francesca's statement, no palinode was required, exactly because its equivocal meaning is clarified by the moral lesson contained in the entire episode. No correction was in this case necessary since, despite all appearances, even when using the same verbal expressions, she does not speak the language of Dante, or of all the poets who, as he says in another canto of the *Purgatorio* (XXVI.99), used sweet and lovely rhymes of love (*rime d'amor usar dolci e leggiadre*).

Nor, despite the Provençal mannerisms of her speech, have we any right to deduce that Francesca's manner of speaking is an echo of the diction of the troubadours. Only Dante himself may help us to find the literary models and the stylistic examples after which he patterned Francesca's discourse. He offers such a help in another part of the canto just mentioned, where he affirms that Arnaut Daniel was the best craftsman of the vernacular word (*Purgatorio*, XXVI.117–119), and surpassed all his rivals in both "versi d'amore e prose di romanzi."

With this simple line, Dante sums up all the main forms of the literature in the vulgar tongue, as it had developed at that time in Tuscany and Italy, as well as in Provence and France. He obviously considers only the forms endowed with formal dignity, addressed to a literate and nonpopular audience, dealing in different ways with the same great medieval theme, which, for the intellectual as well as for the social elite, was the theme of love. There is no doubt that Francesca's speech must be patterned on either one of these two main forms. It is true that Francesca's language is highly literary in character, and has very little to do with popular speech: its very sophistication and complexity stand out against the background of the simple style used by Dante in the narrative parts of the canto and in the whole of his poem. Yet this does not mean that Francesca's manner of speaking is necessarily poetic, especially in the lyrical sense. We have already stated that that language differs from the style which Dante himself called both "sweet" and "new"; and one may add, not too paradoxically, that, although Dante shapes her words and thoughts into the rhythmical and metrical structure of the *Commedia*, she speaks not in verse but in prose. Thus, by making use of the line quoted above, one could say that her forms of expression derive not from the tradition of the poetry of love ("versi d'amore"), either in the *lingua del sì* or the *langue d'oc*, but from the tradition of love fiction ("prose di romanzi") in the *langue d'oïl*. After all, the name "Francesca" means nothing else but "French." Dante's heroine translates into her own terms the idiom she has learned from such French literary sources as the romance of Lancelot; [19] hence the formal conventionality, the rhetorical stylization, of her speech. Almost dialectically, that conventionality and that stylization transform themselves into their very opposites, becoming thus the aptest instrument, the most natural vehicle, of which Francesca could avail herself not only to relate her story, but even to idealize and sublimate it.

This general imitation of the tone of the romantic narratives she used to admire so much does not mean that Francesca imitates in any special way the particular language of the romance of Lancelot, or that, while re-evoking the effect provoked by the reading of that romance, the poet patterned the story of its two readers after the most important episode of the romance itself. Immoral literature may influence life, but not in such a way as to pattern life after itself. When she establishes an apparently perfect parallel between the two first kisses, the one exchanged between Lancelot and Guinevere and between Paolo and herself, Francesca gives the impression of remembering the one as fully as the other: yet Dante knows that she is wrong. The parallelism she implies is partial or relative; and one could say that she unconsciously reshapes the literary kiss to make it better agree with the real one. In other terms, she recollects what she did experience far better than what she read. Her words mislead the reader (if not the poet) into believing that Lancelot and Guinevere too were alone and without any suspicion (*soli e sanza alcun sospetto*), while, in their meeting in the grove at night, they were not only accompanied by Gallehaut, but also attended by the queen's ladies in waiting, who were lingering nearby. What is even more important is that in the book it is the woman, and not the man, who kisses first. As a matter of fact, while the romance fails to mention that the knight returned the queen's kiss, Francesca does the same in regard to her response to Paolo's embrace. The parallel is partly one also of contrast, and the implication of this is so obviously suggestive that we do not need to dwell upon it. These details may, however, point out that Dante cared more for the spirit than for the letter of his text; and this scorn for literalness must be certainly taken into account also in regard to what we have said about his decision to let Francesca speak according to the diction of the love romances.

The very fact that the poet does not adopt the same diction himself, and fails to use it fully in those passages where the character speaking in the first person is not Francesca but the protagonist of his own poem, clearly shows that even Dante the character avoids involving his own views and values in the language employed by his heroine. The man writing this canto is no longer the young literary enthusiast who once so much liked the French romances dear to all the Paolos and the Francescas as to define them "Arthuri regis ambages pulcherrimae," as he did in a famous passage of *De vulgari eloquio*, where however the word *ambages* is rather equivocal, and may mean "fancies" as well as "adventures." [20] Here Dante uses the language of the romances almost critically, or rather as a dramatic device, through which he projects the psychology of Francesca, and within which he encloses her personality as within a shell. Francesco de Sanctis recognized the magnificent total result of Dante's vision and perspective, while ignoring the process or the method by which that result was achieved. In other words, he paid attention to the natural effects, rather than to the artificial components, of Francesca's speech. It is perhaps for this reason that he was led to interpret the canto in tragic, rather than in romanesque, terms. Yet this was at least in part a happy mistake, because it saved him from the far more serious error of reading Francesca's words in a lyrical key. With his profound insight, the great critic felt that, despite all appearances, Francesca speaks not only outside the frame of reference of the "sweet new style," but in opposition to it. This is what he means when he says that Francesca, "this first-born daughter of Dante," is also "the first truly living woman to appear on the poetic horizon of the modern age." Although readily admitting that such a figure could be created only after "a long elaboration of the feminine ideal in the poetry of the troubadours and in the very lyrics of Dante," he ends by saying that Francesca is the opposite of Beatrice. Within the poetic tradition from which the latter derives, "man fills the stage with himself; it is he who acts, and speaks, and dreams; while woman remains in the background, named and not represented, like Selvaggia and Mandetta; she stays there as man's shadow, as a thing he owns, as an object he has wrought, as the being issued from his rib, devoid of a separate personality of her own." [21]

Unlike the Selvaggia of Cino da Pistoia, the Mandetta of Guido Cavalcanti, and all the other women sung by their peers, including even Beatrice, here Francesca fills the stage with her own actions, words, and dreams, while it is the man who remains in the background, "named and not represented," existing as a mere shadow, a shadow without a mind, without a will, without a word of his own. The originality of the figure and the novelty of the situation are such as to break the iconic pattern of the *donna angelicata*, and to give us instead the first modern portrayal of the "eternal feminine." "Francesca has remained," says de Sanctis, "the type wherefrom there issued the dearest creatures of modern imagination." De Sanctis is certainly right in projecting forward the highest feminine creation of Dante's poetic insight, although he goes too far when he equates her, romantically and sentimentally, with Shakespeare's Juliet and Ophelia, and with Goethe's Gretchen. Francesca is more fully and universally understood if we project her backward in time, as well as forward: if we try to understand the literary tradition to which historically and culturally she belongs. I have tried to do so by analyzing her language; and through this analysis I contend that she speaks not like the women of Shakespearean tragedy, nor like the female protagonists of the modern novel, but like the heroines of the medieval love romances. The poetic genius of Dante has been able to give immortal life to the very figure he has created within the framework of a passing form: and De Sanctis glimpsed this truth when, commenting upon the three sentences which Francesca opens with the word *Amor*, he stated that "in these three wonderful lines there is all the eternal romance of love, as woman apprehends it." Here his insight goes very deep, and it does not matter very much that he uses the word "romance" (*romanzo*) in a sense which is neither literary nor literal.

XII

The last clue to Dante's treatment of romantic love is a negative one: Paolo's silence, and the significance of that silence. Paolo has no existence of his own. He speaks no word during the entire epi-

sode; and even when Francesca refers to her lover, the poet pays
no attention to him. Dante seems to notice his presence only at the
end, and does so only to remark that Paolo must have been weeping
for a long time. It was natural for the poet to place Francesca in the
foreground of the episode, and Paolo in its background; yet this
fails to explain the poet's almost absolute indifference to the lesser
of these two protagonists. Such an indifference is not casual, but
deliberate. Dante's scorn is not directed toward Paolo as a separate
person, but toward what he stands for; and as such it involves all
men who like him are the slaves, rather than the masters, of love.
The passionate man, hardly ever as interesting or suggestive as the
passionate woman, is never called hero, while many a woman in
love is a heroine. It is said that love exalts the lowly and humbles
the lofty ones; but this is true only in the sense that the first is the
feminine, and the second the masculine alternative. Especially in
love is "the female of the species more deadly than the male." For
man, even more than for woman, love is almost always a *liaison
dangereuse*. Either one of the two actors or victims of a love story
will look pathetic to the eyes of mankind, but while pathos may
enhance a woman's personality, it lessens a man's stature. A pathetic
hero is a contradiction in terms, since he is made to look not only
unheroic, but even unmanly. This Dante understood well: so,
while raising Francesca to prominence, he reduced Paolo almost to
nought. De Sanctis recognized this very clearly: "Who is Paolo?
He is not the man, or the manly type, such as to form an antithesis,
to establish a dualism. Francesca fills the stage wholly with herself.
Paolo is the mute expression of Francesca; the string trembling at
what she says, the gesture accompanying her voice. The one speaks
while the other weeps; the tears of the one are the words of the
other."

This statement, a perfect aesthetic justification of Dante's conception, implies that the main character of the episode absorbs the
lesser one; that its protagonist is this couple of lovers, even more
than Francesca herself; that the two lovers form a single personality
though such a personality is shaped by its feminine component,
rather than by its masculine one. In this very conception Dante
shows outstanding originality. No poet went as far as Dante in this
reduction to a cipher of the masculine partner of a great passion.
Considered alone, Paolo, a bleak creature whose only action is

weeping, pales nearly to a vanishing point. Love changes man into woman's shadow, and this is true of Paolo not only as the ghost he now is, but as the man he once was. Francesca projects the memory of herself even before the time of her fatal affair, but evokes her lover only during the moment of their sin. And, unconsciously, she fixes him forever in a vision of passive pusillanimity. At least in appearance she describes him in the very moment he acted like a man: when he took the initiative, as he was supposed to do, and kissed her on her mouth. Yet Francesca finds it fit to remember that even in that instant of daring he was trembling in every fiber of his body, like a leaf. Commenting upon the simple and terrible words, *tutto tremante*, by which Francesca recalls the emotions of her lover in the moment of anguish and bliss, Francesco de Sanctis is led to observe that "certainly Paolo's flesh did not tremble out of fright." I am not so sure: I may even be ready to maintain exactly the opposite. Paolo perhaps trembled because he was afraid: of woman and love, or of death and sin; or simply of the unknown, even of his own fear itself. In this passivity and pusillanimity Paolo strangely resembles the character to whom Francesca and the poet liken him. In the second of the two romances of which he is the protagonist, *Le Chevalier de la Charrette*, Lancelot is described as willing to look like a coward, and even to risk infamy, merely to pursue his love object; while in *Lancelot du Lac* the queen kisses him first, as soon as she realizes that he does not dare to do so himself; and, as the text states with comical naiveté, she gives herself the illusion of being the receiver rather than the giver, by taking the knight by his chin: "Et la roine voit bien que li chevaliers n'en ose plus fere; si le prent pour le menton et le base" (XXXI).

All this may suffice to prove not only that Francesca towers above Paolo, but that the poet towers above both. As I have frequently hinted, this cannot be said of Dante the character, whom the author, with great humility and charity, equates with the lesser part of his double creation. This happens at the very ending of the episode, when the reader witnesses at the same time, in two different men, almost the same heartbreak. It is at this point that we suddenly realize that Paolo had been unashamedly sobbing for the entire duration of Francesca's speech; and immediately after this, we learn that Dante has fainted as soon as Francesca has uttered her last word. For a while, at the close of the canto, Dante the character becomes the equal of Paolo, and even of Lancelot, who seems about to swoon himself while talking with the queen of his still unrewarded love. In this brief moment, Dante himself is but a creature of pathos, a victim of the ridiculous, but it is only the timely fall of the curtain which saves the final scene of the episode from an unexpected caricatural effect.

XIII

All this amounts to saying that love cannot ever be the tragic passion par excellence. Tolstoy acknowledged as much when he attributed the following words to Konstantin Levin, the masculine protagonist, or rather antagonist, in *Anna Karenina*: "To my mind, love . . . both sorts of love, which you remember Plato defines in his *Banquet*, serve as the test of men. Some men only understand one sort, and some only the other. And those who only know the non-platonic love have no need to talk of tragedy . . . In platonic love there can be no sort of tragedy . . . because in that love all is clear and pure because . . . But perhaps you are right. Very likely . . . I don't know. I don't know." [22]

Unlike Tolstoy and his hero, Dante was one of those few human beings equally able to understand both kinds of love; and he understood them both as a man and as a poet. He was able to understand the kind of love which stops at sweet sighs, and which is generally expressed in lyric form, as well as the kind that experiences dubious desires, and manifests itself in romantic fiction. In the same way he understood that neither kind can be tragic. Dante is a moral realist, always subordinating pathos to ethos. So it is improper to interpret the episode of Paolo and Francesca in the light of the romantic view of poetry and life, as De Sanctis did, or according to the decadent view as Gabriele D'Annunzio did in his *Francesca da Rimini*. The latter is not a tragedy, but merely a poem of blood and lust (*poema di sangue e di lussuria*), as the author himself so aptly said.[23] In the same way, while using continuously, and almost exclusively, the criterion of tragedy, Francesco de Sanctis gave us an interpretation of the Paolo and Francesca episode far more pathetic than tragic. "Sin is the highest pathos of tragedy, since this contradiction [between the sense of sin and the erotic impulse] is placed not without, but within the two lovers' souls," says the critic, thus reducing the situation to a psychological crisis, even more than to a moral conflict. It is in the sweet sighs, even more than in the dubious desires, that De Sanctis sees "the tragic core of the story, the divine tragedy left unsaid on Francesca's lips, and which only Dante's reverie, so movingly imagined, calls forth and re-enacts," thus showing that he conceives the fall and the ruin of the two lovers in sentimental terms. De Sanctis concludes his analysis by affirming that "pity is the muse of this tragedy, which the poet unfolds only in its main lines, filling the rest with silence and mystery." But tragedy is made not only of pathos and pity, but also of ethos and terror. A full study of De Sanctis' essay reveals that the critic is reading this episode not in the light of tragedy, but in the light of romantic drama: as a story of love and death, stirring our emotions and feelings rather than our moral sense, as an effusion of sentiment so pure as to need no catharsis. There is no doubt that this canto is based on an interplay of passion and compassion: yet neither one nor the other, not even their synthesis, can be taken at its face value.

I have already stated that Dante wrote the episode in the key of the love romances, but even this needs qualification and cannot be taken for granted. In what he did, Dante went beyond not only the form he chose, but also beyond the sentiment which normally inspires or dictates that form. The love romance is primarily, but not exclusively, a medieval genre; it recurs even in modern literature, where it changes its style, replacing the convention of fancy with the conventions of realism, and taking the shape of the novel or of other types of fiction. Yet the new product will remain a love romance if it still expresses sentiment without judging it. This is certainly not the case with such a work as *Anna Karenina*, where the writer condemns his heroine at least by implication, by referring her judgment to the tribunal of God. Such is the sense of the scriptural epigraph that Tolstoy placed at the head of his novel: "Vengeance is mine; I will repay, saith the Lord" (Romans XII.19). Yet the same epigraph would be at least partly improper if placed at the head of this canto, since it would reflect solely the standpoint of Dante the character. In this episode, as in the entire *Commedia*, God has already taken his vengeance, and Dante is a witness of this. Paolo and Francesca have been condemned to everlasting death, to the damnation of their souls: when faced with such a revelation, the most man can do is silently to bow his head. Yet Dante is not to be satisfied with this, and gives to God's verdict the assent of his own conscience, even if he does so without words. Though verbally unstated, Dante's judgment is framed in literary terms; his moral message is implicit in the situation and the structure of the story, so that no further intervention on the poet's part is required to make it meaningful to us.

Dante achieves this result by a dialectical treatment of the romance form — by what one might call a double mirror trick. There is no doubt that the poet derived the idea that the reading of the Lancelot romance had been "the first root" of the passion and ruin of the two lovers, not on the authority of any external tradition, but solely on the inner urgings of his own imagination. If the "how" and "why" of Francesca's fall is an invention of Dante's, then its supposed occasion becomes highly suggestive and significant. The real kiss of Paolo and Francesca follows the imaginary kiss of Lancelot and Guinevere, as an image reflecting its object in a perspective similar and different at the same time. In brief, the seduction scene fulfills within the entire episode the function of a play within a play: more properly, of a romance within a romance. This creates an effect of parody or, if we prefer to use a less negative term, something akin to what in modern times has been called "romantic irony," which in this case operates in an antiromantic sense. This means that the two romances, one of which may be likened to a frame, and the other, to the picture enclosed therein, react reciprocally in such a way as to annihilate each other. In his analysis of *Madame Bovary*, starting from the presupposition that the modern novel is but an offspring of the ancient romance, and that originally the former was but a love story like the latter (as proved by the fact that in French both are still called by the same name), Albert Thibaudet ends by saying that Flaubert's masterpiece is in reality a *contre-roman*.[24] In the same way, the "romance" of Paolo and Francesca becomes in Dante's hands an "antiromance" or, rather, both things at once. As such, it is able to express and to judge romantic love at the same time. While Dante the character manifests his sorrowful regret through the mute eloquence of his bewilderment, and later of his swoon, so Dante the poet expresses his judgment without uttering a word, without even a gesture or a sign of reproof or reproach. Dante does not preach or plead, nor does he need to superimpose an edifying sermon on the structure of his story. His ethical message may be easily read not in the spirit, but in the very letter of his tale. It is Francesca herself that he entrusts with the literary moral of his fable. This moral is very simple, and could be summed up in the statement that writing and reading romantic fiction is almost as bad as yielding to romantic love. This obvious and almost naive truth is all contained in the famous line, *Galeotto fu il libro e chi lo scrisse,* by which, as Francesco D'Ovidio says, the poet confesses his horrified feeling at the thought that he too "could become a Gallehaut to somebody else." [25] But there is no reason for such a fear, since that line helps to destroy the very suggestion on which it is built. It is with traits like this that the poet created this masterpiece, based on the avoidance of tragedy,[26] as well as on the moral sublimation of the romance form.

NOTES

1. All quotations from the episode (*Inferno* V.25–142) follow the text of the Società Dantesca Italiana as published in *Le Opere di Dante* (Florence, 1921).

2. This is the only point where I fail to follow the text of the Dantesca. Instead of closing the verse just quoted with a period, as I have done on the authority of other editors, the Dantesca joins the final sentence with the opening line of the following verse (lines 42–43), in this way:

> E come li stornei ne portan l'ali
>   nel freddo tempo a schiera larga e piena,
>   così quel fiato li spiriti mali:
> di qua, di là, di giù, di su li mena.

3. *Fiato* also means in Italian "wind," but hardly "blast," as Charles Eliot Norton renders it in his translation (Boston, 1891–93).

4. Norton refers to this legend in the following way: "According to the post-Homeric account of the death of Achilles, which was current in the Middle Ages, he was slain by Paris in the Temple of Apollo in Troy, 'whither he had been lured by the promise of a meeting with Polyxena, the daughter of Priam, with whom he was enamoured.'"

5. See *Inferno,* VI.1–2: "Al tornar de la mente, che si chiuse/ dinanzi alla pietà de' due cognati."

6. The textual tradition has preserved another variant, according to which the wings of the doves are not raised, *alzate,* but open, *aperte.* The change does not affect the visual content of the image, nor does it detract in any way from its power or fitness. The metaphor itself is consciously patterned after a famous simile in the *Aeneid* (V.213–217).

7. A main difference between the troubadours and the poets of the "sweet

new style" is that the former celebrate the bride, and the latter, the maiden. The Italians, moreover, unlike the Provençals, do not prize nobility per se.

8. In the essays "Hamlet and His Problems" (1919), reprinted in *Selected Essays* (New York, 1932) pp. 121–126.

9. Such is the interpretation I have chosen to give to *ci tace*: although most of the commentators prefer to interpret the particle in its adverbial and locative sense, as meaning "here," "on this spot," rather than in the pronominal one, as meaning "to us," "for us."

10. It is perhaps unnecessary to remark that in Dante's language, or, more generally, in old Italian, *gentile* means almost without exception "noble," "well born," "of high birth," and the like.

11. These significant suspension points separate the end of ch. 10 from the beginning of ch. 11 in pt. II of Tolstoy's novel, and immediately precede the sudden revelation that Anna has already become the mistress of Vronsky.

12. *I Promessi Sposi,* ch. 10.   ,

13. Francesca's words are a gnomic sentence only in the sense that they paraphrase a famous passage in Boethius' *De consolatione philosophiae* (II.4): "In omni adversitate fortunae infelicissimum est genus infortunii fuisse felicem."

14. [*Publisher's note*. In line 125, the word Mr. Poggioli renders as *mal* should be *amor*. Hence the terzina should read:

> Ma s' a conoscer la prima radice
> del nostro amor tu hai cotanto affetto,
> dirò come colui che piange e dice.

Professor Dante Della Terza of Harvard University has kindly provided the following comment: "The second line of the tercet is a translation of *Aeneid* II.10: 'sed si tantus amor casus cognoscere nostros.' It is interesting to notice that for Dante the Latin word *amor* corresponds to the Italian *affetto*, strong desire, and that *casus*, which means suffering, corresponds to the Italian *amor*. The idea that *amore* is for Francesca the root of evil and suffering, justified by line 93 ('poi c' hai pietà del nostro mal perverso'), seems to have caused an etymological return of Poggioli's memory to the Latin source, *casus,* and the erroneous substitution of *amor* with *mal*. The mistake should be corrected by the reader, but, once Poggioli's identification of *amore* with *male* is accepted, the remarks that it inspired can be considered reasonable and coherent with the general interpretation of the episode."]

15. A few commentators advance the hypothesis that Paris is not the Trojan hero but the medieval knight by the same name, who loved the beautiful Vienna: but the identification must be rejected because the medieval Paris did not die of love. If the hypothesis were to be accepted, it would strengthen my reading of the entire passage. My interpretation would, however, lose validity if one could prove that by calling "knights" the noble heroes of love, both ancient and modern, Dante merely commits an unconscious anachronism. Yet, even if this objection were to be granted, we should still face the fact that the feminine figures of the catalogue represent classical antiquity alone. At any rate, that in Dante's language *cavalieri* is not a generic term but a specific one, to be understood within the frame of reference of medieval culture and its chivalric tradition, is proved by two famous lines of the *Purgatorio* (XIV.109–110), on which

Ariosto patterned the beginning of the *Orlando furioso*: "le donne e i cavalier, li affanni e li agi, / che ne 'nvogliava amore e cortesia."

16. It is from Paulus Orosius' *Historia* (I.4) that Dante takes the formula by which he states one of the sinful deeds of Semiramis: *che libito fé licito in sua legge*. The Orosius passage reads thus: "Praecepit enim ut inter parentes ac filios, nulla delata reverentia naturae, de coniugis adpetendis, quod cuique libitum esset licitum fieret."

17. The expression *libro galeotto*, directly derived from the line, *Galeotto fu il libro e chi lo scrisse*, was to become proverbial in Italian, with the meaning of "erotic book." See, for instance, Boccaccio's masterpiece, the title of which is followed by these words: "*Comincia il libro chiamato* Decameron, *cognominato* Principe Galeotto."

18. *Ibid.*, II.79–84.

19. There is no doubt that Dante read the French medieval romances in the original language. As for Paolo and Francesca, they must have read their *libro galeotto* in the same tongue; for, "if an Italian translation of *Tristan* was already extant from the thirteenth century, there is no proof that Lancelot had been granted the same fortune: moreover, and this is what matters most . . . French . . . was then the courtly language par excellence in the Italian North," according to Pio Rajna's statement in his article "Dante e i romanzi della Tavola Rotonda," *Nuova Antologia*, 1157 (June 1920). The same problem had been studied before Rajna by Paget Toynbee, in his essay "Dante and the Lancelot Romance," *Fifth Annual Report of the Dante Society of America*, Cambridge, Mass. (1886), and, more fully, in his *Ricerche e note dantesche* (Bologna, 1904); after Rajna, by Nicola Zingarelli, in his article "Le Reminiscenze dal 'Lancelot,' " in *Studi Danteschi*, I (1920), 82–90.

All these studies deal in detail not only with the relevant lines in this canto, but also with another famous passage of the *Commedia* connected with the Lancelot romance, to which I have already referred in the present essay. This passage is to be found in *Paradiso*, XVI.13–15, and reads thus:

> onde Beatrice, ch' era un poco scevra,
> ridendo, parve quella che tossio
> al primo fallo scritto di Ginevra.

Here Dante alludes to the same chapter of the Lancelot romance to which Francesca refers in *Inferno*, V; but now he recalls merely a minor incident, preceding the climax of the chapter, which is the kiss exchanged between Lancelot and Guinevere. The one "who coughed" is the Dame de Malehaut, who is also in the grove, during the nightly meeting of the knight and the queen. The Dame is still in love with Lancelot, who was once her prisoner, although he pretends to have forgotten it. Pio Rajna explains the reference, and its connection with the present situation, in the following way: "By coughing, and thus recalling back to herself the attention of Lancelot, the Dame de Malehaut warns him that she is nearby, and makes him understand that the secret he has been so jealously keeping [his love for the queen] is no longer a secret for her. Likewise Beatrice, after having withdrawn a little aside, as feeling estranged from the worldly conversation between Cacciaguida and his descendant, with her laughter recalls Dante to the awareness of her presence, so that he may watch himself; and at the same time warns him that the reason of that proud *voi* had not excaped her."

(Dante, who at first addresses his ancestor with *tu*, shifts to the more respectful *voi* as soon as he learns Cacciaguida had been knighted before his death.)

I have discussed this passage in detail only to have the opportunity of commenting on the highly interesting closing line of the terzina, *al primo fallo scritto di Ginevra*. These words are clearly a definition of the crucial chapter of the Lancelot romance, of the scene ending with the first kiss of the two lovers. The presence of the adjective *primo* may, in our context, throw some light on one of the most famous lines of *Inferno*, V, which is precisely *quel giorno più non vi leggemmo avante*; and make perhaps more valid my interpretation of that line. Even more significant is Dante's description of the romance itself as a *fallo scritto*, sin written down, exactly because such a description sounds like an explicit replica of the moral judgment about romantic literature which this canto states implicitly, and which Francesca herself sums up in the words: *Galeotto fu il libro e chi lo scrisse*.

20. The passage quoted from *De vulgari eloquio* may be found in I. x.2. The double meaning of *ambages* is discussed by Pio Rajna, who prefers interpreting that word in its figurative rather than in its literal sense. This term's equivocal significance seems to anticipate Petrarch's pun on *erranti* ("wandering" and "erring"), discussed elsewhere in this essay.

21. This passage, as well as the following ones, is quoted from the most important of all Francesco de Sanctis' Dante essays, and is given as translated by me. De Sanctis originally published that essay in 1869, under the title *Francesca da Rimini secondo i critici e secondo l'arte*. The essay was later included in the collection of his *Saggi critici*. The text I have used is the one reprinted in the 1952 Laterza edition of *Saggi critici* (VII, 240–256). Though disagreeing with De Sanctis' view, I still feel that his critique of the Paolo and Francesca episode is a masterpiece. Anything the great critic had to say about the *Commedia,* even beyond the famous pages in his *Storia della letteratura italiana,* is worth rereading. Such a task can now be easily done, since the Einaudi edition of the *Opere di Francesco de Sanctis,* made under the direction of Carlo Muscetta, devoted its fifth volume (Turin, 1955) to the *Lezioni e saggi su Dante*.

22. Pt. I, ch. 11 (as translated by Constance Garnett).

23. In the "Commiato," or Farewell Song, which precedes the play.

24. In his *Réflections sur le roman, passim*.

25. *Nuovi Studi Danteschi,* II (Milan, 1907), 531.

26. This concept was first used by Erich Heller, in his article "Goethe and the Avoidance of Tragedy," *The Disinherited Mind: Essays in Modern German Literature* (London, 1952).

PASCAL'S CLASSICISM:

Psychological, Aesthetic, and Scriptural

Poète et non honnête homme

I

Nothing is so central to an understanding of Pascal's notion of human nature as a re-examination of his treatment, in psychological as well as in moral terms, of the classical idea of "the golden mean" — *aurea mediocritas* — or "juste milieu." While researching the validity of all intermediate positions, Pascal seems to infer this principle from the authority of neither sentiment nor reason, but solely from that of opinion: "L'extrême esprit est accusé de folie, comme l'extrême défaut. Rien que la médiocrité n'est bon. C'est la pluralité qui a établi cela, et qui mord quiconque s'en échappe par quelque bout que se soit" (378).[1] It is noteworthy that this *pensée* is preceded by the title "Pyrrhonisme" (Skepticism), by which the author seems to imply that it is merely on pragmatic grounds that he accepts the principle he sets forth. In this, as in many other human issues, Pascal's attitude is that of a doubter, willing to conform, with a mixture of indifference and resignation, to a given state of affairs. Yet, as the rest of the *pensée* makes clear, Pascal accepts the principle also on other, and more solid, grounds: "Je ne m'y obstinerai pas, je consens bien qu'on m'y mette, et me refuse d'être au bas bout, non pas parce qu'il est bas, mais parce qu'il est bout; car je refuserais de même qu'on me mît au haut" (378).

Those who speak all too easily of a Pascalian romanticism would do well to reflect upon this passage, since the frame of mind expressed here reveals an instictive distaste for all extremes, including perhaps that abasement of intellect that is one of the aims of both mysticism and asceticism. Here Pascal seems hardly the same man who recommended *abêtissement* as the road to faith (233). This is not the only case where Pascal's outlook, notwithstanding the problematic character of the statement in question, and despite the Christian substance of his psycho and thought, seems not too distant from that of either the Stoics or the Epicureans: "C'est sortir de l'humanité que de sortir du milieu. La grandeur de l'âme humaine consiste à savoir s'y tenir; tant s'en faut que la grandeur soit à en sortir, qu'elle est à n'en point sortir" (378). Yet to this feeling of revulsion for extremes Pascal often joins an all too modern interest in contradiction, ambivalence, and multiplicity, or at least in all the perplexities or complexities affecting the operations of the human soul:

> On ne montre pas sa grandeur pour être à une extrémitié, mais bien en touchant les deux à la fois, et remplissant tout l'entre-deux. Mais peut-être que ce n'est qu'un soudain mouvement de l'âme de l'un à l'autre de ces extrêmes, et qu'elle n'est jamais en effet qu'en un point, comme le tison de feu. Soit, mais au moins cela marque l'agilité de l'âme, si cela n'en marque l'étendue. (353)

Again, to understand the passage correctly, it is necessary to take into account the sentence preceding these words in the same *pensée*. Here the tendency to view with sympathetic indulgence this inclination of the soul to move in different directions at the same time is still tempered by the conception, both Christian and classical, that the good consists in the very moderation and balance of those virtues that often sprout (as La Rochefoucauld would certainly think) from the roots of the passions: "Je n'admire point l'excès d'une vertu, comme de la valeur, si je ne vois en même temps l'excès de la vertu opposée, comme en Epaminondas, qui avait l'extrême valeur et l'extrême benignité. Car, autrement, ce n'est pas monter, c'est tomber" (353). Thus what might be called the modern idolatry of the heroic — the predilection for all states of tension and agony, the worship of all those individuals who seek to transcend humanity in order to become demons or gods — this is an attitude repugnant to Pascal, who, like La Bruyère, would have perhaps wished to use the term "hero" merely as a technical designation for the man of arms: "Ce que peut la vertu d'un homme ne se doit pas mesurer par ses efforts, mais par son ordinaire" (352). Hence the true man is for Pascal the common man, not in the modern sense of the term, but rather in the medieval and Christian sense of Everyman.

Man is then more human and real the more he stays within the norm: and this is even truer for the Christian or the good man. One might even claim that for Pascal the Christian or the good man plays within the sphere of morality the same role that the *honnête homme* plays within the sphere of social and intellectual intercourse. The task of the *honnête homme* is basically not too different from the one Pascal assigns to man in general: "tout son devoir est de penser comme il faut" (146). Both the *honnête homme* and the ethical man must be ruled by a sense of temperate and balanced universality, by a calm and serene mediocrity: the path they must follow is the middle road of the spirit. Too intransigent a virtue, on the one side, and intellectual fanaticism on the other — these disgusted Pascal no less than Molière was by the intolerance of Alceste or the exaggerations of the *pédants* and the *précieux*: two attitudes that Pascal himself would have viewed as forms of misanthropy based on *amour de soi*, and diametrically opposed to the high truth included in the often repeated principle of "hating one's self" (*se haïr*). But by its very nature, such exemplary normality makes it difficult to distinguish the true Christian soul from the hypocrite (Tartuffe or the Jesuit), or the intelligent man from the professional, the pedant, the cultural specialist.

Les gens universels ne veulent point d'enseigne, et ne mettent guère de différence entre le métier de poète et celui de brodeur.
   Les gens universels ne sont appelés ni poètes, ni géomètres, etc.; mais ils sont tout cela, et juges de tous ceux-là. On ne les devine point. (34)

That the term "gens universels" is as far removed as possible from the romantic conception of "genius" is evident in the text just quoted. The term itself refers to an open intelligence that becomes many-sided by working from the center of things. Pascal makes this clear when, speaking of the diversity and variety of our mental needs, he maintains the utility and necessity of holding intercourse not with exceptional intellects, but with minds of inclusive and balanced awareness, able to satisfy as many as possible of the spiritual demands of their fellow men: "Il faut donc un honnête homme qui puisse s'accommoder à tous mes besoins généralement" (36). In view of this Pascal treats even Plato and Aristotle as if they were nothing less and nothing more than *honnêtes hommes* of antiquity; and here he shows himself fully a man of his time, and even of the following century, freed from even the last residues of the Renaissance idolatrous apotheosis of the great men of the

classical world: "On ne s'imagine Platon et Aristote qu'avec de
grandes robes de pédants. C'étaient des gens honnêtes et, commes
les autres, riant avec leurs amis" (331). Hence the inference that
philosophy, which derives from common sense, is the opposite of
academic and technical thought. Thus, with a phrase that Leopardi
and Nietzsche will repeat, consciously or not, almost verbatim,
Pascal concludes that "se moquer de la philosophie, c'est vraiment
philosopher" (4). In this respect, Pascal's thought hardly differs
from Molière's and La Bruyère's. The philosopher is none other
than the common man who thinks, or the man par excellence, the
creature Pascal himself defined as "un roseau pensant" (346), a
thinking reed. *Homo philosophicus* so understood appears a quite
different species from *homo sapiens* as understood by the Renaissance or the age of science, within which the scientist Pascal would
hardly feel at home.

For Pascal one of the tasks of philosophy, or more simply of
thought, is the attempt to dissolve from man's mind the veils imposed by imagination, which for him is literally *la folle du logis*.
Pascal viewed imagination as a temptress and a seductress, and
condemned it with intellectual and moral rigor, after the manner
of Plato and the Fathers of the Church. Pascal treats imagination
as a purely psychological faculty: imagination as an aesthetic
power will be a discovery of romanticism. And he yet mistrusts
it not only as a Christian and a moralist, but also as a scientist
and a classicist. Descartes, as well as Bossuet, would have ap-
plauded Pascal's indictment:

Imagination: — C'est cette partie décevante dans l'homme, cette maîtresse
d'erreur et de fausseté, et d'autant plus fourbe qu'elle ne l'est pas toujours;
car elle serait règle infaillible de vérité, si elle l'était infaillible du mensonge.
Mais, étant le plus souvent fausse, elle ne donne aucune marque de sa qual-
ité, marquant du même caractère le vrai et le faux. (82)

This passage cannot be understood without realizing that for Pascal
imagination is a denial of reason, and yet is not merely its opposite. As a matter of fact imagination is, so to say, "reason in madness": and this is why it is so often capable of misleading reason
itself. What matters even more is that it operates where and when
reason cannot act. And there it does the work reason cannot do,
thus often seducing with greater ease the clear-sighted and the
wise than the slow-witted and the fools: "Je ne parle pas des fous,

je parle des plus sages; et c'est parmi eux que l'imagination a le grand don de persuader les hommes" (82).

The greatest failure of reason is its inability to regulate what one might call the market of life ("la raison a beau crier, elle ne peut mettre le prix aux choses" — 82), while on the contrary imagination is quite willing and able to "set the price" for all worldly goods: "l'imagination dispose de tout; elle fait la beauté, la justice, et le bonheur, qui est le tout du monde" (82). Whereas the Christian or the ethical man knows that only religion and ethics establish genuine and absolute standards of value, the man of the world is not interested in standards of value, but merely in value judgments (which are, as Kant will say, merely judgments of taste), and it is imagination that dictates such judgments to him. Yet the scale so established is based on wrong measures and on false perspectives, reversing all order of greatness, and destroying all sense of proportion: "L'imagination grossit les petits objets jusqu'à en remplir notre âme, par une estimation fantastique; et, par une insolence téméraire, elle amoindrit les grands jusqu'à sa mesure, comme en parlant de Dieu" (84). In brief, imagination produces not a transvaluation, but rather a subversion, of all values. It represents the "human, all too human," and paves the ground for what logic calls error, morality evil, religion sin. This view of the imagination as a subversive power, which breaks the hard-won and uneasy balance imposed by tradition and custom, by reason and faith, is a projection of what one might call the classical psychology of the culture of which Pascal was a part. In evolving this conception Pascal acts not only as a Christian moralist, but also as a modern skeptic or stoic, still acknowledging the wisdom of the ancient maxim *nil admirari*. While Pascal's emphasis is here primarily ethical and psychological, he shows his classical outlook by the very notion of disproportion that he uses to indict the disorders produced by imagination in the soul and mind of man. This notion, like the positive term it opposes, is native to the domain of the arts.

II

Having brought to light what one might call Pascal's psychological classicism, we must now examine his thought and work to see whether they contain or imply a more obvious and conscious kind of classicism in the literary sense of the term. What we seek lies not in the field of artistic practice, but of aesthetic theory. Yet we should not expect to find a doctrine, or even a cluster of ideas, dealing with such absolutes as art or poetry. What Pascal has to offer in such a context is but a series of casual reflections, not far removed from the direct experience of writing, or a set of observations derived from his contact with other arts. For their quasi-empirical character, and for the very quality of his thought (in the nonreligious domain, Pascal still remains a disciple of Montaigne, at least in part), these reflections and observations are of a prevailing skeptical temper: yet of a skepticism not necessarily directed against aesthetics per se. Pascal does not argue pro or con the existence of aesthetic values: what he puts in doubt is our ability to understand, define, and assess them. As a matter of fact, when meditating about art *in abstracto*, Pascal is far from being a skeptic or a relativist: like all men of his culture and age he believes at least ideally in the objectivity of aesthetic norms, while disbelieving the possibility of formulating them in logical terms. What he really does is to turn his skepticism and relativism not so much against aesthetic theory as against critical practice. Beauty may well be a reality *qua* idea; yet, when we try to recognize its presence in a work of art, we can hardly point our finger at it. In brief, the idea of beauty seems for him unable to produce a workable criterion of judgment: the artistic judge, whether reader, spectator, or critic, has nothing to rely on except a vague insight, often more negative than positive — as is shown by the later definition of that insight, or rather of its object, as merely *un je ne sais quoi*.

To use Pascal's celebrated antinomy — a bit arbitrarily, since its second term is not by necessity aesthetic in essence — one could say that for him the understanding of the arts is a function of the *esprit de finesse*, not of the *esprit de géométrie*: which of course simply means that the objects of such an understanding have a reality that the mind cannot see as clearly as it does a triangle or a circle. It is not a paradox to affirm that Pascal's classicism lies precisely in this; far from anticipating the modern and romantic distrust for the intervention of reason in the aesthetic domain, he shares the dislike of the *honnête homme* for the pretensions of the *esprit de système*, especially in the sphere of value judgments. It is therefore not surprising that Pascal's statements in connection with the most important issue in the aesthetic thought of his time — that of dealing with the notion of taste — sound like mere variants, or vague anticipations, of a famous passage by the writer of the following generation who represents the ideal of the *honnête homme* at its best. That writer is La Bruyère, and the passage we have in mind is one of the aphorisms of the opening section of *Les Caractères*, entitled "Des ouvrages de l'esprit." Here is what La Bruyère has to say on the subject of taste:

> Il y a dans l'art un point de perfection, comme de bonté ou de maturité dans la nature. Celui qui le sent et qui l'aime a le goût parfait; celui qui ne le sent pas, et qui aime en deçà ou au delà, a le goût défectueux. Il y a donc un bon et un mauvais goût, et l'on dispute des goûts avec fondement.

The paradox implied in this utterance consists in its ambiguity or rather in the equal acceptance, on the part of its author, of the opposite claims of the absolute and of the relative. The statement is at once skeptical and dogmatic, so dogmatic as to deny the traditional view that *de gustibus non est disputandum*, and yet so skeptical as to suggest already that beauty is *un je ne sais quoi*.

Pascal thinks likewise that beauty is a real, but elusive, flower, which is easier to sense than to find. Yet he cannot avoid the temptation to assign to it an ideal location in the abstract space of the mind. For him beauty is a point determined by lines crossing at the right moment and place, in a kind of aesthetic *juste milieu*. This conception reveals how much, even when it deals with the values that can be assessed only by the *esprit de finesse*, Pascal's thought is affected by the *esprit de géométrie*. This is evident in his use of such abstract or mathematical notions as *modèle* or *rapport*. Like La Bruyère's, Pascal's aesthetics is both skeptical and dogmatic: he believes at once in the absolute of beauty and in the relativity of taste, a relativity that he reduces, however, to a simple alternative of *bon* and *mauvais goût*. In brief, he thinks with La Bruyère that there exists an exemplary pattern of beauty, which taste seeks and feels intuitively (as we moderns would say):

> Il y a un certain modèle d'agrément et de beauté qui consiste en un certain rapport entre notre nature, faible ou forte, telle qu'elle est, et la chose qui nous plait.
> Tout ce qui est formé sur ce modèle nous agrée: soit maison, chanson, discours, vers, prose, femme, oiseaux, rivières, arbres, chambres, habits, etc. Tout ce qui n'est point fait sur ce modèle déplaît à ceux qui ont le goût bon.
> Et, comme il y a un rapport parfait entre une chanson et une maison

qui sont faites sur ce bon modèle, parce qu'elles ressemblent à ce modèle
unique quoique chacune selon son genre, il y a de même un rapport parfait
entre les choses faites sur le mauvais modèle. (32)

It seems that Pascal emphasizes even more strongly than La
Bruyère the difficulty of determining the where or why of that
point of perfection, of that ideal *juste milieu,* the presence of which
is recognized only through the operations of a sure and refined
taste:

Comme on dit beauté poétique, on devrait aussi dire beauté géométrique
et beauté médicinale; mais on ne le dit pas: et la raison en est qu'on sait
bien quel est l'objet de la géométrie et qu'il consiste en preuves, et quel est
l'objet de la médecine, et qu'il consiste en la guérison; mais on ne sait pas
en quoi consiste l'agrément, qui est l'objet de la poésie. On ne sait ce que
c'est que ce modèle naturel qu'il faut imiter. (33)

Pascal might have said of beauty what Metastasio later said of both
Phoenix and God: "Che ce sia ciascun lo dice, Dove sia nessun lo
sa," thus proving again how Pascal's aesthetics is at once dogmatic
and skeptical, relative and absolute. The reason for this is that
even he could not transcend the intellectualism and psychologism
of the aesthetic thought of his time. That thought demanded an
abstract notion of beauty, while viewing the operations of the
aesthetic principle and its effects on the beholder, as the workings
of the pleasure principle. It is in this combination of intellectualism and hedonism that neoclassical aesthetics finds at once its
inner resort and its outer limit.

The literary practice of a writer is not necessarily identical with
his aesthetics. In the case of Pascal, this practice coincides with the
cultural and moral outlook of the *honnête homme,* and it makes of
him a *moraliste.* Like all other writers of that breed, Pascal observes
man in the unique generality of this or that of his passions or vices.
The *moraliste* is then not a moralist, but a psychologist; and it is
qua psychologist that he must rely on the *esprit de finesse.* The
latter is required even when we look at man in general: the human
world cannot be understood like the world of nature, with the
esprit de géométrie. This is evident; yet the famous passage dealing
with the two *esprits* (1) remains an equivocal text, even if the
reason for this may lie more in the denseness of the interpreters
than in the author's obscurity. It is worth remarking that in a related *pensée* (2) Pascal prefers to use, for *esprit de finesse,* the

term *esprit de justesse*, to which he attributes the task of *jugement* (4), by which he means something not too different from what Kant will define by the same term. This suggests that the *esprit de finesse*, while being meant as the opposite of the *esprit de géométrie* as a category of knowledge, is also supposed to check and to correct within its own sphere the ravages produced by Pascal's *bête noire*, the imagination. One might even say that Pascal treats the *esprit de finesse* as a psychological equivalent of taste, which fulfills within the moral domain a task similar to the one that taste fulfills within the aesthetic one. This *esprit* is a kind of insight that perceives the realities and the values of the human world in the same way that the *coup d'oeil* of a connoisseur recognizes the qualities of a work of art: "il n'est question que d'avoir bonne vue, mais il faut l'avoir bonne" (1). Reason and logic are then not the right instruments for the study of man:

J'avais passé longtemps dans l'étude des sciences abstraites; et le peu de communication qu'on en peut avoir m'en avait dégoûté. Quand j'ai commencé l'étude de l'homme, j'ai vu que ces sciences ne sont pas propres à l'homme et que je m'égarais plus de ma condition en y pénétrant que les autres en les ignorant. (144)

It is the *esprit de finesse* that gives us an immediate and genuine knowledge of human reality: yet, precisely because each of them is the proper tool in its proper sphere, the *esprit de finesse* and the *esprit de géométrie* must not be understood as outright antitheses. Either one is but a special variation of common sense, which for Pascal, as for Descartes, is the universal root of all intellectual understanding. That Pascal thinks so may be seen by studying the meaning that he gives to the word *esprit* when using it singly (it is evident that in the two compound formulae the term *esprit* is a synonym of "faculty" or the like). *Esprit* without qualification will soon take on in French thought some of the meanings of Italian *ingegno* or English *wit*, thus designating all forces of creative or artistic talent, as shown in the formula by which La Bruyère will soon define all artistic and imaginative works: *ouvrages de l'esprit*. But for Pascal the word *esprit* still designates a yet undifferentiated native intellectual gift, and this will help us to interpret and evaluate more properly a famous *pensée*, all too often misread as an anticipation of Rousseau's notion of psychological originality, or of the romantic conception of genius: "A mesure qu'on a plus d'esprit,

on trouve qu'il y a plus d'hommes originaux" (7). Similar misunder-
standings have been provoked by the stand Pascal takes in the most
vexing of all the questions of neoclassical poetics, which is the
question of "rules." It is true that he denies their validity; but he
does so not as forerunner of the romantic conceptions of unre-
strained spontaneity, of the absolute freedom of poetic inspiration
and artistic creation. His denial of rules or precepts is that of a
relativist or a skeptic. It is certainly as a relativist or as a skeptic
that, discussing a problem of style (whether repetition be merit
or defect), he settles the issue with the categorical statement: "il
n'y a point de règle générale" (48). Yet he still remains convinced
that such a rule should exist, as when, in a stroke that would make
a nice detail in a *caractère* after the manner of La Bruyère, he
mocks those who judge "sans règle" by comparing them to a man
who tries to tell the time without a watch (5).

Pascal's literary ideal is, then, that of an informal philosopher,
of an essay writer à la Montaigne. In the terms of De Quincey's
famous antinomy, what attracts him is "literature of knowledge"
rather than "literature of power." In brief, he wants to be not a poet
but a prose writer, deriving his matter and style not from imagination or fantasy, but from reflection and experience. When he criticizes without the least compunction the fountainhead of all poetry
by claiming (628) that "Homère fait un roman" (a term that, like
all his contemporaries, he uses in an utterly derogatory sense), he
dispraises not only classical epos and modern romance, but poetry in
general. Just as he detests the romanesque as both sentimental and
fantastic, so he disdains the purely representational, whether plastic
or picturesque: any sort of external imitation impresses him as
frivolous decoration, as ornamental pomp devoid of function and
sense. Pascal is an aesthetic and intellectual puritan or, if we prefer, a Jansenist of literature. It is only from the standpoint of a
literary conception wholly alien to any form of invention and fancy,
as well as totally averse to the mimetic illusion itself, that we can
properly understand his notorious artistic blasphemy: "quelle vanité
que la peinture" (134).

In the formal and stylistic sphere, the central point of Pascal's
literary thought is his rejection of what he calls *figure* — a term
that at least in part he uses in the medieval sense, so well explained
by Erich Auerbach in his important essay on the subject.[2] Such

rejection involves the poetic as well as the rhetorical aspect: Pascal rejects *figure* both as an instrument of poetic falsehood and as the favorite device of eloquence, which in its turn is but the favorite vehicle of the faculty that is the foremost object of his hatred, imagination. It is as an enemy of rhetoric that Pascal singles out for outright condemnation the figure called periphrasis, which for him seems to replace denotative simplicity with connotative exaggeration by refusing to call a spade a spade — by referring to Paris as "capitale du royaume" and to the king as "auguste monarque" (49). By speaking thus men veil sincerity and truth; the effect of that trope, as Pascal says, is to "masquer la nature et la déguiser." In another passage he conveys his dislike of a second rhetorical figure, antithesis, with a homely and comical parallel: "Ceux qui font les antithèses en forçant les mots font comme ceux qui font de fausses fenêtres pour la symétrie: leur règle n'est pas de parler juste, mais de faire des figures justes" (27). Pascal's scornful attitude toward any kind of trope is summed up in another *pensée*, where again he condemns periphrasis, concluding with the ironical observation: "et on appelle ce jargon beauté poétique" (33).

III

By *figure* Pascal means not merely rhetorical tropes or conventional metaphors but all those verbal and figurative devices that we call by such different terms as imagery, symbolism, or allegory. We must therefore not be surprised that the pages where he brings to the extreme limit his indictment of all such devices are those where he attempts to present his interpretation of the Scriptures, and to explain the differences between the New and the Old Testaments. The passages in which Pascal criticizes or interprets Scriptural typology cannot, however, be understood without first examining some of his ideas about Christianity and religion. In this context we must reject the common error of thinking that Pascal overemphasizes the mystical aspects of belief, or reduces the whole of faith to the assent of sentiment. As a matter of fact, he warns us from the temptation of all extreme positions even in the religious sphere: "Deux excès: exclure la raison, n'admettre que la raison" (253). He sees one of the highest virtues of Christianity in its power to balance the opposite claims of the mind and the heart, or the contrasting requirements of an inner or outer sanction for one's beliefs: "Une religion purement intellectuelle serait plus proportionnée aux habiles; mais elle ne servirait pas au peuple. La seule religion chrétienne est proportionnée à tous, étant mêlée d'extérieur et d'intérieur" (251). For this very reason divine truth is revealed and concealed at the same time, thus attracting us both into belief and into doubt:

> Je regarde de toutes parts, et je ne vois partout qu'obscurité. La nature ne m'offre rien qui ne soit matière de doute et d'inquiétude; si je n'y voyais rien qui marquât une Divinité, je me déterminerais à la négative; si je voyais partout les marques d'un Créateur, je reposerais en paix dans la foi; mais, voyant trop pour nier, et trop pour m'assurer, je suis en un état à plaindre. (229)

The mystery of the divine, at once absolute and relative, is an essential necessity; yet is equally essential and necessary for the human mind to understand why that mystery is needed: "Dieu étant ainsi caché, toute religion qui ne dit pas que Dieu est caché n'est pas véritable; et toute religion qui n'en rend pas la raison n'est pas instruisante" (385). The mystical moment, the moment of blind faith, is thus joined with the theological moment, which always tends toward a theodicy, toward the attempt to justify the ways of God to men. Man reacts to mystery and obscurity by seeking truth and clarity: it is toward such a quest that even in religion the human spirit must always strive. Precisely because "Dieu ne se manifeste pas aux hommes avec toute l'évidence qu'il pourrait faire" (556), we must use all the faculties we possess, except possibly the imagination, in order to raise ourselves toward God. While it is true that, when confronted with the metaphysical, human reason should become "critical" in the Kantian sense, which means also self-critical or fully aware of its own limitations ("la dernière démarche de la raison est de reconnaître qu'il y a une infinité de choses qui la surpassent" — 267), yet it is also true that there are moments when our understanding has the duty to doubt and to argue, no less than to acquiesce and to yield: "Il faut savoir douter où il faut, assurer où il faut, et se *soumettre* où il faut" (268).

In other words, man is faced with problematic truths, which he may attain through the *esprit de finesse*, or which he may confront with a *doute* that is not merely *méthodique*, in the Cartesian sense of the term; with rational or logical truths, which he may examine by means of the *esprit de géométrie*, or verify through mathematical proofs; and with categorical or dogmatic truths, which he may apprehend only with the passivity of a blind faith, with the docility of an immediate belief. Thus, as far as the Scriptures are concerned, we must admit that "il y a de l'évidence et de l'obscurité, pour éclairer les uns et obscurcir les autres" (564). This obscurity, perhaps in order to humble the exalted, or the proud intellects, and to raise the lowly, who are sunk in ignorance, works not only beyond the level of reason, but also beneath it. It is both transcendent and immanent, commensurate to the powers or weaknesses of the heart, but incommensurate, by excess or by defect, to the mind of man.

The name God gives himself in the Scriptures, says Pascal (194), is *Deus absconditus*; and he hides not only far and high, but also near and low. It is by means of ambiguity and obscurity that God veils his very revelation. This is done through the very language of that part of the Holy Writ that is sacred also for the Gentiles, but that historically was meant for the Jews alone. In order that he might speak to the Hebrews, God concealed his own truth in images, symbols, allegories, or, to use Pascal's terms, *figures*, such as might strike the fancy of "ce peuple charnel":

Les Juifs avaient vieilli dans ce pensées terrestres, qui Dieu aimait leur père Abraham, sa chair et ce qui en sortait . . . qu'il les nourrit de la manne dans le désert; qu'il les mena dans une terre bien grasse; qu'il leur donna des rois et un temple bien bâti pour y offrir des bêtes. (670)

This and other passages clearly reveal that Pascal makes no distinction between metaphors and tropes, between poetic images and rhetorical figures, or verbal and literary symbols, on the one side, and rites and ceremonies on the other. What is even more important, he fails to differentiate between legends and fables, between allegories and myths, between analogies and metaphors — in brief, between all the different and even contrasting forms of the visionary imagination and of figurative speech. He treats all these as similar manifestations of one and the same thing, as *figure*, by which he means an obfuscated truth, half-hidden and half-revealed by the poetic veil that envelopes it. As such, it is inferior to a higher kind of truth, which takes the Cartesian form of *idées claires et distinctes*. The former may acquire a limited validity only as a shadow or reflection of the latter. God, not wishing to reveal his own verities to the nation that claimed to be his chosen people, and who were unworthy of those truths, "les a quelquefois exprimées clairement, mais abondamment, en figures, afin que ceux qui aimaient les choses figurantes s'y arrêtassent, et que ceux qui aimaient les figurées les y vissent" (670). In other words "les choses figurantes," the verbal icons of the divine, satisfied all too easily the sensual fancy of an archaic or barbaric people. But by its very nature imagination fosters deception, and is liable to self-deceit. This is why the Jews took the prophecies for promises — and yet were unable to recognize that the carpenter of Nazareth, the son of Mary, was the Messiah. This is why they failed to realize that the expected Kingdom had finally come true as prophesied: "Les Juifs ont tant aimé les choses figurantes et les ont si bien attendues, qu'ils ont méconnu la réalité, quand elle est venue dans le temps et en la manière prédite" (670). Imagination denies both reason and sentiment, although all too often men mistake its false claims for the demands of the latter: "Les hommes prennent souvent leur imagination pour leur coeur" (275). Poetic imagery is likewise falsehood, illusion, or at best a shadowy truth. "Dans les Juifs, la vérité n'était que figurée," says Pascal (673), and precisely for being addressed to that nation, "l'Ancien Testament n'est que figuratif" (659). In conclusion, it was because they were a poetic race that the Jews failed to see the truth.

This conception is in total contrast with the postclassical and preromantic view of the Scriptures. Since Vico, the Bible has been seen not only as a sacred book, but also as a folk epos of great power and beauty: a power and beauty based on that figurative character so scorned by Pascal. At the threshold of modern times, the pious Herder was destined to fall in love with the oriental splendor and primitive vigor of the sacred writings of the Hebrews. Yet it is precisely against what we call the poetry of the Old Testament that Pascal's taste rebels. What he likes there are the rare flashes of light that break for an instant through the clouds of passion and the senses. He goes so far as to claim, at least once, that the Old Testament is at times as dense and absurd as the Koran: "Je veux qu'il y ait des obscurités qui soient aussi bizarres que celles de Mahomet" (598). And it is with the complacent assurance of a *honnête homme*, basing his balanced judgment on the canons of good usage and good taste, that he dares to submit God's early written word to a criticism understood in the old-fashioned manner of correction and censure: "Il y a des figures claires et démonstratives, mais il y en a d'autres qui semblent un peu tirées par les cheveux" (where we find worth remarking the colloquialism of the stricture).

As we have already pointed out, Pascal views the poetic or figurative element of the Old Testament as a concession made by God to human frailty. He seems almost to imply that what is divine in the Old Testament has been dictated not by the Holy Ghost, but by a Logos not yet made flesh. What counts there for him are the clarity and evidence of the thought of God, which thus give idea and sense even to what Descartes would have called *idées obscures et confuses*, and which seem to abound even in Holy Writ: "ce sont les clartés qui méritent, quand elles sont divines, qu'on révère les obscurités" (650). Thus Pascal's intellectual puritanism leads him toward an iconoclastic attitude even in the field of verbal symbolism, and makes him reject as idolatrous mankind's tendency to translate into an anthropomorphic imagery even the vision of God. What he cannot tolerate in the Old Testament is, however, not merely the clothing of divine revelation in metaphors appealing primarily to the senses, but also the inconsistencies and contradictions by which it reports the word of God. Pascal's *esprit de géométrie* abhors such irrationalities or absurdities, which he thinks can be resolved and reconciled if reduced to the common denominator of a single meaning. Such a meaning may be hard to find, but it obviously exists, and Pascal bases his conviction of the presence of such a meaning not on the belief that the Prophets were insufflated with the Divine Spirit, but on the rather prosaic and worldly argument that otherwise one should suppose that the Prophets were devoid of common sense. The hypothesis seems preposterous to a contemporary of Descartes, who certainly shared with him the opinion voiced at the beginning of the *Discours de la méthode* that "le bon sense est la chose du monde la mieux partagée":

Tout auteur a un sense auquel tous les passages contraires s'accordent, ou il n'a point de sense du tout. On ne peut pas dire cela de l'Ecriture et des prophètes; ils avaient assurément trop bon sens. (684)

The rites, symbols, and fables of the Hebrews, which are so offensive to the Christian spirit, must thus be viewed as intimations of the high religious truths that God made evident to the mind of man; if this were not the case, they would be senseless falsehoods or nonsensical oddities. In these matters Pascal seems to speak almost like a representative of rational Protestantism: or, to remain within the Catholic fold, as a forerunner of modernism. Unable to accept on historical or intellectual grounds the literalism of the religious tradition, or the complexities of creeds or rites equally alien to the demands of his mind or the scruples of his heart, Pascal has no alternative but to conclude: "Tous ces sacrifices et cérémonies étaient donc figures ou sottises. Or il y a des choses claires trop hautes, pour les estimer des sottises" (680).

The very task of the New Testament was then to bring light into this obscurity, into these shadows. The Messiah did not appear in all his glory and men did not recognize him. But the true light does not dazzle, it illuminates. Basically the message of Christ, the Gospel or the Good Tidings, was nothing but a truthful message: technically what modern communication theory would call a message in the clear. Christ thus came not only as the Savior or the Redeemer, but also as an *éclaireur*, an *éclaircisseur*. Since it was the frame of mind Pascal here represents in so typical a way that helped to form the eighteenth-century spirit — a culture bound to deny his most cherished values — we may be forgiven for saying, with a pardonable anachronism, that his conception of Christ is that of an educator of man's moral and intellectual understanding, of an *illuministe* or *Aufklärer* of the spirit. But when Christ appeared, mankind was not ready for the illumination or enlightenment of which he was the bearer, and this made necessary the intervention or mediation of an interpreter. That interpreter was Saint Paul:

Le monde ayant vieilli dans ses erreurs charnelles, Jésus-Christ est venu dans le temps prédit, mais non pas dans l'éclat attendu; et ainsi ils n'ont pas pensé que ce fût lui. Après sa mort, saint Paul est venu apprendre aux hommes que toutes ces choses étaient arrivées en figure. (670)

For Pascal the Scripture must be considered as a cipher to be decoded twice, in order to resolve the double difficulty arising from the worldly sensuality of its imagery and from the "contrariétés manifestes dans le sens littéral" (678). It was Saint Paul who gave us the key to decode that cipher: "La lettre tue; tout arrivait en figures" (683). Saint Paul taught us that the tradition of ritual and myth is but a veil that takes substance from the meaning hidden beneath it. We must be grateful to Saint Paul and all the interpreters of the Scripture; yet we must not forget that the decoding key had already been offered us by Jesus and his disciples:

Combien doit-on donc estimer ceux qui nous découvrent le chiffre et nous apprennent à connaître le sense caché, et principalement quand les principes qu'ils en prennent sont tout à fait naturels et clairs! C'est ce qu'a fait Jésus-Christ, et les apôtres: ils ont levé le sceau, il a rompu le voile et a découvert l'esprit. (678)

In a sense even the sacrifice of Christ was also a symbol and a sign: redemption was but the vehicle of revelation. The miracle of his descent and advent consisted in the lifting of the seal, in the breaking of the veil, in baring forever what to open eyes was already a self-evident truth. Christ is then to be seen as an uncoverer or a discoverer, as a Columbus or a Galileo of the soul. The necessity of his coming and of his passion arose from the fact that men have eyes and do not see, have ears and do not hear, that they behave as if they were blind and deaf. In fact the spiritual meaning of the Scriptures

a été couvert sous le temporel en la foule des passages, et a été découvert si clairement en quelques-uns; outre que le temps et l'état du monde ont été prédits si clairement qu'il est plus clair que le soleil; et ce sens spirituel est si clairement expliqué en quelques endroits, qu'il fallut un aveuglement pareil à celui que la chair jette dans l'esprit quand il lui est assujetti, pour ne le pas reconnaître. (571).

The failure of men to see the verities of religion arises from the power of the imagination, which misleads them even when searching the good and the true. Only faith and love can help us to recognize divine values; all others are false values, *vanitas vanitatum* or, as Pascal puts it: "Tout ce que ne va point à la charité est figure" (670).

Never elsewhere in religious thought have ethical and intellectual rigorism been so strictly joined. Even Pascal was, at least historically, an *enfant du siècle*: and it is evident that such an outright rejection of religious mythology and mystical symbolism could arise only in the age of a Nicole and of a Descartes. The extremity of Pascal's stand is made more evident by contrasting it on the one side with the medieval position, strongly based on the acceptance of the dualism of the literal and the allegorical, of letter and spirit; and on the other with the modern view, deeply rooted in the worship of creative imagination and in the romantic and postromantic rehabilitation of symbol and myth. The latter view is becoming almost universal, so as to be now acceptable even to the orthodox mind: it may suffice to think of the Abbé Bremond, the great historian of religious sentiment in France, who as a literary critic or theorist went so far as to view poetry as a form of prayer, as a step on the ladder of mystical insight. It was obviously the classical and rational epoch in which he lived that made it possible for Pascal to look at the Old Testament as if it were a divine *roman à clef*, and so reduce hermeneutics to the level of mere exegesis.

As he does with the Old Testament, with the word of the Father, so sometimes Pascal treats also the Gospel, or the word of the Son, as if it were a book or, to use La Bruyère's formula, an *ouvrage de l'esprit*: "Jésus-Christ a dit les choses grandes si simplement qu'il semble qu'il ne les a pas pensées, et si nettement néanmoins qu'on voit bien ce qu'il en pensait" (797). Who, reading these words, can miss the echoes of the ancient and modern commonplaces about the simple and the natural, or of such maxims as Horace's "difficile est proprie communia dicere" (*Ars poetica*) or Boileau's "ce que l'on conçoit bien s'énonce clairement" (*L'Art poétique*, I)? It hardly sounds blasphemous to take this Pascalian statement about the Gospel as the judgment of a literary critic, praising the style of an author he has just read, according to the aesthetic and stylistic criteria provided by the rhetorics or poetics of his own time.

In a sense the Pascalian definition of the mission of the Redeemer, "Jésus-Christ, qui est venu ôter les figures pour mettre la vérité" (665), involves among many other things a complete reversal of the traditional hierarchy of literary values. At least by implication, Pascal views Christ as the great denier of poetry, who came to dethrone it, and to put prose in its place. In such a conception of the word and teaching of Christ, all the different aspects of Pascal's personality join together in a single bond. His Biblical and Evangelical "criticism" is the natural outcome of a combination of many trends and traits; yet the decisive factor may well be the tendency of classical reason to abstract and generalize, while glossing over all that is concrete and particular, exceptional and unique. It is obvious that Pascal simplifies and exaggerates by reducing the Gospel to a literal, lucid, and unadorned discourse: no better proof of this than the fact that he hardly faces the issue that would have put into question his very interpretation of the style and language of the Gospel, Christ's use of the parable, which may well not be a genuine metaphorical and allegorical device, but which still has the literary and poetic qualities of such homely figures as the apologue and the fable.

Pascal's spontaneous and deliberate disdain for the errors of psychological imagination and the vagaries of poetic fancy made him assume toward the Old Testament an attitude very different from that of the great tragic poets of his time. For at least two of his tragedies Racine took his subject from the Bible; and both he and Corneille were so seduced by the magnificent lyricism of the Psalms that they tried to reattune some of their accords to the rigid strings of French classical verse. In his literary outlook, Pascal is certainly closer to Boileau than to Corneille or even to his fellow Jansenist Racine. Like Boileau he would have considered a Christian tragedy at once ridiculous and absurd, and therefore an act of both literary and religious impiety: Christ the Redeemer cannot be a *deus ex machina*. As for Boileau, he rejected the literary use of the *merveilleux chrétien* for the same reasons that made Pascal exalt the New Testament over the Old. Boileau's rejection was based on the belief that mythology is falsehood: a falsehood admissible as a pleasing decoration in a pagan or profane subject, and even necessary in the epic poem, where the employment of the fable is made mandatory by the exemplary precedent of the great ancient masters of that genre. Yet Boileau (*L'Art poétique*, III) finds the use of the Christian supernatural objectionable in any case, proscribing it even in the treatment of a religious theme, for the very reason that "De la foi d'un chrétien les mystères terribles / D'ornements égayés ne sont point susceptibles." Boileau holds myth to be undisguised fiction: any fable that had not been used by any canonical, that is, classical, poet is for him but the product of a superstitious imagination or barbaric taste. If Boileau accepts mythology for given literary ends, or for definite poetic effects, it is only because he treats it as if it were empty *figure*, containing no truth, and therefore devoid of sense and purpose.

Pascal of course goes further than Boileau, because he denies not only the mythical, but even the poetic, as a deceitful illusion or as a dangerous charm. Yet the similarity between his position and that of Boileau is quite evident. This is so true that when Pascal

salutes the advent of the Savior his words strongly remind us of
the phrase by which Boileau was to greet the arrival on the scene
of the literary lawgiver destined to redeem the tongue and the
poetry of France from the obscurity and barbarism of his predecessors: "enfin Malherbe vint." There are many passages in the *Pensées* where Christ's mission is treated as if it were a *rappel à l'ordre,*
to the very order of classicism, or to the order of a law both eternal
and new. (One must not forget that Pascal came from the *noblesse
de robe*, from a family of magistrates and civil servants, and that
he saw in Christ also a legislator, speaking the lucid language of
a lofty jurisprudence.) In terms of what one might call without
blasphemy the literary vocation of the Son of God, Christ becomes
for Pascal the *grand moraliste*, the prose writer par excellence:
or, since we are in the century of Descartes, the divine *raisonneur.*
Through many Pascalian pages, Jesus seems almost to utter to man
the very words addressed by one of Dante's devils to the saint with
whom he successfully argues, like a lawyer or a schoolman, for
the mastery of a sinner's soul (*Inferno*, XXVII.123): "Tu non
pensavi ch'io loico fossi." What is even more important is that, for
the first time in the history of Christian thought, someone seemingly treats the sacred text as if it were a classical text as well. The
Middle Ages and the Renaissance, which worshiped both "antiquities," even if not at the same level, had yet always distinguished
between them. In Pascal the distinction disappears because the
word of Christ is treated as if it were that of a modern classic.
Since we have constantly fallen back on this noun and its adjective
to describe the frame of mind of an age that Pascal both expresses
and represents, at this point we might perhaps sum up our argument by saying that in his case we may speak not only of a literary
classicism, but of a religious classicism as well.

IV

Pascal's interpretation of the Scriptures derives its authority from
the Pauline tradition, which is also the source of medieval scripturalism. The antinomy of letter and spirit is as inherent in the
medieval conception and interpretation of Holy Writ as in the
Pascalian antithesis of Old and New Testament. Nobody stated
more cogently than Dante the reason why man must first receive

the word of God through the vehicle of sensual imagery (*Paradiso,*
IV.40–45):

> Così parlar conviensi al vostro ingegno,
>   però che solo da sensato apprende
>   ciò che fa poscia d'intelletto degno.
> Per questo la Scrittura condescende
>   a vostra facultate, e piedi e mano
>   attribuisce a Dio, ed altro intende.

Yet it is evident that for Dante this necessity is permanent and
universal, that it obtains for both Jews and Christians, for the moderns as well as for the ancients, applying equally to the Biblical and
to the Evangelical tradition. What matters most is that for Dante,
as for the medieval mind as a whole, letter and spirit are a duality
rather than a dualism. Dante views the letter (*sensato*) as the first
step, and the spirit (*intelletto*) as the last, on the ladder of religious
understanding. They are the two phases of a single process, the
final outcome of which is a change in the quality of comprehension,
reached, however, only gradually. In brief, medieval scripturalism
does not humiliate the letter while exalting the spirit. This is the
very reason why allegory and symbolism are such an integral part
of medieval culture even outside the purely religious sphere. A poet
of our time, T. S. Eliot, has been so affected by medievalistic longings as to complain that modern culture cannot avail itself of what
Pascal calls *figure*. The allegorical symbolism that has become a
practical impossibility for the modern mind has for Eliot such
power that he has desired to reverse the Pauline principle, proclaiming that it is the spirit that kills, and the letter that gives life. The
paradox is the more significant since Pascal, whom that poet greatly
admires, opposed symbolism and allegory, and denied medieval
scriptualism by converting into a dualism the duality of letter and
spirit. One could say without punning that the letter of Pascal's
Biblical and Evangelical criticism is old, but its spirit is new: the
new wine that he puts into the old bottles is the hardly concealed
impatience with which he must accept, along with the blessings
of the spiritual, the necessary evil of the literal. Pascal's insuffer-
ence of the latter is so thinly disguised that he seems almost willing to treat the material promises and the intellectual ambiguities
of the Biblical prophecies with the contempt expressed by Dante
for the equivocal and deceitful oracles of the pagans (*Paradiso,*
XVII.31–33):

Né per ambage, in che la gente folle
già s'inviscava, pria che fosse anciso
l'Agnèl di Dio che le peccata tolle.

Nothing shows more clearly the contrast between the medieval scripturalism of Dante and Pascal's scriptural modernism than their views of the relations between religion and literature. Dante, while accepting both, is yet able to distinguish, in the letter to Cangrande, between "the allegory of the theologians" and "the allegory of the poets," even though he chose the former over the latter as the vehicle for the higher meaning of his poem. On the other hand, at least in practice if not in theory, Pascal confuses the two while denying them both, rejecting in one breath the allegorism of theology and the allegorism of poetry.

The originality of Pascal's position may be seen in two things: in his treatment of the Bible not only as a revelation but also as a literary work; and in his sharp critical differentiation between the Old Testament and the New. Most moderns have followed his example on both accounts, while diverging at least in two directions from the path marked by him. The first divergence is that many, while following Pascal in treating the Bible as a book, have regarded it even more as a classical than as a sacred text. The second divergence, which is by far more important, is that almost all have reversed Pascal's opinions, praising the Old Testament over the New. The first significant example is Chateaubriand's: even if the author of Le Génie du christianisme never dared to draw an invidious comparison between the two revelations, yet he chose to exalt the poetry of the Old Testament, which he called simply "la Bible." It matters little that Chateaubriand based his exaltation on the absence from the books of the ancient revelation of any mythology in the Greek sense of the term, which he viewed as a purely anthropomorphic illusion, as a kind of "pathetic fallacy" belittling the joint grandeurs of nature and God.

The same predilection for the Old Testament is to be found among unbelievers or enemies of the Christian religion. In the case of Nietzsche, this predilection dictated a well-known passage in *Jenseits von Gut und Böse* (section 52):

Im jüdischen "alten Testament," dem Buche von der Gerechtigkeit, gibt es Menschen, Dinge und Reden in einem so grossen Stile, dass das griechische und indische Schriftenthum ihm nichts zur Seite zu stellen hat . . . der

Geschmack am alten Testament ist ein Prüfstein in Hinsicht auf "Gross" und "Klein" . . . Dieses neue Testament, eine Art Rokoko des Geschmacks in jedem Betrachte, mit dem alten Testament zu Einem Buche zusammenge-leimt zu haben, als "Bibel," als "das Buch an sich": das ist vielleicht die grösste Verwegenheit und "Sünde wider den Geist" welche das litterarische Europa auf dem Gewissen hat.

(In the Jewish Old Testament, the book of divine Justice, there are men, things, and words of so high a style that the literatures of Greece and India have nothing to put beside it . . . the liking for the Old Testament is a touchstone in regard to "great" and "small" . . . To have joined into a single volume with the Old, as "Bible" or "Book per se," this New Testa-ment which from every standpoint is but a Rococo of taste: this is perhaps the greatest transgression and "sin against the Spirit" which literary Europe has on its conscience.)

We might well have expected such a statement from Nietzsche the Antichrist, who even among the gods of the pagans chose to worship Dionysus over Apollo. Yet we shall meet an almost iden-tical opinion in the work of a member of the Christian denomina-tion that calls itself the Orthodox Church, the Russian writer Vasili Rozanov, who felt in closer communion with the Biblical than with the Evangelical, with the faith of the Father than with the faith of the Son. Rozanov's opinion may be found stated in one of the many aphorisms of his last published work, *Apokalipsis nashego vremeni* (The Apocalypse of Our Time), which he wrote during the Revolution. The peculiar significance of this aphorism is that its author unfolds, and concludes with an opposite judg-ment of value, the Pascalian antinomy of the Old Testament as a book of fancy and the New as a book of vision:

In the Gospel there are many parables, but where is the prayer, the hymn, the psalm? Why did Christ never take into his hands, not even once, the harp, the cither, the pipe? Why did he never "intone"? . . . By what in-explicable mystery have men never realized that the Gospel is a book reli-giously *cold*, not to say religiously *indifferent*? where nobody sings, nobody rejoices, nobody is exalted or contemplates the sky? . . . No one has real-ized that if there is something surprising or striking in the Gospel, it is its religious *moderation*, already close to rationalism.[3]

Praying is the religious act par excellence, continues Rozanov, and in the Gospel it is precisely prayer that has disappeared:

All one does is talk. Hence the suspicion that from now on David's harp, Apollo's lyre, and Marsyas' pipe — *which may well sum up the whole of the ancient world* — will give way to theological arguments. It is conceivable that the mysterious principle of the Gospel and of the entire Evangelical undertaking consisted in the replacement of the music of prayer by the "cogito ergo sum" of theology.

Precisely through speaking as a believer, Rozanov here conveys with utmost intensity the ultimate denial of Pascal's scripturalism. Yet there has been at least one modern writer who took a stand similar to Pascal's, even if he drew, from almost identical premises, different and even unorthodox conclusions. That writer was another Russian, older and greater than Rozanov, Leo Tolstoy. Tolstoy resented so strongly the irrationalities and the obscurities of the Old Testament, its hidden organic ties with a wholly alien tradition, that he was forced to deny immediate relevance and permanent significance to the Biblical Word. What he decided to do was simply to ignore that word, as he makes clear in the introduction to "Issledovanie Evangeliya" (An Examination of the Gospels):

I do not consider the Old Testament, for the question is not what was the faith of the Jews, but in what does the faith of Christ consist . . . The faith of the Jews, foreign to us, is interesting to us as is, for instance, the faith of the Brahmins. But the faith of Christ is the one by which we live.[4]

Tolstoy took the Pauline distinction between the dead letter and the living spirit as seriously as Pascal, or rather more so: he refused to accept the letter even as a necessary evil, as an unavoidable *pis aller*. He went further than Pascal also by claiming that the spirit that gives life is present not in the whole of the New Testament, but solely in the books that report directly the good tidings of Christ's truth: "The source of Christian teaching is the Gospels, and in them I found the explanation of the spirit which guides the life of all those who really live." For Tolstoy Christianity is Evangelical only in the strictest sense of the term. In this his position differs from Pascal's merely as a matter of degree: but he breaks with him by maintaining that even the Gospels are oppressed by the dead weight of the letter, which he identifies with many other rational and anti-ecclesiastical Christians, as the residues that the Gospels still preserve of un-Christian superstitions, or as priestly doctrines arbitrarily superimposed on the Evangelical text. Tolstoy reacted against such a corruption of the clear and direct preaching of Christ with a revulsion evident in the very image that he chooses to convey his protest: "But together with this source of the pure water of life I found, wrongfully united with it, mud and slime which had hidden its purity from me: by the side of and bound up with the lofty Christian teaching I found a Hebrew and a Church teaching alien to it." [5]

With a parallel and even more stringent metaphor, Tolstoy compares his first serious reading of the Gospels as tradition had handed them down to us with the experience of "a man who receives a bag of stinking dirt," and who "only after long struggle and much labour finds that amid that dirt lie priceless pearls." It was in order to spare his fellow men that ordeal henceforth that he decided to sift forever Christ's pearls from tradition's mud. He did so by compiling an Evangelical harmony of his own, not through the ancient method of consolidation but by the criterion of selection, expunging from the text of the Gospels as uncanonical interpolations the frequent passages to which he refused the assent of his emotions or of his intellect. By doing so, Tolstoy killed both the letter and the spirit, dispensing with Christianity as well as with religion, both of which he reduced to the level of an ethical code that, beyond history and revelation, could be found eternally engraved in the human spirit: "I regard Christianity neither as an exclusive divine revelation nor as an historical phenomenon, but as a teaching which gives us the meaning of life." What speaks in this plain and apparently modest statement is the pride of a self that recognizes no other authorities than the inner voices of reason and feeling: and it is evident that Pascal would have repudiated with horror the blasphemous arrogance that resounds in these soft-spoken words. Yet, paradoxically, the devout Pascal must shoulder a large measure of responsibility for the line of scriptural thought that reaches its extreme manifestation in Tolstoy's pseudo-Christian Evangelism.

What strikes us most forcibly here is the realization that Tolstoy attained such views of Scripture by means of a conception of literature very similar to Pascal's. Tolstoy's literary outlook is that of a modern classicist in the sense that he prefers the simplicity, the sincerity, and the naturalness of prosaic discourse over the complexity, the falsity, and the artificiality of the poetic one. Tolstoy has left the most resounding indictment of the poetic (which he identified with the conventional, with what he called "borrowed") in a famous passage of *Chto takoe iskusstvo?* (What Is Art?). "Thus, in our circle," he says,

all sorts of legends, sagas, and ancient traditions are considered poetic subjects. Among poetic people and objects we reckon maidens, warriors, shepherds, hermits, angels, devils of all sorts, moonlight, thunder, mountains, the sea, precipices, flowers, long hair, lions, lambs, doves, and nightingales.[6]

This passage suggests by implication how Tolstoy was bound to dislike the passionate imagery in the Old Testament, from which, in another passage of the same book, he singles out for special praise the straightforward narrative of the adventures of Joseph and his brothers, an all too human and extended parable, where the spiritual and the literal merge into one.

We may then conclude that in the case of both Pascal and Tolstoy the preference for the Evangelical over the Biblical is, among many other things, also a question of taste.[7] The taste that determined that preference was in either case austerely classical, seeking its ideals of perfection in prose, and finding a supreme standard of excellence in the very utterances that four of the Apostles wrote down in the Gospels. From such a perspective Christ seems to emerge as a divine, or at least sublime, Monsieur Jourdain of the spirit, speaking prose and talking sense not only for everyday life, but for eternity itself.

NOTES

1. The number at the ends of the quotations and paraphrases from Pascal are those of the *Pensées* in the edition of Léon Brunschvicg in Les Grands Ecrivains de la France (Paris, 1904, 1923), which has provided the text here used.

2. "Figura," *Neue Dantestudien* (Istanbul, 1944), pp. 11–71; English version in Auerbach, *Scenes from the Drama of European Literature,* trans. Ralph Manheim (New York, 1959), pp. 11–76.

3. Translated from parts 8 and 9, section entitled "Strangeness."

4. Trans. Aylmer Maude, *Tolstoy Centenary Edition* (New York, 1929), vol. 11.

5. This quotation, as those in the following paragraph, is from the preface to Tolstoy's *Kratkoe izlozhenie Evangeliya* (The Gospel in Brief); trans. Maude, *Centenary Edition,* vol. 11.

6. From section XI; trans. Maude, *Centenary Edition,* vol. 18.

7. I had already sketched the parallel between the scriptural views of Pascal and Tolstoy which closes the present essay in "A Portrait of Tolstoy as Alceste," from my book *The Phoenix and the Spider* (Cambridge, Mass., 1957); see especially pp. 98–100.

CRITIQUES OF THE MODERNS

TOLSTOY AS MAN AND ARTIST

More than fifty years ago, on a day in November 1910, Leo Tolstoy left his estate of Yasnaya Polyana to seek that freedom of the spirit which he was to attain only a few days later, when he met his death at the station of Astapovo. George Orwell found it fitting to compare Tolstoy's death to that of King Lear; Sir Isaiah Berlin, to the end of Oedipus at Colonus. These two parallels reveal different and yet similar insights; they seem to complete each other and to illuminate evenly, although from different angles, the mournful and lofty scene. Those who witnessed it saw dying, in the humble surroundings of a stationmaster's house, a rare, or rather a unique, human being: someone who had been a king, like Lear, and who, like Oedipus, had become almost a saint.

The paradox of Tolstoy's death is but the last of the many paradoxes of his life. The series opens with the paradox of his birth. It would be unwise to forget that he was born a nobleman, and that he remained aristocratic in temper even after he had embraced the cause of the common man, and had started exalting the Russian peasant over all other classes and types of human beings. It took the plebeian and proletarian Gorky to guess that not even the trauma of conversion had stifled within Tolstoy the unconscious feeling of belonging to the breed of the masters: to find out that even though he would live, dress, and act like a man of the people, refusing to be addressed as "Count," the old man remained at heart a Russian *barin*, accustomed to being obeyed, served, or, at least, revered. There is no doubt that Tolstoy's personality can be fully understood and assessed only by taking into account the role that pride played in his behavior or in his make-up: and by keeping in mind that in him the pride of the self was never wholly severed from the pride of blood and breeding.

The second paradox is that both his birth and temper made of him a conservative, while reason and faith turned him into a radical. Tolstoy was a moral, not a social, radical: a fact which may have been not fully clear to many Tolstoyans, but which did not escape the lucid observation of Lenin. The latter maintained that Tolstoy's thinking and preaching were patriarchal and autocratic in character, and reactionary in spirit. Whether or not this is true, we must confess that the sociopsychological formula which the radical critic Nikolai Mikhailovski coined in order to define Tolstoy and the members of his class who followed his teachings was, at least as applied to him, rather inept. The Tolstoy who developed after the writing of *A Confession* was no "repentant nobleman": he rather resembled a feudal lord who had exchanged the sword for the cross, while preserving his haughty nature under a monk's cassock.

Tolstoy's ethical and intellectual radicalism never implied the belief that man could transform his own being and transcend himself. The only change he viewed as both necessary and possible was a "change of heart." He had himself undergone such a change and felt that his fellow men could do what he had done. He was willing and even eager to help them while they were striving toward that end: but his aid consisted more in words than in deeds. The most he would do was to set an example, and he thought that this should be enough. This is why his action was on the whole more negative than positive in character. In the Europe, or rather in the world, of the end of the nineteenth century and the beginning of the twentieth, he played the role of a supreme conscientious objector. By using our terms merely in their etymological sense, we could say that he was more of a "protestant" or a "dissenter" than a "reformer."

What Tolstoy preached was in effect that others should convert themselves as he had converted himself. In practice, as a convert and a converter, he gave nothing more, and nothing less, than a "counsel of perfection." His ideal was that each man could forever feel as Konstantin Levin, one of his favorite heroes, did feel at a given moment of his own personal experience: "He felt himself, and did not want to be anyone else. All he wanted now was to be better than before." These words seem to prove that Tolstoy never thought seriously that human nature could be fundamentally changed. The idea of "changing life" never held for this conservative in radical dress the seductive attraction it had for many of his contemporaries, such as Nietzsche and Rimbaud, or his fellow Russian, Dostoevski. Yet, paradoxically, it is precisely one of the commands of Nietzsche — *Werde der du bist,* Become who you are — which best conveys the Tolstoyan view of the conversion process: a view which betrays the aristocratic conception of the supreme worth of the separate person, as well as the Christian conception of the absolute value of each individual soul.

Perhaps because we know that he was a spiritual disciple of Jean-Jacques Rousseau, or of a man who had been born a Calvinist, we are tempted to find protestant elements in Tolstoy's beliefs. Whether or not we are right in doing so, we can certainly point out that, outside Russia, his religious ideas affected the English and the American spirit far more deeply than, for instance, the French intellect, or the Latin mind in general. At any rate, it seems evident that there are protestant components in Tolstoy's idea of the self. He viewed the self primarily as "heart": as a heart moved by both ethos and pathos, ruled by sentiment as well as by conscience, ceaselessly echoing the urgings of its inner voice, which is also the voice of the spirit. He felt that man is really human only when he listens to that voice; and thought that he who understands it aright will never go wrong. In order to hear its promptings, man must constantly turn toward his inner being: hence the practice of introspection, with the consequent habit, in Tolstoy's own case, of keeping for most of his life those diaries which were the very mirrors of his soul. In this we see another of Tolstoy's paradoxes: such lifelong preoccupation with one's psyche reveals at once the humble shame of the sinner and the proud glory of the chosen, inextricably joining self-hatred and self-love in a single knot.

Yet Tolstoy's idea of the self is based on a cult of the person which avoids the pitfalls of the "cult of personality." This great Russian always exalted the unique, native originality of every human being: a birthright which man could easily lose by conforming too strictly to the conventional patterns of social life. It is obvious that Tolstoy understood that originality in a psychological, rather than in an intellectual or cultural, key. He founded this conception not on the romantic notion of "genius," but on the Rousseauistic and eighteenth-century notion of *génie.* The second of these two terms indicates not a complex organization of the highest faculties, nor an extraordinary endowment of exceptional powers, but the inarticulate virtues of simplicity and freshness, marking a "temperament" which relies only on its innermost resources.

It was in accordance with such a view that Tolstoy molded and shaped practically all his creatures, his negative no less than his positive character, those who are untrue to their nature as well as those who are loyal to it. He placed together on one side, without distinguishing too much the ones from the others, the figures which are "romantic" and those which are merely vulgar, such as Olenin and Prince Andrei, or Aleksei Vronsky and Aleksei Karenin. He placed on the other side the all too many for whom truth is a question or a quest, and the fewer who have attained a wisdom of their own, such as Pierre Bezukhov and Konstantin Levin, or Uncle Eroshka and Hadji Murat. He loved fully only the latter, especially if they were naive and humble, unaware of their rare worth and dignity, like Platon Karataev, or Gerasim, the faithful servant of the dying Ivan Ilich. It is in the portrayal of such characters (the more exalted, the more they abase themselves) that Tolstoy seems to fulfil better than anybody else the demands of the Russian genius. It was according to such demands that Dostoevski sought to elevate on the highest pedestal of his art the meek and saintly figures of Alyosha the novice, Zosima the elder, and Prince Myshkin, the fool of God; yet, against his intention and beyond his will, he instead achieved the opposite feat, raising his most magnificent statues to such somber heroes as Raskolnikov and Ivan Karamazov. Tolstoy, however, succeeded where Dostoevski had failed: it fell to him to accomplish what D. H. Lawrence considered the chosen task of Russian literature, to depict "the phenomenal coruscation of the soul of quite commonplace people."

The man exalting the inner voice is a fanatic of a sincerity which might be defined as subjective truth. He constantly tends to confuse sincerity with objective truth, and this is why he is frequently tempted to identify both qualities with beauty, as well as with goodness. "The hero of my story," wrote the young author of *The Tales of Sebastopol*, "the one I love with all my soul, which I have tried to depict in all its beauty; which has been, is, and will for ever be beautiful — is the truth." The older Tolstoy knew how to distinguish between subjective and objective truth, and realized that the latter is rarely beautiful. Yet he never ceased to believe that the former is always good. In short, he remained for all his life a fanatic of sincerity. In this he resembled Molière's Alceste, who becomes a misanthrope precisely because he learns, through the trial of experience and the ordeal of social intercourse, that reality and sincerity rarely meet, or do so only in strife and contest.

The misanthrope à la Alceste is a mere disappointed and embittered lover of mankind, who ends by hating his fellow men because they are false to themselves as well as to the moral code. Despite his philanthropic bent, Tolstoy all too often behaved like a misanthrope of this kind. He turned his *saeva indignatio* primarily against society and its institutions, including religion and culture, following in this the example of Rousseau, but going further than his master in the indictment of the sciences and the arts. His wrath did not spare individuals, especially those exercising social functions, like politicians and bureaucrats, career officers and professional people, lawyers and judges, teachers and priests, and even writers and artists. At bottom he never fully believed that man is born good, and that his only corrupter is the world. If Tolstoy remained a Christian, it was above all in his inborn suspicion of the old Adam in himself, as well as in his fellow men.

Tolstoy's misanthropy was then a matter of both his mind and his heart, being equally rooted in the lucid pessimism of his observation and in the noble idealism of his ethical vision. In view of this one should correct in at least this instance Coleridge's famous aphorism, according to which every man is either an Aristotelian or a Platonist. In Tolstoy's case one should say that he was the one and the other at the same time. One could even modernize this statement by asserting that, while there is something of either Pascal or Voltaire in each human being, in Tolstoy there was something of both. The truth of this is evident in his writings of evangelical exegesis and scriptural controversy. When Tolstoy is able or willing to take a positive attitude toward a given aspect of the Christian tradition because it seems to agree with the demands of his conscience, he gives that aspect the docile and total assent of his heart, like Pascal. But when he feels that he must take a negative stand against another aspect of the same tradition because he finds it irreconcilable with the demands of his mind, then he rejects that aspect with the rebellious and uncompromising denial of his reason, which he utters with the bitter mockery of a new Voltaire.

How simple-minded and straightforward was Tolstoy's "grammar of dissent" may be shown by a single example. There is a passage in *A Critique of Dogmatic Theology* in which he attacks the credibility of the account in Genesis of the creation of the world. In this attack Tolstoy did not hesitate to employ, with the sarcastic grin of heavy irony, one of the most obvious and trivial arguments of positivistic polemics against Christianity. If "there was a morning and an evening on the first day," but "there was no sun until the fourth," said Tolstoy in a crucial phrase of that passage, then "God must have himself shaken the illuminating matter so that there might be a morning and an evening." We find it highly significant that Dostoevski had once chosen to report the same argument, but with an opposite intention: not to challenge the word of God through the lay authority of science and reason, but to expose what religion calls a "scandal," in this case the scandal of a cheap blasphemy, of a vile incredulity. After rephrasing and refashioning it into the shape of a rhetorical question, Dostoevski attributed the argument in his great novel *The Brothers Karamazov* to the still childish but already base mind of the flunkey, Smerdyakov. It is with an impious sneer that the latter questions his devout tutor who is reading aloud from the Scriptures: "Where did the light come from on the first day if God created the sun and the stars on the fourth?"

The fact that in his quest after truth Tolstoy was never repelled by the pettiness or the bad taste of common-sense reasoning is a sign of strength, not of weakness. Yet the search itself caused a perpetual conflict between his reason and his sentiment, between his intellect and his conscience. This conflict was far more serious and painful than another of his inner rifts, the one in which most of his biographers saw the supreme crisis of his life, the climax of all his contradictions and paradoxes. For the last thirty years of his long existence a steady conflict, apparently without truce or issue, seemed to arm against each other Tolstoy the preacher and Tolstoy the writer, Tolstoy the moralist and Tolstoy the artist. We think that too much has been made of this conflict. Tolstoy had always been, even before his conversion, a writer with a message; and even after his conversion he magnificently performed his artist's task, as he had himself defined it at the time when he was writing his two greatest novels: "A writer's aim is not to settle a question once and for all, but to compel the reader to see life in all its forms, which are endless."

Yet it remains true that this great and splendid writer despised literature as a profession; and that even when he took his calling seriously, he never thought that art has no end but itself. For this reason he appears to be the only exception, among the main literary creators of the modern age, to a rule once laid down by Rainer Maria Rilke that "the writer is the poet of a world which differs from the one of which he is the prophet." The world of Tolstoy the creator and the world of Tolstoy the prophet may not fully coincide, but they are closely related to each other. Even those who find that the digressions on history mar such a masterpiece as *War and Peace*, or that the tract on marriage spoils the effect of *The Kreutzer Sonata*, must admit that, only by being as opinionated as he was, could Tolstoy have written what and how he did. This was obscurely felt by the same Rilke, who in his youth had visited Tolstoy. Despite his conviction that an artist must sacrifice everything to his craft, the Austrian poet admitted in one of his last letters that Tolstoy's creative figure had remained "touchingly valid and safe even when rebelling against his greatest and most evident duties."

The unity of Tolstoy is thus to be seen in a consistent interplay of all the contrasting factors of his extraordinary personality. There took place a constant dialogue and exchange, as well as a continuous controversy and debate, among the many souls dwelling within his breast. At times he was keenly aware of the problematic, as well as of the dialectical, character of his own nature: on such occasions Tolstoy the *heautontimoroumenos* would unexpectedly reveal the serenity of an almost godlike being. This happened once in a Crimean grove. The old man, who was in Gorky's company, suddenly heard, and immediately recognized, the song of a little bird. He then spoke glowingly to his younger friend of the mating habits of the tiny creature. The literal-minded disciple could not refrain from remarking that in *The Kreutzer Sonata* the master had spoken far differently of the not too dissimilar sexual mores of humans. To which, Gorky relates, the wise old man replied, with an olympian smile: "But I am not a chaffinch."

If he was not a chaffinch as a creature, neither was he one as a creator. He built most of his literary creations on a maze of contradictions, at times of a labyrinthine complexity. Yet he never got lost in their meanderings or ambiguities: he always held in his hand a sort of Ariadne's thread. He knew his way out as well as his way in, being endowed with a strong sense of orientation and direction, always sensing in what part of the sky he could find his bearings. To change the metaphor, one could say that his greatest merit or virtue was that he consistently took sides, and it matters little whether they were right or wrong. They were right in most cases: at all events one could fairly claim that even in his most spontaneous writings Tolstoy was in a sense a tendentious writer who wanted to make a point and generally succeeded in making it.

Let us look for instance at an early tale, the mediocre *Two Hussars*, where the point fails to come through. This story, significantly, is composed like a diptych. The two hussars of the title are father and son. More or less at the same age, but at an interval in time of about thirty years, they happen to arrive in the same place, to become the guests of the same family, and to meet, in a different manner, the same incidents. The symmetry of the situation and the sharp contrast between the two different outcomes appear all too deliberately contrived. The writer makes the first of the two officers behave like an attractive rake, and the second like a repulsive cad. Tolstoy does so precisely because his aristocratic and conservative temper compels him to feel a sentimental indulgence for the dashing behavior of the nobles of the old generation, and an utter contempt for the mean and calculating conduct of their degenerate offspring. This is perhaps the only one of all Tolstoy's works in which he takes an outright romantic stand, based essentially on prejudice. Here Tolstoy plays with loaded dice; and we acknowledge the retribution of poetic justice in the author's failure, in the artist's loss of his entire stake.

It is evident that Tolstoy plays the same sort of high-handed game in another early tale, which is also a diptych, *Domestic Happiness*. Yet there is no doubt that in this case he gets away with it and wins his wager. The first part of the story evokes the bright poetry of sentimental love to make only more striking the representation in the second part of the grey prose of married life. The happiness of marriage and family life is for Tolstoy a reality, while romantic love is only a passing illusion of youth. Yet that happiness may well seem without glamor when wrongly compared with passion, or rather with its dreams. This is the moral of the fable: a moral which is ultimately drawn by the feminine partner, whom Tolstoy makes, with supreme irony, the narrator of the story and the reluctant witness to his masculine truth. The description of the *fiançailles* and the evocation of the protagonist's virginal emotions are so astoundingly beautiful that it would be difficult to find more ecstatic pages in all the literature of romantic love. This is why many critics tend to think that the two parts contradict each other, and that the artist should have been satisfied with the first, or more poetic, half of his diptych. Such a view shows a complete misunderstanding of the author and his work. D. H. Lawrence once said that one should trust not the writer but the tale. In this case we are forced to trust both, even though we know that *Domestic Happiness* was inspired by a personal experience and dictated by a personal *parti pris.* That experience was a betrothal which failed — as Tolstoy wished to believe — through the fault of the girl. Only Tolstoy could have succeeded in creating a masterpiece out of a misguided and wrongheaded attempt to prove that, had the marriage taken place, it too would have failed, and again through no fault of the man.

Notwithstanding its autobiographical basis and despite its author's personal bias, *Domestic Happiness* ends by winning over the reader with the simple wisdom of an apologue or a parable. This fact is significant, since it reveals that Tolstoy's liking for the apologue or the parable was a matter of taste, which later found a higher justification or sanction in his pedagogical theories or evangelical doctrines. It was in a well-known passage in *What Is Art?* that Tolstoy was to define the parable as the purest and the highest of all literary forms. Yet he had written parables far earlier, even before composing his folktales or the moral fables he later collected in his school readers. It was not only as moralist but also as artist that Tolstoy cherished that literary vehicle. T. S. Eliot once surprised and persuaded us by affirming that the medieval drama which goes under the name of *Everyman* is indeed a "classical" work. There are in Tolstoy's canon many works which are classical in the same sense — works which are at once moral parables or even morality plays like *Everyman.* Such are *The Death of Ivan Ilich* and *Master and Servant*, both of which treat the supreme Christian theme, which is the response of Everyman to the challenge of mortality. In both, Everyman finds his own transfiguration in the epiphany of death: he seems to follow literally Goethe's command — *Stirb und werde,* Die and become — since he fulfills himself and understands the meaning of life only when his life ends. In these, and in other pieces of the same kind, Tolstoy, this classic of modern realism who distrusted all sorts of mysticism and symbolism, this Christian who doubted eternal life and disbelieved in the immortality of the soul, was able to convey an allegorical vision the like of which the Western world had hardly seen since the waning of medieval culture and the decline of religious art.

This implies that Tolstoy was endowed with a lucid critical outlook, as well as with a deep poetic insight. All too few of his interpreters have given due credit to the keenness of his literary flair, to the conscious and deliberate craft with which he handles and hammers literary forms. One of the most cherished theories of that group of Russian critics who called themselves Formalists, and who briefly flourished during the early years after the Revolution, was that literary genres are born, grow, and die through the dialectics of imitation and parody. Such a process (which for them took place within the broad framework of literary history, beyond the limitations of individual writers or separate works) seems to reproduce and to repeat itself, as it were in a nutshell, in several of Tolstoy's creations. In at least one case the process appears so complex as to involve more than a single genre. This is what happens in *War and Peace*, a composition so vast and so manifold as to suggest the reworking of three different genres, each one of which ultimately defeats or transcends itself.

Tolstoy's masterpiece is in the first place a historical novel "debunking" history and denying that historical development has any purpose or sense; then an epic indicting warfare, deglamorizing military valor and the martial virtues, tearing glory's laurels from the brows of the false heroes who presume to hold the destiny of the world in their hands; finally, a national or universal drama which through the ordeal of blood, sweat, and tears ends by yielding to the sweet routine of daily life and turns into a family idyll. Most critics tend to emphasize its epic quality, and in so doing they find support in the authority of Tolstoy, who defined his masterpiece as "Homeric." After admitting the fitness of the epithet, we must reject the author's further claim that *War and Peace* is a new *Iliad*. It is rather a new *Odyssey*, resembling the second Homeric poem in theme and tone, and retelling the same story, which is the belated but happy return of the warrior to his land, his farm, and his home.

By spreading over an immense range of human experience, *War and Peace* gives the impression of an enormous polyptych. Yet, if we look closer, we shall see that in effect we have to do with an almost endless series of diptychs. The novel's narrative structure is based on the regular alternation of events and scenes which contrast with each other in both subject and mood. Most observers have remarked that warlike episodes alternate with peaceful ones. Few, however, have noticed that, in the sections dealing with war, actions on the battlefield suddenly break off to give place to activities unfolding in the rear, at headquarters or in the barrack room. In the sections dealing with peace the representation of city life likewise yields in its turn to the evocation of the simpler life of the countryside. Urban life itself is depicted in parallel scenes, opposing in succession the mores of St. Petersburg, courtly, bureaucratic, and European in character, to those of Moscow, old-fashioned, patriarchal, utterly Russian in spirit.

All these reciprocal oppositions are subordinated to the most inclusive and significant of all contrasts, which underlies the whole work and sets two rival worlds against each other. The first is the public world, which includes not only politics, diplomacy, and war, but also society, with its manners, its culture, and its arts. The second is the private world, exemplified by the family and its way of life, within which the individual finds his proper place, like a bird in its nest. The first of these two worlds stands for all that is artificial in the human condition; the other, for all that is natural in men and things. Despite its title this book does not celebrate the victory of Kutuzov or the defeat of Napoleon, the triumph of the Russian people or the catastrophe of the French, but the tides of being, with their ebbs and flows. In brief, this immense poem in prose sings only of the perennial resurrection of life from the ashes of the historical process. Thus even this purest of all Tolstoy's masterpieces is up to a point a tendentious work. One might claim that the whole edifice rests on a single rhetorical device: on the recurrence of a series of invidious comparisons which make the wars and peaces of history look vain and petty when confronted with the peaces and wars of life and nature, which are love and death.

The foundations of *Anna Karenina* are grounded on the opposition of the ethos of family life and the pathos of unlawful love. Thus the structure of the second of Tolstoy's great novels is very similar to that of the first. Even here the fundamental opposition merges with parallel and lesser contrasts, such as those between town and country, the new and the old capital, the frivolities of "high life" and the labors of the fields. Here we have, however, a novel of modern life, without hopes for a better future or longings after a better past. The reader is confronted with two dramas, the one public, the other private. Socially *Anna Karenina* is a tragedy of manners, or, as Dostoevski would say, a "drawing-room tragedy." But morally it is another version of what the old Tolstoy, in a conversation reported by Gorky, was to call the worst of all tragedies: the "tragedy of the bedroom." But it was chiefly in the discreet treatment, and indirect representation, of the latter that Tolstoy again showed that his talent consisted in a unique fusion of literary intelligence and ethical insight.

It is evident that Tolstoy projected Anna's drama through a double perspective, based on the sublime absurdity of the Christian injunction to love the sinner and to hate his sin. He wanted the reader to be merciful, not merciless as was society, which punished Anna not for sinning but for confessing her passion before the world; yet he wanted him to be severe, as well as merciful. Anna was to be pitied but not absolved; nor was her guilt to be forgiven. Tolstoy realized, however, that in order to determine such an ideal moral balance he had to pass over in silence the fatal moment when Anna yields once and forever to the seduction of sin. For a psychologist like Tolstoy, who looked with clear eyes at the "facts of life," and who later dared to tear all veils from the realities of sexual love, this was not an easy thing to do. Yet, had he done otherwise, he would have hardly escaped one or the other of two pitfalls: on one hand the naturalistic portrayal, on the other the romantic idealization, of the sexual act. Tolstoy knew that Anna Karenina could not undergo the self-inflicted indignities of an Emma Bovary. He also knew that she could be neither a Francesca nor an Iseult: that neither she nor her creator could speak aloud of her sin. This is why, with great intellectual courage, he made an act of renunciation, motivated not by puritan scruples but by an artist's concern. In brief, he resisted the temptation of describing Anna's fall. Anna's fall takes place outside the novel, behind closed doors: and the author reports it, anticlimactically, as a *fait accompli*. We are informed of what has just occurred by a series of suspension dots, which open a chapter dealing only with what happens immediately afterwards.

Notwithstanding the "domestic happiness" of Levin and Kitty, *Anna Karenina* does not end, like *War and Peace*, on a note of serenity. The second of Tolstoy's great novels conveys a sense of crisis, which seems to threaten the foundations of being and puts into question all that men live by. Yet *Anna Karenina* is not a tragedy, even though we earlier employed in connection with it such formulas as drawing-room tragedy and tragedy of the bedroom. The former is in reality a tragicomedy, while the latter is too sordid to deserve that lofty name, as Tolstoy well knew. If even *Anna Karenina*, which is ruled more fully than any other creation by the "high seriousness" of its author's inspiration, cannot be characterized as tragic, then we must infer that Tolstoy's genius tended to that "avoidance of tragedy" which according to Erich Heller marks all that Goethe thought and wrote.

We can see the triumph of that negative tendency in *The Kreutzer Sonata*, in *The Powers of Darkness*, and in the third and last of Tolstoy's novels, *Resurrection*. It would be hard to find a more tragic subject than that of *The Kreutzer Sonata*, into which Tolstoy also introduced the Dionysian theme of the mysterious bonds between love and music. It may suffice to compare the *Sonata* with the pathetic imitation and involuntary parody on the same theme which Thomas Mann wrote in his *Tristan*, to realize that in Tolstoy there is a far deeper sense of evil than in any of the naturalistic or decadent masters of the West. Yet, by representing sex as a repulsive disease of both body and soul, he made of *The Kreutzer Sonata* a hybrid work, "contaminating" the Christian parable and the naturalistic *tranche de vie*. The same can be said of the so-called peasant tragedy, *The Powers of Darkness*, a morality play written in a naturalistic key. As for *Resurrection*, the tragic curve of transgression and retribution is there replaced by the straight line of a new "pilgrim's progress."

There were two primary reasons why Tolstoy felt alien that tragic vision of life which was so congenial to the imagination of Dostoevski. The first was a strong sense of the realities of nature, based on the inexorable and ineluctable law of the death of all things. The second was the eighteenth-century quality of his mind which, in a sense and up to a point, was that of a *moraliste* and a *philosophe.* This last factor motivated his avoidance of the tragic even more than his evangelism. Like Alceste, he was a *raisonneur*: or, if we prefer it, a kind of modern Socrates, always refusing to heed Nietzsche's summons to the old Socrates, to "learn music." It was this rejection of "the spirit of music" that determined the nihilistic tendencies of all Tolstoy's aesthetic and critical writings: his denial of poetry and art; his condemnation of some of the most classical works of the Western tradition; his libels on Beethoven and Shakespeare, and other luminaries of the human spirit.

We may resent his strictures against Beethoven and Shakespeare, but we are willing to admit that he was far from wrong in indicting some of the artistic trends of his age, which is also ours. He was certainly right in uttering his anathema against that modern heresy, the idolatry of art. Yet in order to do so he did not need to become an aesthetic iconoclast. The same can be said of his unfair mistrust of cultural values in general. Yet, if he tended to paint "the grey tree of thought" even greyer than it is, it is only because he also tended to paint "the green tree of life" with hues far brighter than its natural ones. Charles Du Bos once said that "if life could write, it would write just as Tolstoy did." We find these words misleading, even though we understand what the French critic meant by them. When he rewrites life, Tolstoy enriches and enhances it. He always conveys our sense of being with greater intensity and fullness than we apprehend it in reality.

The midsummer-night dream of a girl, retelling that dream to her friend, while they gaze from the window of a villa at the starry sky and at the darkness of the empty fields; the intimate conversations of two friends, broken by spells of silence sealing the reciprocal understanding of their souls while they are crossing a river on a ferry at dusk; the wild sledge ride of a Christmas party of young men and women, caressed by the cold wind and lulled by their bliss: all of us have experienced such moments at least once in our lives. Yet neither our perception of them, nor their rehearsal through imagination and memory, seems to possess the magic quality which marks their reflection in the mirror of Tolstoy's art.

Most critics overemphasize the median and moderate temper of Tolstoy's realism, without realizing that this miracle-worker makes art more real than nature and more vivid than life. When Tolstoy looks with smiling love at the things surrounding him, he turns what he likes into something bewitching and fanciful. He himself seems to have hinted at miracles of this kind in a charming episode in *Childhood*. The boy-protagonist tells the reader how he decided once to draw a hunting scene. He had at his disposal only blue paint and wondered whether he could paint a hare in that color. He then consulted his father, who resolved his childish doubts by reassuring him that there are also blue hares in the world. We now know that blue hares do indeed exist in the world of Tolstoy's art, and that the bluer they are, the truer they look.

Yet Tolstoy is Tolstoy not merely because he loved and re-enacted all the most vital aspects of human experience, or because he created more than anybody else — after God and, of course, Shakespeare. Even among modern writers there are after all many creators who have loved the human and the real, perhaps more unwisely, but no less well. As a matter of fact it was one of them who once declared, in the jargon of the prize fighters, that he felt ready to challenge all the champions of European realism, for example Turgenev and Flaubert, but that he would never dare to meet Tolstoy in the ring. The writer who spoke these words must have obscurely realized that love of life alone cannot lead to that summit which Tolstoy, alone among the moderns, seems to have attained.

Another man of letters of our time stated once, lucidly and epigrammatically, that it is literature that makes a work literature, but that something else makes it great. This "something else" may well be the urge, on the writer's part, to seek the meaning of the life he re-creates through the wonders of imagination and the portents of love. This is perhaps the truth contained in the statements just cited, which belong respectively to an eminent novelist, Ernest Hemingway, and to an outstanding poet and critic, T. S. Eliot. The case of Tolstoy, at once exemplary and unique, seems the most convincing proof of such a truth: no other artist loved both life and the meaning of life with so much joy and despair as he.

PIRANDELLO IN RETROSPECT

During the period between the end of the last century and the First World War, two great Italian novelists, and one of them undoubtedly the greatest, were islanders: Giovanni Verga, the Sicilian, and Grazia Deledda, the Sardinian. While the most famous authors of their generation were striving, often in vain, to approximate universality either by withdrawing from experience or by offering their readers refined and frequently false quintessences of life, Verga and Deledda achieved universality almost without conscious effort, by turning toward what to others seemed too humble and restricted a form of existence.

Those who wished to ape Europe or Paris succeeded in being merely provincial. But these two writers, each of whom had no thought but for his own island, amply asserted their right to enter the temple of *Weltliteratur.* They had encompassed universal values by stressing their own regionalism. In evangelical terms, we may say that they entered heaven through the narrow gate. Of these two couplings, Deledda–Sardinia and Verga–Sicily, the second is of greater interest here, not on account of Verga's superiority, but because Pirandello, with whom I am concerned, stems from Verga and Sicily.

D. H. Lawrence helps us to clarify the origins of Pirandello, who was a Sicilian like Verga, and his spiritual son: for Lawrence knew both Sicily, where he lived for a while, and Verga's work. He decided to translate some of Verga's writings and published two volumes of the Italian's short stories in English, as well as the great novel *Mastro Don Gesualdo.* For the translation of the latter Lawrence wrote an introduction which remained unpublished until after his death. At that time Lawrence was profoundly affected by his reading of the great Russian writers, and made use of the impression which that reading had left on his mind to convey more sharply, and by way of contrast, the unique temper of the Sicilian spirit and of Verga's art:

In *Mastro Don Gesualdo* you have the very antithesis of what you get in *The Brothers Karamazov.* Anything more un-Russian than Verga it would be hard to imagine, save Homer. Yet Verga has the same sort of pity as the Russians. And, with the Russians, he is a realist. He won't have heroes, nor appeals to gods above or below. The Sicilians of today are supposed to be the nearest thing to the classic Greek that is left to us; that is, they are the nearest descendants on the earth.

In order further to emphasize the relationship between Verga and Pirandello delineated above, I shall quote the testimonial of the French critic, Benjamin Crémieux, who once stated that "Pirandello's humoristic subject begins where the naturalistic subject of Verga ends." Actually, it is in Pirandello's social and moral experience rather than in his art that Crémieux's statement is true, for Pirandello's Sicilians are no longer ancient Greeks, but modern men. They no longer belong to the generations which could recall the rule of the Bourbons, as did the characters of I Malavoglia; they are citizens of the Kingdom of Italy. They are no longer peasants or shepherds or men from distant farms, but the inhabitants of villages or small provincial towns. In short, from Verga's pastoral world we are taken to the world of the petit-bourgeois, from the shepherd's crook and the nomadic life to the pen and the table of sedentary people, whether they dwell in Palermo, the island's metropolis, or in Rome, the capital.

Verga's shepherds and Pirandello's petit-bourgeois represent the artistic synthesis of two contrasting generations or, more accurately, the historical and social evolution of Sicily during the last sixty years. In part, Pirandello's task consisted in pointing up the psychological changes brought about by the transition from country to province, from the simple, almost feudal relationship between citizen and state. Pirandello traces the course from a life of innocent ignorance to that of a sad awareness. In other words, the playwright aimed at showing that the Sicilians felt rising within them those terrible diseases designated by Lawrence as "intellect" and "soul."

Though Verga's Sicilians were, indeed, deprived of a consciously developed intellect, we must admit that they too possessed a soul of sorts. Thus we cannot push the critical game of paradox to its logical conclusion. Verga's heroes, immersed in the flow of events, are idyllic spirits, epic and tragic at times, but without drama, without history. Unlike Pirandello's description of his own heroes, their souls do not watch themselves live, but are simply *souls that live*.

Pirandello's heroes, too, will let themselves be swept along by the current, but they are directed not by the laws of nature but by those of society, conscious that their time is no longer reckoned by the agricultural calendar of the seasons, but by the bureaucratic timetable of a daily servitude.

Something similar to the phenomenon that had taken place among the Sicilians of Verga's generation, transforming them into the Sicilians of Pirandello's, took place also among the inhabitants of another island, Corsica. As soon as it became a part of the French nation, this island gave its most adventurous sons to the administration of France and her empire. From a pastoral idyll, praised even by Rousseau who at one time cherished a dream of becoming the Moses of the Corsican people, its inhabitants had turned to a life of action. Since Buonaparte, every Corsican leaves the island, not with a dream, but with a Napoleonic program.

Sicily fulfilled a more useful, though less brilliant, role. After sending her strongest sons to America, she detailed the remaining share of her human crop to the administration of the Italian nation; but, unlike Corsica in its relation to France, Sicily has given Italy great writers and remarkable philosophers, as well as statesmen.

Sicilian emigration to America and the continent had, for a long time, the same effect on the social life of the island that the steady pursuit of a new frontier toward the Far West had had in the history of the United States. But finally the Sicilians too found their California, and not at the extreme border, but at the very heart of their island. Unmerciful Nature suddenly proved that even volcanoes and geological catastrophes may be in some way useful. It revealed to the islanders their own volcanic and phosphorescent gold, sulphur. The Sicilians knew they owned sulphur, but had never realized that it could be turned into gold. The beginnings of a primitive industry had already been noted by Verga who, after the *Malavoglia*, gave us *Mastro Don Gesualdo*. At that time the self-made men of the new industry began to appear in Sicily. In fact, the two men who were to become Pirandello's father and father-in-law were among the owners of sulphur mines.

This social evolution is artistically evidenced in a synthetic way, and not by analysis, in Pirandello's early works. I shall point to this evidence, not as to simple historical documentation, but as to an indication of the real nature of Pirandello's art, too often regarded as abstraction or cerebral fancy. Aside from the literary experience terminating with Verga, Pirandello's starting point was also, I repeat, a new social and moral experience that Verga had barely discerned. Crémieux wisely warns readers and critics to remember this "realistic, experimental, and unideological basis of the art and thought of Pirandello."

In one of Verga's short stories, "La Roba" (Property), the author describes the vast tracts of land owned by Don Mazzarò, an illiterate peasant, who has become rich through toil and sacrifice. Wherever one went, one learned that the surrounding land belonged to Don Mazzarò. Verga remarks, with epic humor: "It seemed that Don Mazzarò was spread out as wide as the surface of the earth, and that we were walking on his belly." Don Mazzarò, in grabbing as much land as possible, was not motivated by covetousness or avarice, but by the impulse which moves others to the conquest of love or power. His pride of acquisition was of such purity that he submerged his own identity in the object conquered: "After all, he did not care for money; he said it was not real property and, as soon as he had accumulated a certain sum, he bought land. He wanted to own as much land as the king and be even better off than the king, who can neither sell it nor call it his own." Mazzarò's feeling for property is that of a primitive man, part patriarch, part pioneer. The fact that he does not consider money as wealth shows that he still belonged to that social prehistory when the conception of *homo economicus* had still to be evolved.

Let us consider now one of Pirandello's short stories, which he later developed into a one-act play of the same name, "La Giara" (The Jar). The hero, Don Lollo, could be Don Mazzarò's brother. He too loves the land and, like Don Mazzarò, oversees the peasants who are lazy and negligent in their work. He treats them badly, punishes them whether or not it is warranted. One day, Don Lollo buys a large jar which is to hold the surplus oil expected from a bumper crop of olives. The jar is enormous, and Don Lollo is so proud and jealous of it that he forbids anyone to touch it for fear that it might be broken. Suddenly some peasants discover that the jar is cracked. At first, Don Lollo is infuriated, but then he becomes resigned to having it repaired by Don Zima, who is expert at this kind of work. Don Zima has invented a magic putty which, according to him, will make the jar as good as new, with no trace of a crack. But Don Lollo insists that he repair it the old way by stapling the parts together with wire. Protesting, Don Zima obeys. He climbs into the jar to mend it from within and when he wants to get out, he realizes that the neck of the jar is too narrow for his shoulders. At the sight of Don Zima, imprisoned in the jar much as Jonah was in the whale, Don Lollo is once more infuriated. He feels that this is an entirely new situation, an "interesting case," to use legal jargon. Rather than set Don Zima free, he sends for a lawyer.

The lawyer advises Don Lollo to free Don Zima, in other words, to break the jar again; otherwise, Lollo will be guilty, by definition of law, of sequestration of person. Don Lollo concurs, but points out that it is Don Zima's own fault that he has been caught inside the jar. The lawyer's judgment is worthy of Solomon; he decrees that Don Lollo is to break the jar and Don Zima is to pay for it. Don Zima objects that the jar is worthless, first, because he found it broken and, second, because Don Lollo insisted that it be repaired in his own way. The lawyer then decides that Don Lollo must break the jar and Don Zima pay a third of its value. Don Lollo gives in, but Don Zima refuses to pay and prefers to remain in the jar until Don Lollo changes his mind. Don Lollo goes off in a fury, but Don Zima gaily sends for some wine and settles down to joking with the peasants dancing about his prison. Don Lollo, finally seeing that they are making fun of him, rushes down in a rage and kicks the jar to pieces amid the laughter of the peasants and a bellow of triumph of Don Zima.

What is the difference between the worlds of Don Mazzarò and Don Lollo? Don Mazzarò conceives of property as a relationship between men and things, a struggle between men and nature. Don Lollo, instead, regards it as a relationship between men and society, a contest between man and man, a right that can be conferred or removed by law. He conceives of the law, not as an expression of justice, but as the sanction or denial of a privilege. He plays the law against the law to maintain or to defend a privilege, to enforce the subordination or even the humiliation of a rival, of a competitor, in other words, of a peer. Don Zima, in order to oppose Don Lollo's legalism, falls back on obstructionism and crawls into the jar, like a snail into its shell. From this haven, he proves to his adversary that the law may be a blunted weapon, a useless instrument. In literary terms, we may say that we have passed from the epic austere world of Verga into an ironic, dramatic world; or, in sociological terms, from a primitive, patriarchal society into the world of bourgeois civilization. We have passed from an old feudalism which maintained itself by the law of violence to a new feudalism which defends itself by the violence of the law. And at least sometimes the law is defeated and broken into as many pieces as the fragments of the jar.

Pirandello describes this world with a malicious smile which lurks, like Don Zima, at the very bottom of the jar. From there the author smiles unnoticed at Don Zima, but mostly at Don Lollo and the lawyer. On closer observation, however, Pirandello's position is revealed as not too different from that of the lawyer, who listens to the argument rather indifferently. That indifference is a skeptical reflection on the law of which he is the representative and interpreter. Pirandello, in his turn, smiles because he realizes that men always act like puppets, whether they be moved by the strings of instinctive passion or by those of the indirect and repressed emotions which burgeon beyond the pale of the law.

The true discovery in the short story "The Jar" is that law is not a rule which tends to discipline and check the strife between men but is, of itself, a new instrument for strife. Pirandello took the legal and social battle symbolized by the Sicilian Don Lollo as a point of departure, and from that battle he later evolved the eternal dissent, not between man and man, but between the very soul of man and man himself. Thus a new dissension was revealed, of which the author was to give us further proofs in deeper and richer personalities.

From Verga's final position, which was a return toward the simple, Pirandello moved in the opposite direction toward the heterogeneous and complex. Although his goal was different, Pirandello's itinerary coincided, in direction at least, with that of so many men from his island who abandoned the white houses of the Sicilian countryside for the uniform gray beehives of the capital. In this hostile world, Pirandello's Sicilians defend themselves with dialectics, as did those of Verga with a knife.

The really important word is "dialectic." Contrary to what his father probably wished him to do, Pirandello did not choose a law career, a career considered by simple minds both useful and dignified, like the army or the priesthood. He chose, instead, to fol-

low the road of literature and culture, not as a journalist or ama-
teur but seriously, as a philologist and a scholar. He went from the
University of Rome to that of Bonn in Germany, where he gradu-
ated as a Doctor of Philosophy with highest honors. In his final dis-
sertation, Pirandello had reconciled the love of his island with the
love of science in a work of scholarly research on the systematic and
historic phonetics of the dialect of Girgenti, his province. In Germany, he continued to write poetry and began to read the classics of
philosophy. Perhaps it was at that time that the shadows of abstract
ideas and the romantic seeds of modern thought began to take
shape in his southern soul.

Although written much later, a true synthesis *a posteriori*, "The
Jar" appears to us today a symbol of his awakening consciousness.
Between his experiences of the period and his new studies, there
was the same transition, we might say, that there is between legal
and pragmatic dialectics and pure oratory. Yet Pirandello the student of philosophy, as well as Pirandello the artist, was always to
retain a little of the wrangling dialectic of Don Lollo. That skepticism which was later to form the basis of his logic was to lead that
same logic to the most abstract and general conclusions. But the
force which had first started that skepticism in motion will always
be the force that the heroes of the master, Verga, left as inheritance
in the souls of the Sicilians portrayed by his disciple, Pirandello.
That force is the instinctive suspicion felt by every simple soul
when faced with official justice and its instruments, that is to say,
the police, courts, judges, and official documents, and the suspicion
felt toward that very justice which is, in the final analysis, govern-
mental authority.

The shadow of law and government power is present in Verga's
stories too, but it remains in the background. In most of Verga's
tales, the predominant passion is not a desire for possession, but for
love. If the instinct for possession finds in man's law or in nature's
catastrophe its own sentence (earthquakes, landslides, floods like
the one which was to inundate the sulphur mine of Pirandello's
father and to destroy his wealth), then too the violent and volcanic
instinct of love carries in itself its own implicit punishment, jealousy. However, in almost every instance, the instinct for possession
as well as for love, is dominated and checked, despite its strong
compulsion, by a supreme law, a noble and unyielding moral code,

the code of honor. The Malavoglia family does not suffer and work in order to get rich, but in order to pay back its debts, to win back public esteem. In "Cavalleria rusticana" the rustic duel is fought to erase with blood the wound inflicted on honor. Everybody knows the subject of "Cavalleria rusticana." It is one of Verga's many short stories, which, according to Lawrence are, "one after the other, stories of cruel killings . . . it seems almost too much, too crude, too violent, too much a question of mere brutes." As a matter of fact, the judgment is unjust. Turiddu is not a brute; nor is Alfio. Both are men of sensitive and even honorable nature. Turiddu knows he is wrong and would even let himself be killed, he says, "but for the thought of his old mother." When Alfio discovers that Turiddu is his wife's lover, he challenges him to a duel without harsh words and with an extreme moderation of gesture. Turiddu accepts the challenge, thoughtfully, almost silently, with only a nod and a half-phrase. Their instinctive and primitive self-mastery acquires a character of epic spontaneity and dignity when compared to the sophisticated elegance of a "gentleman" in an affair of honor. And they tread, not with the heavy step of a peasant or a carter, but softly, like shadows, to their death or to inflict death for love and honor.

The same eternal theme of adultery and jealousy is the theme of Pirandello's comedy *Il Berretto a sonagli* (Cap and Bells), and of the short story from which it grew. But here we see enormous changes at the very outset and in every detail. In Verga's tale the villagers witness, in a respectful and stern silence, the scandal and drama unfolding before their eyes. Blood and sin are matters too grave to be the subject of much conversation, but the crux of Pirandello's plot is gossip. It is through slander that Beatrice, the wife of Mr. Fiorica, learns that her husband is carrying on an intrigue with the wife of one of his clerks, a humble bookkeeper, Ciampa. During the latter's absence, arranged by Beatrice herself, she has his house raided by the police and the lovers are caught, but not precisely in a compromising situation. Ciampa returns just in time to witness the outburst of scandal. Poor Ciampa had known that his wife had been unfaithful to him for years, but he had always pretended to be unaware of it and by this feigned ignorance, which made him the object of universal pity, he had provided himself with a mask of respectability. Once the scandal becomes public knowledge and everyone is aware that his wife's unfaithfulness can no longer be unknown to him, Ciampa finds himself cornered and faced with two alternatives: the primitive law of honor and vengeance, or the supine acceptance of the accomplished fact and the consequent dishonor. Unlike Alfio, Ciampa hesitates before bloodshed, but his extreme awareness of society prevents him from choosing the second alternative.

Then, in a moment of brilliant lucidity, he decides to exploit Beatrice's jealousy which, though justified, is so morbid and exaggerated that it carries her to the verge of insanity. With this to work on, he convinces the wretched heroes of the petty scandal that the only solution lies in establishing Beatrice's insanity and in asserting that, in her insanity, she has taken for fact something that was but a figment of her imagination. With devilish ability, carried by suggestion and logic to the very verge of absurdity, Ciampa succeeds in convincing everybody that Beatrice is mad and that she must be sent to an asylum. Thus, instead of Ciampa's being forced to wear the mask of dishonor, it is Beatrice who is forced to wear on her head the cap and bells of folly.

The vulgar knife as an instrument of honor and revenge is here replaced by a sharper and deadlier instrument, the razor blade of logic, so keen and sharp as to split a hair. Before we examine the development of this new use of logic as an arm of defense and of vital offense, as it was to become in subsequent compositions, let us first review some of the most original and significant of Pirandello's works.

First of all, let me emphasize the author's originality. The assertion that Pirandello derives from Shaw, from the Scandinavian writers, or even from the Russians is mistaken. The preceding pages are a sufficient proof, but let me add in confirmation that Shaw himself has dubbed *Six Characters* the most original play ever written. The predominant motive in Ibsen's work is the heroic struggle against reality of men following the flag of the ideal. In Pirandello's work, there is room for neither ideal nor ideology. As regards the Russians, one may even say that Pirandello at least once stepped ahead of one of their greatest writers, Leo Tolstoy, who acknowledged that the theme of his play *The Living Corpse* was inspired by the Russian translation of *The Late Mattia Pascal*.

There is always something personal and characteristic in Pirandello's art, that is to say, the experience of the southern Italian faced with the more disciplined and modern life of central and northern Italy. As Crémieux cleverly pointed out, "even when he is away from his island, Pirandello, the quiet Sicilian, enjoys observing the follies of his compatriots." Accordingly, the writer's best work is that in which the principal motive is the description of the "follies of his compatriots," namely, the series of tales in which the background is formed by the experiences of the Sicilians who crossed to the "continent," that is, to Italy proper. It is these tales which will authorize the future reader to place Pirandello in the same category as the greatest Italian fiction writers: Boccaccio, Manzoni, and Verga. At present, for lack of space, I can consider only three of his recognized masterpieces, a novel and two dramas: *The Late Mattia Pascal, Henry IV,* and *Six Characters in Search of an Author.*

Il fu Mattia Pascal, published in 1904, was written under strange circumstances. Hard-pressed for money, Pirandello had sold it before it was written to the literary journal *La Nuova Antologia,* and the whole book was composed with one chapter already at the printer's, the next in the process of composition, and the third in his mind. He did not know himself what the ending would be; yet the novel has great artistic coherence.

Mattia Pascal, a librarian in a small provincial town, is tormented by an unbearable family life and by constant bickering with his wife and mother-in-law. Following an angry scene, Pascal flees from his home, intending to return after a short period of escape. However, he reads by chance in a newspaper that the corpse of a drowned man, recovered from a nearby river, has been identified as himself, presumably a suicide, since he had been missing from his home for several days. Mattia Pascal decides to take advantage of this opportunity to start life afresh. He then assumes the name of Adriano Meis and, after winning a small fortune at gambling and having wandered about freely for a time, decides to settle down in Rome. Subsequently his landlord's daughter falls in love with him, and one of his fellow guests steals his money. Suddenly Meis realizes that he is completely beyond the pale of society. He can neither marry the girl nor denounce the robber, because Adriano Meis never existed and Mattia Pascal exists no more. In order to revive Mattia Pascal, Adriano Meis must be killed by means of a second pretended suicide. Meis gives way to the resurrected Pascal and decides to return home. But here he is faced with another surprise. His wife, thinking herself a widow, had remarried and now has a child by her second husband. The story ends with the tragic and grotesque impression created by this new trick of life.

Benedetto Croce, who did not like the novel, ironically described its plot and meaning as the "victory of the legal state." But Pascal's drama lies precisely in this and arises from the initial chapters, that is to say, from the normal life Pascal led before the pretended suicide and his transformation into Adriano Meis. The vulgar episode of his wedding, the haunting description of his daily life, the hypocrisy of the friend who after Mattia's supposed death marries his wife, all make us conscious of the potential unfaithfulness in wife and friend alike. By a trick of fate their union will, after a legally proved widowhood, become legal unfaithfulness blessed by the marriage tie. Actually, they betray only Mattia's memory. The blindness of life and destiny makes possible what might have been prevented by social prejudice. The final, grotesque surprise for the revived Mattia Pascal appears to us a revelation of the secrets of the human soul. The euphoria of the transformation into Adriano Meis does not last long, and the episode of his winning at the gaming table is not, as many have thought, a *deus ex machina*, a trick devised in order to continue the course of events. It is, instead, a symbol of the chance happenings characterizing the hero's existence. In a world so little heroic as Pirandello's, where there is no place even for practical will power apart from heroic efforts, events can be directed only by chance.

Mattia Pascal's adventure proves the impossibility of escaping society, or proves that at most it might be possible if a man succeeds in changing himself into a nonentity, into that passive witness of life represented by Adriano Meis before sorrow and love stir him again. Mattia Pascal, guilty of no crime, since he did not even pretend his own suicide, experiences the life of an outlaw, of an escaped convict, with his flights from town to town, his changing of clothes, his altering of features, of personal papers and name. This is the very essence of Pirandello's thought. He wants us to realize that society regards as a criminal or as a "living corpse" all who escape from her bosom and that it is impossible, therefore, to evade the tyranny of the legal state. The strength of this novel lies in the odyssey of that impossible escape, which offers only two alternatives: either no social or vital living or a return to prison. The irony of fate leaves Mattia to close the cycle of his adventures with a combination of the two solutions: return to a prison where there is no place for him.

The Late Mattia Pascal is a novel, but the two other recognized masterpieces of Pirandello are plays. Before examining them, let us discuss the problem of the late revelation of the author's playwriting ability, which has puzzled many biographers and critics.

From the time he went to live in Rome, Pirandello's life seems to fall into three main divisions. The first phase consisted in a calm family life, relatively independent from a financial point of view, and marked by his continued activity as a writer who had great difficulty in finding readers, publishers, and critics. During the second phase, following the loss of his father's entire fortune, Pirandello was forced into the teaching profession and was chained to his literary labors, while he suffered from the first manifestations of unjustified jealousy on the part of his wife. The third phase coincided with the war, the recognized insanity of his wife, and the beginning of his career as a playwright. These three phases, corresponding to the crescendo of a crisis, were followed by the beginnings of fame and success, which were to last from 1920 until his death. The more important events of the last period were the founding of the Teatro d'Arte, Pirandello's successes on the stages of Paris, London, New York, and Berlin, and finally, shortly before his death, the "official" recognition of the Nobel Prize. The mysterious delay in the assertion of Pirandello's theatrical vocation has been explained by G. A. Borgese in terms of the scruples of an *erudito* and a scholar who mistrusted the noisy ephemeral glories of the stage, and whose taste did not run to the modernistic extremes of the drama and stage direction of the time, despite all contrary appearances. This estimate is partly true. Like all conscientious Italian writers, Pirandello had begun as a classical poet by translating the Roman elegies of Goethe and imitating them in his own *Elegie renane*. But in reality Pirandello started to write comedies, dramas, or tragedies only when his interest in the intellectual elements, for logic and emotion and their contradictions, began to haunt him. And we should not forget the personal and human element which caused this change of trend and form. The beginning of his dramatic career coincides with the height of his psychological and personal crisis when, through daily experience, he saw in his wife's mind all human, vital logic replaced by the logic of insanity.

The theme of *Enrico IV* is, specifically, the relationship between logic and insanity. The events preceding the tragedy are narrated with great virtuosity in the opening scenes and consist in a strange and terrible incident. Many years earlier, for a pageant on horseback, a rich young gentleman had dressed as Henry IV, Emperor of Germany, and the woman he loved had apparelled herself as the Countess Matilde of Tuscany, ally of the Pope in his victorious fight against the Emperor. A man named Belcredi, who was also in love with the woman, had startled his rival's horse. In the fall, the young man had landed on the back of his head and, as a consequence, had become insane. The madness, by a trick of fate, had imprisoned him forever in that moment of masquerade and illusion. From that time on, he had earnestly believed himself to be Henry IV. His relatives had wanted to satisfy all the whims of his insanity and had him live in a medieval castle surrounded by servants dressed in historical costumes who, in order to obtain their positions, were required to learn the history of the German Empire during the eleventh and twelfth centuries by heart.

With amazing ability, Pirandello keeps us waiting for Henry IV's entrance until late in the first act. He prepares for it by a slow, provocative succession of recitals of the preceding facts, dialogues and humorous scenes like those which point out the contrast between the electric bulbs in the outside hall, the servants smoking cigarettes surreptitiously, and the medieval costumes and the historical speeches of the roles they recite. One day the woman who had taken part in the pageant as Matilde arrives at the castle. She is accompanied by her daughter Frida, her lover Belcredi, who had caused Henry IV's insanity, and a psychiatrist. The four together decide on a last attempt to cure the poor madman and, on the doctor's advice, they dress up in medieval costumes. Frida, who resembles greatly her mother when young, is to appear suddenly before Henry IV dressed as Matilde, so as to restore to his mind, which had stopped like a broken clock, the sense of time, of the contrast between past and present. While they are preparing for the execution of this trick, we witness an even greater surprise. Henry IV reveals that he is no longer insane. A few years before he had suddenly become cured but, realizing that he could no longer take his place in real life, he had decided to continue to act the role. When Frida appears dressed as Matilde, the shock makes him dizzy. The resemblance to the woman he once loved makes him dream for a moment that the past can be revived. But when the trick is discovered, in a desperate attempt to grab the life which has already run by him, he tries to kidnap Frida. Belcredi intervenes, but Henry kills him with his sword. Then, in order to save himself, he re-enters immediately the world of fiction, to put on again, and this time forever, the mask of Henry IV.

From this résumé one may think that the play *Henry IV* is based entirely on capriciousness. But the element that erases this impression is the extraordinary ability of the playwright and, above all, the great words formulated by an extremely keen intelligence, which produce, by their depth, a sustained emotion. The audience has the feeling that nothing is impossible in this fourth dimension within which Pirandello's thought and imagination move. Nietzsche said there are "unreal" truths; Unamuno said there are "arbitrary" truths. Here Pirandello shows us one or some of these truths.

The occurrence that forms the basis of *Henry IV* is quite credible, I should say natural, because it springs from a vision which is at once foresight and imagination. Henry IV is Pirandello's own thought transformed not into flesh and blood but into tears and nerves. "Every speech he utters," writes the British critic Walter Starkie, "contains words of profound wisdom and there are some critics who call him the Hamlet of the 20th Century." The specialists in Shakespeare assure us that there is no Hamletism in Hamlet, and that Hamletism is a later invention of the imaginative critics and romantic poets. But we are right in asserting that there is Hamletism in *Henry IV*, even if it is born long after the Prince of Denmark. Very seldom could Pirandello rid himself of the limitations of the world in which he was living as successfully as in this drama. No one has realized here the presence of another element, the negation of history that has become masquerade, myth, real madness.

Whether the works we have examined up to now or those we are about to study convince us of Pirandello's originality, the study of his sources is substantial proof. *The Late Mattia Pascal* may have derived from *La Morte civile* (Civil Death), a mediocre melo drama of the end of the century, while Henry IV reminds us of Hamlet's great example. *Sei personaggi in cerca d'autore* belongs to that series of plays about the theater written by men of the theater, which includes such masterpieces as *Il Teatro comico* by Goldoni, or *The Critic*, by Sheridan, and resumes the old Elizabethan and Shakespearean motif known as the "play within a play." But in *Six Characters in Search of an Author* the old formulae of the "play about the stage" and of the "play within a play" are enlarged beyond the restricting limits of caricature or make-believe, to become revelations of the obscure ties which bind imagination to reality or, in Goethe's words, bind truth to poetry.

We see a bare stage, during the rehearsal of a play. The rehearsal is a failure and makes the manager furious and the actors impatient. Suddenly six persons appear on the stage: the Father, the Mother, the Stepdaughter, the Stepson, and two children. They are six real, living creatures who want to act the tragi-comedy of their existence. The manager starts to drive them out but then decides to exploit this *tranche de vie* to his own profit. The Father, in telling their story, says that the four younger people are not his children. The wife had deserted him and had them by another man. One day the Father met the Stepdaughter in a house of prostitution, where they recognized each other only by chance and just in time. The Stepdaughter confirms the episode but does not explain it in shame like the Father, but rather with contempt and disgust. The Father frees himself of reproach by saying that all men are sinners in the most shameful way, but that they conceal their shame under the mask of respectability and proceed indifferently by pretending that nothing really has happened, only because they have buried all recollection in their subconscious. The Father's tragedy lies in the fact that he was discovered by his Stepdaughter. He had been marked forever by the stamp of shame, catalogued forever under that label, or rather, since a label can always be torn away, branded with a more lasting identification, because a man who has once been caught on the hook of scandal will never be able to free himself.

The manager is impressed with the story and wants his actors to recite it immediately and spontaneously. But the six characters protest that they want an author who will understand them, and not actors who will betray their meaning. No one knows but they themselves what has happened and how it should be presented. The manager and the actors must give them a free hand. While the Father and the Stepdaughter are acting their own scene, a shot is heard. The Stepson, a timid and silent adolescent, had killed himself backstage to escape forever from the shame weighing on his family. As the confusion, the sorrow, and the terror of the actors become hysterical, the curtain comes down, giving us the feeling that, rather than the shot itself, the only *deus ex machina* capable of terminating this story is the curtain.

In this drama, the interplay of art and irony unfolds at the same time against three different backgrounds: the background of life, the background of art, and that of the theater. The six characters are first of all human beings, then characters, and lastly interpreters. As human beings they judge themselves and others. But the Father's judgment is directed by humbleness and pity, while in the Stepdaughter's judgment there is only rebellion and disgust. In the Mother, humbleness and pity have become passive submission, but in the Stepson they have been transformed into the will for self-destruction.

As characters, they speak a philosophical and polemical language. This latter form is probably meant for the men of letters and the Italian audience of those years, and it advises them to remember that real life is bare and gray and sorrow is a serious, everyday matter. Writers should not waste time in the fireworks of rhetoric. Audiences should not expect from the theater only vulgarity and happy endings. The philosophical advice has a larger scope and tells us that the great writer must remain in some way subordinate to his characters. A great writer always hides behind his characters like God behind his creatures. A great writer never gives a personification aroused by the contemplation of his own ego, or by the infinite reflections of his own image, as seen in a maze of mirrors. The artist must follow the examples of life and nature, which create without affixing their own signatures or branding with their stamp the infinite objects they produce from shapeless matter, from true nothingness. Here is what Pirandello says in the foreword to the first edition of this play: "Nature uses instruments of human fantasy in order to achieve her high creative purpose. A character in a play comes to life just as a tree, as water, as a butterfly, as a woman . . . And he who has the fortune to be born a character can afford to jeer even at death, for he will never die . . . Who was Sancho Panza? Who was Don Abbondio? And yet they live on eternally as pulsating beings, just because they had the fortune to find a fertilizing womb." This is why the characters cry out at all times: "We want to live . . . The drama is in us . . . We are the drama, and we are eager to act it; our inner passion drives us to this."

In D'Annunzio's art, as in all aestheticism, the center of the art is the poet, the artist himself, while the center of Croce's thought is the artistic and literary work itself, and often not as a whole, but in the rare elegance and cleverness of a stanza or a page. But in Pirandello's aesthetics, the center of art lies beyond the artist, beyond his work. It lies in what makes him the rival of nature and equal to man, the life-giver. It is in his own characters, in the eternally alive human personifications which the artist gives humanity as an everlasting token of himself.

And we now arrive at the third background, that of the relationship between drama and stage, between art and interpretation, between imagination and conventionality. Here, too, Pirandello presents a double-faced attitude. First, he smiles ironically at the professional vanity of the actors and at their poor ability to understand the lessons of life and the hidden purpose of the author. But his more indulgent attitude is that of the experienced playwright who knows that all interpretations or performances, even the most noble and serious, are still unfaithful to the truth, to the essence of his work. As regards this fact, Pirandello, in a note to the second edition, expressed all his pride as a creator and perhaps also the resentment of the poet toward his interpreters when he defined the six characters as "more real and consistent than the voluble actors."

The razor-sharp logic of *Cap and Bells* has become, in *Six Characters*, the lancet of the surgeon who is vivisecting himself, a sort of X ray which throws light on the anatomical secrets, the very skeleton of the imagination. Now that we have seen it in the extreme forms it has reached in Pirandello's works, we must know how Pirandello conceived that logic which was perhaps his only Muse.

One of the characters explains it to the heroine of *Ma non è una cosa seria* (But It Is Not Serious): "Do you know what logic is?

Well, imagine a kind of filter pump. The pump is here (he points to his head). It stretches down to the heart. Suppose that you have an emotion in your heart. The mechanism which is called logic will then pump it for you and filter it; then that feeling at once loses its heat, its muddiness; it rolls upward and becomes purified — in a word, it becomes idealized and flows wonderfully well, because, I tell you, we are outside life, in abstraction. Life exists where there is muddiness and heat, and where there is no logic. Do you understand? Does it seem logical that you should weep now? It is human." While we see here logic replaced by sentiment, often it is logic which replaces sentiment, that is to say, the two elements alternate in active and passive position. To Pirandello, man's life is but a parasitic symbiosis of logic and sentiment.

How did he reach that symbiosis, how did logic become a vital element to such an intellectually simple man as Ciampa? Or, if we take the image used for the hero of *Cap and Bells*, how did we pass from the logic of the ancients, which worked like a sword or a plow, to this razor-blade logic?

Logic or reason, according to the classics of philosophy, had always had a universal value, equally valid for each individual of the human race. By this universality, reason had acquired a transcendental essence. The Encyclopedists and the Illuminists adored it with the same faith that they ridiculed, as evidence of moral disease or a product of ignorance, the believers in positivistic religions. Their spiritual children, the Jacobins, dreamed at the height of the Terror of making reason a goddess.

Pirandello does not believe in reason as an absolute and transcendental value. Since he sees logic everywhere, he cannot consider it an eternal and superior value. Between him and the theologians of reason lie romantic thought and modern relativism. At the most, he considers it a social function. It may render the social life of man easier (or more complicated), but it will never be the basis of a moral code. Man knows and feels that logic and reason are not beyond, but within, himself. He realizes their existence only by introspection. He exploits them without having much respect for them. He uses them to defend himself against others and, above all, against himself, as well as to assert his own personality, to give color and taste to his interior life. He considers them, at the same time, the justification and the instrument of his happiness.

For the "modern" man, therefore, reason is a practical activity or, if the term does not sound contradictory, a sentimental activity. But to the "ancients" it was a moral rather than a practical guide. For Kant, universality of reason is the basis of the categorical imperative of the conscience, which teaches man to direct his actions according to a principle that might become a universal rule. Socrates teaches the same truth. For Kant and Socrates, reason determines the action, guides the will, gives a general and moral sanction to the work of the individual. From this classic rationalism determining morality, we have reached modern rationalism (which some dissenting critic may call intellectualism), of which Pirandello is one of the greatest interpreters. Actually, in his work logic is only a reasoning machine which spins its wheels in the void, or turns them without gaining ground, eroding and sharpening itself in a continuous, useless attrition.

The machine which is out of order in Pirandello's world, a world equally dominated by logic and instinct, is the will. In his characters, logic has become a second nature, another instinct. When Pirandello was narrating his life to his future biographer, he said he had been born in the country, near a wood that the Sicilians, in Biblical style, had named Chaos. Not only had he been born, but he lived, thought, and worked in chaos, because chaos signifies a universe regulated neither by man nor by God, a cosmic jungle where the will either does not exist or cannot operate. The chaotic nature of reason, undisciplined by any law, the slave to the whims of instinct and, like it, bound by the vain, strenuous pursuit of happiness, is the predominant motif of Pirandello's works. Very few critics have realized this fact. Most of them have stopped at that point where reason itself, in the futility of its search, becomes the cause of unhappiness.

In the first place, logic attempts to furnish the individual with the weapons he needs in his fight against society. Its first duty is to provide man with social respectability. Before it becomes the source of individual illusions, logic is to be regarded as a machine rationalizing what every man conceals deep in his subconscious because, according to society's judgment, it is shameful or mean. But man, by acting his social role, comes to believe it to be real and often confuses the mask he wears with his real features. Logic has become a true logic of the irrational. The romantics and the analytical novelists had already written of the "logic of passions" or, to use another romantic phrase, the logic which through the constant supply of a vital warmth becomes the "eloquence of the passions."

Dialectic and eloquence, the latter the body and clothing of the first, are terms which occur frequently in a discussion of Pirandello. Reason always attempts to convince others or itself. Recalling the image of the unfortunate lawyer of "The Jar," we see that in Pirandello the unfortunate man is his own lawyer, now defending, now accusing himself, often doing both with such detachment as to regard himself a legal case. Pirandello's characters do nothing but accuse or defend themselves before a hypothetical tribunal. When their dialectic reaches the level of confession, we see Pirandello in his greatest and most human light, and all sophism disappears in a yearning for purification. But even then the confession of his characters does not resemble that of a guilty man or of a sinner who is elated by the humiliation of an act of mystic contrition, as happens in the great Russian novels. They are not inspired by God, but by the obscure fatality to which they are subject. In this sense, the writer who resembles Pirandello most is Franz Kafka, who was haunted by the life of the conscience, not as a confession, but as a ceaseless trial.

The "demon" of logic and reason in Pirandello is much more powerful and diverse than is the intelligent, indulgent one Socrates heard within himself, in whose advice he found the inspiration of truth and the words for explaining it. It is not a demon, as understood by the Greeks, but the devil himself, as conceived by Christianity: the Evil One who does not convince, but seduces; the Serpent of the Garden of Evil, the one who called sin the tree of knowledge. Pirandello's demon belongs to the same race as the demon in Dante's *Inferno*, who fights with an angel for the soul of a sinner. He succeeds finally in winning it with brief, brilliant reasoning and then says to the angel, with an ironic smile: "Thou didst not think I possessed such logic."

In the lucid, skeptical spirit of Pirandello, whom thought and imagination had led beyond the circle of his father's faith, this conception of intellectual guilt is a profound reminiscence of Christianity. Original sin is the corruption of the conscience. It is the sin of pride; from it arise some of the greatness and all of the misery of man. The Christian considers it sin and describes it. For

Pirandello, it is sin transformed into sorrow, and therefore he regards it with mixed pity and horror. But in the face of the nobility which every human sorrow arouses, the pity in Pirandello's world overcomes the horror. As long as the struggle between pity and horror continues, we have the Pirandello of comedy and farce, humorous and grotesque. But when pity wins the battle, his art substitutes for the comic mask of buffoonery the severe and solemn mask of tragedy. Then the teaching of the poet who may seem one of the most cruel and violent critics of humanity rings out like the evangelical words: "Judge not."

All the sadder and more profound characters appearing in his works seem to repeat those great words. They no longer seem Catholic, because they rebel against being judged and condemned for eternity according to their "deeds." Even Rousseau, who regarded the Calvinistic conception of grace as a convenient spiritual alibi, refused to be judged according to his deeds. His narcissism led him to believe that man can be saved by the mystic merits of his personality, if he possess a sensitive soul, satisfied with the peaceful contemplation and adoration of itself. In this doctrine, that very pride constitutes election and predestination. It is, in short, a new idolatry.

However, Pirandello's man not only rebels against being judged according to his deeds: he does not even want to be judged for the real or apparent virtues of his soul. He knows that his feelings and thoughts are just as weak and subject to the same slavery as his body. While Rousseau's man seems to say, "Forgive us our sins and love our soul," Pirandello's man whispers, cries out, and repeats: "Judge us not. There is nothing in us worth saving!" When he is not swept on by the flow of sentiment, Pirandello's man feels his soul, his intelligence, and his body overwhelmed by an absolute, unique feeling of shame.

Most of the time, Pirandello's characters try vainly to fight it. Sometimes they reveal it cruelly in the souls and lives of their fellow men. Sometimes they bare it in themselves and with such sincerity that it seems like immodesty. The feeling of shame dominates them because of the instinct of modesty which is still strong and deep in their nature, as it was in the souls of Verga's Sicilians. Pirandello shows that moral modesty is similar to physical modesty. "Each of us, sir," the Father tells the Manager in *Six Characters*, "in society before the others, is clothed in dignity." The moral and social logic proves that the soul, too, possesses a body, a body it must conceal. The garment which hides the body of the soul is falsehood. But shame or life almost always destroys this mask. There lies the tragedy of existence which inspired Pirandello with the paradoxical and meaningful title under which he has gathered together the body of his dramatic works, *Naked Masks*. This idea of mask and nakedness always tormented his imagination and is manifest in other titles, such as "Life in Its Nakedness" and "Clothe the Naked." The lack of physical modesty and unexpected half-nakedness have been permanent elements of vulgar humor from the earlier farces to modern pochades. But from these offenses done to modesty Pirandello has drawn all the grotesque, tragicomic play of his humor, symbolized by the hook which the Father in *Six Characters* describes. In his Stepdaughter's eyes, the Father will always remain caught on the hook, as Dostoevski would say, of "an obscene episode": "She then insists on attaching to me a reality which I could never expect to assume for her in a fleeting, shameful moment of my life." He will console himself with the fact that, in her eyes, he has lost forever social honor, the reason for life, or what the hero of another play of the same title calls "the pleasure of respectability."

The Father of *Six Characters* is one of Pirandello's many creations who, in the ceaseless process of living, defend themselves by denying the judge the right to condemn them. They seem to be telling him: "Either you are one of us, and therefore you cannot condemn us or, if you are different, you cannot understand or judge us. Anyway, you could not condemn a soul or a life eternally because of one cheap and vulgar incident." "A fact," Pirandello says elsewhere, "is like a sack which will not stand up when it is empty. In order to make it stand up, we must put into it the reason and sentiment which caused it to exist." An artist may possibly discover the sentiments and reason which impart the essence and the value to a given fact, but a judge never. The judge looks on the accused or guilty man as an individual, that is, as something integral and permanent. Pirandello and his characters, instead, are perpetually haunted by the many and fleeting aspects of personality. Under the disintegrating force of logic and life, the human personality dissolves into a sort of atmospheric dust, filled with countless grains and atoms now disappearing into the shade, now revealed in different colors and vibrations in response to the particular sunray which falls on them. In Pirandello's own words, man is at the same time "One, No One, and a Hundred Thousand."

Borgese was the first critic who contrasted Leibnitz's idea of the monad with Pirandello's conception of the infinite divisibility of personality. We can extend the comparison still further and assert that Pirandello does not believe in pre-established harmony, but in a pre-established disharmony. But this profound mistrust in the harmony of life, this basic doubt which is a fundamental of Pirandello's art, is not the doubt of a Mephistopheles, which denies all human values. Pirandello's characters arrive at the denial of all truth only because they are pursuing, anxiously and desperately, *the* truth. Although his art often reveals the humorous or the grotesque, it is never cynical or damning, but almost always pathetic and tragic. For this reason, Starkie's likening of Pirandello to Swift is not sound.

The fundamental austerity of Pirandello's spirit withstands even the difficult trial of the obscene elements in his works. In some, for example in *Man, Beast and Virtue* or even in *Liolà*, the plot revives situations found in the old Italian short stories from Boccaccio to Bandello, or in the plays of the sixteenth century from Aretino to Bibbiena. But Pirandello emphasizes the humorous element in such a way as to give the impression that the good-natured licentiousness of the classics has been contaminated or vulgarized by the "gags" of the *commedia dell'arte*. As in Machiavelli's *Mandragola*, the saraband of the passions is not observed with any kind indulgence, but with a detached clarity which actually becomes disgust and contempt. By presenting this aspect of the exciting, shameful adventure in the intricate jungle of consciousness and instinct, the author of the *Novelle per un anno* may be considered the author of *The Thousand and One Nights* of the modern soul. Similarly, the complicated, mysterious plots of the longer stories and of the novelle read like the countless installments of a serial murder story of the subconscious.

Because it is a continuous process of argument and questioning, Pirandello's style seems like the faithful transcription of thought born and evolved only to be expressed orally. Like lava, it is shaped by internal fire. Pirandello the writer is at times nothing but the feverish stenographer of a rapid, violent voice dictating to him from within himself, and he seeks to reproduce its constant crescendo, its reticences and pauses, its interjections of surprise and doubt. Because of this oral element, Pirandello's thought does not proceed by synthesis, but by syncopes, and that explains the frequency of pauses and dashes on his pages.

The balance between dialogue and narration weighs in favor of the second, in his novels and short stories as well as in his plays. The brief moments of pure action develop much as in a moving picture (Pirandello showed some curiosity and mistrust toward this new art in his novel *Si gira*), but the core of the story or novel is the meditation which either precedes or follows the action. The drama is nothing but dialogue. According to Valéry, rhyme and verse are the exclusive characters of poetry. For Pirandello, the alternate beats of conversation and arguments become more important than the speakers and assume the real roles of protagonist and antagonist. Thus Pirandello reminds us that, as etymology teaches, dialogue and dialectics are one and the same word.

The conversational bent of his imagination is revealed in his titles. Almost always they have the quality of an interruption, of a proverb used to silence or finish off one's opponent, or of a bitter and wise "last word" offered by a skeptical spirit as advice or admonition: *All for the Best*; *Each in His Own Way*; *Each of Us His Own Part*; *Think It Over, Giacomino*; *Right You Are, If You Think You Are*; *As You Desire Me*; *We Do Not Know How*; *But It Is Not Serious*; *Same as Before, Perhaps Better*; and so on.

The inquiring nature of his inspiration endows his writing with a constant spirit of research, not scientific or chemical research, but the magic, vain seeking of the alchemist for the philosopher's stone. It is in this constant moving from formula to experience, in the intertwining of hypothesis and supposition, that his thought assumes a tortuous pattern suggesting to Starkie his clever reference to Hamlet's remark, "All is oblique," and which reminds us also of Ibsen's myth in *Peer Gynt*, "The great curved one."

In Pirandello's world, life and death become true theatrical climaxes, taking the form of human reactions to biological catastrophes. Truly biological is that conception which envisages man in a continuous process of transformation and destruction of an infinite number of spiritual cells, this process either stimulated by the germs of logic or destroyed by its microbes. This associative and disassociative nature of intelligence also continuously creates and destroys the ties between man and man, "Men gather together only to fight," says one of the heroes of *La Nuova Colonia* (The New Colony), an imaginative drama about the founding of a new utopian town by a group of outlaws. In this play, the complete failure of the enterprise proves that the religion of the group (of the masses) is destroyed by a spirit which does not even believe in the religion of the individual.

The idea that there can be no progress, deriving unquestionably from Catholic doctrine, is deeply rooted in the Italian spirit. Christian progress is individual, but it has meaning and form only in God, that is, beyond the earthly life. Before Baudelaire, Giacomo Leopardi had ironically praised "magnificent, progressive destinies." Pirandello understands life as a succession of rises and falls, and doubts the possibility of any final, perfect ascension. The spirit can achieve stability only on the plane of art. But art, as well as logic, aims at creating a vital illusion, although it creates that illusion without any practical end in view. It is the one pure, unhindered, and free form of the intelligence. The artist alone has the right to believe in and respect the phantoms of his imagination, precisely because they are not used for any purpose, because they hide nothing; they are not machines or masks, but real and true creatures. It is in this sense that Pirandello reconciles himself, through a profound historical synthesis, with the major tradition of Italian culture, that is, the primacy of art over all other activities of the human spirit. Pirandello does not affirm such primacy in the humanistic terms of Croce, or in the aesthetic narcissism of D'Annunzio. He states it humbly, like the workman who sees himself subordinate to the beautiful work he has created with his own hands. The center of his art is always its humanity. Unlike Ortega y Gasset, he never aimed at the "dehumanizing of art." The heroism and nobility of his life as an artist lie in his constant search for characters who are real people, not merely reflections of people. It was modesty, not pride, that prompted him to entitle his most famous work *Six Characters in Search of an Author*. In reality, he was an author who constantly sought new characters. And it is through them that he will acquire an immortality less ephemeral than that which he attained in his lifetime through his successes on the stage, the award of the Nobel Prize, or his membership in the Royal Academy of Italy.

A NOTE ON ITALO SVEVO

Ettore Schmitz was born in Trieste in 1861 of a family of German-Jewish descent, which had paradoxically Italianized itself in the great harbor city of the Austro-Hungarian empire. The future writer was bound to feel the dualism of the elements composing his intellectual and psychological background, and chose to express it by selecting for his literary work the pseudonym Italo Svevo, or Italus the Swabian. He left incompleted his studies in Germany and returned to his native city, first to work as a bank clerk and, later on, to become a rather prosperous, even a rich, businessman. Death caught him in a car accident in 1928, a few years after the writer had tasted, too briefly, the wine of success.

Svevo was about thirty years old when he wrote his first literary work. It was a novel which belonged more to the tradition of French realism and naturalism than to the corresponding Italian school, Capuana's or Verga's *verismo*. Naturalism meant in France the depiction of urban life, of the working classes on one hand, on the other of the bourgeoisie, while its Italian counterpart coincided almost completely with southern regionalism, with the representation of the primitive life of the shepherd, the peasant, and the fisherman.

The literary sources of the first Svevo novel are betrayed by its title à la Maupassant: *Una Vita* (A Life); by its story, which is nothing else but another *roman d'un jeune homme pauvre*, with the difference that it is not concluded by a happy ending (as a matter of fact, the protagonist ends in failure and suicide); finally by its intentions, which were of narrating another *éducation sentimentale*. But Svevo's Frédéric Moreau, whose name is Alfonso Nitti, is not only far more provincial, gray, and dull than Flaubert's hero, his Parisian model: he is also a more introspective and literal self-portrait, as is proved by the milieu, which is the banking world, seen from inside and from below.

In spite of the fact that it was published only locally, the novel did not pass completely unnoticed in Italy, though it was soon and easily forgotten. Nobody paid the slightest attention to Svevo's first masterpiece, *Senilità* (A Man Grows Older), published five years later in 1898. The fault lies to a certain extent with the author himself, who was unable to realize, like all amateurs, that even literature is a business of its own. Perhaps the first admirer of the second novel of Svevo was James Joyce, who read it in 1906, when Ettore Schmitz found a tutor of English in the person of the future author of *Ulysses*, then an obscure language teacher at the Trieste Berlitz School.

The first of the many surprises this second novel, which is autobiographical, offers the intelligent reader is its title. Its protagonist, Emilio Brentani, is nearing middle age, but is still not too far from the years of youth. In a charming and moving preface to the second edition (1927), the already famous but still unspoiled Svevo cites the opinion of Valéry Larbaud, according to whom the title was not suited to the work. The author confesses his repugnance to follow the advice to change it, even if it comes from such a connoisseur. We think that the distinguished French critic was wrong, and Svevo right. *Senilità* is the novel of senility understood not as a physical or psychic state, but of old age as a second nature, as a vocation.

The last works of Svevo, written shortly before his death and published posthumously — such as the novelette *La Novella del buon vecchio e della bella fanciulla* (The Tale of the Good Old Man and the Beautiful Girl), a masterpiece; or the beautiful short story "Vino generoso" (Heady Wine), translated, but little known in English; or finally the unfinished novel *Il Vecchione* (The Oldster), of which we have only a few pages of the beginning — are again variations on the dominant theme of old age. *Senilità* is therefore an anticipation, a prophecy; and it apparently intends to show that people are not *made* but are *born* old. And the man born old is nothing else but a psychological counterpart of that type which, when seen from a social viewpoint, is called a bourgeois.

It is not extraordinary that *Senilità* passed completely unnoticed in Italy, since Italian is the only modern literature that could be defined as one for which the bourgeois, as a sociological condition or a state of mind, does not exist. It is not extraordinary either that Svevo's work went unrecognized in spite of the fact that its center was Trieste, a city so dear to the Italian heart. If the man, Ettore

Schmitz, was an Italian patriot always active in the agitation for the reunion of that city with Italy, the Trieste of the writer, as Svevo sees it and feels it, has nothing to do with the Trieste of Italian *irredentismo*, of the national dream. The Trieste of Svevo seems to an Italian reader a foreign city, not because there are Austrians or Slavs (who almost never appear in Svevo's world), but merely because it is a city of burghers, very similar to the Lübeck of Thomas Mann's *Buddenbrooks*.

For a cultivated Italian it is very easy to understand, but almost impossible to appreciate, the Italian of Svevo, perhaps the least literary and even the least literate, certainly the least polished, Italian ever used by a man of letters in our time. It is not, like the Sicilianized Italian of Verga, influenced by the local vernacular (in Trieste's and Svevo's case, a stronger variant of the singing Venetian dialect), but it is a kind of Italian Esperanto or pidgin Italian, an instrument of commercial exchange, a modern *lingua franca*. The poet Umberto Saba stated recently that Svevo could have written as well (or as badly, if one prefers to judge from the viewpoint of linguistic pedantry and grammatical purism) in German as in Italian, and that if he chose to write in Italian, he did so to show his predilection for Italian culture. We rather think that if Svevo chose to write in Italian, he did so to be a Triestino of his own kind and class. The Italianism of Svevo is a social and psychological case rather than a cultural and literary one.

It is therefore not extraordinary that the very few Italian critics who understood from the beginning the value of his work were peripheric Italians like him, for instance Silvio Benco; or later, sophisticated, cosmopolitan European minds, like that of Eugenio Montale. But it was only natural that the real discovery of his work was by foreigners, first James Joyce and, in the second place, Valéry Larbaud who, together with Benjamin Crémieux, presented to the French public in an issue of *Le Navire d'argent* a partial translation of the second masterpiece of Svevo, *La Coscienza di Zeno* (The Confessions of Zeno), which had just appeared, after a quarter of a century of silence, in 1924.

His early recognition by Joyce, with the latter's good memory for works and men, was the prime mover of the French rediscovery of Svevo and the reason for the writer's European success. In the preface to the second edition of *Senilità*, Svevo spoke of that rediscovery as his own "resurrection of Lazarus." It made him humbly grateful and innocently happy for the few remaining years of his life, and he always considered it as more than a bad debt which poetic justice or the literary exchange had belatedly but dutifully paid him, rather as a wonder and a miracle, an act of grace and an act of God.

In all his works Svevo's real protagonist is the bourgeois soul. But the bourgeois of Svevo is a very different kind from the type described in sociological or ideological literature. He is always being studied during his free time, while he does not work. The best definition which may be given of the bourgeois, on both the social and the psychological plane, is perhaps the one according to which the bourgeois is that type of man for whom time is money. In the novels of Svevo there are no instances of a problem so frequently treated in the novels of Balzac and Zola, the *question d'argent*. Of Zeno Cosini and the anonymous old man who is the protagonist of the *Novella del buon vecchio e della bella fanciulla* we merely know that they are rich; of Alfonso Nitti and Emilio Beltrani, that they are poor. Generally it is a matter of indifference to know whether Svevo's heroes have money to spare: the only important thing is to realize that they always have little or plenty of time to lose. And Svevo tells us how they employ their time, how they lose or kill it.

Actually some of his heroes, like Alfonso Nitti, have little time to spare. But Svevo always has time for them, even if he visits them preferably when they are free. He is not, like Mann or Proust, preoccupied with the old man Chronos or, like Kafka, with eternity. He is interested only in that aspect of our time's consciousness which Bergson used to call *durée*, and which could be defined as the very antithesis of the quantitative conception of time, of time as *duration*. Time is the terror of youth. But Svevo, always a wise man, looks upon time as a foolish and amusing prankster, a clown or a practical joker, playing everybody a kind of recurring and successful hoax, *una burla riuscita*, to use the title of one of his most amusing works. A hard-headed businessman, Svevo also knows that man too can play with time and against it, that for each one of us time is always both *perdu* and *retrouvé*. We must merely accept it as the medium in which one breathes and lives.

The English translator of *La Coscienza di Zeno* was well advised in changing its original title to "The Confessions of Zeno," because the common noun in that title means both conscience and consciousness, and its suggestion and cogency lie in the equivocal meaning of that very word, which no literal translation in a non-Latin tongue could render. In a certain sense one might say that the aim of Svevo's works is to express conscience in terms of consciousness, and consciousness in terms of conscience.

If there is a writer for whom the resurrected William James formula ("stream of consciousness") and its French and literary equivalent, coined by Valéry Larbaud (*monologue intérieur*), are particularly apt, that writer is Italo Svevo. But his method and imagination have nothing to do with the method and imagination of Joyce and Proust, either from the viewpoint of effective influence (which does not exist) or from the viewpoint of the congeniality of kindred spirit (which may be argued or even denied). The world of Joyce is a world where the bourgeois spirit withdraws into the background for intellectual reasons; in Proust's, for sentimental ones. Leopold Bloom and Swann are not actors but marionettes of that world, not protagonists or heroes but antagonists and victims, not subjects but objects. The bourgeois spirit is in Svevo's fiction both its actor and marionette, its protagonist and antagonist, its hero and victim, its subject and object.

The only intellectual influence that may have been decisive in Svevo's writing, at least in the case of *Zeno*, is psychoanalysis. As we know, he was directly acquainted, thanks perhaps to the uninterrupted cultural relations between Trieste and Vienna, with Freud's teachings and the medical treatment of his school. Certainly he used psychoanalysis more literally than Joyce, for instance, ever used the doctrines and methods of Jung. But if we look at *Zeno* with attention, we see that in that book psychoanalysis is more a matter of content than of form.

Psychoanalysis is par excellence a bourgeois fad. From Molière on, the bourgeois has been often depicted as the only social type who may become that very sick kind of man generally called *malade imaginaire*. In the modern world only the bourgeois may afford himself the luxury of being psychologically and physiologically ill, like Hans Castorp in Thomas Mann's *Zauberberg*. Proust's bourgeois characters are too snobbish, Joyce's too bohemian, for this. Zeno, being a member of the leisure class, uses his leisure to torment himself. And the greatness of Svevo lies in that, after a century of romantic spleen, he was the first one to consider, like the ancients, the type of the *heautontimoroumenos*, the self-tormentor, as essentially a comical one.

In *Zeno*, Svevo does not operate with psychoanalysis, but on it. It is true that the novel was written under the impact of the discovery of Freud by the man Ettore Schmitz: but it is equally true that the writer Italo Svevo psychoanalyzed psychoanalysis itself. In other words, his writing, or at least his vision, has always been potentially or actually psychoanalytic. Ettore Schmitz and his heroes, who are, at least in part his self-portraits, had always been doing psychoanalyses, as Monsieur Jourdain made prose all the time without knowing it. But Svevo the writer has never been unaware of this and therefore is able to give a caricature of both psychoanalysis and himself. Such a detached self-awareness was his lifelong amusement and contentment. One might say that Svevo was that wonder, a bourgeois really interested in his own soul; however, being a wise man, he used to consider one's soul, rather than imagination itself, *la folle du logis*.

To speak in scholastic terms, the human soul is not for Svevo a substance, but merely a series of accidents. The most important accident in the substance of life is love. Love is life both perpetuating and destroying itself. In this conception Svevo has been certainly influenced by his early reading of Schopenhauer. But for a bourgeois Schopenhauer, love is neither a chaotic force nor a cosmic evil: it is merely something both charming and bad. It is not a sin, but a forbidden fruit in the literal sense of the word. It is not forbidden by one's priest, but by one's doctor, who knows better than his patient what is good for him, and who orders him to abstain from it as from that "heady wine" from which the protagonist of the story so entitled gets drunk and sick. Sometimes, as in the matter of smoking, abstention is self-inflicted, like a taboo perpetually violated and reinstated by the patient himself. Love is a temptation dangerous to one's peace of mind and health of body. But temptation is real only to those who yield to it. Love is like the last cigarette of Zeno: Man, a creature eternally condemned to death, lights it up again and again.

In other words, Svevo looks always at love, at least beginning from his second novel, which was written in his early maturity, from the viewpoint of old age, from the perspective of an old man. This attitude is not merely social and psychological, but sexual as well. Like Leopold Bloom with Gerty MacDowell, Svevo's heroes are fascinated only by young girls. This predisposition also leads to logical consequences on the practical plane: Zeno and the protagonists of Svevo's last works regularly keep young mistresses. While Zeno's wife conspires with others, for her husband's good, to prevent him from managing his fortune, and thus treats him like a minor, Zeno supports Carla with his pocket money. In other terms, he becomes at the same time the protector and the father of his mistress, and the son, ward, and protégé of his own wife. The latter situation, not less than the former, is an evident symptom of his spiritual if not actual senility. Old age is very often nothing else but a second childhood. Like an adolescent and an old man, Zeno is interested especially in the beginnings of love; later, only in his own torments and feelings, doubts and self-deceit.

For Ettore Schmitz the man, and for the characters depicting or mirroring him, love is very often nothing else but a tonic and an intoxicant for the nerves. The other hobby, literature, seems rather to be an opium and elixir for man's brain. Both activities or pastimes are treated as habits, manias, or fixed ideas, like a not too harmful drug addiction or a rather innocent vice. In other words, neither literature nor love acquires, in the psychological economy of his characters, an obsessive quality; and this is the reason why the work of Svevo is far less consciously "aesthetic" and "morbid" than the work of Joyce and Proust. The literary experience of his protagonists, even if, as in the case of *Una Burla riuscita*, it is very often based on Svevo's life, is nevertheless less autobiographical (or at least less literally so) than any other element in their *curriculam vitae*.

The author has been able to reach such a paradoxical result by dissociating Svevo the writer, not from Ettore Schmitz the man, but rather from the man of letters who was in Ettore Schmitz and in his heroes. Practically all his characters, perhaps with the exception of Zeno, are men of letters in their spare time. Such is the case of Alfonso Nitti in *Una Vita*, of Emilio Brentani in *Senilità*, of Mario Samigli in *Una Burla riuscita*. In other cases, like the protagonists of "Vino generoso" and *La Novella del buon vecchio e della bella fanciulla*, they are naive reformers or ineffectual idealists. They are never without some intellectual interest (in Zeno's instance, psychoanalysis). But generally, with the exception of Zeno, who after all is not a writer, they never denounce, reflect, or betray the intellectual interests of their creator: Alfonso Nitti, Emilio Brentani, and Mario Samigli limit their literary curiosities and sympathies to Carducci and traditional Italian literature, without revealing in the first case that Svevo was interested in French naturalism and Schopenhauer; in the second, that he had been reading Russian writers; in the third, his recent acquaintance with Freud.

Is it arbitrary to affirm that the writers who are his characters are to a certain extent a satire of the contemporary Italian literary mind, exactly as Zeno is a parody of psychoanalysis? The Mario Samigli of *Una Burla riuscita* perhaps entitles us to think so. The suspicion seems reasonable because in that story Svevo also makes fun of the writer within himself. Even more interesting is the fact of the appearance in one of his last works of the "good old man" of the novelette so entitled, a character affected by literature without knowing it, and who writes a pseudo-philosophical and edifying work by which he belatedly tries to save the soul of his young mistress and to teach her the conduct of life, even after his own death. In the literary vocation of his heroes, therefore, Svevo seems to see an attempt to escape from life, perhaps from consciousness, and even from conscience itself. By this attitude he did not mean to condemn literature; as a matter of fact, this is the very reason he approved of it.

This explains why between the literature of Svevo and the literature of his characters there is neither relationship nor contrast. The conflict between the bourgeois spirit and the literary mind is perhaps the dominant theme of modern and contemporary writing. The ideologist and the reformer on one side, the aesthete and the individualist on the other, solve that conflict by submitting the bourgeois spirit to the literary mind. Such was the solution of Flaubert and Nietzsche, of Wilde and Shaw, of Joyce and Proust. Thomas Mann reversed the position, granting the bourgeois spirit the right of questioning the validity of the literary mind and of opposing it. But Svevo was perhaps the only one among modern writers unable even to conceive of such a conflict. He accepted the bourgeois spirit as a frame or state of mind, as a datum or fact, as our own version of what Montaigne used to call "the condition of man."

Exactly because he does not judge the bourgeois spirit, Svevo amuses himself, tremendously and naively, by looking at it. A perfect bourgeois as a man, as a writer he is almost alone in not looking like one. Instead of descending or condescending to the bourgeois spirit within his own soul, he raises and uplifts it along with himself to the sphere of imagination, to a world of fancy and dream, which is at the same time the world of reality itself. Once Stendhal asked for a literature written by bankers and industrialists able to understand, lucidly and cynically, the economy of life, the business of society, the value of man. Svevo was certainly a writer of this brand and, furthermore, was endowed with such bourgeois honesty and common sense as to refuse to transform his indulgent egoism into any set of theories, any "egotism." A kind of innocent wisdom was the real source of his greatness and originality. He was with everybody, including himself, a man of the world. This makes him, more than an Italian Joyce or Proust, a kind of contemporary Henry James, without the latter's snobism and narcissism.

This is why from the naturalistic and Schopenhauerian pessimism of his youth he gradually grew to a kind of olympian serenity, and acquired that "merry wisdom" which is so alien to the modern mind. His first novel is gray and sad: in his second, there appears already what Gogol used to call "smiling through tears"; in *Zeno* and in his last stories, one may see the very uncommon realization of that poetic ideal which the German poets of the beginning of the past century used to call "romantic irony." This explains why the man born old always grew younger with time: and the same is already happening to his work, through the wonders of glory and the miracle of death. In the annals of contemporary literature very few books will remain so youthfully fresh as the pages of a writer like Svevo, who spent all his life in drawing a "portrait of the artist as an old man."

LEO FERRERO'S *ANGELICA*

From Leo Ferrero's parents we learn that *Angelica* was written during the first months, if not the first weeks, of the young Ferrero's exile (winter of 1928–29). Pages from a journal kept a few years earlier, several scenes left us from an experimental, youthful drama, allusions to the effect that the reading of Schiller's *Conspiracy of Fiesco* had aroused in the young author, and, lastly, a scenario that served as the first draft of the play: these facts constitute the evidence revealing how the idea of *Angelica* had begun to mature in the mind of Leo Ferrero from the first years of Fascist oppression. His first letters from Paris, written at the same time as the first version of the play, speak of *Angelica* as if it were an "outburst," a word used consciously to indicate his desire to sublimate in an artistic catharsis the repressions which so fine and delicate a nature had suffered in Italy, under the moral and political whip of dictatorship.

The original manuscript was discovered by his father among Leo's unpublished papers about a month after his death. The drama was first performed several years later in French, when, produced by the company of George and Ludmila Pitoëff, it opened with great success in Paris on October 22, 1936, at the Théâtre des Mathurins. The opening, followed by a long run, elicited general approval by the French critics who were, for the most part, extremely enthusiastic, and the success it enjoyed in Paris led to its being produced in Switzerland and South America.

The author's father, the historian Guglielmo Ferrero, in the beautiful and moving preface which he wrote for the first Italian edition of the play (*Nuove Edizioni di Capolago*, Lugano, Switzerland, 1937), reveals in a few words the content and meaning of the masterpiece left by his beloved son. According to the father's interpretation, *Angelica* is a "prophetic poem . . . a fantasy of aerial structure" which suggests "Shakespeare, Musset, Aristophanes," and which evokes "in its every aspect . . . the greatest drama of history, the struggle of man for the conquest of liberty." Subsequently he defines the aspects and the phases of this struggle as "the sophism . . . by which despotism imposes upon [masters] the conniving weakness of its victims," as "the whole tragicomedy of man who, in his struggle for liberty, shows himself still to be a contradictory being . . . and falls back into slavery" because "free men are not worthy of their liberty."

This masterly exposition, which could be described as an ideological summary of the drama, delineates the architecture of the play with extraordinary precision. But a structural study of *Angelica* interests us less than an examination of the emotional impulses and of the psychological elements which motivated that construction; we must study the foundations, rather than the external structure. In my opinion, the sources of *Angelica* should be sought in a series of notes entitled "For the Play." Through the devotion of the author's parents, these have been preserved and made available to interested critics, having been published as an appendix to the first edition of the play. Gleaning from this little harvest of notes, we will be able to reconstruct perhaps the spiritual attitude and motives which gave birth to *Angelica*.

I

The first group of these aphorisms concerns the relationship between morality and politics, that same problem which Machiavelli had not solved but had unhesitatingly abolished with his formidable negation. "Politics will never be able to free itself from immorality," says Leo in a statement that rings like a reply, like a vigorous refutation of Machiavelli's negation, "because it seeks its laws from within itself rather than in a principle beyond itself." This idea conforms readily to the general orientation of Leo's thought, which thirsted constantly after superior and universal truths, and it is one of the many forms assumed by his struggle against certain tendencies, or rather deviations and maladies, of Italian culture and civilization. At first glance, such an idea may appear to be a commonplace, except that there are no commonplaces for the conscience of a moralist, or for the soul of a believer. Its significance must be evaluated only by a synthesizing diagnosis of the essence of what is called the Italian genius. Leo's originality consists in the eloquence with which he has repeated lamentations uttered many times before him; he has repeated them with the despairing faith of the voice crying in the wilderness.

From Dante to humanism, the Italian spirit was saturated in universality. It believed in an international art, which was termed classical. It believed in a single faith, in a fusion of the concept of cosmopolitanism with that of Christianity. Beyond the one Church, Dante had dreamed of one Empire. But by a paradoxical anachronism, we can say that, from the Renaissance onward, Italian culture has instead helped to realize *ante litteram* what later, in terms of Crocean idealism, was to be called the dialectic of distinctions. In an excellent preface to the English edition of *The Ruling Class*, the principal work of the Italian sociologist Gaetano Mosca, the American critic Arthur Livingstone points out with great acumen that the most original Italian contribution to modern European culture consists in a rigorous and precise designation of the diverse spheres of influence of the various activities of the mind. And in fact Machiavelli came first to tell men that politics is not moral, but something else, and was the first to formulate specific laws for politics. Machiavelli was followed by Galileo, who affirmed that there exist two truths, that of the Bible and that of scientific speculation; while seeking to define the meaning and significance of the latter, he was very careful neither to violate nor to deny the former. And finally Croce appears, to declare that action and ethics are two concepts, supplementary but different; that art is knowledge, but knowledge of an autonomous kind, if not the antithesis of that which is attained through philosophic speculation and the exercise of the intellect.

All the work, indeed all the life, of Leo Ferrero was consecrated to the struggle against this dialectic of distinctions which is the fundamental *forma mentis* of Italian culture. Instead of particular principles, he sought always universal and transcendent ideals. Just as his book *Leonardo o dell'Arte* is devoted to the search for a principle which does not identify itself with art, but transcends it, so *Angelica* is the tragedy of a spirit which seeks, even through sacrifice to itself, to transform necessity (politics) into liberty. In Ferrero's soul there is a continual preoccupation with a catholicity which strives to overcome the dualism of historical Catholicism, spirit and matter, a dualism which, in the humanistic doctrine of

Croceanism, persists under the form of a distinction between the ethical and the practical.

It is this concrete idealism which inspires another series of notes collected before and during the composition of the play. The thought of Leo Ferrero seeks a real, possible, human order of things. He declares himself struck by "the admiration of power which characterizes all moderns" and admits not understanding "why honest people so much enjoy the spectacle of dishonest people's breaking the very laws which they observe." In the interrogative form of doubt, Leo has postulated here, in its passive and active aspects, the psychology of Fascism. But continuing, his voice rises nostalgically toward the absolute, when he says that "in order to distinguish between good and evil, it would be necessary for the criteria of good and evil to be established beyond man by a kind of tribunal, which might pass judgment according to principles that do not concern us . . . In order to be free, one must be, to a certain extent, bound, for the man who is bound aspires to liberty."

II

The first question with which *Angelica* confronts the reader and critic is why the author chose as his characters the fixed and recurrent types of the *commedia dell'arte*. Many different formulae have been advanced in answer. Though very few interpreters have considered the question as nonexistent or secondary, they have treated the masks either with complete indifference or with the excessive attentiveness with which the purported reality or humanity of fictional or dramatic characters is often studied.

Among the most sensible critics are those who have defined the masks as animated symbols or those who have seen them as general or collective types, "not individuals, but species," identifying them as representatives of social classes in the more or less Marxian sense of the word. In regard to this last conception, we may recall that the tendency to present on the stage social archetypes instead of individualized characters goes back further than Shaw, indeed directly to Diderot. To his dramatic theories we owe the present-day substitution of the type of the priest, the soldier, the intellectual, and the financier for the comic or tragic examples of personality reduced to a consuming, all-absorbing passion, such as the jealousy of Othello or the hypocrisy of Tartuffe. This allusion is necessary but not adequate to explain the adoption of masks in *Angelica*, because social mythology or, if you prefer, classical mythology could assume either more normal or different forms.

Another point of view seems more nearly true, that of recognizing in the adoption of the masks one of the means by which Leo Ferrero attempted to remain faithful to the cultural heritage of his country, to that tradition which he cherished in his meditations and in his writing. In my opinion, the truth is to be found in this direction, although on a more elevated psychological and intellectual plane. Leo chose masks as his characters for formal and interior reasons. Such a choice is based primarily on his favorite conception of a culture built on what he called "implied presuppositions," which we might compare in a very positive sense to the meaning Valéry gives the word "conventions." Adopting the conventions of the masks, Leo sought to achieve a profundity and a greater expressive intensity, either in spite of or because of the fixed lineaments and the precise limitations dictated by a tradition crystallized for all time. Secondly, the adoption of the masks freed him from the obstacles and dangers inherent in every inspiration which is marked by its contemporary nature, or what is popularly called (with a meaning far different from Goethe's) occasional poetry. In short, the masks allowed the author to transcend the narrowness of a polemical or a political attack, and to give an admirable example of what the sage of Weimar meant in his formula of *Gelegenheitsdichtung*: that is, a vision inspired by the fleeting moment but which, through its grandeur, projects the moment into eternity.

The special nature of Leo's masks is easily made clear by contrasting them with the three protagonists, who are figures suggested by earlier characters, very different from those of *commedia dell'arte*. Orlando and Angelica were offered to Leo's imagination by one of the most precious of literary galleries, that of Ariosto's fantasy. This reversion to imaginary and already defined characters has a motivation similar to that of the adoption of the masks; the difference of origin, however, gives the hero and heroine a very different flavor from that of the minor characters, the extras who are, almost without exception, re-created in the pattern of the fixed types of *commedia all'improvviso*. It almost seems as if the

Ariel-like lightness of Orlando and the frivolous but genuine femininity of Angelica were intended to give us the impression that they are two more mobile and vital creatures than the traditional forms among which they act, that they are the only ones capable of autonomous movement, without masks and without strings, in a world of puppets. This literary contrast, oscillating between the opposite poles of learned and popular art, gives the dialogue and action an agreeably contrapuntal movement, and the temperament, or the individual origin, of the third character of the drama, the Regent, contributes to this harmony. As we will attempt to point out, the Regent is nothing more than a caricature of the D'Annunzian hero, an example of that deteriorated D'Annunzianism which persists, for example, in the historical figure of Mussolini.

The *dramatis personae* of *Angelica* are furnished, therefore, by three different spiritual worlds, by the gallery of Italian masks, by the Ariostan version of knightly legends and fables, and by present-day Italian politics and culture, that is, the myth and prophecies of D'Annunzio, all treated as half-chronicle, half-fantasy. In D'Annunzianism, understood here according to *Goliath, The March of Fascism*, by G. A. Borgese, as the most important mythical, literary, and rhetorical ferment of Fascism, it is easy to recognize the principal enemy against which the author's irony and the protagonist's fervent faith are struggling. Once again Leo's work is conceived, like the work of the ancient philosophers, as partly destructive and partly constructive, but the two are so intimately fused as to give a positive meaning even to negation, and condemnation becomes here the affirmation of faith. Thus just as, through its implied presuppositions of the anti-Croce polemic, the book on Leonardo seeks to formulate an integral concept of art, so *Angelica*, conceived as a poetic pamphlet against spiritual and political tyranny, against D'Annunzio and Mussolini, attains by virtue of its art to that supreme sphere where every human voice, even that of mockery or imprecation, is transformed into a hymn, a chant, a prayer.

III

Before studying Orlando, the hero, let us examine his antagonist, the Regent, in order to show above all the latter's symbolic identity with D'Annunzio and the D'Annunzian hero. The first to point this out, although only in passing, was the Argentinian critic, José

Bianco. And following is some of the evidence which bears out this obvious thesis.

In his discussion with Orlando, the Regent confesses that he is "a pagan poet," he speaks of "supermen," he uses an ornate style in which he makes great show of recherché Latin and Greek expressions. Even from the stage directions describing his appearance, we see that the author had the D'Annunzian iconography in mind: "small . . . elegant . . . voluptuous . . . cruel." Meneghino claims to have been imprisoned only for having made public a literary "plagiarism" of the Regent's. It is well known that a group of critics, headed by Thovez, accused D'Annunzio of the same thing. Lastly, the Regent, like his model, makes excessive use of imperial rhetoric and displays an eroticism *ex lege* similar to that of which the Imaginifico gave such celebrated examples, both in his life and in his art. Also the actual impulses which moved D'Annunzio in his search for "beautiful death" in combat, to heroic undertakings in the air and at sea, and finally to the expedition of Fiume are summed up with masterly wit in the compendious phrase by which the Regent concludes a brief dialogue with one of his captains: "Perhaps you understand tactics, but not choreography."

This felicitous hit welds, as it were, the D'Annunzio-Regent equation with the equally valid Regent-Mussolini combination. The choreographic element, the stage setting, the skillfull preparation of a public meeting as if it were a choral group, the necessarily theatrical touches with which modern dictatorships attempt to transform coercion into the ritual of a new faith, are perhaps the most interesting and provocative aspects which the political movements of our day will offer to the study of the artists, psychologists, and thinkers of the future. The ferocious irony of the Regent's figure, an irony truly romantic in the sense that the author alone recognizes it, suffices to show to what point those critics who thought they recognized in the Regent a so-called "charming character" have misunderstood the intentions of the poet. The Regent is grotesque, grotesque without knowing it, for he lacks completely that sense of humor which in the other characters springs forth with great emotional or imaginative vigor, deriving either from their very characters or from the symbolic humanity that constitutes their mutual discord or harmony. Perhaps the critics have failed to recognize the grotesque character of the figure precisely because the author, with great finesse, was careful not to emphasize it; we have our best proof of his sense of proportion in the significant misinterpretation by some critics who see a sympathetic portrayal in the character of the Regent. The world of *Angelica* is a microcosm of puppets where a monstrous or animal-like caricature, on the order of a King Ubu, can find no place. The Ariel-like temper of Leo's inspiration prevented the caprices of a too heavy imagination, and the "fren dell'arte" vigilantly prevented his trespassing into absurd or amorphous buffoonery.

As clear as the historical symbol exemplified by the Regent is the moral and emotional message entrusted to the person of Orlando. Up to a point one could maintain that the Leo–Orlando equation is as valid as that of Regent–D'Annunzio. This has been suggested by many critics, without insisting unduly upon it. Like Leo, Orlando declares he found his own ideas in the books of St. Thomas and Confucius, and with few changes the character describes himself in terms which had already been written in the diary of the author. The famous farewell pronounced by the dying Orlando is only a variation on the salute to Italy written by Leo at the moment of his departure into exile. The originality of this twofold farewell to fatherland and to life, which is transformed from a private document into the impersonal voice of poetry, is by no means denied or disproved if one recognizes in it a clear echo of Manzoni and the famous, moving apostrophe of the fleeing Lucia: "Addio, monti sorgenti dall'acque" (Farewell, mountains rising from the waters).

If the conflict between Orlando and the Regent exhausts the full meaning of the drama, the conflict itself has validity only in relation to the mysterious personage who gives the play its title. And truly Angelica is a sphinx. Following are only a few of the numberless symbolic and allegoric interpretations with which a veritable army of critics has attempted to solve the mystery. According to some, Angelica is "false liberty," that is, "license"; also "reality"; also "the crowd or masses." Before studying them individually, let us grant that in each there is a shadow of truth; and this is due less to the acumen of the critics than to the inspired profundity with which the poet conceived his character.

As we know, allegory goes hand in hand with personification, and often prefers to invest itself with a feminine appearance and characteristics. From time immemorial, thinkers and poets, with a facile mythology of passions, have assigned the attributes of femininity to almost all abstract concepts, now in a positive, now in a negative sense. In dealing with Angelica, the majority of commentators have industriously striven to construct a whole series of connections between the character and the idea of liberty. But the discerning reader cannot overlook the Sybilline words which Angelica herself speaks to the dying Orlando, the very Orlando who had presented her to the people as the symbol of liberty: "I am not Liberty, I am Angelica."

The hypothesis which makes of Angelica a symbol of the crowd is attractive, and Leo's idealistic position regarding the modern myth of the masses gives it added credibility. Perhaps the hypothesis can be further substantiated as a reminiscence of Freudian ideas about the femininity of the crowd which is now mystically unleashed, now mystically subdued. Other critics claim that in Angelica we see also the symbol of the human, social reality of life as such, of instinct personified, of the joy of living, or the ego's self-preoccupation, or what Leo elsewhere referred to mystically as "love of self."

But to understand Angelica one must not lose sight of her *curriculum vitae* as a literary character; then it will be remembered that, in Ariosto's poem, the madness of Orlando is due to the fact that Angelica prefers a stupid and handsome young man to the prince of heroes, the most noble of the noble. In Leo's drama the relationship between the protagonist and his female antagonist can perhaps be reconstructed through the Nietzschean antinomy of Apollonian and Dionysian. On the basis of this reference, we can better judge another of the current interpretations, which recognizes the symbolic identity of Angelica with Leo's native land and its people, with Italy and the Italians. The fact that it is Angelica who transforms the hero into a martyr seems to furnish valid corroboration to the hypothesis. Nonetheless, I believe that Angelica holds a meaning at once more vast and restricted, more specific and universal. She can be a symbol of an ethical nature, as is partially suggested by the Nietzschean antinomy mentioned above. Angelica actually represents nothing but the old, uncontrollable Italian sensuality, oscillating between the two extremes of *dolce far niente* and *joie de vivre*, now the blind slave of physical love, now the prisoner of an indulgent skepticism, capable of doubting not only the ideal but also the reality of the concrete. Angelica is the symbol of that sensuality which has found classic interpreters, now tragic, now comic, in every century of our artistic and literary tradition, from Boccaccio to D'Annunzio, from Marino to Salvatore di Giacomo, from the melodies of Rossini to the songs of Piedigrotta. In his preface, Guglielmo Ferrero, after discussing the "passive perversion" of Angelica, asks himself, "for what reason is it a woman who kills the liberator?" I believe my hypothesis can give the most nearly complete answer to that question. Angelica is a Delilah who kills the Samson she does not love. She kills him lazily, almost without reason, without rancor. "Her greatness extenuates her," says Orlando, speaking of Italy. We might say the same of the beauty of Angelica. This interpretation of Angelica is most strongly corroborated by the masculine character who most resembles her, Harlequin, when he describes her with smiling, poetic precision: "She is a falling star, Orlando." Actually, not even the knightly Orlando, who, more than a visionary, is a prophet, is deceived as to the true nature of his Dulcinea.

IV

The minor characters are more simple. They represent not only typical Italian voices, but the universal prejudices and passions of men and classes. Thus, for example, Pantalone is the hypocritical, egoistic industrialist who pretends to work for the good of the community, but who accepts a formal, theoretical liberty in order to deny the liberty which comes to fruition in practical activity and in the game of interests: actually he is a liberal and a protectionist. "I respect free thought," he says, "but free trade is nonsense." For him, the promise of a modification in the tariff is enough, as for Valerio the mirage of a brilliant diplomatic career is sufficient, to cause him to accept in thought and deed the prostitution of his daughter Angelica. Dr. Balazon, who is a doctor in the *commedia dell'arte*, has become a professor and university president; he represents the ambitious intellectual, ready to change colors at the first shifting of the wind, or prone to transform the bitterness of his deluded ambition into a feeling of theoretical opposition. He hides meanness and opportunism under a formula which he frequently repeats in the course of the action, and this formula is all the more felicitous for the mockingly allusive flavor the author infuses into it: "We must wait for the natural solidification of events." Who can fail to recognize under the cloak of an hypocritical wisdom, under the mask of scientific serenity or historical platitudes, the pet phrases fashioned by the conservative liberalism of Giolitti, of the bourgeoisie? Or perhaps also an ironic echo of the pedantic formulae with which Gentile's philosophy, the *idealismo attuale* from which Fascist ideology was born, seeks to hide its moral vacuity and its worship of success?

The figure of Scaramuccia, modern variant of the old comic type of cowardly, swaggering soldier, is truly admirable. The physical dastardliness concealed under the Spanish arrogance of the Captain and Matamoros, replicas of the *miles gloriosus* of Plautus in the human gallery of *commedia dell'arte*, is transferred by Leo to the social and moral plane. Scaramuccia is the modern officer and soldier, a bourgeois and a bureaucrat whose only interest is in the bare business of living and whose days are eternally obsessed by the fear of losing his job, of no longer being in a position to fulfill his duties as paterfamilias. In his *Meditazioni sull'Italia* Leo had observed how, ever since the Tridentine Council, the one center of activity and concern for the Italians had become the life of the family. As a direct result, ever since the sixteenth century civic conscience and public life had been almost completely annihilated. It was indeed an happy inspiration to take an army man as the example of that subordination of all political and civil rights, as well as of military honors, to those obligations which in a primitive, etymological sense of the word would be called proletarian, that is, concerned with the producing and raising of children.

A state employee like Scaramuccia, but on the lowest rung of the bureaucratic ladder, is Stenterello, a popular mask born in the Tuscany of the grand dukes and posterior, therefore, to the *commedia dell'arte*. The poet raises poor Stenterello to the stature of a martyr; actually he dies to save Orlando or, better, to redeem the meanness of his life by offering it as a sacrifice, in token of the dignity of man, to the ideal of devotion and of liberty.

Lastly the drama presents two anonymous characters, whose

personalities are distinguished not by proper but by common names; at least one of them deserves particular, profound study. They are the Worker and the Padrona.

About the latter, as about Angelica, the most varied and contradictory hypotheses have been bandied about. Just as some critics saw in Angelica the negative symbol of the crowd and the masses, others of opposed political leanings thought they recognized in the Padrona the positive allegory of the people. But Leo, insensible to Marxian religion, considered any such entity a symbol itself. Then there have been critics so ingenuous and indiscreet, infatuated to such an extent with nationalistic rhetoric, as to see in the Padrona a familiar tribute to or, better, an adulation for the country which had extended hospitality to the exiled poet. Briefly, the Padrona would be an allegory of France, and at least one French critic maintained this opinion. We will not be guilty of the same sin if we affirm the contrary. No, the Padrona is not the symbol of the admirable French nation which the poet celebrated later in his *Paris, dernier modèle de l'occident*. Instead, she represents the clear, precise antithesis of Angelica. For that reason alone we may see in her the vision of another Italy, different and opposed to that symbolized by the figure to which she herself is contrasted: Italy, popular but not plebeian, wise but not skeptical, prudent but not indifferent or calculating; Italy that loves glory and life, knowing still how to respect sacrifice and death. And we know that this Italy is equally true, more true and lasting, than the other, although for so many years, weeping and suffering in silence, she has been shrouded in darkness. And when the Italy of Angelica has been so despised and discredited as to seduce no one any longer, the Italy of the Padrona will rise to pronounce her great word to the world and to reveal her chaste beauty to all men.

Of the figure of the Worker there is little to say, but he will always remain engraved on our heart and memory for the simple, ingenuous reply he makes to Orlando when the hero asks him what he thinks of liberty: "That it is sweet, sir."

V

The spark of the drama bursts forth in *Angelica* from the Regent's having re-established the famous feudal custom of *jus primae noctis.* Obviously this is treated only as a symbol. But the choice of such a symbol suffices to indicate at once the Italian nature of the play. In the passage in the *Meditazioni sull'Italia* to which I have already referred, Leo observes that, from the seventeenth century on, through the influence of the Spanish Domination and the Counter-Reformation, the concept of honor which previously had had so broad, human, and chivalrous a meaning had become restricted to the narrow, mean orbit of conjugal fidelity, purity of sisters, chastity of daughters. If we contrast these pages of the *Meditazioni* with the plot of *Angelica,* and above all with the behavior of the father Pantalone and the fiancé Valerio who, before the decisive intervention of Orlando, were quite willing to sell Angelica, the one for interest, the other for ambition, we cannot help feeling the extraordinary bitterness which moved the poet in writing his theatrical satire. With the lucid brutality of an Inquisitor, he seems to want to say to his people: Italians, do not be deceived. He who renounces his rights as man and citizen, who deludes himself into believing that he can transform collective injustice into individual profit, who hopes to be able to shut himself up like a snail in the supposedly inviolable fortress of four walls and a domestic life, this man sooner or later will be obliged to renounce the most intimate privileges, even the holy prerogatives of personal and private liberty, even the honor of father and husband. Actually, before the intervention of Orlando, *Angelica* is merely a tragicomedy of humiliation and shame, which are carried to the last limits of acquiescence before every form of violence.

When Angelica confesses to Orlando that really she would not have been too displeased to submit to such violence and tells him, "I, like all women, love power," it is not Angelica or her cynicism that offends us. We are offended, rather, by those men incapable of ideals and of spiritual education who have created this type of woman by their lack of faith, by their subjugation to sensuality and the pleasure of living. In this sense, Angelica truly represents Italy, that Italy which "will belong to no one," which flirts with conquerors, enslaves and cajoles them, and which, in the very act of surrender, eludes their clasp forever.

The most interesting personages in the drama are, in the good and bad sense of the words, poets and artists. Angelica herself is, in a certain sense, the symbol of beauty. And it is very provocative to have a poet (for Orlando, as mouthpiece of the author, can only be a poet) demand, stupefied, of one of the characters: "Do they put poets at the head of the government in this country?"

Like Plato, Leo Ferrero wants to drive poets from the Republic. However, his is an ostracism dictated not by philosophy but by moral conscience, and perhaps by a more elevated conception of poetry. There are three poets or artists in this play: Orlando, the Regent, and Harlequin. The latter is a sculptor who has been entrusted to do a bust of the Regent; he is afraid of being taken for a communist and considers life, including the blood and tears shed by men, only as material for art. "For me," he says, "the world is only a diverting spectacle, and I have no desire to compromise myself. I am in no way obligated to protest in favor of morality, because I am concerned solely with aesthetics." And elsewhere: "Nothing is so amusing for me as a revolution . . . a battle . . . the people unleashed." Harlequin typifies admirably the traditional type of Italian writer and artist whom we find from the Renaissance up to the present: the type of cynical or indifferent virtuoso, the immoral aesthete, prince of form, and the slave naturally of miserable, daily reality, ready to write a new ode for each new master. In short, the type of Vincenzo Monti.

The Regent, on the other hand, seeks to be the so-called artist of action, the modern bandit, the man who creates a state or empire as one creates a work of art. Italy has produced several examples of this type, from Cesare Borgia to Buonaparte, from D'Annunzio to Mussolini. In *Goliath*, Borgese has given the best psychological and historical synthesis of this recurrent type in Italian history. In the heroic, imperial megalomania, in the cult of action, he perceived the rancor and spleen of the poet who is a failure or, to use the Freudian vocabulary, a sublimation of the inferiority complex of the unsuccessful artist.

Let us say, once and for all, that this type must not be confused with the Machiavellian ideal of the Prince. Leo certainly did not confuse the two, although a French critic tried to see in *Angelica* a "reflection of Machiavelli." If such a reflection exists, it is not where the French critic wishes to find it. Orlando, victim and hero of the drama, is not a "disarmed prophet." Before dying he says something which could suggest disillusion and negation, but which instead rings out like a note of hope: "I have come too soon." And in one of the notes Leo wrote concerning the composition of the play, there sounds the same note of distrust for the present and of intrepid faith in the future: "In this country [the country of Angelica, Italy] the truly great are treated as charlatans and buffoons, while the buffoons become heroes. But it would be too fortunate for the great if, besides being aware of their own greatness, they should have the joy of seeing it recognized by others. Perhaps, one day, these things will come to pass."

The reflection of Machiavelli does perhaps exist in the sense that, with the exception of Orlando and of some minor figures, all the characters are seen as expressions of that political and social evil which the Florentine secretary called the "interest of the particular" or, as we would say, the egoism of individuals or of groups. Leo, as we have seen, preferred to call it "love of self." But the one who transcends the personal interest is not the Regent, that is, the Prince, the man invested with the authority of the State, but a "particular" of noble and generous spirit, the rebel who is to be overcome, Orlando. A truly Machiavellian phrase, although spoken for the first time by the greatest of all Germans, is put in the mouth of Dr. Balazon who repeats it continually throughout the drama: "I say with Goethe, better an injustice than disorder." But the cry of the moral conscience which the poet gives wisely not to the hero Orlando, but a common man, Gianduia, the prudent, right-thinking bourgeois, proclaims on the stage the opposite, far more noble truth: "No, better disorder than an injustice!"

Thus it is the bourgeois Gianduia who protests against the word of a poet, which Dr. Balazon, the typical academic intellectual, repeats with the hypocritical unction of *ipse dixit*. In Gianduia morality and good sense protest against the villainy of an elite incapable of fulfilling its own mission. The words of Orlando, instead, are the heroic protest of another and rarer elite, capable of devotion and sacrifice. I believe that Leo Ferrero chose for the protagonist of *Angelica* the most celebrated and popular of the Paladins precisely because, in the delightful fiction of Ariosto, the hero of the Faith becomes mad for love, and to restore his reason the adventurous Astolfo must take a trip to the moon, where the sanity of Angelica's poor lover is preserved in a phial. The lunatic, quixotic nature of Orlando gives us a sense of the poetic irony with which the poet conceived his own hero. But let us not forget what poet and character tell us, that "the law is the basis of the dream." Criticism can justifiably reverse the phrase into an apparently contradictory but actually equivalent formula: the dream is the basis of the law. Every founder of a city is an ideal citizen of Utopia. Orlando's head often wanders in the clouds, but his heart is rooted to earth and to life; his body is lovingly bound to his earthly homeland: "I too was born in this city."

Through his concern for truth, Orlando is opposed less to the crowd or masses than to those spirits which worship an idol, instead of serving an ideal. Born of Leo's profoundly religious spirit, Orlando functions in this drama as the living antithesis of those skeptical, egoistic natures, enamoured only of themselves: Angelica, the Regent, Harlequin. In the name of an exalted and pure idea of beauty, he rebels against the dominating heresy of the Italian spirit, the fetichism of art. He desires that the harmony of poetry be for men the token of a more sublime harmony, the harmony of justice.

In one of his most celebrated poems, "The Mob," the great Russian poet Alexander Pushkin makes admirable use of the old theme of *procul este, profani.* The Mob anxiously questions the Poet who, solitary and absorbed, touches the strings of his lyre:

> If you are heaven-sent,
> use this blessed gift of poetry
> for our relief; else what would be its virtue
> could it not heal our woes?

But the Poet replies, with pride and contempt:

> Be gone! What cares my sonorous lyre
> for you? Never will its voice, o lowly multitude
> infuse life into your stony spirits,
> Great gifts have been bestowed upon you,
> *whips, scaffolds, prisons,*
> all to tame your wayward minds.
> We are not born for action, nor gain, nor army service;
> only for inspiration, sweet sounds, and prayers.

No one has expressed with such vigor the ideal of poetry as the "divine right," the lofty and superb religion of art. The Regent and Harlequin, mediocre disciples of a gross D'Annunzian aestheticism, defend a much more despicable right: the right of tyranny over art, or the servility of art. Leo, differing with the Poet of Pushkin, conceives poetry not in the religious sense of a ritual, but in the mystical, heroic sense of sacrifice. The poet must be more than a priest; he must be a saint. Like Orpheus, who calmed monsters and quieted wild beasts with a song, the poet must be a magician who must cause yokes to fall, who can beat down scaffolds and open prisons. Orlando is neither a Lorenzaccio nor a Marquess de Posa. His role is neither to kill nor to illuminate the tyrant; he wishes to show the Prince, his subjects and his fellow men, that the grace of intelligence justifies itself only through charity and justice.

VI

Charity asks no reward, nor any recompense beyond itself and, for this reason, contrary to what many claim, there is no contrast between the hero and the crowd in *Angelica*. The relationship between Orlando and the characters of the crowd is of a tragic, not a dramatic, nature. They are controlled, not by social or human dynamics, but by a superior fatality. Actually, Orlando seeks merely to be the prophet of a future elite or, rather, of an ideal elite; that is why, when he is dying, he confesses that he has come too soon. The concept of the elite was one of Leo Ferrero's constant preoccupations and differs fundamentally from Pareto's definition of the term. In Leo's essays and theoretical writings, he never tires of defining the elite as the creative minority which can give men a new and nobler sense of life, which can point out unknown roads and reveal worthier ends to its own generation. The elite is not an already formed ruling class, eager to assume the burdens and honors of power, but an exceptional group ready to pay for its responsibility and vision with the sacrifice of its finest members.

The fundamental problem in *Angelica*, as of every other work of Leo Ferrero, is the religious ideal. In essence the moral ideal of Orlando is that of the Crusader, the Templar, the Knight of the Faith. As a direct consequence of the religious nature of his thought, the social type of the priest is missing in the "human comedy" of *Angelica*, whereas one does find the prototypes of the industrialist and bureaucrat, of the academic intellectual and professional soldier. In spite of his partially Jewish origin and lay education, Leo was ceaselessly tormented throughout his short life by an uneasy nostalgia for Catholicism. If he had introduced the priest type on the stage (which for obvious reasons would not be found among the masks), he would have had to deform him as he did the other characters along the grotesque lines of caricature. But he could only conceive of religion as a positive value and therefore entrusted to Orlando the full message of faith. An intelligent director of the play would perhaps do well to crown the head of the protagonist with one of those simple aureoles which in primitive paintings surround the youthful head of St. George. The "edifying" nature of Orlando is also recognized by his own adversary when the latter calls him the "innocent shepherd of a sickly flock."

The sickliness of the flock and the holy innocence of the shepherd, these are the elements that make *Angelica* truly "the drama of heroic sorrow" and of "the tragic paradox of liberty." Thus Leo's father defined it. "The problem of liberty which we thought answered," the historian continued, "has scarcely been stated, and still remains to be solved." When the Italians, together with their brothers of so many other nations, come to see happier days, they will perhaps remember that *Angelica* was the first poetic warning of this hard truth.

But for us, its contemporaries, *Angelica* reveals minor truths of great value in our everyday struggle. For example, we can never forget the episode of the English philosopher and the American journalist, which is a satiric condemnation of the tourist Fasciophilism of so many foreigners in love with the Italy of the postcards and the opera. The effectiveness of this scene lies entirely in its fleeting character, in the absolute absence of exaggeration or emphasis. The French critic Crémieux may be thinking of such an instance when he says that the best of Ferrero is his lightness. The word must be taken in an unusual, positive sense, as if it meant capacity for elevating, strength for freeing men and things from the doom of gravity: a lightness which is fashioned, like all miracles, from extraordinary seriousness.

Such strength is apparent from the very first stage directions which, with easy unconcern, are directed more to our understanding than to giving a series of helpful suggestions for performance. When Leo advises us to construct, with scenery and ropes or, better still, with imagination, "the square of an imaginary city, where houses, trees, inhabitants, costumes, revolutions, and governments are a little simplified," he gives us the secret of his art. If his position as a moralist is to conceive of men as puppets, his position as an artist is to use the marionettes as basic, naked, synthesized human types. His is a simplified vision, rendered thereby supremely intense. Even when he is analyzing the cast, we realize that he is giving more than instructions to a stage director. The phrase, "soldiers and members of the crowd can be represented by puppets," is understood in its full symbolic context only if we compare it with two remarks exchanged between Harlequin and Brighella before the appearance of Orlando: "One man would be enough . . . a hero." These words, together with the stage instructions mentioned above, synthesize the whole allegorical moral of the play: a real man, that is, an ordinary, normal man, must know when he too must become a bit of a hero; otherwise there will be room on this earth only for supermen and for puppets.

THE ITALIAN SUCCESS STORY

Up to very recent times, Italy had been playing on the American scene the role of the Cinderella of European culture. Nobody seemed to know or to care whether in contemporary Italy there were a few writers and artists deserving at least part of the attention being paid to their brethren of France and England, of Germany and Russia, of Spain and even of Latin America. To be sure, Italy is still acting Cinderella's part — but after the reversal of her role, after the obscure kitchenmaid has left forever the fireplace to become a radiant princess. The American audience has thus witnessed a new performance of the old success story, following the usual pattern so well expressed by the phrase "from rags to riches."

What happened has indeed the quality of a fairytale: the rewarding discovery of the hidden virtues and charms of the humble heroine implies not only a recognition but also a metamorphosis. This is the symbolic meaning of the magic wand, which reveals the real worth of a thing or being by changing it, and which translates an epiphany into a palingenesis. What I mean to say is that Italy gained the sympathy and the admiration of an alien world only after she started acting and feeling like Cinderella: and that, before doing so, she had failed to tear the veil of foreign ignorance and indifference, having chosen to play the part of Cinderella's stepmother or stepsisters.

It is my contention that foreign literary opinion turned its back on the cultural values of modern Italy, not through any lack of intellectual generosity on its part, but rather because of Italy's inability to win, or to woo, non-Italian hearts. If this is true, then the explanation for her present triumphs must be found elsewhere than in the triumphs themselves: in yesterday's failure as well as in today's success. In the long career of the Italian nation, glorying in a cultural tradition spanning several centuries, "yesterday" means of course not merely the recent past; that simple word implies the historical proximity, or even permanence, of events which happened a long time ago.

I

In spite of its antiquity, the culture of Italy is not one of those which we may understand only by wandering again "in the dark and backward abysm of time." One could even claim that, like Athena, the culture of Italy was born, adult and armored, from Jupiter's head. And because of this precocious maturity, it was able, during the era opened by Dante and closed by Galileo, to shape the European mind in its own image. Arnold Toynbee went so far as to claim that Italy has played for the moderns a role similar to Greece's among the ancients; and that Western civilization may rightly be defined "italicistic," in the same sense that we call "hellenistic" the culture of the Roman world.

But after the Renaissance, Italy lost her greatness, without ever forgetting it. While other cultures, by developing and transforming her intellectual inheritance, succeeded in creating a new Europe and even a new man, Italy remained apart and aloof, in a not too splendid isolation. Those cultures found their spiritual power on the cornerstone of new social and political forces. They created the national state; and while the genius of Machiavelli had conceived its theory, Italy reached that status four centuries later, when that institution was already surviving its usefulness. On the moral plane, the foundation of the national state coincided with the invention of the idea of the "great fatherland": and to that invention also Machiavelli contributed more than anybody else.

Italy, the daughter of Rome, always cherished the idea of an even greater fatherland, conceived in the sense of either imperial or catholic universality, in supranational and even metapolitical terms. Now, this greater fatherland, universal, eternal, and singular, was a spiritual entity without body or flesh, while the great fatherlands, temporal, national, and plural, were material and real, rich in iron and gold, which are the signs and sinews of power on earth. The ancient mistress was unwilling to learn the practical lesson now taught to her by her former pupils and she saw her soil invaded and despoiled by stronger neighbors. The shock of this new world of European reality, made of power politics and historical necessity, turned Italy back to the old world of her ideal dreams. Incapable of rejecting forever the ancient vision of a universal fatherland, she found escape from the nightmare of history into a patriotic myth of her own.

This patriotic myth was a retrospective utopia, sentimentally identifying the present with the past, and confusing modern Italy with ancient or eternal Rome. When Italy was confused with the Rome of Caesar, there emerged the dangerous illusion of *romanità* (romanity), a chronic disease that affected the Italian mind up to D'Annunzio and Mussolini. When Italy was confused with the Rome of Peter, the self-deceit thus created took the form, if not the name, of "romanism," an intermittent fever recurring again in the thin blood of the Christian Democratic Party, now ruling the Italian Republic. How strange that it was the last prophet of "romanity" who made possible, through his pact with the Vatican, the present resurgence of "romanism"! While still open, the "Roman question" had at least saved the Italian Kingdom from this.

Only once, in the noblest of all cases, was Italy confused with both the Rome of Caesar and the Rome of Peter, and subordinated, like any other human tribe, to the one and the other. This happened with Dante's medieval utopia, suprapatriotic in character and dividing the estate of man equally between the temporal monarchy, ruled by the sword of the Emperors, and the spiritual kingdom, ruled by the cross of the Pope. In practice this meant that Italy had to submit to the authority of the German emperor, a shepherd who was wont to abandon to the wolves his flock beyond the Alps. Yet, except in Dante's harmonious vision, the conflict between "romanity" and "romanism" was never healed, and remained the typical schism of the Italian soul. This may be seen in the rift that, at the beginning of the Risorgimento, rent asunder the party of the fatherland into two opposing factions, which defined their respective positions with the medieval terms of "neo-Ghibellines" and "neo-Guelphs."

From Petrarch to our times, the main task of Italian literature was to express this national dress, molding it in monumental forms, draping it in magnificent clothing. But the poets of Italy, while their heart's desire was to celebrate that idea in the noble and sacred accents of the ode and the hymn, were often forced to descend to the lower tones of the humble elegy when, confronted with the brutal lessons of history, they had to avow that the fatherland was neither great nor true. Thus the epinicion of old would become a new threnody: they would sing not of the eternal life of the fatherland but of her temporal death, or at least of her present sleep. Their complaints would invariably end with the prophecy of an awakening or a rebirth, which often was but a pious wish. It is after this pattern that so many men of letters, from Petrarch to Filicaia, from Leopardi to Borgese, wrote their numberless *canzoni all'Italia*, all of them re-echoing in their last lines the closing statement of Petrarch's poem, which even Machiavelli quoted at the end of his *Prince*, that "the ancient valor was not yet dead in Italian hearts."

II

Yet the Italian soul could not live wtihout a shadow of glory, without an illusion of greatness. When a proud people loses its independence, it may bear patiently its political misfortunes; it may even admit to being the inferior of its masters in warfare and statecraft, in practical skills and mechanical arts. But, as soon as it has done this, that people claims its own superiority in the moral and intellectual sphere, in spiritual things, or at least in the liberal arts. The Greeks reacted in this way against their Roman rulers, who repaid their vanity by calling them *Graeculi*, an epithet of scorn. Today, those European intellectuals who still refuse to realize that the old continent is no longer the axis of the globe, and that the centers of world power have shifted east and west, find some cheap consolation in the thought that Americans and Russians are the "barbarians" of modern history. There is no better sign of the decline of the old European world.

Vico, the eighteenth-century thinker, recognized very early that beside "la boria delle nazioni" there exists also "la boria dei dotti"; and in his *New Science* he thundered against both. As soon as the Italians felt that they could no longer indulge in the vainglory of the nations, they were quick to resort to the vainglory of the learned. Thus they replaced the idolatry of a fatherland without reality or territory with the idolatry of a fatherland that was half false and half true: a thing *of* the mind, rather than a thing *in* the mind. The great fatherland became, quite simply, Italian intelligence; from a moral idea it descended to the level of a purely mental notion, while a patriotism that had been almost religious in temper declined into a kind of intellectual jingoism. Such a process had already started with those Renaissance men of letters who persecuted the Belgian humanist Longueil (Longolius), a disciple of Erasmus, for having protested against the pretension of an Italian monopoly in the art of writing Latin with Ciceronian perfection and Attic elegance.

This attempt to convert a complex of political inferiority into a complex of intellectual superiority dominated the Italian psyche from the Counter-Reformation to the Risorgimento and the age of Fascism. Sometimes the conversion was effected on a nobler plane, as when Vincenzo Gioberti proclaimed, in the title of a famous book, even more than their intellectual hegemony, the "civic" and "moral primacy" of the Italians. Normally, however, the national ego felt quite contented with far less than this, and the self-respect of the Italians found enough satisfaction through the belief of their leadership in the more pacific and specific fields of poetry, music, and the arts. The Machiavellian ideal of *virtù*, understood as lucidity of vision and strength of will in the realm of action, degenerated into *virtuosità*, or the technical skill of the interpreter or performer of the creations of others. Italy thus became the promised land of native and foreign aesthetes: not a mother of men, but the mother of the arts.

This was another illusion, which lasted long, to be shattered when Italians had to recognize (better late than never) that the barbarians of the North had also made giant strides in the letters and the arts. It seemed that Italian pride could not recover from this blow, when the unexpected triumph of Croce's aesthetics gave it a new lease on life; the new opportunity was eagerly grasped, and all Italy claimed that, even if she had lost her old supremacy in the realm of artistic creation, she still retained leadership in the field of critical thought.[1]

A pretension of this kind would have been utterly alien to the highest critical mind that Italy ever produced: Francesco de Sanctis, whose greatness Croce had the merit to rediscover. De Sanctis was one of the few modern Italians able to see signs of the present misery even in the ancient grandeur, and who, although devoid of any ambitious illusion, never despaired for the future of the nation just reborn. He wrote the last chapter of his famous *History of Italian Literature* at the very moment the royal troops were entering Papal Rome; and in the conclusion of his masterpiece, which re-echoes in its turn the ending of *The Prince*, he framed a program for the literature of Italy in democratic and European terms, asking the new writers to be realistic and modern, and to cultivate the neglected forms of the novel and comedy, as well as to exorcise the sublime but ghostly visions of the poetry of the past.

III

Those visions, however, had never been able to enslave the Italian mind completely. Man has to work and act in the daytime, and to do so he must forget the fanciful monsters which the feverish waking hours in the heart of the night generate in his imagination. After all, it was impossible for the writers and artists of Italy to forget that their bodies were dwelling in a series of small but real fatherlands, very different from the ideal one they inhabitated in their dreams. Dante, for instance, was never able to erase from his mind the memory of that Florence where he was born, and which he would call proudly *la gran villa* (the great city) or, endearingly, his "nest." That citizen of the world remained forever in his heart the citizen of the Florence that had exiled him. He could not help thinking of her even when he was in sight of the glorious city of his quest. When possessed by a noble feeling of pride for having completed his "poema sacro," the only reward he dreamed of was to return to his town to receive from her the poet's crown in the church of his baptism. At the very culmination of his heavenly vision, he was still so full of loving hatred for her that he chose to describe scornfully his "pilgrim's progress" not only as a journey from mankind to the Godhead, or from time to eternity, but also as a journey from Florence to Heaven, from a city of fools and knaves to the city of the saints.

From this, as from other standpoints, Dante greatly differed from Petrarch, who had no other fatherland than the ideal one and who could live anywhere, without calling any place his home. Like the later humanists, Petrarch wandered in Italy and Europe, as a citizen of the Republic of Letters, aware that he would give luster to the principality or commonwealth where he had chosen to stay. But after the Renaissance, and in more recent times, many writers turned again toward the small fatherlands of the peninsula. This change of attitude found expression in the literature in various Italian dialects, which from the nineteenth century on produced a rich body of works, unfortunately still inaccessible to foreign readers, not because of linguistic difficulties, but rather the mistaken presupposition that they have no merit but local color or a sense of the picturesque.

Nothing is farther from the truth than the idea that this kind of literature cannot satisfy more than a mere ethnographic interest. After all, the classical literature of Italy started from the vernacular: Dante had rejected the temptation of writing the *Comedy* in Latin, the *patrius sermo*, preferring to use what he called the "vulgar speech" and the "mother tongue." The poems, and more rarely the plays, written in the Italian dialects (they include almost no fiction or prose), while more popular than the writings in the standard language, have nothing to do with "popular poetry" in the romantic sense of the term. Folklore itself is a factor of far greater importance in the works of the great regional novelists in the tradition of *verismo*, like Giovanni Verga and Grazia Deledda, who wrote in literary Italian, although strongly affected by local speech, and who found again a homeland in their native islands of Sicily and Sardenia, those severed members of the Italian mainland so dear to the heart of D. H. Lawrence.[2] The small fatherlands of the writers in dialect were, instead of the regions, the provincial capitals: cities like Milan and Venice, Naples and Rome, the last now conceived as *urbs* rather than as *orbs*.

The literature in dialect may be seen as a minor branch of the main trunk, as a complement of the major tradition, dealing with values or themes which writers in Italian would scorn or neglect. Its task was to describe everyday life rather than its ideal or timeless counterpart: to evoke the *vera città* (true city), not in Dante's meaning, but in the sense of modern realism. Thus the writers in dialect painted their home town, as Dante his Florence, either in the dark colors of satire or in the light shades of the idyll. It was in the plebeian speech of his fellow citizens that Gian Gioacchino Belli, perhaps the greatest satirist of modern times, represented in all its vulgarity and misery the life of Papal Rome.[3] It was in a refined version of his native dialect that Salvator di Giacomo, one of the purest lyrical voices to appear in Italy after Leopardi, evoked Naples as a city of pathos and *melos*, where love meant a passion for real and living women rather than the adoration of veiled phantoms like Laura and Beatrice.

Sometimes the discovery, by the poets in dialects, or the small fatherlands of the present was accompanied, in the poetry in standard language, by the rediscovery of the little fatherlands of old. This was one of the tasks of Giosuè Carducci, who hated the two modern Romes of the King and the Pope, and who, of the two Romes of the past, loved Brutus' more than Caesar's. Still loyal to the Republican dream of Mazzini and Garibaldi, and an enemy of neo-Ghibellinism as well as of neo-Guelphism, he glorified medieval Italy for those city-states which had challenged the power of both Emperor and Pope. Once, in a sonnet exalting Dante's poetic greatness, he proclaimed his hatred for Dante's "Holy Empire"; later, he wrote his epic masterpiece in *The Song of Legnano*, describing the town meeting of the Milanese, on the eve of the battle in which the soldiers-citizens of that free city defeated in the field the armies of Barbarossa, Dante's "good Frederick"; while in his old age he described beautifully, in *The Rustic Commune*, the democratic dignity of a peasants' council.

IV

Carducci's little fatherlands were still conceived in literary and historical terms: and for this reason even he could never forget the dream of the great fatherland. This is even truer of the two main poets of the following generation, who called themselves Carducci's disciples. One, the mild Giovanni Pascoli, lost his head when he heard the roar of a gun. He saluted the war with Turkey for Libya as a holy war; and in a naive speech, where Italy was called "the great proletarian nation on the move," trying to find "a place in the sun" (two slogans which Mussolini would later put to new use), he showed his inability to distinguish between the popular and the imperial fatherland, as well as between the two Italies of overseas, one made of colonial adventurers, the other of workers and emigrants. The other poet, the wild Gabriele D'Annunzio, converted all the heroic memories of the past, from Rome to Venice, into a bloody empire of his own; fought the first world war as his own duel against the world; ruled Fiume as if it were his lordly manor; finally, built his Gardone villa into the decadent temple of a barbaric worship, where he was priest and god.

It was D'Annunzio who paved the way for the patriotic ideology of Fascism, through which the old literary ideal of a great fatherland changed into a totemic symbol, a tribal fetish. This new idolatry could not tolerate more familiar cults: and Mussolini showed his hatred for the little fatherlands of old by discouraging local pride and by forbidding cultural regionalism. At the same time, the Fascist regime fostered a state-supported drive for the export of official Italian culture abroad. This intellectual imperialism failed even more miserably than the dreams of political hegemony and of territorial expansion. The nemesis of all this was that, under Fascism, Italian culture declined to a mediocrity never reached before.

Fascism claimed to represent the Italy of the past and the Italy of the future. Its failure to gain recognition for the Italian culture of the present was due to this very fact. The arts and letters of Italy are ignored abroad not only when they rely on the prestige of antiquity, but also when they base their claim on a pretense of modernity. When the foreign observer sees through it, he finds beneath that modernity either a frivolous snobbery or a vulgar provincialism. Such was the case with the Futurist movement, which gained a short-lived triumph beyond Italy's borders but which, in order to do so, in a compromise galling to Italian pride, had to resort to the use of a foreign vehicle and to publish its manifestoes in the French tongue. Futurism was bound to show its real nature by consenting to be buried under official recognition, when its leader Marinetti joined the Academy which the Duce had felt compelled to found.

This was also the case with the so-called Novecento or "twentieth-century" group, which, like Futurism, had to translate its self-advertisements into French. The Novecentisti, who naively exalted the modern metropolises which in Italy do not exist, deserved the scorn of those Fascist writers who raised in fun against their mythical Stracittà (Ultra-City) an even more mythical Strapaese (Ultra-Village), representing the Italian, or rather the Fascist, negation of any kind of Europeanism and cosmopolitanism. It is highly significant that nobody took this controversy very seriously, and that the only writer of that time who gained a reputation abroad was Luigi Pirandello, who raised his Sicilian pathos to the level of a universal anguish.[4]

Fascism's attempt to destroy the small fatherlands had a purpose of its own. Italian life is so organically connected with its local communities that only by severing those ties could the regime transform the Italian people into a herd. Fascism claimed to serve the whole nation and the cause of its greatness, while in reality its fortunes were inextricably bound to the interests of those whom medieval Florence called *popolo grasso* (fat people), and could do so only by oppressing the *popolo minuto* (thin people). While proclaiming to have destroyed class divisions, Fascism tried to reimpose old slaveries under new names on that "fourth estate" which had just emerged from centuries of neglect. It was that great leader and teacher, Gaetano Salvemini, historian of medieval Florence and of the French Revolution, who, choosing again the path of exile, told to foreign, and often unbelieving, ears the ordeal of the common man "under the ax of Fascism."

As Italian emigrants had done, so Salvemini and the exiles who followed him created first in the old, and later in the new, continent a "little Italy" of their own. It was one of the members of this new community, G. A. Borgese, who became a writer in English to expose in his *Goliath, or The March of Fascism* all of Italy's past and present cultural sins. There, and in other books, he reinterpreted in modern and democratic terms Dante's idea of the world as the "city of man," transforming Dante's medieval monarchy into a federal republic, where Italy could have her rightful place by serving the "common cause." He echoed in *Goliath*'s final appeal the closing pages of both De Sanctis' *History* and Machiavelli's *Prince*, asking for a new synthesis of the two contrasting Italian political myths, the national and the universal one.[5]

v

In this vision of the single human fatherland of the future, the great fatherland of the past stood condemned, while the small fatherland of the present remained forgotten. The task of redeeming the latter was fulfilled, more than by the thinkers, by the creative writers of emigré literature. Within the framework of a "veristic" tale, Ignazio Silone put his *Fontamara* on the map of Italy and the world, raising the pathetic and grotesque image of that fictitious town to the level of a transparent allegory of Italian life. Within the framework of the fantastic play *Angelica*, where he mixed freely the most Arielesque creatures of Italian poetry with the stock characters of the *commedia dell'arte*, Leo Ferrero contrasted Ariosto's Angelica, as the figuration of fatuous and literary Italy, with the Padrona, the generous and motherly innkeeper, impersonating all the best qualities of the Italian people.[6]

A similar view of Italian reality was slowly maturing in the minds and hearts of those writers of the younger generation whose eyes had not been hopelessly blinded by the stage lights of the Fascist show, now a *grand guignol* and again a vaudeville. Thus, immediately before the war, Elio Vittorini published his novel *In Sicily*, which was translated into the languages of occupied Europe, to be withdrawn after it was reviewed in an underground Belgian paper as a great anti-Fascist novel, strangely written in a Fascist country. Using the old theme of the quest, the author follows his young hero home for a visit; crossing all of Italy from north to south, he vainly looks for the happiness and justice which had been promised to the people, only to find that these qualities are still alive as longings and hopes in the hearts of the poor and the simple.

Sicily, the goal and end of the journey, becomes the symbol of an all too pitiable, all too lovable fatherland. Yet it was not merely to deceive a rigid and gullible censorship that Vittorini stated that the Sicily of his book was a mere "name" rather than a "local habitation"; and that it could be replaced by any other geographical designation, for instance, Venezuela. After all, he concluded, "all manuscripts are found in a bottle." His bottle, however, was full of the bittersweet flavor of a heady Italian wine: and what the writer meant was that his Italy and his Sicilians were as poor and miserable as any land and people on this earth. Thus he found an even broader symbol than Sicily in his hero's mother, who represents the "everlasting yea" of life, while the hero's father, a dreamer and poet, signifies literary intelligence with its irresponsibility toward man's earthly tasks. The cold, mental world of paternal values was thus replaced with the warm, cordial world of motherly love, while Italy was changed, from a fatherland, into a motherland.

Even the final, and decisive, revelation of this new view of Italian reality took place under Fascism, although it was made public, to Italians and non-Italians alike, only after Italy's defeat. Shortly before its fall, the regime had banished to a forgotten corner of Lucania, the most archaic and backward province of the south, Carlo Levi, a painter and writer who was also a physician and anti-Fascist. Even a man like him had to lose his freedom to be able to see, under the mask, the suffering face of Italy and the sorrow of her soul. The testimonial of that discovery was a book which, under the title of *Christ Stopped at Eboli*, was crowned with a sudden and lasting triumph both in Italy and abroad.

In that book Levi proved that Italy and the south were one and the same thing, that Lucania and the peninsula are a godforsaken land, neglected by the Fourth Rome of the Duce and the Third Rome of the King, forgotten by the Rome of Peter, so that, in the words of a local proverb, Christ himself had never set foot on it. The writer maintained further that even the First Rome — the Rome of Caesar — had left hardly any trace on that blessed and accursed land. Feeling powerless to convey this revelation in words of his own, Levi merely stated that he had found again that "humble Italy" which Dante hoped to see redeemed by the Hero whose coming he had announced in the prophecy of the Hound:

> Di quella umile Italia fia salute
> per cui morì la vergine Cammilla,
> Eurialo, Turno e Niso di ferute.[7]

The real Italy was therefore so ancient and different that she had existed before the foundation of Rome, and she was still alive after centuries of oblivion, having survived all destructions of Rome and by Rome. She was not the Italy of Romulus, or even the Italy of Aeneas, but the Italy of Turnus: an ancient and primitive land, but not the prehistoric wilderness dreamed of by D. H. Lawrence and by other retrospective prophets of our time.

VI

It was in the wake of these two books that there was formed in Italy a lively school of young writers of fiction who came to be designated as "neorealists." I shall mention here only those whose works or names are already well known to the American audience. Since Carlo Levi is more of an essayist, it was Elio Vittorini who was recognized as the unofficial leader of the school. Next to him, the most influential member of the group was the late Cesare Pavese, who had started his career as a translator of the modern masters of English and American fiction, from Joyce to Gertrude Stein, from Melville to Dos Passos,[8] while Vittorini had devoted his attention to Faulkner, Hemingway, and Lawrence.

The favorite backgrounds of Vittorini's fiction are two. The first is southern Italy, or more generally his native Sicily, which reappears in his novel, *The Women of Messina*, where the tie between the "humble Italy" of the present and the "humble Italy" of the past is evident in the epigraph, a fragment from a popular poem of the twelfth century exalting the bravery and the sacrifice of the Messina women of old during the ordeal of a siege. The second background of Vittorini is the urban center of Milan, his adopted home: yet he does not glorify that city in its prosperity or pride, but in its poverty and courage, as the proper place for the mass events he relates in *Men and Not-Men*, the most important narrative of the Italian resistance; or for the private crisis of a family of workers as described in *The Twilight of the Elephant*, which is perhaps the only proletarian novel ever to appear in Italy. His *Red Carnation* was saluted by American critics as a poetic document of the joys and sorrows of a precocious youth.

The locale of Pavese's last tale is his native city of Turin and the Piedmontese countryside, where he unfolds again the pathetic chronicle of the civil war, as mirrored in individual souls.[9] The scene of Giuseppe Berto's *The Sky Is Red* is a bombed city of the north, where youth builds again a sort of life among the ruins. The young Florentine writer, Vasco Pratolini, has chosen as his arena neither the modern nor the ancient Florence, but the old one, with its slums and its *popolino*, disfigured but not defiled by the Fascist plague. In *Chronicle of Poor Lovers* and *The Girls of San Frediano* (one of the poorest quarters of the city), Pratolini proves that the flowers of love and beauty may grow even from the manure of life: that even a low, narrow window in a squalid tenement flat, looking only into a filthy courtyard, may open unsuspected vistas for an innocent heart.

The Italy of these writers is very different from tourist Italy, with her sunny squares and her sleepy museums. It is another country, at once strange and familiar, one on which even Italians had not set their eyes before. These novelists are able to see her anew exactly because they look at their land with an equanimity of which their elders are still incapable. Each of them is more of a real Italian for refusing to call himself, with the title of Malaparte's collection of jingoist jingles, an "arch-Italian." They are even good patriots, better than the vocal ones, since their patriotism is neither more or less than Dante's "carità del natio loco."

It is this very "love for the place where one is born," rather than a longing for old glories, that led an older writer, Riccardo Bacchelli, to resurrect the historical novel in *The Mill on the Po*, written after the great models of Tolstoy's *War and Peace*, Stendhal's *Charterhouse of Parma*, and especially Manzoni's *Betrothed*. As a matter of fact, it is worth remarking that the success of contemporary Italian fiction has revived the memory of Manzoni's masterpiece, which has reappeared in a new English translation.[10] In Manzoni's as well as in Bacchelli's historical novel, the Italian Odyssey is retold with serene emotion, with no thought of revenge or any trace of hatred. The same applies to the neorealists of today who, when describing the war along the peninsula, with its medley of armies and races, fail to differentiate between enemies and allies: sometimes even between Germans and Italians. Yet they always distinguish sharply between human beings who are really human and human beings who are such in name only, between *uomini o no*, to use the title of Vittorini's novel. In other words, they divide mankind, like Manzoni, into the powerful and violent, on one side, and the weak and meek on the other; or, at least, they try to avoid confusing the just with the unjust, as Carlo Levi does in *The Watch*, when he separates all Italians into the two opposite species of "peasants" and "little Louies," *contadini* and *Luigini*.[11] By using a similar and yet different antithesis, one could say that while all too many writers of the preceding generation paid attention only to "father's sons" (in bourgeois parlance *figlio di papà* designates, not without indulgence, the spoiled youth or rich playboy who is a typical member of the privileged class), the new writers prefer to deal with "mother's sons" (in popular speech, a *figlio di mamma* is that defenseless creature who seems destined to bear all the burdens which social injustice and state power impose on the poor and the meek, in peace and war).

Another young storyteller, Ennio Flaiano, shows that the new writers of Italy are able to discriminate between the just and the unjust even when the situation is reversed, when it is the Italians who are the aggressors or the oppressors of a humbler or smaller fatherland, when it falls to another people to play the passive role of "the insulted and the injured." Flaiano chose a corner of invaded Ethiopia as the scene of his novel *The Short Cut*, which has some of the qualities of Camus' *The Plague*. In this novel, the original title of which is *Tempo d'uccidere* (*Time to Kill*), the meaningless brutality of the colonial adventure is raised to a high symbolic plane, and is translated into the trials of the hero, who is contaminated forever by the sins and guilt of all.

VII

The writers mentioned above prefer to focus their attention on the "poor in spirit," on men and women of good will. Flaiano, however, is not alone in choosing his models among the cruel, the wicked, and the guilty. So, in his *Hero of Our Times*, Vasco Pratolini has drawn the profile of a plebeian Fascist bully, while Alberto Moravia has painted in *The Conformist* the full-sized portrait of a Fascist bureaucrat, who becomes a spy and a murderer out of a longing for security and respectability. Moravia, a lucid observer with the temper of a moralist, often misjudged as cynicism, had already earned a reputation abroad for being the only Italian writer of his generation consistently representing, from his early works up to now, from such books as *The Indifferent Ones* to *The Wheel of Fortune*, from *Two Adolescents* and *The Woman of Rome* to *Conjugal Love* and *The Conformist*, the mean and yet universal fatherland of the modern average man: the middle class.

Moravia's foreign admirers may fail to recognize that the middle class he describes is peculiarly Italian in character, and that it can be identified with the petty-bourgeoisie of eternal Rome, that is, of the most provincial capital in the world. It was that same kind of social milieu that Giacomo Leopardi had known in his *natio borgo selvaggio* (wild home town) in the Papal States a century ago, and which he had condemned for its vulgarity and emptiness in his *Observations on the Manners of the Italians*, published a long time after his death and forgotten ever since. The shallowness and irresponsibility of the group which forms, not Italy's elite, but merely her ruling class, had already been the unconscious theme of Pirandello's stories, deserving the same recognition which his plays, more vague and abstract, were granted by literary opinion abroad.

Nowhere is that class more uprooted and rotten than in the south of Italy, where it survives like a legion of ghosts. It is this kind of life which another Sicilian, Elsa Morante, who is the wife of Moravia, has chosen to evoke in her extraordinary novel *House of Liars*, probably the wildest romance ever penned by an Italian hand. This book, frenetic as a tale of horror and fantastic as a tale of wonder, is entitled in Italian *Menzogna e sortilegio*: in its most magical pages the public "lie" of daily life is indeed replaced by the private "witchcraft" of wishful visions and dreams. This Italian "Fall of the House of Usher," as it were, unfolding against the volcanic background of Sicilian passions, ends with the Wagnerian thunder of a new twilight of the gods.

A work of this kind, essentially lyrical in character, directs our attention to the field of poetry, where there has taken place a transformation, less radical, but not very different from the one which has affected Italian fiction. The ordeal of the war, even when not creating new poets, has changed the old ones. Lyrical inspiration has rejected the temptation of narcissism forever, while replacing the old monodic tone with a kind of choral mode. Thus, for instance, Giuseppe Ungaretti, the master of a poetry of illumination and ecstasy, has not hesitated to convey in his last book, *Sorrow*, an autobiographical and yet universal experience: the grief of one of the many fathers who have lost a son in the tempest. Eugenio Montale, often called the Italian T. S. Eliot, has evoked in his *Finisterre* the apocalypse of the war, representing the historical crisis almost in theogonic terms, yet choosing as victims of the cataclysm the familiar objects surrounding every man.

While younger poets do not fear to use as themes their experiences behind barbed wire or dungeon walls, the old Umberto Saba, exiled from his beloved city, sings again of Trieste with elegiac nostalgia, but without the rhetorical frenzy of any new *irredentismo*. The hermetic and esoteric Salvatore Quasimodo has found accents of classical purity in his *Day by Day*, to evoke the pathos of destruction, hatred, and bloodshed. The poet says that one cannot sing "with the stranger's foot upon one's heart": yet he sings. He sings day by day, not of the dark pageant of history, but of the chronicle of life, of its griefs and pains, of its shames and ruins.

This poetry seems as ancient and still as young as Italy herself. It aims at a peculiar blend of traditional and modern elements, at a harmony without dissonance, which may sound alien to ears accustomed to voices more discordant and sybilline. Yet international literary opinion is now giving the poets of Italy their due. Their poems, while part of "the modern experiment," [12] derive from the main lyrical tradition of Italy, marked at opposite ends by the names of Petrarch and Leopardi. And these new disciples have rejected forever that "grand style" which in the academic tradition of Italian poetry was the aesthetic equivalent of the dream of the great fatherland.

VIII

Even more than by its realizations in the fields of fiction and poetry, the vitality of a literary culture may be gauged by its achievements in the public form of the drama: and it must be admitted that the present Italian Renaissance has failed to pass this test. Yet there are signs of rebirth even in the theatre, as shown by the dramas of Ugo Betti, and even more by the plays of the Neopolitan Edoardo de Filippo, who still follows the traditions of the drama in dialect, combining in one person the functions of the playwright and the star of the show. In spite of its organic ties with the local and the popular, his work has a universal appeal and a modern ring, as Eric Bentley was quick to notice in a brilliant article in *The Kenyon Review*.

Although realizing that the theater and the movies are two different arts, I feel we can safely assert that in today's Italy the revival of dramatic inspiration has taken place not on the stage, but on the screen. We must not forget that the Italian success story started with the triumph of Italy's postwar films. After all, the label of neorealism was originally coined to designate the new cinematographic school, and its attempt to transform into an imaginative style the documentary itself. Thus, for a larger audience, the vehicle of the rediscovery of great little Italy was not the book but the moving picture; and it is highly significant that the original title of the first Italian movie to gain the admiration of the world was not *Open City*, but *Rome Open City*, as if to emphasize the poetic justice of the tragic fact that war does not spare even those cities which claim to be the hub of the universe.

Nothing could be more different than *Open City* from the heavy archeological machinery of the Fascist film, full of political propaganda and historical rhetorics, like that monstrous *Scipio Africanus*, where an operatic *romanità* plays a role similar to that of Wagnerian mythology and of Great Russian patriotism in the *Nibelungen* of the Nazis and in the *Ivan the Terrible* and *Peter the*

Great of the Soviet film. How pale is the melodramatic heroism of those monumental screen plays when compared with the ordeal of the children of *Shoeshine,* the private drama of a worker's family in *Bicycle Thief,* or the tragic scene of *Paisan* when we see the floating corpse of an executed partisan, bearing a sign of infamy in place of a crown of glory or a Christian cross!

If there is no literary revival without a living theater, so there is no true Renaissance without a school of accomplished masters in the field of the visual arts. Here, too, there has been a great awakening, which is finally getting the international appreciation it deserves. The poetic still-lives of Giorgio Morandi, the dramatic figures of Renato Guttuso, the mystical statuary of Giuseppe Manzù, the plastic groups of Marino Marini, are now filling the private and public galleries of the world. They are replacing forever the traditional exports of Italy's academic art, with its murals and monuments spread in official buildings and public squares all over the world. Similarly, in the field of music, the compositions of the young master, Luigi dalla Piccola, are already replacing the old operatic exports.

Based as it is on a quasi-magic fusion of the old and the new, this artistic revival is very like in temper to the changes which have taken place in the realm of poetry. The Italian artist of today derives his strength from the sources still giving power and insight to the hand and the eye of the humble artisan. Like him, the artist looks back not at the glorious and universal empire, but at the forgotten provinces of Italian art. He finds his masters and models not in the Renaissance and the Baroque, but among the primitives and the archaic Etruscans. He is well acquainted with modern art, but more with Cézanne than with Picasso. This is why the abstractionists, once persecuted under Fascism but now free to show their works, have little to contribute to the revival of a tradition for which living forms, even more than "things of beauty," are the grace of nature and the wonder of the world.

I X

This revelation of the worth and dignity of Italian contemporary culture could not have taken place earlier. Italy had claimed for too long to be a great fatherland, even when she was no fatherland at all. Men dislike being reminded of the existence of fatherlands other than their own. If they ever look with sympathy at their greatness, it is only when it becomes a thing of the past. Only now, at the very moment that "the white man's burden" is no longer oppressing his shoulders and the shoulders of those whom he used to call "lesser breeds," is it possible for non-English ears to listen with equanimity to the notes of Kipling's *Recessional.*

It is not only the self-love of the fatherlands but also their self-pity that may alienate a foreigner from their culture and art. While the literature of Russia became a spiritual power by describing the human condition in Russian terms, the national pathos of Polish poetry prevented its masters from touching human hearts everywhere. And the literature of the small Scandinavian countries has affected the modern mind more than the literature of Germany, too preoccupied with the "German man" or with the "blood and soil" of the German fatherland.

Our own is still the age of nations and national cultures, even if we dream of "one world." This is why, when we are haunted by the Goethean ideal of a *Weltliteratur,* we think of it in terms of diversity as well as of unity: as a chorus where each singer performs a solo in his turn. We can no longer conceive of a universal literature in a universal language, where men of all tribes celebrate as their fatherland an *urbs* which is also an *orbs.* Literary patriotism, even if its object is the "city of man," holds no appeal for us. We prefer to hear of the miseries, rather than of the glories, of the numberless fatherlands of Everyman. If American literature is now popular abroad, it is because it is not concerned with America's destiny but with man's fate in American terms: with Dreiser's "American tragedy" rather than with Mr. Luce's "American century."

The artists and writers of Italy had been so preoccupied with the "Italian centuries" of the past that it is not surprising that up to yesterday no one outside Italy paid any attention to them. This applies even to those who lived on her soil and tried to love her. Think of Ezra Pound, indifferent to any Italian literary value after Cavalcanti, although he fell in love with the ghostly Italy of Mussolini, a guilty error which prevented him from seeing, if not the tragedy, at least the farce of Fascism. Think of James Joyce, who claimed that Italian literature had died with Dante, and who took mischievous pleasure in discovering a great modern Italian writer in Italo Svevo, the obscure Triestine merchant to whom Italy granted grudging recognition twenty years afterward.[13]

If all this is true, then Italy's moral and cultural revival could take place only in the wake of a defeat. This, however, does not mean that the artistic and literary triumph of Italy on the American scene is but a repetition of the phenomenon described by Horace with the formula of *Graecia capta*: as if the American conqueror had been in his turn captured by the graces of the land invaded by him, as it happened to the Romans of old after their conquest of the sister peninsula of Greece. As a matter of fact, it has been argued that the victory of the defeated was achieved by using the feminine weapons of imitation and flattery, whether unconsciously or not.

Strangely enough, this has been attested by Italian, rather than by American, witnesses. Thus the young critic Pasinetti stated in *The Sewanee Review* that the American reader may enjoy in today's Italian fiction the same gusto for violence that marks the native school of hard-boiled realists; while the older scholar, Mario Praz, has asserted in *Partisan Review* that the idiom of Vittorini and his peers is but an inferior copy of Hemingway's diction and style.[14] This of course, is not the whole story. The American example emancipated Italian fiction from the cant of a shabby gentility, from an old-fashioned mannerism in matters of gesture and dress.[15] Yet I remain convinced that the Italian success story has been made possible by causes other than merely literary ones: that in the main it has been the outcome of the change of heart described above.

Because of its very spontaneity and inevitability, the new outlook may even lead into blind or dangerous paths. Nietzsche, who claimed that the small state is the only ground from which the human plant may fully grow, also maintained that an excessive compassion for one's unfortunate country may become a heavy chain for the mind of man. This may be true when pride feels its self-inflicted wounds more than the real wounds in the body of the fatherland. But, for the Italian artist and writer of today, Italy is not an object of pity but of love. Instead of being intoxicated by the morbid passions of old, he is now exhilarated by a kind of "joyful wisdom."

Once Novalis said that "it is comedies that one ought to write after a lost war." The place of tragedy is in the moment of prosperity and victory, when man needs to be reminded that happiness and success are always threatened by the envy of the gods. Thus, starting from the very climax of the catastrophe, the authors of Italy have been writing, almost in collaboration, the "human comedy" of Italian reality, of Italian life, of the Italian people. This explains why they do not indulge in any recrimination or complaint, and why they have forever abandoned that "poetry of ruins" which was so dear to their forefathers: a poetry which Du Bellay mocked in his *Antiquités de Rome,* and to which even a poet like Leopardi had to pay tribute.

The new writers do not utter lamentations even about the ruins of the present, since they do not look for glory but for life, because they are no longer haunted, as the poets of old, by Italy's graveyards. They do not think, like Foscolo in his *Sepulchres,* that one can build a secular religion on the tombs of the great, as the altars of a noble form of hero worship; nor do they feel the need to prove, like Giusti in his *Land of the Dead,* that Italy is still alive through the survival of the great shadows of the past. They realize that there is truth in Carducci's affirmation that the Italian people is endowed with manifold existences: yet they conceive of that vitality in human, rather than in historical, terms. This is why, unlike Carducci, they have decided to bury their dead. They know that, while the land of the father is forever inhabited by family ghosts, the land of the mother may really live only in the expectation of children yet to be born.

NOTES

1. Since the task of these pages is to tell the American "success story" of Italian letters, it is perhaps fitting to remark at this point that Croce has been taken less seriously in England and America than in Germany and Spain, although more than in France. The impact of his school of thought, as distinguished from the attention paid to it, has been almost negligible, in spite of the fact that there has just appeared a new reprint of the old translation (by Douglas Ainslie) of the *Estetica.* Aesthetics and criticism, at least in bulk, are far less exportable than fiction, or even poetry; yet it is worth noticing that modern Italian culture has failed to leave its mark abroad in the very field where it felt it was in the lead. American thought, for instance, has been far less affected by the aesthetic doctrines of Croce than by the political and social ideas of Gaetano Mosca and Vilfredo Pareto.

The death of Croce has naturally provoked the writing of many commemora-
tive pieces; but they were high tributes to the figure of the master, rather than
reassertions of the permanent value of his thought. Such an attitude may
imply an unfair reflection on Croce's achievement: yet it ought to be accepted with humility by his Italian followers, who are still hardly aware of
what has been done during the last quarter of the century outside of Italy in
the aesthetic and critical field. They seem to ignore even the contributions
made by some of the foreign disciples of Croce, for instance Karl Vossler;
and they have never even heard of Russian Formalism, of Anglo-American
New Criticism, of the German and Spanish school of stylistic analysis,
without speaking of all the attempts to relate art and literature with linguistics and semantics, with psychology and mythology, with anthropology
and other social sciences.

2. Lawrence translated into English a good selection of Verga's stories
and his second best novel, *Mastro Don Gesualdo*. The first adequate translation (by Erich Mosbacher) of Verga's masterpiece, the novel *I Malavoglia*,
has been published under the title, *The House by the Medlar Tree*. It is quite
significant that this revival of interest in the highest achievement of the
master of *verismo* has been made possible by the previous revelation of the
young "neorealists," who are Verga's not too distant offspring.

3. Belli has been recently introduced to the American reader through the
article *G. G. Belli: Roman Poet*, by Eleanor Clark (*The Kenyon Review*,
Winter 1952), later reprinted in Miss Clark's book *Rome and a Villa*.

4. Pirandello the storyteller, who deserves comparison with Chekhov and
who is certainly superior to the epigones of the latter, is unfortunately still
practically unknown abroad. We are instead now witnessing in America a
resurgence of his reputation as a playwright, as shown, among other things,
by the publication of the volume *Naked Masks — Five Plays*, splendidly
edited by Eric Bentley. [See also, "Pirandello in Retrospect," in this
volume.]

5. These lines were written before the noble life of that great master and
dear friend was cut short, a few months after he had settled again in Italy,
near the city of his, and of my, youth.

6. [See "Leo Ferrero's *Angelica*," in this volume.]

7. "He will be the salvation of that humble Italy for which the maid
Cammilla, Eurialus, Turnus, and Nisus died from their wounds" (*Inferno*,
I.106–108).

8. The best testimonial of Pavese's activity as a critic of American literature is the posthumous collection *La Letteratura americana ed altri saggi*
(Turin, 1951).

9. At the time these pages were written [1953], Pavese was the only
first-rate Italian novelist of his generation still untranslated into English.
This oversight has been corrected with the publication of his last, and perhaps best, novelette, *The Moon and the Bonfires*, with a foreword by Paolo
Milano. Movingly and simply, the prefator retells the story of Pavese's
suicide, due both to personal and to political reasons, reminding us of the
suicide of F. O. Matthiessen, about whom Pavese had written beautiful
pages which can still be read in his collection of American studies. But the
end of Pavese may remind us also of the end of Mayakovsky; as a matter of
fact, the words "no gossip" in the last note he wrote were an echo, conscious

or not, of the same recommendation in the farewell letter left by the Russian poet.

10. The translator, Archibald Colquhoun, has significantly inscribed his version "to the Italians of the Second Risorgimento of 1943–45."

11. The nickname *Luigino* suggests in Italian the idea of hypocrisy.

12. This formula belongs to Sir Maurice Bowra, who revealed Quasimodo to the English reading public in one of the last issues of *Horizon*. The same writer has again quoted from him, and referred to other Italian poets of today, in the article "Poetry in Europe, 1900–1950," *Diogenes*, I (1953). The translations from Saba, Ungaretti, Montale, Quasimodo, and *tutti quanti*, which have been appearing from the end of the war up to now in English and American little magazines or other periodicals and publications are too numerous to be mentioned here. For reasons of brevity I have also failed to mention in this survey other Italian writers whose works of fiction have appeared in American editions.

13. New Directions has reprinted in recent years Beryl de Zoethe's excellent translations of *The Confessions of Zeno* (1948) and of *As a Man Grows Older* (*Senilità*, 1950, with a preface by Edouard Roditi). The owner and director of this press, James Laughlin, has undoubtedly been the first and most active publisher of the task of acquainting the American reader with the Italian letters of today. [See also, "A Note on Italo Svevo," in this volume.]

14. It is worth noting that Hemingway wrote a preface for the American edition of Vittorini's *In Sicily* (*Conversazione in Sicilia*).

15. This function, perhaps the most important aspect of the American influence, was already pointed out by Cesare Pavese in one of his American essays, and by Paolo Milano in his foreword to Pavese's *The Moon and the Bonfires*.

Postscript, 1960. As I have stated in the Foreword [see instead the quoted paragraph in the preface by Harry Levin], I have avoided the temptation of updating the articles collected in this volume. The temptation was particularly strong in this case. Almost ten years have passed since this piece was first written, and during this period of time we have witnessed the constant renewal, in America and elsewhere, of that eager curiosity for Italian things which made possible the "success story" here described. It would have been all too easy to add new names (such as those of Dino Buzzati Traverso and Natalia Ginzburg among many others), as well as new titles (first among them that of *The Leopard*, the posthumous best-selling novel of the Sicilian aristocrat Giuseppe Tommasi di Lampedusa). And it would have been all too inviting to observe, from the privileged perspective of hindsight, that the collection of poems by Salvatore Quasimodo which here I had singled out for special praise was perhaps the one that in 1959 earned for the Sicilian poet the Nobel Prize. If in the end I have chosen to reprint the present essay as it was originally published, it is merely because its only merit is to be a faithful mirror of the mood and situation which dictated its pages.

THE POETRY OF ST.-J. PERSE

Duc d'un peuple d'images à conduire aux Mers Mortes

I

Nothing could be more exotic, more hermetic than the name chosen by Aléxis Léger to hide the mystery not only of his person, but also of his poetry. Has the interpreter any right to try to solve the riddle? "St.-J.," the form in which the pseudonym first appeared, evidently stands for Saint–John, and we fancy that among the saints of that name the poet meant Saint John the Baptist, the prophet whose voice vainly echoed in the wilderness. If so, why choose the English form of the prophet's name? We shall ask ourselves a question which may be naive but which may therefore be devoid of any irony: what does John the Baptist have to do with England? Perhaps there was irony, rather than naiveté, in the mind of the poet: let us not forget that before choosing the pen name he had already written a series of poems on Robinson Crusoe. Robinson Crusoe too had lived in a wilderness of his own, in a wilderness where the only voice speaking to him had been the voice of the Bible. In one of those poems St.-J. Perse describes Robinson back in his London, opening the Bible and trying to hear again, from the pages of the Book, the voice of the wilderness calling him back to an irretrievable experience. Still, at all events, what relation has the myth of Saint John the Baptist to the story of Robinson Crusoe?

As for *Perse*, where does it come from? At first we may think of the Asiatic experiences of Aléxis Léger, of his journeys through that Persia which before him had already seduced another French writer and diplomat, the prophet of the inequality of races, the Comte de Bobineau. But it seems that this is not the case. Reliable witnesses, including Aléxis Léger himself, tell us that among his literary preferences were two Roman writers, Tacitus the historian and Persius the satirist. An anecdote, attributed to Léger, claims that when his literary friends obtained from him, after many entreaties, permission to publish some of his poems, he set the condition that they appear without his signature. The poet was asked to find a pen name for himself, and he selected *Perse* because his eyes chanced to meet, on one of the shelves of his library, the satires of Persius.

If this is true, the irony is merely the irony of chance. Perhaps it is better for us to give up the attempt to satisfy our indiscreet, all too human curiosity, and to face instead the far more formidable enigma of the poetry of St.–J. Perse. It may be that only at the end of our task shall we be able, O Poet, "de décliner ton nom, ta naissance, et ta race."

Whatever the origins of his pen name, it seems of itself to indicate a sympathy for exoticism. Such a sympathy is demonstrated also by a cursory examination of the poet's work. Nothing could be more exotic than the inspiration of *Anabase*, his masterpiece, or of those poems which later became part of his first book, and which were written when the name of the poet was not yet St.–J. Perse. Still, the poet is right when, in his letter to Archibald MacLeish (which we shall often quote in these pages), he reminds his correspondent: "you are acquainted with . . . my fierce hatred of literary exoticism." [1] The exoticism of St.–J. Perse, as a matter of fact, is not literary in the sense that it has anything to do with the aesthetic exoticisms of the romantics, such as Hugo and Gautier; it has even less to do with the exoticism of a Parnassian poet like Leconte de Lisle, who was born, as Perse was, on a distant island of colonial France.

The exoticism of St.–J. Perse is neither conventional nor decorative. Even less is it idealizing or sentimental, unlike the exoticism of many an outcast from Western civilization, for instance, Lafcadio Hearn or Gauguin. He reminds us a little more, especially in his first book, of the naive exoticism of *Paul et Virginie* and, in contemporary poetry, of those poems, as charming as old-fashioned prints, which Francis Jammes devoted to the life of merchants who long ago traded with the lands of spices. In other words, the exoticism of St.–J. Perse is essentially the discovery of a mode of life which, in spite of being localized by history and geography, is perhaps human existence at its best. In his latest works St.–J. Perse may even seem to us a modern Chateaubriand, with a similarly splendid evocation of nature's least familiar landscapes, though less occupied with his own self.

The inspiration of St.-J. Perse is lyrical; yet his lyricism can operate only when it is filled with an epic and a cosmic breath. This is especially true of *Anabase*, which is a "song of experience" rather than a "song of innocence." But literary exoticism has always been a song of innocence, except for the case of Rimbaud. In a certain sense, St.-J. Perse brings to fruition some of the dreams of Rimbaud. He is, of course, a less subjective and more archaic Rimbaud: a Rimbaud who travels counter to the *bateau ivre* and its pilot. For St.-J. Perse, all roads lead not to Rome, but to Paris. From the dreamlands of the East, he always returns to his West. Because spiritually his native island was not Saint-Léger les Feuilles, but the Ile-de-France. At times his return seems really the return of Rimbaud: Europe becomes also for St.-J. Perse the puddle in which a child sails his paper boat. This, in fact, is the theme of his series of poems on Robinson Crusoe.

But Paris remains the harbor toward which he casts his *bouteilles à la mer*. As a matter of fact, all the islands which St.-J. Perse loved were either *Petites* or *Nouvelles Frances*. In the letter already quoted, he says as much to Archibald MacLeish: "Nor shall I speak to you of the Antilles where my childhood was profoundly affected by the animal and vegetable life of the Tropics and which have remained none the less an essentially French experience, and my oldest one." In the same text, he evokes the glorious impression he felt when, on a Polynesian island ruled under another flag, he attended a performance of Racine's *Esther*, recited in the original language by a cast of native girls who understood no French, though educated by a mission of French nuns.

II

It is not strange that such a poet should start his literary career with a lyrical version of the fable of Robinson Crusoe. He dedicated to that fable the cycle "Images" which appears, reversing the chronological order, at the end of the first part of *Eloges*.[2] In "Images" the poet speaks with the voice of a voluntary exile, of a Parisian Crusoe who has returned from his island to the urban civilization of the white man. The protagonist of the cycle is a man suffering from a paradoxical *mal du pays*, a youth dreaming of a real island, and not those islands of which we read in books of travel and adventure. In another cycle, "Eloges," the title piece of the collection, the poet evokes through the magic of memory, with a more serene and objective inspiration, his past life on the island where he was born. It was only natural that in the logical order of the complete work the cycle expressing the phase of nostalgia should follow, rather than precede, the cycle of reminiscence and evocation.

In a certain sense, the "Images" are a continuation, and a reversal, of the story of Robinson Crusoe. They are an account of the homecoming, of the aftermath. Following the lucky shipwreck near an unknown island, we witness here the unlucky shipwreck of Robinson Crusoe on the waters of society and civilized life. Robinson realizes that he had been happy and free on his wild and deserted island, while now he is a prisoner on the *terra firma* of the metropolis, a slave such as his good man Friday never was. Whereas the child of Baudelaire's "Voyage" dreams by the light of his lamp of imaginary travels suggested by the book he is reading, "l'astre précaire de sa lampe" makes pale in the mind of Crusoe the real splendor of his past adventures. That the poet thinks not only of the reality, but also of the dreams, of his childhood is shown by his use of an episode from Jules Verne's *The Mysterious Island*. Here too we have to do with a reversed myth. Who, among those who read that novel in their youth, does not still remember the episode of the marvelous discovery, in the pocket of one of the survivors of the shipwreck, of a grain of wheat, and the harvesting of an immense crop from that one seed? But the grain found by Robinson in his sheepskin has been planted not in the virgin soil of his island, but in the sterile dirt of a flower pot, where "elle n'a point germé." Together with a parrot and a slave, that seed is the only inheritance left to the dispossessed king of an island far more real than Barataria: now Robinson himself, no less than his good man Friday, is but "un bon sauvage déchu."

The *Eloges* cycle starts with two lyrical series which were probably written later than the other poems of the same work, and which are entitled "Ecrit sur la porte" (four stanzas long) and "Pour fêter une enfance." The poet celebrates his childhood in a spirit very different from many modern literary evocations of childhood (see, for instance, Alain-Fournier's *Le Grand Meaulnes*). Here childhood is not a half-forgotten and forever-lost paradise, but an earthly paradise still alive in the memory of the poet's body and soul. The protagonist is not so much the child as the way of life the poet experienced, as part of a whole, in his childhood. This way of life is centered in patriarchal institutions: in the house and the household, in the family and its servants. Childhood is not seen in the splendid isolation of the soul of the child; it is always integrated with a concrete vision of life, within a definite social framework. The child is a microcosm within the macrocosm of the family, a planet turning around the sun of the house: "la Maison durait, sous les arbres à plume."

This mode of life is archaic; and childhood itself is described in a spirit more akin to ancient than to modern poetry. The real hero is therefore the father represented as a calm and quiet lord, protecting his family and servants, taking care even of the domestic animals of his household, satisfied with his destiny and his condition. A man of this kind cannot be affected by the Mallarmean dream of the *azur*, since he possesses:

> toutes choses suffisantes pour n'envier pas les voiles des voiliers
> que j'aperçois à la hauteur du toit de tôle sur la mer comme un ciel.

In that kind of life there is no room even for the dreams nourished by children who are destined to become prodigal sons. Here children travel by sea on real boats and do not need to rely on their imagination or on their paper fleets: "Ce navire est à nous et mon enfance n'a sa fin."

The glorification of this primitive, and yet aristocratic, mode of life is the leitmotiv of the entire book, especially of the cycle "Eloges." The very title of the book and the cycle is significant; the theme of praise reappears on every page. In each poem one continually finds words like *fêter, vanter, louer, louange*, and *éloge*. The *refrain* most frequently repeated by the poet is: "O j'ai lieu de louer." His eulogies are of a heroic or epic, more than of a mystical, order. The tones which the poet himself calls *les rhythmes de l'orgueil* are dictated by the pride of lordship and lineage, perhaps even by the awareness of "the white man's burden" with respect to "the lesser breeds." Such awareness is evident in the words of the father: "Mon orgueil est que ma fille soit très-belle quand elle commande aux femmes noires."

The pride of the wellborn transforms itself very often into the psychological and physiological pride of the thoroughbred: the poet honors equally, among men and animals, all creatures without mixture or impurity. It is this quality or state that, both in life and nature, St.–J. Perse defines by the term *haute condition*. The value thus exalted by the poet could be called vital nobility, natural purity, primitive innocence. Precisely for this reason he often praises what the modern man would loathe. He is not affected by modern prejudices, either sentimental or hygienic; he sees beauty where others would only feel disgust. A horse sweats; the poet says, "c'est briller." Female flesh gives an acrid smell; the poet says, "le sexe sent bon." It is in the same spirit that the child establishes relationships of equality, intimacy, and friendship between himself and the most insignificant beings, to which he pays a tribute of courtesy as if they were his peers: "un insecte m'attend." Brotherly communion is extended even to inanimate things: the poet, or the child, makes "une alliance avec les pierres veinées-bleu." All this does not exclude the archaic and aristocratic horror for impure mixtures and contaminating contacts: "j'ai retiré mes pieds." A primordial and yet naturalistic wisdom, a sense of sharing in the life of the organic world: such are the psychological roots of the work. For the child, as for the poet, "tout n'était que règnes et confins de lueurs."

It is with equal pride that the poet glorifies the culture and the civilization of the primitive society he belonged to in his childhood: its temporal and spiritual institutions, the simple and yet magical techniques through which it dominates the external world, its mythical or theogonic beliefs: "nous avons un clergé, de la chaux." In this context Perse inaugurates one of the recurring forms of his songs of praise, the enumerative and celebratory catalogue of all human castes and classes, crafts and trades. Catalogues of this kind will appear again and again in his work, especially in the long poems, *Anabase*, *Exile*, and *Vents*. We will find them to be constructed around the idea of a spiritual and technical hierarchy, at the head of which the poet sees those privileged individuals whom Gobineau would have called "fils de roi." It was therefore only natural that one of the cycles of *Eloges* be consecrated to the sovereigns of the spiritual and of the temporal, to "la gloire des rois."

"La Récitation à l'éloge d'une Reine" glorifies the splendid kingdom of matter and the flesh. The Queen symbolizes the *Erdgeist*, earth as a mother and nature as a female. She is burdened with a magnificent fatness, which is the sign of biological vitality, of animal fecundity, of physiological warmth. She is fatter than Penelope or Molly Bloom: she is the fleshly idol to which the poet sings his own pagan and barbaric litanies. The titanic disproportions of her body do not convey the monstrous and morbid suggestions of the *géante* of Baudelaire; her limbs do not repose with the cowlike passivity of the neoclassical swift Sybils of Picasso's famous painting.

Equally magnificent praises ("et la louange n'était point maigre") are sung by the poet, in the cycle "Amitié du Prince," to the thin, emaciated Prince of the Spirit, who reminds us, if not of Hamlet, of Mallarmé's reinterpretation of him in "Igitur" and in "Un Coup de dés jamais n'abolira le hasard." That we have to do with reminiscences deriving from the second of these two texts ("Igitur" was perhaps still unknown to the poet at the time "Amitié du Prince" was written) is proved by the apostrophe, "ô Prince sous l'aigrette," which recalls the "solitaire aigrette éperdue" of "Un Coup de dés." The Prince sung in this cycle seems destined to be dispossessed of his earthly kingdom by a regent or usurper: in contrast to temporal power, he represents spiritual power; rather than the aristocracy of blood and will, he symbolizes the aristocracy of the heart and the mind. He anticipates the recurring figure that St.–J. Perse celebrates in his later works under the name of Sorcerer or Stranger; in the Prince, as in the later forms, it is easy to recognize an allegory of the mysterious and fatal calling of the poet. "Enchanteur aux sources de l'esprit! . . . Bouche close à jamais sur la feuille de l'âme!" — such are the litanies with which St.–J. Perse sings and celebrates him. The Prince, like the Sorcerer and the Stranger, is the chosen vessel of a higher wisdom, the carrier of a deeper message. In relationship with and contrast to the historical and collective culture of his race, he represents the individual and universal culture of the Self, the very ideal and substance of poetry as understood by modern man. Within the work of St.–J. Perse, he is the personification of the lyrical element, while the awareness of other ties and duties expresses itself through the choral voice of the tribe or of the clan. The author himself is the judge or the arbiter, solving or pacifying the conflict between these two elements.

This is why the author, although he speaks in the first person and becomes himself a character of his own fictitious world, never identifies his person and mission with the person and mission of the

Prince. He acts rather as his *confidant* (literally, as the *confidant* of the protagonist in a classical tragedy), as someone trying to gain the friendship and understand the mind of the hero. Such a role is necessary because the conflict is tragic in nature, being the conflict between an ancestral culture, based on tradition and authority, and culture understood as free creation, as affirmation of the self. Yet it is almost with a Nietzschean accent that the poet addresses to the Prince the significant apostrophe: "ô Dissident!" The theme is extraordinarily important, because it is one of the legacies the young poet of *Eloges* will leave to the older poet of *Anabase, Exil,* and *Vents.*

Such is *Eloges* in its ideal substance, in its garland of fables and myths. But what is its style, or its form? What kind of world does the reader of the book inhabit? It is a splendid and original world, shaped by the will of the poet into forms of transcendental objectivity. The poet speaks with the voice of all things he loves. Each object or creature seems to sing its own praises — praises which are at the same time so eloquent and discreet that they seem an organic element of their natural essence. Every thing seems to radiate, as an electric light, the awareness of its beauty; every living being seems to emanate, as a vital fluid, the consciousness of its own nobility: "Et puis ces mouches, cette sorte de mouches, vers le dernier étage du jardin, qui étaient comme si la lumière eût chanté!"

In this book, perhaps more than in the following ones, the spectacle most affecting the poet is the contemplation of nature in its continuous organic and biological metamorphoses, in the everlasting and ever-changing phases of its growing and becoming, even in the agonizing stages of degeneration, corruption, and death. Each one of these phenomena is evoked with teeming seminal images which remind us, again and again, of Rimbaud. Very often St.–J. Perse becomes a *voyant*, not according to the theory of the "Lettre du voyant," but rather to the concrete, evocative processes of the "Bateau ivre" ("j'ai bien vu des poissons" is an evident reminiscence of the *j'ai vu* formula so frequently used by Rimbaud in his famous poem). Sometimes we find images which recall some of the most powerful still lifes of the poetry of Rimbaud: "la tête de poisson ricane," St.–J. Perse says once, and that animal head resembles very much Rimbaud's "tête de faune."

The tropical landscapes and the equatorial seascapes of St.–J.

Perse are, of course, visions, while the same tableaux are in Rimbaud only dreams. But the technique through which St.–J. Perse stimulates the power of his memory is very similar to the technique through which Rimbaud produces his voluntary hallucinations. In other words, the method of St.–J. Perse is still the method of Rimbaud's *Illuminations*. His own "illuminations" are clearly the illuminations of a reader who knows not only Rimbaud, but also Claudel. It is from Claudel that the poet has, for instance, taken his medium, a versicle always noble and inspired, neither too rhythmical nor too loose, which avoids the rhetorical and declamatory pitfalls of that form.

III

It was in this medium that St.–J. Perse composed all his works; and it was in *Anabase* that he transformed it into an instrument peculiarly flexible and rich, personal and inimitable, giving at the same time the impression of something very ancient and very new.[3] In that poem the poet's versicle became both an architectonic and a musical element. The structure of *Anabase* reminds us of a great tapestry, or, better, of a series of powerful bas-reliefs like those, all of them scenes of war and hunting, in the ancient art of Persia, which are still to be seen in the ruin of the royal palace of Persepolis. The geographical background is no longer the New Indies of *Eloges*, but eternal and ancient Asia, the Asia of great deserts and plateaus, inhabited by nomadic peoples, and conquered by the most reckless and daring cavalries in history. "Of Asia, and especially of Central Asia," says the poet in his letter to Archibald MacLeish, ". . . I can say to you, like a pedant, that it gave me a vaster gauge of space and time." Central Asia: perhaps the western marches of the Celestial Empire of Mongolia. Or maybe Turkestan, or the Pamirs? It is a region for which one does not need to find "a place or name," even if the poet should see it with his own eyes. What is important is that we place it, though only negatively, either within or without our cultural geography. Perhaps it is enough to say that the region is not one of those territories reached, in their historical anabases, by the Greeks of Xenophon or Alexander.

Just as the colonial tropical islands were for the poet of *Eloges* not the lost paradise of childhood but an Eden of original purity, likewise the deserts and plateaus of Central Asia, still unknown to the white man, are for the poet of *Anabase* a kind of historical limbo. They are traversed by bands of conquerors who do not carry, like the *conquistadores* of Hérédia, Claudel, and MacLeish, a rapacious symbol of adventure embroidered on the white banner of the faith: their sword is not at the same time a cross. Nor do adventurers after gold, caravans of traders, expeditions of wealth seekers, hunters of profit, push on in the wake of their incursions. In other words, the Asia of *Anabase* is not yet, and seems never to become, the Asia of the merchant, of the imperialist, or of the Western missionary: it is an archaic and almost prehistoric Asia; to use an expression we shall find in *Neiges*, it is *hors chrétienté*. The primordial barbarousness of that mythical region is contemplated by the poet not from without but from within, again in a spirit of understanding and praise. In the letter already quoted, the poet states his attitude toward civilization and culture in the following terms: "my hostility to 'culture' . . . has something homeopathic: I believe only that it should be carried to the point where of its own accord it retires, and, untrue to itself, is made void." In other words, the decadent learning of the West should humbly accept the lesson of simple wisdom from the barbarian. It should incline toward that which transcends history and culture itself. In these extremes which touch each other, Paris and the Antilles, the mandarin of Pekin and the camel driver of the Gobi desert, is the message of Perse.

If the images be translated into concepts, this message says that history should give way to prehistory. Indeed, Perse seems to be the poet of what might be called, paradoxically, the consciousness of prehistory. If in *Eloges* he was the poet of blood loyalty, of what we might define as genealogical anamnesis, here he is the poet of ancestral memory, of a collective awareness, buried but not extinguished: "Au point sensible de mon front où le poème s'établit, j'inscris ce chant de tout un peuple, le plus ivre."

Ancestral remembrance is the opposite of historical memory: the former is of a mystical nature, and in its incarnations makes the latter pale, and makes it seem remembrance of what is transient, common, irrelevant. In contrast to history (a memory at one and the same time individual and generic, cultural and rational, we might say, intellectualistic), the other reveals itself as memory of the flesh and of instinct, as memory of the absolute, the universal, the eternal: thence its synthetic character, its ability to intermingle epochs, its marvelous power of temporal ubiquity, its indifference to any sort of chronology. And symbolically the poet has put across this character by introducing willful and suggestive anachronisms.

Prehistoric reminiscence, or a repeated evocation of the archaic, differs from archeologic memory, and leads to anthropology and paleontology: for the poet does not seek relics of art and culture, but the fossils of life, the eternal and primitive objects, still almost blind nature, which *homo faber* has adapted with his hands for the delight of his body, for the pride of his spirit. Here too the letter to MacLeish offers us a valuable testimony: from all the museums of Europe the poet claims to have visited for courtesy's sake, he confesses to have retained in his mind only the images of such items as the "pre-Columbian skull of crystal in the British Museum."

What inspires the poet is therefore, once and for all, the voice of the blood: but here, rather than sentiment, it is poetry alone that makes of him, according to the famous definition of the historian left to us by Friedrich Schlegel, a "retrospective prophet." Beginning and ending with two independent poems, *Anabase* is divided into ten distinct units, for which the French critic Lucien Fabre and, following his footsteps, though with more discretion, T. S. Eliot have given a sort of thematic scheme. To find an explanatory title or compile a short summary of each of these units would be neither difficult nor impossible, but inappropriate and perhaps wrongheaded: after all, a theme rarely becomes exhausted in a single or entire division, but appears elsewhere in the form of a prelude or recapitulation, or repeats itself in more than one section, according to the musical method of the leitmotiv. But what is more important, every restatement gives the mistaken impression of a dramatic or epic structure in the logical unraveling of an action that goes in the direction of catastrophe or disaster, capable of being divided into cantos or episodes, into acts or scenes.

The spirit of the work is epic-lyrical, but its structure is rhapsodic. The poet gives us the feeling of rhapsody by means of an incomplete juxtaposition of fragments, always necessary and sufficient, almost standing by themselves, but with needful and intentional lacunae. Perhaps, in the Greek sense of the word, *Anabase* may give the impression of a "theory"; that is, of a figured procession, in which nevertheless some images and figures are absent or lacking. Or in a different image: a necklace made of strong thread, but which has lost many pearls or gems along the way, or which has had its filigree broken. The gaps manage intentionally to give the work an air of fragmentary style in the modern taste and, at the same time, in the manner of an ancient literary monument, mutilated and rhapsodic.

The image of the necklace, whose ends are locked in a single clasp, finds justification in the two songs at the opening and at the close of the work. The first begins with the vision of an equine birth, of a colt born with a destiny in man's wars: "Il naissait un poulain sous les feuilles de bronze." In the second appears a courser or steed, perhaps that very colt now old enough for the bit and saddle, which rests and waits for other raids or incursions, for other marches or for other battles: "Mon cheval arrêté sous l'arbre plein de tourterelles." Along with the parallelism in animal figuration we find added a parallelism in human figuration. In each song, alongside the horse we see the Stranger appear, another variant of the character we have already found in "Amitié du Prince," in whom we have recognized the alter ego of the Poet, the friend of Poetry. In the first song he gives us a forecast of the future poetry, of the poetic ferment, upon which, after the action, the poet will impose a law of order and harmony: "Bitume et roses, don du chant! Tonnerre et flûtes dans les chambres!" In the second song he celebrates his brother poet, now far away, who has seen with him the anabasis of the flesh and of the spirit, the triumph of life and death; and he gives us the annunciation, that the miracle of poetry has been consummated: "Et paix à ceux, s'ils vont mourir, qui n'ont point vu ce jour. Mais de mon frère le poete on a eu des nouvelles. Il a écrit encore une chose très douce. Et quelques-uns en eurent connaissance."

According to the summary to which we have already alluded, the theme of the first fragment should be the arrival of the conqueror at the site of the future city. Less literally, this is the canto of human strength, not in the moment of action, but in the moment of potentiality, of conscious and self-satisfied mastery, of relaxed will, without impatience. More than a city, the conqueror establishes a law or, better, lets it irradiate from himself, since it is the very law of nature, of maturity, of supremacy. The nomadic conqueror stops to found a pastoral society; he still does not wish to violate the fields with his plow, or contaminate the land with growths of tile or brick. It is not yet time to take down the fragile and glorious tents of the encampments still planted on the hillsides; it is not yet time to dissipate among new undertakings the strength which his warriors had gained on the deserts and savannahs. Nor should his people mingle with other peoples, with the hybrid tribes from the other bank. As we see, the motive of purity continues.

It is a time of quiet, of self-possession, of spiritual noontime. The conqueror does not let himself be seduced either by those who want to settle down permanently and become farmers, merchants, artisans, or by the adventurous and the impatient, eager for booty, anabases, raids, those whom the poet calls: "ô chercheurs, ô trouveurs de raisons pour s'en aller ailleurs!" It is the canto of the incorruptible heavens and of the sun, true god, designated only through suggestion, whose name should be superstitiously avoided: "le soleil n'est point nommé, mais sa puissance est parmi nous." It is the canto of a peace, not social and political, but physiological and spiritual, whose opposite is not war, but the fever of city builders and founders of civility, the fever of history. It is the canto of life at its peak, of what the ancients called the fullness of time, the canto of "l'éternité qui bâille sur les sables."

Upon the canto of sobriety and of solarity follows, in the second fragment, the canto of the first morbid intoxications, of physical and spiritual crises, of dissatisfaction and impatience. The second fragment functions as a sort of transition or intermezzo for this change of tone. Indeed here we find all impure desires, gnawings of envy of the great, sexual temptations, obsession with fornication and incest: "Et peut-être le jour ne s'écoule-t-il point qu'un même homme n'ait brûlé pour une femme et pour sa fille." Here is a forecast of calamities or of future catastrophes: "Il vient, de ce côté du monde, un grand mal violet sur les eaux." This motif reaches its culmination in the third fragment. The theme is discord, ambition, rivalries, the decision to build the new city for the passions and the pride of man. The season is the harvest time of barley, and therefore of the making of intoxicating drinks. The harmony between man and nature is now broken: man, gone mad during the dog days, is

in impious discord with the very sun, which he now dares to call
by name in order to curse it, which he now invokes only to fling
accusations at it, to make it responsible for his own revolt: "Va!
nous nous étonnons de toi, Soleil! Tu nous as dit de tels mensonges!
. . . Fauteur de troubles, de discordes! nourri d'insultes et d'es-
clandres, ô Frondeur!"

It is the time when the word, when eloquence, triumphs:
whence come prevarication and sophistry. It is the time of dema-
goguery and tyranny, of disorders and ferments. The primitive
aristocracy decays and dissolves — even the priest, the man called
upon to interpret omens, the depository of the great secrets of nature, of the mysteries of destiny, is now a plebeian, a descendant of
slaves, no one's son, no hidalgo:

> Et un tel, fils d'un tel, homme pauvre,
>   vient au pouvoir des signes et des songes.

And he reads the augury in favor of the founding of the city, of
the transformation of the ancient blood nobility into mercantile
oligarchy, of the abandonment of primitive purity for new mixtures,
for the triumph of gold instead of for the triumph of iron: "Tracez
les routes où s'en aillent les gens de toute race." The dead patri-
archs, who were cavaliers, now rot under the sand, and the only
horse that appears is merely carrion or a skeleton: "ce crâne de
cheval."

But for the author of *Eloges*, the office of the poet is to celebrate
and sing, not to accuse or curse. The poet is always the bard of the
deeds or the glories of the race. And in the fourth fragment he
glorifies the founding of the city. At first he watches with a resigned
and doubtful eye the disappearance of the encampments from the
hillsides, the stone walls and bronze statues that rise heavenward
from the plain, the slow metamorphosis of the very countenance of
the earth, which has rendered the horizon unrecognizable to the
glance of navigators. It is a moment of passive acceptance, perhaps
of indifference: "C'est là le train du monde et je n'ai que du bien à
en dire." But every trace of hostility and doubt disappears once
and for all, and gives way to a hymn of mystic enthusiasm and epic
joy for the new city, for the city of his people, in which he suddenly
discovers a sense of virginal life, of fresh creation, another nobility

and another purity, the sudden radiation of a morning innocence. symbolized in the exotic sound and hidden meaning of a name he does not tell: "Ainsi la ville fut fondée et placée au matin sous les labiales d'un nom pur." And we see the merchant ships sail up the river to the new city; we see the artisans who open up their shops, the architects and the philanthropists who hasten to construct buildings and institutions of charity; we see a new race of men appear, to watch the treasures amassed by the new men; we see alliances and minglings with the people on the other bank, the inauguration of the reign of commerce and the influx of tribute.

Right at the height of enthusiasm, the poet's sense of participation begins to decrease, and finally becomes lacking once more; and we see the coming of a new dissidence, this time very ethical and intimate, the sense of a now irreparable divorce between man and nature, of an incurable disease rooted forever in man's spirit. The distant and solitary canto is the symbol of a poet, and likewise the sadness of the child whose tamed bird flees from his hand and forever returns to its home among the branches of the trees, because it does not want to make its nest in stone and mortar.

The fifth fragment is the most excellent expression of this dissension and this nostalgia. The Stranger gives voice and rhythm to his dream and to his need for spiritual adventure and virile action, to his longing for another earth, for other times, for other life. "Pour mon âme mêlée aux affaires lointaines" there is no physical limit to the dimensions of its longings. He dreams of conquering in spirit and the flesh and the stars, while his partisans are content to plan the conquest, by iron and by fire, of a portion of our planet, of other older and richer cities: "nos pensées déjà campaient sous d'autres murs." All the inhabitants are pervaded by the same or a different madness, symbolized in the abandoned and demonic obsession of a summer night, with its presentiments and terrors, its vigils and its hallucinations, its incubuses and its deliriums, on a poetic page which is one of the most intense and most noble in the work.

The sixth fragment is an invitation to adventure. The military aristocracy, the phalanxes of horsemen, has risen and seized power. The dream of adventure and of empire is given flesh and bones. The horsemen, fuming at the delay, listen to the words and the notes of "une histoire pour les hommes, un chant de force pour les hommes," which captivates them all, and tempts even the lazy and sedentary with the promise of new war booty, of a victorious peace which would open up to them the profits of other sorts of trade, the opulent *fondaci* of distant metropolises. The people are conquered by that fiery appeal: "Ceux-là qui en naissant n'ont point flairè de telle braise, qu'ont-ils à faire parmi nous?"

The seventh fragment opens with the decision to depart, in which a tone of regret vibrates: "Nous n'habiterons pas toujours ces terres jaunes, notre délice," and with the vision of the mountains compared to nomadic camels newly sheared, which culminates in a lyrical apostrophe that reaches one of the highest poetic summits of the entire work. The excellent eighth fragment, almost necessary to quote completely, summons up again the desert march. In the ninth we see the new country appear, an Eldorado heralded by the chimneys of the first houses. The fragment culminates in the hymn, sung by a soloist with choral accompaniment, wherein the ladies of the new land sing of temptation and sensuality, of the eternal motive for the mingling of the sexes, of the passions, and of the blood. It closes, in a fading light, with the vision of epic bestiality:

> — et debout sur la tranche éclatante du jour, au seuil d'un grand pays plus chaste que la mort,
> les filles urinaient en écartant la toile peinte de leur robe.

The tenth canto is the canto of conquest, and of the insatiability it generates, of the perpetual invitation to other exploits or adventures. For the second time, and not the last in his entire work, the poet takes up again one of his favorite themes, that of the catalogue of professions, arts, and trades, of "toutes sortes d'hommes dans leurs voies et façons" — among which the genealogist now appears, the annalist, the narrator: "combien d'histoires de familles et de filiations?" But this time the nomads of the earth do not settle down either to cultivate or to build: "Terre arable du songe! Qui parle de bâtir?" Their chief, the Stranger or the Conqueror, now turns his thought to the fortune and condition of the navigator. And the poem closes with the declaration that voyages and cruises will follow the marches and the raids, that the nomads of the land will be transformed into nomads of the sea, into colonizers and corsairs, into Phoenicians or Vikings, into Venetians or Englishmen. The anabases will give way to odysseys.

IV

The poet did not know that fate destined him to be himself the Ulysses of an unforeseen odyssey, of which he must have given us poetic testimony in *Exil*.[4] The assumed biographical element of *Anabase* has been the intellectual experience of a man confronting a past almost outside history; it is equivalent to saying that the work would not have been written without the "connaissance de l'Est." But the assumption of *Exil* is actually autobiographical, an experience of an actor rather than a spectator. And the substance of that experience is here the present, history which has been lived, which will become sentiment, avoiding once again, but along different lines, the chance of becoming written history, chronicled record.

The transition from *Anabase* to *Exil* is in a certain sense the transition from epic to lyric; or better, from the manner of celebration to the manner of lamentation. The conversion is perhaps spiritual more than poetic. The rhapsodist, the bard, the composer of paeans and victory songs, becomes now the singer of threnodies, perhaps the poet of psalms. The singer of might and conquest now sings the plaint of his ill fortune and that of his people.

The migration has thus become an exodus. Conquest has given way to captivity and to persecution. The nomad is now a refugee. The stranger, horseman and wanderer, now gives way to the passer-by or to the pilgrim. The poet is no longer an exile or refugee from the realm of fantasy, but a man proscribed who walks the streets of the real world. The song, which was at first the song of collective action, is now the song of inaction, of passivity, of individual solitude. It is not the history of man, but the history of the spirit which follows upon prehistory: "Il n'est d'histoire que de l'âme, il n'est d'aisance que de l'âme." The conversion from the poet of *Anabase* to the poet of *Exil* is, one may say, a conversion from primitive barbarousness to a Christian and Hebraic spirit, perhaps above all to the spirit of the Old Testament. The feeling which dominates here is not at all that of sin or guilt, but rather of error and of secular erring: "L'exil n'est point d'hier! l'exil n'est point d'hier!"

Poetry becomes a song of humility. The celebrator and the

founder of cities now prefers a most beautiful lament, beside his wailing wall: "J'ai fondé sur l'abîme." The bard and leader of cohorts, the singer of the god of hosts, now expresses the vanity of military glory with a potent Biblical image: "Où furent les grandes actions de guerre déjà blanchit la mâchoire d'âne." And it is with an image of a great mystic poet that he sings also of life as *vanitas vanitatum*, of the earth as *lachrymarum vallis*: "Ainsi va toute chair au cilice du sel." Thus, even the Christian and evangelical spirit appears here, the most individual and most human story in the New Testament. Here we have the assertion that in this world, through the exile of the poet and of man, is gained no promised land: "A nulles rives dédiée, à nulles pages confiée la pure amorce de ce chant." Here is a restatement on a less symbolic, though just as earthly, plane of the parable of the prodigal son, who here returns, even if only in a dream, to the haven of his family and his home, to the island of his childhood (see the fifth fragment). Also Christian in spirit is the appeal to the "mère du Proscrit": upon which follows a human, all too human, appeal to the also distant wife (see the seventh fragment): "Tais-toi, faiblesse, et toi, parfum d'épouse dans la nuit comme l'amande même de la nuit." And when he takes up his favorite motif of the catalogue of human conditions, arts, and trades, he does not direct his appeal to the shepherds of the people and the sovereigns of intelligence, but to the flock itself, to the simple creatures under the same curse of emigration and sweat: "Ceux-là sont princes de l'exil et n'ont que faire de mon chant."

Exil is a religious poem in the sense that lamentation becomes sublimated in purification and expiation. It is no longer the primitive purification from contact with the ignoble and the unclean, but purification of the spirit from the evils and errors of the spirit. It is purification from the very pride of poetry, from the cult of the Word, *flatus vocis* compared with the voice of the spirit, of the Logos: "Renverse, ô scribe, sur la table des grèves, du revers de ton style la cire empreinte du mot vain." Instead of the names of terrestrial cities, the poet will now inhabit the city of the spirit: "J'habiterai ton nom."

This does not mean that he will cease to be the poet of loyalty to family, fidelity to race; rather, he will be so in the name of filial respect and spiritual brotherhood. Indeed the moment of revelation and confession has now arrived for him: "Et c'est l'heure, ô Poète, de décliner ton nom, ta naissance, et ta race."

v

Exil, as the allusions to Numidia and Taurus demonstrate, as the refrain "l'exil n'est point d'hier" demonstrates, still breathes poetically the atmosphere of *Anabase*. If in the latter work poetic inspiration itself, as well as its objects, is seen in the light of a remote poet, in the succeeding poem the present is seen in a similar light of timelessness and eternity.

The originality of *Neiges* (the most important of the lyrics composed after *Exil* and before *Vents*) lies in its being among the *poèmes nés d'hier*, occasional poetry in the highest sense of the word, dictated by an authentic American vision, dedicated to a new season.[5] In *Exil*, as in *Eloges*, as in *Anabase*, the season was the torrid summer of the old continents and of the tropics; here, on the other hand, is the northern winter of the new world, the season of meditation and of despair in the coldness of solitude.

In *Neiges*, the still solemn and oracular lyrical quality of *Exil* becomes completely private, even intimate. The landscape, however much etherealized and sublimated, is still recognizable. Here at last one can assign local names to the ideal geography of Perse. The vision of the gray dawn, of the white snow that falls upon the profile of a city seen on the horizon, makes us think of the skyline of the largest and most fabulous American metropolises: the river and the harbor suggest perhaps the Hudson and the port of New York, seen from the periphery or from a distant suburb.

Solidly anchored in space and time, the poem gives us, like a picture, the sense of weather and hour: it is a winter morning when men are going to work, when the call of the factory whistle sounds. The local color, the picturesque concreteness of an intuitive and immediate experience, re-created later in the sensitive memory, reach us by means of particulars realistically precise, such as the Negroes gathering garbage, the snow shovelers, the chains by which automobiles seek to overcome the hindrance of ice.

But the imagination of the poet does not stop here. It goes beyond, to the heart of the American continent, toward the Great Lakes and the Middle West, toward the interminable plains, still untilled though already dominated by factories, darkened with smoke, transfixed with telegraph poles, violated by railroad tracks. Cold and cruel nature and the same harsh industry of men who run, as always infected with an eternal fever, after their own shadows, are for the poet *hors chrétienté*, as the poet says concerning the blizzard. They live, that is, not in the innocent ignorance of spiritual barbarousness, but in a malevolent and hostile cosmos.

But the song and the soul of the poet are not "outside Christianity." Like the long poem that preceded it, this lyric is also a song of exile, of solitude and separation. Yet *Neiges* is also a song of love and charity, of expiation and reconciliation. The vision of the mother who folds her hands in prayer, across the ocean, is the vision of a new Mater Dolorosa. The "chant de pur lignage" becomes the song of a nobility of pain. In a league of new human brotherhood appear, instead of the queens or the women of a certain time, chaste and humble ladies, eternal sisters in Christ: the ladies of France betrayed by the weakness of men, the ladies of every race who are weaving with a shuttle fresher linen "pour la brûlure des vivants."

Here, in contrast to *Exil*, appears a promised land. The promised land is not only the abandoned country, but also the country of exile, America, "sous le plus pur vocable, un beau pays." And the other promised land turns out for the poet to be language, the archaic treasure of the human word, true idiom of the eternal and the ineffable, the tongue, adamic and divine, in which there are "pas de mots distincts pour 'hier' et pour 'demain.' "

Among the other poems written in America, *Pluies* is that which logically follows *Neiges*, in spite of the fact that it was written before.[6] Here too the inspiration is essentially lyrical. But the theme of *Neiges* is the acceptance of a new experience, the abandonment of the soul to every voice it hears within and without itself. The theme of *Pluies* is exactly the opposite: the soul of the poet recoils against itself. He now disdainfully rejects the temptation of poetry, inasmuch as poetry is sentimental autobiography, pathetic lyricism. This is shown by such recurrent phrases as *l'imminence du thème, l'évasion du thème, l'impatience du poème*. The poet is in that feverish state when the soul is possessed by the nightmares of insomnia, by daydreaming and wishful thinking. Within him, from that sterile soil and against the check of judgment and the control of will, grows, like a fascinating monster, "la rose obscène du poème."

The poet prays to his god that he be liberated from the corrupting danger of a poetry that is the fruit of self-love and self-pity, the alarming symptom of weaknesses in his own soul: "Seigneur terrible de mon rire, gardez-moi de l'aveu, de l'accueil et du chant." He resists seduction, he beats back temptation. But the soul has been contaminated, and the poet must purify it. Just as for the body ablutions alone can cleanse the soul. Water alone can conquer the aridity and the sterility of his masculine spirit, for water is the feminine element in nature and in the world. The poet wants to be cleansed by those free and natural waters which sky and clouds unloose on every earthly thing.

The poet addresses a magnificent apostrophe to the rains of spring. They are daughters of nature or, as he describes them, "grandes gerbes non liées." But the unbound sheaves are transformed into feminine figures, into maids and girls in the service of everything noble in earthly existence. They are, in the words of the poet, the *suivantes, guerrières, danseuses, nourrices* of man's heart. The downpour of rain means the regeneration or rejuvenation of all primordial forces: "C'est la terre lassée des brûlures de l'esprit," and may also cleanse "la face des vivants," may wash away the stains left by history and culture on the body and soul of man. It forms an obstacle separating us from a no-man's-land upon which the spirit cannot trespass. The Ego must not proceed any farther into the desert of the Self: the written word stops "au seuil aride du poème," which will remain unwritten.

This attempt on the part of the poet to depersonalize his experience is to be seen also in *Poème à l'Etrangère*.[7] The poem, as can be gathered from the words "Alien Registration Act" which follow the title, was inspired by the poet's appearance in 1940 before an Alien Registration Board. The apparent protagonist is another foreigner, a Spanish-speaking lady, whom the poet calls by the Americanism *Alienne*. But the real protagonist is the sentiment of the poet who, by carrying out that legal act, feels he is no longer a member of the community in which he was born. A man may become prisoner even of love for his fatherland, as Nietzsche had already said. And he must sometimes be freed even from what is dearest to him: the poet describes himself departing "à mon pas d'homme libre, sans horde ni tribu."

Poème à l'Etrangère is important because, up to a certain point, it anticipates the state of mind in which *Vents* will be written. As we shall see, *Vents* is both a reinterpretation of the American myth and a statement of the poet's decision to return spiritually to his home, to accept the new destiny of his fatherland. The theme of *Vents* will be the purification of the historical men living still within the poet's soul, just as the theme of *Pluies* is the purification of his individual and poetic soul.

Perhaps for this reason, in the collection of American poems (the poems written from 1941 to 1944 [8]), *Poème à l'Etrangère*, which was written after *Exil* and before *Pluies* and *Neiges*, closes the series. Another poem St.–J. Perse published in America is not included in that collection, because it was written after 1944 and because it is quite different in spirit and form from the other American pieces. This poem, *Berceuse*,[9] returns, except in its style and rhythm, to the inspiration of *Eloges*. It is a highly stylized and impersonal complaint, in the form of a lullaby, concerning the birth of a girl into a royal household which had been expecting a boy.

VI

Vents, the latest poem by St.–J. Perse, is the longest and perhaps the most ambitious piece he has written.[10] It takes up, in a very different spirit, the themes of both *Anabase* and *Exil*: like the former, it is a poetic statement about the migration of the human race; like the latter, it is a poetic statement about the wanderings of the poet's soul. It is more lyrical than *Anabase*, and more epical than any of the poems written before *Anabase*. Like the other poems written in America, it is inspired by exile and absence; like *Pluies*, its most important motif is the self-purification of the poet.

The means of purification are no longer the rains of spring, but a far greater elementary cosmic force, the powerful winds sweeping the American continents from north to south, from coast to coast. The purification now takes place within space, rather than within time. St.–J. Perse again becomes the poet of geography;

historical memory itself here becomes merely a function of the sense of geographical extent, of physical space. The winds are also the symbol of a new life, wider and freer, unconfined by territorial limits or by the chains of time. That new life thrives on the present and the future, and rejects the sterile food of the past.

Every purification involves the rites of burial and rebirth. For the poet and his brethren, the winds are the sign of the approaching palingenesis of man. Perhaps for this reason the poem begins with a reminiscence from the poetry of T. S. Eliot, the author of *The Waste Land*. As in the case of purification by water, the object of purification by air is the countenance of every creature; but in the process of purification by air, the winds batter and destroy everything not deeply rooted in the soil of life. This is why they batter and destroy those whom St.–J. Perse calls *hommes de paille,* that is, the hollow men; and with them they batter and destroy the hollow trunk of civilization, the dead plant of historical time and historical consciousness. It is only through the miracle of art that the hollow trunk may again be transformed into the living tree of language and poetry.

The protagonist of the poem is once more the Narrator, who is described, as before, as a stranger and as a magician. Perhaps for the purpose of alluding to the experience which dictated *Anabase,* the Narrator or Stranger here is a Siberian sorcerer, a shaman. The poet surprises him while he is looking, from the ramparts of the city, into present and visible space, and into absent and invisible time. Yet he speaks to the men of his age and tells them of the new forces and ideas, wishes and longings, needs and desires, which he seems to hear in the voices of the winds. The winds are destroying and regenerating everything we believed in "au tournant de notre âge," our fixed material and spiritual borders, our artificial bulwarks, our temples and monuments.

The Narrator, the Stranger, the Sorcerer, is a priest and a clerk, chained to the beliefs and the creeds, the lore and the science of the past. He is a prisoner of the Serapeum of Science, the library or the museum, almost buried under the dead weight of his books which are but "cendres et squames de l'esprit." If he wants to be carried away by the vitalizing force of the winds, the librarian or the scholar must die to himself. His death will be his life: "S'en aller! s'en aller! Parole de vivant!" Before leaving, he must exorcise the past; he must accomplish the ritual of burial and rebirth. The poet states the intention with an image which is a reminiscence from Baudelaire's "Recueillement": "Nous coucherons ce soir les saisons mortes dans leurs robes de soirée." The books are thrown into the river, the lamps into the street. The temple of learning will be sanctified again by what for others would seem a profanation: by exposing under its open dome the nude body of a young woman, who will give us truths without words.

The Sorcerer, having "dépouillé toute charge publique," is now free to listen to the message and lesson of the winds, which give him a counsel of force and violence. He becomes their voice for other men; and he gives to other men their command, which is both the command of action and the command of dream. But the new dream must be different from the old one: modern man must renounce forever "les grandes invasions doctrinales," the utopias and the ideologies of his forefathers. Action must be real movement out in the open; it must be adventure and risk — not the private and sedentary life of our fathers, who were satisfied in cultivating the small garden of their individual existence. With an apocalyptic inspiration, and with a paradoxical image based on alliteration and equivocal etymologies, the poet asks men to listen to the new voices of the winds, not to the old human prayers and hymns, but to "l'antiphonaire des typhons."

The poet describes the roaming winds, with a simile which reminds us of a famous line of Rimbaud, as the "grands essaims sauvages de l'amour." The Sorcerer must follow them, "Allant où les hommes, à leurs tombes." To hear their prophecy he must follow them into the open space of the American continent. Like them he must turn his face westward and look for new lands. Here we witness the reappearance in French literature of the America of Chateaubriand, which, in the case of St.-J. Perse, is the sort of America that can only be crossed traveling by car, by train, or by plane. It is the old America of nature and the new America of technology. It is the America of prehistory and also the land of the American dream, which is the dream of man, the dream the poet defines with the term *l'An Neuf*.

Only the winds may reveal this America, which is symbolized especially by the Middle and the Far West. The poem is essentially an immense "ode to the west wind." But the poet also sings the South, the South which Chateaubriand sang and loved best — which is both newer and older than the East and West. There the poet sees all the wounds of nature and history, the delta and what he calls "l'ulcère noir." He feels the presence of a gap dividing two ages: from underground he seems to hear "croître les os d'un nouvel âge de la terre." Especially here he feels how strong nature is and how weak man is, and he expresses his feeling with an image which reminds us of Mallarmé: "Les vents sont forts! la chair est brève!"

Still, in the past there were also men able to listen to the call of the wind, to the call of the American wind. They were all those who left Europe for the New Atlantis. The first of them were adventurers, pioneers, explorers, especially the Spanish *conquistadores* already sung by the poet's friend Archibald MacLeish. St.–J. Perse calls them "les grands Itinérants du songe et de l'action." They were followed by hunters for wealth and honor, traders and slaveowners. After them came "les grands Réformateurs" and "les grands Protestataires," and those whom the poet calls "les hommes de lubie," those who in Europe were slaves to their own ideas or ideals and who came to this country to become their free servants. After them came the men of science (here it seems that one must read into the poem even an allusion to the atomic bomb). And finally came the poet.

The poet accepts, like all the other men, the winds of his own time; he finds that his own mission is essentially a spiritual and communal mission, which he defines in the following terms:

> Son occupation parmi nous: mise en clair des messages. Et la réponse en lui donnée par illumination du coeur.
> Non point l'écrit, mais la chose même. Prise en son vif et dans son tout.
> Conservation non des copies, mais des originaux. Et l'écriture du poète suit le procès-verbal.

Now the winds suddenly cease. During the spell of silence and calm, the poet looks back on America and its civilization, but even this historical contemplation ends with a geographical vision, with the sight of the immense expanse of the Pacific Ocean. The poet cannot follow any other wind; here his pilgrimage is forever consummated. The circle is closed. From the American Far West he looks toward the Asiatic Far East where he had begun his personal anabasis. Now it is time to turn back toward the American East, and from there, at least in spirit, toward the European West. The temptation of abandoning allegiance to Europe and France is rejected. When the prodigal son decides to start his voyage home, the winds rise again and accompany him on his way back. He seems to hear in them the voice of another command: "Que nul ne songe, que nul ne songe à déserter les hommes de sa race!" Those same winds will regenerate the French spirit and the French soul; the life of the French peasant and, even more, the life of the inhabitant of French towns and cities, the mean bourgeois and provincial existences. A new man will be born from the poet's tribe; from the soil of the homeland, a new life and a new poetry will grow, "un autre arbre de haut rang."

That tree is a metamorphosis of the tree of language which has already appeared at the beginning of this essay, and which the poet has already described as "peuple d'oracles." The same could be said of the poem and of its language. But oracles always have double, and even contradictory, meanings; this is no less true of *Vents*. It seems at the same time to exalt the American dream and the European myth, nature and history, civilization and culture, the modern machines for living and the traditional art of life. This ambivalence is betrayed even by the style of the poem, as well as by its content. There is perhaps no poem written in French which contains more foreign words, Anglicisms and Americanisms, more obscure biographical references and allusions to current events — all this in spite of the fact that the inspiration is, as always with Perse, exotic, prophetic, hermetic. The author is aware of the equivocal character of his poem, not only from the linguistic and stylistic point of view, but also from the point of view of the poet's heart and mind: "ô Poète, ô bilingue . . . homme parlant dans l'équivoque!"

But such ambiguity is not new; it is the usual ambiguity of St.-J. Perse, which might be defined as his continuous oscillation between the opposite poles of the lyric and the epic. In *Anabase* the epic element is, as ideal and form, dominant; in *Exil* it is rather the lyric element. Here they are equally present, almost in the same measure: and this is perhaps the reason why *Vents* seems to me inferior to the other two great poems. We have already quoted the passage where the author gives a splendid definition of the epic mission of the poet. It is surprising, but not unnatural, that in another passage of the poem he looks at the poet, as man and as subjective artist, with a far more critical eye: "je t'ai pesé, poète, et t'ai trouvé de peu de poids." This attitude may explain why *Anabase*, where the lyrical hero is reduced to the level of an interpreter of the glories of man and the destiny of his race, still remains the masterpiece of St.–J. Perse.

VII

As *Vents* easily shows, as the closing section of *Neiges* so clearly states, the myth of the Word is among the most important in Perse's work. Contrary to the decadents and symbolists, he contemplates the mystery of the Word not from the point of view of the poet but of the Word itself. In this sense his conception of poetic language is nearer to Valéry's than to Mallarmé's, though, in order to define the object, it would be impossible to think out a better formula than that which Mallarmé himself offers to us appropriately and so readily: "les mots de la tribu."

For Perse language is the *sancta sanctorum*, the inexhaustible thesaurus of the human spirit. He does not follow the workings of a wholly mystic or arbitrarily individual set of symbols in his attempt to penetrate into the secrets. On the contrary, he treats words with literal, almost superstitious respect. Every *nomen* is for him *omen* and *numen*. For this reason he never divulges the names of his imaginary cities. What seems to include most of the apostheosized *numen*, the Lares or the Penates, is not the place, but rather the geographical name. All the lands of his choice and adoption lie under the protection of the name of a "plus pur vocable," or "sous les labiales d'un nom pur," which the poet does not profane by pronouncing aloud, by the physical vibration of the lip. Exile itself finds in him no other definition than change, not of country, but of word.

That explains the poet's obsession for linguistics. Linguists appear in the catalogue of professions and vocations in *Exil*: allusions to glottology and philology recur, even in scientific and technical terminology, at the end of *Neiges*. But in this respect the passage that always remains the most suggestive is that which we might call the *envoi* of *Exil*, which we have cited before: "Et c'est l'heure, ô

Poète, de décliner ton nom, ta naissance, et ta race." Here we seem to be able to discover, outside of a profound symbolic and auto-biographic significance, the philological game of an erudite poet. Who does not recall the last verse of the *Chanson de Roland*, with which the epic of French heroism and misfortune closes: "Ci falt la geste, que Turoldus declinet." In this verse, which some con-sider an interpolation, thousands of interpreters have found the most diverse meanings for that mysterious final verb. The geste closes because Turoldus is declining in age and health, is old and sick, someone has said. The geste closes that Turoldus is reciting or expounding, say others. Is it paradoxical to assert that in Perse's *décliner* we have an intended reminiscence of that mysterious word and of all the meanings interpreters have wished to attribute to it; and this together with a final play on words, the grammatical sense of "decline"?

Here we should say something about the particular forms which the art of Perse assumes in these works of his maturity, as we have already done for *Eloges*. Each is a mine of images, and the col-lector or guardian of lyrical relics can derive something, can always derive something, from the treasure which the poet generously pours into the torrent or into the crucible of poetry.

Solid and virile as always, the art of Perse in the long poems bestows a still more potent objectivity, which radiates around itself, without dissonance, a lucid metaphysical halo. In *Anabase* it is worthwhile to quote an example of paradoxical realism, the vision of "la ville jaune, casquée d'ombre, avec ses caleçons de filles aux fenêtres." Instead of a picture of the ancient and remote East, we have a picture of the near and modern Orient, a picturesque im-pression of the slums, with laundry in the windows, of a port in Asia or Africa or perhaps even Mediterranean Europe. As we see, the art of Perse knows the virtues not only of anachronism, but also of ubiquity, of placelessness.

In the scene of the desert march, there is the vision, at once apocalyptic and allegorical, powerfully plastic, of a natural phe-nomenon: "Nos compagnons ces hautes trombes en voyage, clep-sydres en marche sur la terre." Alone capable among the moderns of what the ancients called Pindaric flights, the poet gives us this excellent image in *Exil*: "J'élis un lieu flagrant et nul comme l'ossu-arie des saisons." And what reader of *Neiges* would be able to deny, not the personification, but the animal incarnation of dawn into a bird, of "l'aube muette dans sa plume"?

In spite of his cult of the Word, the poetry of Perse is in modern French literature the least inclined to become the poetry of poetry; above all, it least aspires to establish a poetics alongside the work or to make a poetics of itself. "On the subject of literary doctrine," says the poet in his much-quoted letter, "I have nothing at all to state. I have never relished scientific cooking." All his poetics is negative; he himself says of the Poet, in *Exil*: "Et la naissance de son chant ne lui est pas moins étrangère." Contrary to Mallarmé and Valéry, Perse is not the poet of the consciousness of poetry. It seems as if Perse has wished to anchor his work in certain biographical experiences which he has objectified and transcended. Neither the Antilles of *Eloges*, nor the Asia of *Anabase*, nor the America of *Exil* or *Neiges*, nor the continents of *Vents*, should deceive us: as he says in the third, all these works are "un grand poème né de rien, un grand poème, fait de rien," precisely in the sense of those "airy nothings" that are the substance of poetry, according to Shakespeare's king in *A Midsummer Night's Dream*. All this means that poetry nourishes itself neither from the life of the poet nor from the words of poetry, but from those "nothings" that are the very life of man.

In his use of language, felt as a mine of spiritual wealth (for addition and, perhaps, for plunder), Perse resembles more an artist like Joyce than the French moderns, despite the fact that such a formula as that with which Valéry defines language ("discours prophétique et paré") appears to have been written expressly for his poetic language. From the point of view of content, we find the same originality and novelty; here again, more than of his own compatriots, Perse makes us think of an Anglo-American, T. S. Eliot, whom we know to have translated *Anabase*, and above all, naturally, the Eliot of *The Waste Land*.

This does not mean that he has not a French spirit. To those who have doubts in this regard, Perse himself has replied in his letter to MacLeish: "About France there is nothing to say: it is myself and all of myself. It is for me sacred and the only means by which I can conceivably communicate with anything in this world that is essential. Even if I weren't an essentially French animal . . . the French language would still be my only imaginable home, the perfect rest and hiding place, the perfect armor for defense and offense."

The testimony is important, all the more because it documents his conception of poetic language as a veil covering and expressing not only the mysteries of culture and poetry, but the very mystery of being and person. The poet is a knight who defends not only honor, but the very intimacy of man. The poet does not decipher but masks, at times unveils, the secrets of the soul. Thus the mystery of the pseudonym is understood, and the later decision to *décliner* the name of the poet.

But the document is full of meaning even from another point of view, in the casual expression, "French animal." Inadvertently the poet tells us that what interests him is the French animal, the pure blood of the race, not the beast of burden of civility and culture. Thus his love for Racine is understood, for the most perfect French animal we know. The elementary and essential Racine, of blanching and blinding passions, of the queen Phèdre and the prince Hippolyte, of Ariane and Thésée; the poet now of the torrid desert, now of the pure heavens of the soul. And it is with an image that reminds us of Racine, with the words of the poet, that we are satisfied to suggest the mission of his work, the message of his poetry: "Duc d'un peuple d'images à conduire aux Mers Mortes."

NOTES

1. Fragments of this letter were for the first time made public, in an English translation, by Archibald MacLeish himself, in his article "A Note on Aléxis Saint Léger Léger," which appeared in *Poetry*, March 1942, pp. 330–335, to accompany the original publication of *Exil*. The same Note was reprinted as a preface to the American edition of *Eloges*, and, in French translation, to *Quatre Poèmes* (see notes 2 and 8). It is to this Note that we may refer the reader interested in knowing something more about the life of the poet St.–J. Perse, or, better, of the man Aléxis Léger.

2. The first cycle of *Eloges*, entitled "Images à Crusoé," appeared for the first time in the August 1909 issue of the *Nouvelle Revue Française,* the magazine which, in the following year, also published some of the other cycles of *Eloges*. The two parts formed the book *Eloges,* published in 1911 by the *NRF* (Marcel Rivière) under the signature "Saintléger Léger." "Amité du Prince," signed "St.–J. Perse," privately printed in a facsimile edition in 1924 and published the same year in *Commerce,* enriched the second and definitive edition of *Eloges,* which included the other cycles of

La Gloire des Rois and was published in 1925 by Gallimard in Editions de la *NRF*, under the name of St.-J. Perse. The text of this edition was reprinted in 1944 by W. W. Norton as *Eloges and Other Poems* (New York). The volume was introduced with the biographical note written by Archibald MacLeish (see note 1); the original text was accompanied by Louise Varèse's English translation of the poems. Rainer Maria Rilke translated into German the "Images à Crusoé," and Rudolf Kassner the *Eloges*; both translations were privately printed and are no longer available.

3. Fragments of *Anabase* appeared for the first time in January 1924 in the *Nouvelle Revue Française*, which in the same and in the following year published the entire poem in two separate editions (Gallimard). The first translation into Russian, by G. Adamovich and G. Ivanov, was published by Povolotsky (Paris, 1926), with a preface by Valéry Larbaud. The original text of this preface was printed in January 1926 by the *NRF*. The German translation, by Walter Benjamin and Bernard Groethuysen, never appeared. The preface Hugo von Hofmannsthal had written for that translation was published in German in *Neue Schweizer Rundschau* (Zurich, May 1929); and, in French, in *Commerce* in the same year. The English translation, *Anabasis*, by T. S. Eliot, with the original text and a translator's preface, was published by Faber and Faber (London, 1931). An identical American edition appeared in 1938, with the translation revised by Eliot (Harcourt, Brace, New York). The Italian translation, by Giuseppe Ungaretti, which was published originally in *Fronte*, vol. 1 (Turin, 1931), is included in the Italian poet's collection of *Traduzioni* (Rome, 1936), where it is accompanied by a short preface. Almost all these prefaces were reprinted at the end of an American edition of the original text of *Anabase*, published by Brentano's (New York, 1945).

4. The writing of *Exil* took place at Long Beach, New York, and was finished in June 1941. The original text was published for the first time in *Poetry*, March 1942, with a note by Archibald MacLeish, to whom the poem is dedicated (see note 1). The first edition in book form is that published in a special edition of *Cahiers du Sud* (Marseilles, May 1942) and by *Lettres Françaises* (Buenos Aires, July 1942). The same poem was published again in 1944 in the collection *Quatre Poèmes* (see note 8), and in Paris by Gallimard (1945). In America *Exile and Other Poems*, original text and translations into English by Denis Devlin, was published by Pantheon Books (New York, 1949).

5. *Neiges* was published for the first time in *Lettres Françaises*, July 1944. It is included also in *Quatre Poèmes* (see note 8). An Italian translation of the poem, by the author of this essay, appeared in *Inventario*, vol. 1, no. 1 (Florence, 1946).

6. *Pluies*, after having been published in *Lettres Françaises*, October 1943, appeared as a *plaquette*, published by the same review (1944). An English translation, by Denis Devlin, appeared in *Sewanee Review*, October 1944.

7. *Poème à l'Etrangère* was published for the first time in *Hémisphères* (New York), vol. 1 (Summer 1943). In the same issue there is an article by Roger Caillois: "Sur l'art de Saint-John Perse."

8. All the poems writen by St.-J. Perse from 1941 to 1944 (except *Berceuse* and including those mentioned in notes 4–7 above) were collected

in *Quatre Poèmes*, published by Editions des *Lettres Françaises* (Buenos Aires, 1944). The same poems were published in Paris by Gallimard (1945).

9. *Berceuse* appeared for the first time, in its original text, in an American publication, the international review *Mesa* (Aurora, New York, edited by Herbert Steiner), August 1945. The same text was reprinted by *Partisan Review*, September–October 1946.

10. *Vents* was published by Gallimard (NRF) in 1946. Fragments of the poem can be read in *Mesa*, Winter 1947.

Postscript, 1960. This article was written in Italian in 1947 and was published for the first time in *Yale French Studies*, 1948, in a translation of the manuscript made by Lowry Nelson, here reproduced with a few little changes, which could hardly be called corrections or revisions. I have since then published a few more items in French and Italian about the same author: but in this case I have refrained from reusing this material, and from rewriting it into a few additional pages which might have covered the production of St.-J. Perse up to the present time. The present study reflects my views of the poet's work up to the end of his moral, and even literary, exile: up to the moment when his national and international reputation started to grow, slowly but steadily rising up to a higher, and more natural, level. The beginning of such a process coincided with the publication of *Vents*, the poem treated at the end of this essay, which was also the first of the poet's postwar productions to appear again in a French original edition, printed by Gallimard, St.-J. Perse's prewar publisher, in 1946. To this I shall add for the information of the reader that the same publisher issued in 1953 the first volume of Perse's *Oeuvre poétique*, which was followed in 1957 and 1959 by two new works, *Amers* and *Chronique* (the latter published for the first time in 1959 in *Cahiers du Sud*, the next year by Gallimard). *Amers* was published also in a bilingual edition by Pantheon Books (New York, 1958) as *Seamarks*, translation by Wallace Fowlie. Gallimard issued the second volume of the *Oeuvre poétique* in 1960. I shall close this brief account of St.-J. Perse's later career by reminding the reader that in 1960 the poet was awarded the Nobel Prize.

MYTHOLOGY OF FRANZ KAFKA

The search for a habitation, which we know under no other form but that abstract and conventional one of an address, can sometimes assume the dimensions of a discovery or an adventure. Thus once when I was wandering in that section of Prague which is enclosed between the Old City square and the banks of the Moldava, the whereabouts of the domicile I was looking for seemed to me an allusive and encouraging prelude to the acquaintance and conversation that I was so impatient to begin. The person who was expecting me was Max Brod, a Jew by birth and a German by tongue, a journalist and a writer, legatee to the work and memory of Franz Kafka, and the impulse which moved me toward him was the piteous anxiety to visit the spiritual relics of a departed confrère. His house was half way along the last building of an ugly and twisting little street, which grew wide only to shelter in a little square a few steps away the old Synagogue with its little roof of bricks looming over your shoulders like the top of a dormer window, the seat of the ancient Jewish community, as charming and comic as a carillon or a cuckoo clock. Indeed a sweet and polished little remnant of the ghetto, one of those corners which must have been preferred in the Middle Ages by the most fanatical and reflective Israelites, in that ancient and curious Prague which has been revealed to us by Meyrink.

The sound of the bell, a dark corridor, and the sweet and warm voice of the hairy little man who cordially offered me his hand aroused me from my reveries and recalled to me at once the object of my visit and the questions to be asked him. The little man answered me less with words than with documents and with facts, and exhibited a small and tattered collection of photographs; they were all pictures of Kafka. Franz as a baby, a grammar-school pupil, and at the university; Franz in sports, on a walk with his friends, in the country; Franz sick, in a sanatorium, dying. Within me now from the sight of so many mementos there remains only a single and confused recollection: a typical face of a Jewish schoolboy of

Central Europe, with normal lineaments, or even common ones. But the forehead, under the brushcut hair, radiated a sweet and precocious sense of old age from the noble and anxious furrows which gave to the face a strange sense of harmony and beauty, while the vivid and dreamy eyes under the wide and neat curtain of his eyebrows revealed traces of a devastating and monomaniac reflectiveness. I remember well that Brod guessed my thought and anticipated a hesitating and still unexpressed question from me. "Franz was very happy and used to laugh very often. He used to talk a good deal, and in a strong voice, and he died of tuberculosis of the larynx." Then I endeavored for a moment to imagine the sound of that voice and of that laugh, and I was astonished when, as if by an illumination, I felt they must have been like the laugh and the voice of Svidrigailov. And then I understood that the world and the art of Kafka could not be explained except by Dostoevski's myth.

Do you remember one of the most obscure and deceiving passages of the dialogue of Raskolnikov with Svidrigailov? Svidrigailov enters like a phantom into the room where Raskolnikov is feeding on rancor and solitude. He presents himself to him, tells him of his own life, speaks to him of the continual apparitions of his dead wife, and says to him, "Who knows that the other world is not peopled with spiders or with something of the same sort? . . . For us eternity is not only an incomprehensible idea, a thing enormous and immense. But why immense, I ask? And if instead it were only a dark recess, a sort of bathroom crammed with spiders in all the corners? I sometimes imagine it to myself in exactly that way." And when Raskolnikov asks him: "Is it possible that you don't know how to imagine anything less desolate and more just?" Svidrigailov responds, "More just? But it can also be granted that an eternity so constituted is very just; nay, if I have to say so, that's exactly the way I would make it." To which Dostoevski adds that Svidrigailov pronounced these words with "an abstracted smile."

The first revelation that the thought and image of Svidrigailov are flashing into the reader's mind is that a similar idea of eternity as a little gray and dusty room full of spiders is nothing but a metaphysical projection of the scenario in which all the characters of Dostoevski live. In fact all the critics of his work from the positivist Mikhailovski through the mystic Merezhkovski, who was the first person clever enough to contrast the myth of the author of *The*

Brothers Karamazov with that of the author of *Anna Karenina*, have noted that the pages of Dostoevski never disclose to us the rustic and natural landscapes of Tolstoy, and that the only background against which his creatures live, act, and discuss is constituted by the four walls of a rented room, by the stairs of a tenement house, or at most by a poor section of the most artificial and absurd city that men have constructed on the face of the earth: Petersburg. The work of Dostoevski has been the first to make us feel the terrible imprisonment of stone and lime, and it is precisely from this that is born, in correlation with the exterior signs of urban progress and with the vulgarization of its myths, that narrative epidemic of the first postwar period which was called "literature of asphalt." The novels of Dostoevski and of Kafka are really, as a critic has said apropos of the writer from Prague, "novels of human solitude," of a solitude which expresses itself materially and spiritually in the one dimension of a brick pavement or an inlaid floor, in the eternal fatality of a trip around one's room, a trip not even cheered or eased by the familiarity with one's own furniture or with the loving and intimate contemplation of one's own things. Dostoevski's and Kafka's characters live in rooms that do not belong to them, anonymous and unadorned, and certainly not very clean: their thought and their manner of existing are nothing but a magnetic ebb and flow set free from their brain, which are reflected and refracted on the four walls that surround and enclose them. The cosmos of Dostoevski's creatures is a monad of bricks and lime, and, as you know, monads have no windows at whose sill one can press one's face to enjoy the spectacle of the world and through whose blinds and panes the perfume of the flowers or the light of the sun can penetrate. That is why many of his creatures perceive only shadows and believe that these are the only reality of life, thus renewing the Platonic myth of the cave. But the Platonic cave, natural and primitive, intended to symbolize the errors of logic and the limitation of experience, represents precisely in this the obscurity of ignorance and the darkness of instinct, while the four walls of Dostoevski, constructed by will and artifice, a fruit of the practical reasoning which teaches us to protect human existence from the offenses of inclement weather and the elements, mean nothing other than the narrow, inexorable, and perpetual prison of conscience. Civilization, beyond constructing them, has illuminated houses with candles and oil; later the gas burner and the electric light were the generators of a thousand shadows on the smooth porous walls of our grottos of masonry or cement. But if the caves of instinct defy the weather by ignoring it (because their destiny, written as it is on the book of nature and of geological cataclysms, is signed in hours and in dates which are not those conventional ones of the calendars of society and the clocks of history), the houses of men are subjected instead to ruin and to destruction, and it is in this sense, in Nietzsche's, that their inhabitants are "decadents." But by a law of fatality and compensation, notice how those ruined walls, those walls dusty and full of spiders, arouse in the mind of their extravagant lodgers the sense of the infinite and the eternal, and it is this fatality which a pupil and an interpreter of Dostoevski, Leo Shestov, called "second sight," a light which makes even the opaque transparent.

Now Kafka is one who has succeeded in making a similar sense of the eternal live again, that dangerous virtue of reflecting on an infinite series of mirrors which is exclusive of the conscience, in an atmosphere quite different from that in which the creatures of Dostoevski act: we are no longer in the capital of the North and in the last century, but in a great city of Central Europe and of our own day; we no longer have anything to do with hungry students or with decadent nobles who live in the great populous agglomerations of Petersburg, but we find ourselves before bank clerks or salesmen from Prague or Vienna, who live in furnished but comfortable rooms, near some good average or moderately rich family. In a word, Kafka has transplanted Dostoevski's drama of conscience from the barbaric and mystic mold of orthodox Russia into the gracious flower vase which adorns the windowsill of so many petit-bourgeois apartments of our oldest Europe. The particular tragedy of the novels of Kafka is that the catastrophe takes place in almost crepuscular and "intimist" circles, at times even *gemütlich*. And if the sense of prison emanating from the work and fantasy of Dostoevski is a hundred times more universal and grand, that depends not only on the force of the art but also on the fact that, beyond the walls and under the foundations of his houses, is fermenting all that boiling spring of a spiritual existence as vast as the steppes, of a mystic and uncultivated Muscovite barbarism which multiplies the echo of conscience in the very grottos of a more domineering and savage instinct. It can almost be said that the skepticism and the anti-Europeanism of Dostoevski are the amplifiers of a voice which does nothing but repeat the latest and most absurd words of the logic of the Occident. On the contrary, the widest spiritual center within which the vibration of Kafka's word branches forth occupies the narrow limits of a well, of a tradition which is vertical and obscure, that of the Jewish soul, which outside its own rooms and habitations presupposes no human societies vaster than the ghetto. As in Svidrigailov and in Dostoevski, Kafka's sense of guilt forces him to recognize that an eternity thus formed (that of the *dark recess* and the *spiders*) is the only fatal, possible, and just one; but the weight and the importance of the condemnation are precisely limited by the fact that he underlines unconsciously in the cosmic recognition of original sin that principal flaw of a people merely local-minded, which is his world, the Jewish, and of a predominantly bourgeois civilization, which is the modern world and ours. Kafka has forgotten that the sinful fruit of good and of evil has been plucked from the tree of science, and has identified the greatest fault of the moderns with the reduction of the concept of eternity to the sole dimension of time. Dostoevski's conception of the eternal, more abstract and I would say almost geometrical, is perhaps the only just and possible one, according to Svidrigailov, because in his famous image he determines the prison of being as a punishment which tends to limit liberty of movement; and that preoccupies him much more than the thought of his duration: man for him is not the "detained" (a temporal criterion), but the "recluse" (a spatial criterion) in the secrets of the universe. And his taskmaster is nothing else but his intelligence.

And it is only on this plane that Kafka's two masterpieces, that is to say, "The Metamorphosis" and *The Trial*, can be understood. Both begin in the same way: in one just as in the other, the protagonist one fine morning wakes up in his own bed, and notices that something unexpected and extraordinary has happened to him. In the case of Gregor Samsa, the traveling salesman of "The Metamorphosis," just as in the case of Joseph K., the bank clerk of *The Trial*, an unexpected and curious accident suddenly determines another life and another destiny: nay, since the only and supposed preliminary fact of their existence is reduced to the norm of habit and the daily round, we can say without further ado that this new fact determines for the first time their true life and their real destiny. This extraordinary event, which is implanted on the recurring fatality every twenty-four hours of the cessation of sleep, consists in the sudden necessity of wakefulness and insomnia; and indeed they perceive that it will no longer be permitted them to close an eye until their eyelids yield to the sleep of death or that of nothingness: since in them took place that morning the most tragic and the most surprising of awakenings, that of conscience. In Gregor Samsa such a spiritual catastrophe is expressed in his unforeseen notion of having been converted during the night into a monstrous insect, into an unclean animal; in Joseph K. it is manifested by the unexpected notification made to him by two unknown men who have the air of being policemen, that he is under arrest and in police custody for an unknown crime which he has (or has not) committed. Therefore, all at once, you have prisoners of a miraculous and terrible event, whose range is measured in terms of the fact that it canalizes immediately the existence of its own victims into one logical track and one tight-packed with consequences, necessities, and habits, which in and of themselves are banal, natural, and common. And just as the protagonist of "The Metamorphosis" must submit to the bare and crude exigencies of animal and vegetable life, so that of *The Trial* is inexorably forced to enter into the great conventional game of judicial customs and penal procedure. They have suddenly become two men of the underground, and as such judged and condemned for eternity.

Gregor Samsa has been transformed into a cockroach only because the sense of eternity and of sin, the awakening of conscience, reveals to the man his own bestiality; and because only to a cockroach can a room, a wall, or a bit of furniture seem infinite. Joseph K. is submitted to a judicial proceeding and is put under arrest because the man who begins to observe himself living immediately becomes a man accused; and because the tribunals of men, dirty and dusty, anonymous and habit-worn, unjust and absurd, monstrous fruits of the civilization of the four walls, are one of the circles which most resemble the eternity of Svidrigailov.

The extensive and lucid artistic intent of Kafka is completely directed toward making it possible for the reader never to imagine, for example, that a Gregor Samsa has been changed into a cockroach through an act of magic or enchantment. A traveling salesman, a man of everyday life, an average citizen completely given over to comfort and to thrift, immersed up to his neck in logic and practical reasoning, can be miraculously and monstrously changed into an impure bug, but it is not possible for his soul to be purified or changed through the catharsis of the miracle and of the fabulous: in the days of fairies, kinglets could be changed into animals by the treacherous arts of a sorcerer precisely because they retained the hope of a magic wand which would restore them to their original state. But the average citizens and the moderns do not believe in fairies, and for Kafka even the prayers of Solveig would be impotent to remove the Troll's tail from Peer Gynt. The metamorphosis of Gregor Samsa and the trial of Joseph K. are irremediable internal catastrophes, tectonic earthquakes which change the structure of a spirit once and for all. This is the sense of Kafka's work, extended to three dimensions to describe without pity the hard prison of our logic, a prison from which has never been heard the echo of a prayer or the song of a prisoner. The times of the myths are over, and when men discontented with nature wanted to build a city (so goes a common Balkan legend apropos of the foundation of Scutari), the genii every time used to destroy that which had been constructed by day, and in the end the founders understood that it was necessary to placate them by a human sacrifice. Then they walled in alive into a structure the young wife of one of their number: and she lived for months and months in that way, shedding infinite tears and giving milk to her child through the openings of the wall. But the new and modern victims of the four walls, those walled in alive by conscience, are no longer bound by anything to nature and to life, and it is for this reason that they do not know regret.

The other works of Kafka also discuss the same problem, which we might call the squaring of the vicious circle of conscience. But in respect to "The Metamorphosis" and to *The Trial*, they act in an indirect and marginal way and, to continue the image of the circle, I will say that they are limited to the matter of delineating various tangents. Indeed they study the spiritual forces which are centrifugal, peripheral, and eccentric, that is to say, those that tend toward evasion and liberation or that seek desperately to resist the gulf of conscience. Some instead are directed toward the describing of states of mind which precede and present the awakening, those which we would call the drowsy state of conscience, when even instinct collaborates unconsciously in its own ruin and lets itself be seduced by phantasms of the dawn and the last sleep. A typical work of the first sort seems to me to be *Amerika,* which describes the vicissitudes of a rather simple adolescent put into contact with the marvels of mechanics: it is Kafka's least successful book because, in spite of the fact that here too the marvelous is limited to the field of possibilities and of conscience, the fantasy of our author is a curious balloon — or better a football — which is held in check and cannot get poised at its proper height without the ballast of the real and the everyday, understood in their most bourgeois, crude, and worn-out sense. Apropos of this book it is worth remembering perhaps, without claiming to give to the observation any allusive value, that when Svidrigailov is about to be killed, to the sentinel-soldier who is interrogating him on his manner of acting, he replies that he is going to America.

A characteristic example of the second current of Kafka's works seems to me rather *The Castle,* which merits a longer treatment, since it also is a sort of pendant of *The Trial,* if only because here too the family name of the protagonist is designated by a simple K. This time K. is a surveyor who depends on the inhabitants of a mysterious castle, where, without anyone's attempting to hinder him, he will try to enter but always in vain. But in contrast to the protagonist of *Amerika,* in the K. of *The Castle* the ingenuous curiosity for the fabulous, which can be recognized also in the initial and thoroughly literary device of the work, not unlike that of a detective story (a form which, as is well known, prefers above all others atmospheres that are of an ancient and mysterious mannerism), is tempered and I would say almost solidified into a vulgar, common, and bourgeois sentiment; this gives the book the vigor of a drawing, and constitutes the thoroughly provincial and *arriviste* ambition of K. to enter, to take part in, a loftier world and a superior society. But that the artistic proceedings of Kafka tend to make the spark of the fantastic rise from the flint of reality is magnificently attested by a famous fragment from "The Country Doctor," entitled "Bucephalus," the only one which gained strength from an ancient myth, that of Alexander's horse, projected in the figure of a lawyer of our time, likewise a slave of an unknown tribunal and the victim of some metamorphosis or other. This continual irresolution on the thread that divides the concrete from the abstract is sufficient to demonstrate, contrary to the opinion of one or two critics of Kafka (who seem to be incapable of following their own advice), that an author so constituted is not explained either by aesthetics or by psychoanalysis, but resolutely and in medieval fashion by all possible symbolic researches and on the suggestive and deceptive plane of allegory, that supreme abstraction which is the only cornice, background, and relief possible to the obscure realism of all his proceedings as a narrator; an allegory which, under the form of anxiety about the transcendent, filters like a sun's ray through the only but very necessary crack that cuts through the compact, sordid, and gray wall of Kafka's creation.

Such a creation, I repeat, is conceived in the absolute and in the abstract as a series of corollaries to some one of the more lucid postulates of Dostoevski: but often the symbolic and metaphysical precedent of the great Russian is concentrated in literary reminiscences, which result especially from the plain and gray text of the individual works of Kafka. Let the example of "The Metamorphosis" suffice for them all, since its moral and fantastic motif is anticipated by the following words of the protagonist of *Notes from Underground*: "I declare to you solemnly that many times I have wanted to become an insect . . . I swear to you, gentlemen, that too much conscience is a sickness, a real and proper sickness." But there is a page from *The Idiot* which stands as a sort of *avant-lettre* to its first printing, and it is where Ippolit, dying, is obsessed in the delirium of his agony with the vision of Holbein's "Dead Christ": "Looking at such a picture, one perceives nature as an immense, merciless, dumb beast, or more correctly, much more correctly speaking, though it sounds strange, in the form of a huge machine of the most modern construction which, dull and insensible, has meaninglessly clutched, crushed and swallowed up a great and priceless Being, a Being worth all of nature and its laws . . . The picture expresses and involuntarily suggests to one the conception of a dark, insolent, unreasoning and eternal Power to which everything is subject . . . I seemed almost to see . . . that blind Power, that deaf Being, obscure and mute. I remember, it seems too, that someone, carrying a candle, showed me an enormous and repugnant spider, seeking to convince me that it was really that dark, deaf and omnipotent Being, and laughing at my disdain." It might almost be said that the last image alludes to the very art of Kafka, which with the sole help of a candle, and laughing at our shuddering, makes us descend into the sewers of being, and guides us across the subterranean labyrinths of conscience.

A fatal sense of myth invests and interprets something which is worth more than books, and that is the very soul of Kafka, which is a special soul, one of those which could not have been born before our time, because through monogenesis the fantasy of a great modern writer, Dostoevski, has begotten it: men believe that a great literary hero is capable of having only a certain number of new-born children baptized with his name during the epoch of his fame and fortune, and they do not know that his example can become a norm and an ideal of life and can generate creatures which resemble him. Now it can be truly said that Kafka is the first living exemplar of the men of the underground, as the autobiographical touch of that very K. may demonstrate, that touch with which he designs two of his principal personages; and I suppose that the critic Groethuysen wanted to suggest to us a similar hypothesis when he spoke these words about him: "A lucid spirit, he knew how to give us news of the abandoned world in which he had lived." But the necessities of art and the laws of life have so acted that in the series of those individuals he appears as a particular and complex example: that which in the work of Dostoevski is represented by the dramatic and dialectical relation of Raskolnikov and Porphyry becomes with him the desperate monologue of a soul, the "voice of one crying in the desert," of a man whose vocal chords are diseased. The futility of his cry for help suffocates every religious breath and extinguishes every possibility of demiurge in Kafka's universe. It was thus that I understood how a creature so constituted would even after death be always alive in the pitying memory of a friend, and how he could not have been born and lived except in that old section of Prague, where still lives the wandering shade of the fabulous rabbi who constructed the Golem by force of clay and cabala.

TROTSKY'S DIARY IN EXILE

The most vivid and lurid personal drama of contemporary history is the struggle between Stalin and Trotsky, which for one of the two rivals ended in crime and triumph, for the other in death and defeat. Future historians will be bound to consider the winner as the protagonist of that drama, and the loser as its antagonist. On the other hand, the poets of the future, if attracted by such a theme, will reverse the roles and assign to Trotsky the major and nobler part. This is another way of saying that they will be tempted to see a tragic agony in that struggle, and a tragic hero in the character who lost the fight and paid for this failure with his head. From the viewpoint of the personalities involved, they will be right in doing so. But from a more universal viewpoint they will be wrong. Taking Hegel's definition as a norm, tragedy is the conflict between a higher and a lower law. Yet in that struggle or drama Stalin and Trotsky represented and upheld one and the same law; and it matters little that the former played the same role far more crudely than the latter. The tragic hero is such in public as well as in private terms: his personal catastrophe warns us of the evils which threaten the social fabric, or the condition of man. But those evils would have equally affected the destinies of Russia, as well as those of the West and of the whole world, even if Trotsky had won the fight instead of losing it. That is why the drama of his life and career may be viewed as a tragedy only if we look at it from the perspective of individual, rather than of general, values; if we treat it as a biographical accident, not as a historical event.

Nothing proves this point better than the only extant journal of Trotsky, which, significantly enough, he kept during the sixth year of what he himself called his "third exile," which was also to be the last. That exile had started in 1929 when, deported from Stalin's Russia, he had found his first refuge in Turkey; and it was to end in 1940 when, unprotected even in his Mexican sanctuary, he literally fell under the ax of Stalin's executioners. Trotsky wrote this diary for the most of 1935 or, more precisely, from February 7 to September 8. The period so covered coincided with the closing phase of his two-year stay in France and with the opening phase of his stay in Norway, which was to last for more than another year. In all, seven months: four of which were spent in the French provinces, in a little town near Grenoble, and three in the surroundings of Oslo, the Norwegian capital. Because of this shift from one residence to another, as well as the worsening of his health, Trotsky was far less faithful to the daily task of diary writing during the second half of this period of time: he failed, for instance, to enter a single notation in his journal for the whole month of August.

After his death, the three notebooks in which that journal had been jotted down were deposited in the Harvard University Library, as part of that Trotsky Archive which preserves all the papers he had managed to salvage since the revolution. With the permission of his widow, Harvard University Press published the journal for the first time in 1958, in a little book simply entitled *Trotsky's Diary in Exile, 1935*. This precious volume contains in the appendix a moving testament that Trotsky wrote in 1940, between February 27 and March 3, or less than six months before his violent end, which occurred on August 27 of the same year. This document, too, is made public for the first time. Both testament and diary are given in the excellent translation of Elena Zarudnaya, which is at once highly readable and fully reliable. They are presented to the reader with a publisher's foreword, uncommonly discreet and predominantly factual. The translated text is provided with a set of useful notes, gathered and compiled by several competent hands.

The importance of this diary is to be seen not only in the great figure who wrote it, but also in the events which dictated most of its entries. 1935 was, in the life of Trotsky, as well as in the history of contemporary Europe, if not a crucial at least a critical year. Having risen to power two years before, Hitler was then rearming Germany, while the Western powers were already blindly developing their suicidal appeasement policies. Frightened by the riots and the armed leagues of the Right, France was reacting to the internal and external menace by establishing the Popular Front and by signing a treaty of friendship with Stalin. Soviet Russia was becoming fashionable and respectable abroad, and seemed to be willing to serve the cause of peace within the framework of the League of Nations. Yet at home Stalin was submitting the revolution to a bloody Thermidor, and was destroying his enemies in the merciless purges which followed in the wake of Kirov's assassination during the preceding year. Not content with hounding Trotsky's followers, Stalin was about to persecute the relatives whom the exiled leader had left in Soviet Russia, including his son Seryozha, who was to be arrested while the diary was being written. The journal reflects all this, as well as the aging and the ailing of the writer, his material hardships, and his sense of psychological estrangement and moral loneliness.

Yet the author seldom treats these pages as if they were the report of a personal ordeal, or the mirror of his own intimate self. In the opening lines he defines this journal as a kind of political *pis aller*: "The diary is not a literary form I am especially fond of; at the moment I would prefer the daily newspaper. But there is none available . . . Cut off from political action, I am obliged to resort to such ersatz journalism as a private diary." A month and a half later, realizing again that he had been keeping "a political and literary diary rather than a personal one," the writer observes: "And could it actually be otherwise? For politics and literature constitute in essence the content of my personal life. I need only take pen in hand and my thoughts of their own accord arrange themselves for *public* exposition." Unable to write polemical pieces or political leaders for a mass audience, Trotsky writes here his own journalism for himself, while becoming at the same time a critical reader of the journalism written by others. This is why he fills this diary with pasted clippings from many newspapers, all of them unfriendly ones. After all, such a man cannot fail to be deeply interested "in the working of the deeper social forces as they appear reflected" in what he calls, with an image probably taken from Gogol's epigraph to *The Inspector General*, "the crooked mirror of the press."

We may define as journalistic in the best sense all the polemical pages in which Trotsky expresses his judgments, opinions, and attitudes in regard to the current political situation in the West. His *bête noire* is Western socialism, especially in its French version, so typically represented for him by such a figure as Léon Blum. Its alliance with the Third International and Moscow confirms Trotsky's view that Western socialism is the accomplice of both Stalinism and Fascism. To prove, almost *ad absurdum*, this view, Trotsky does not hesitate to cite no less an authority than his main enemy: "Stalin once delivered himself of an aphorism: Social Democracy and Fascism are twins! Nowadays it is Social Democracy and Stalinism — Blum and Cachin — that have become twins. They are doing everything in their power to ensure the victory of Fascism." A Western reader not committed to Marxist and Trotskyite ideology can hardly accept this judgment, or approve of the ferocity with which Trotsky treats Léon Blum; yet to blame Trotsky for this, one would have to forget all that happened in the years that followed, from Munich to the Nazi-Soviet Pact.

This is another way of saying that Trotsky seems to have sensed the turn of events: and this is enough to save the diary from becoming entirely dated, as such documents usually do. Since these pages are already so many years old, it is no wonder that many of Trotsky's observations have grown stale and meaningless. History has run faster than ever in the last quarter of a century, as we know all too well. Even Trotsky's foresight may occasionally fare all too badly when confronted with a hindsight for which we are still paying dearly. Yet, in the main, one could apply to Trotsky's predictions what Trotsky himself says of Engels' "prognoses," as he calls them: "Not infrequently they run ahead of the actual course of events." But, "In the last analysis Engels is always right." Thus Trotsky's claim that "the machinery of neo-Bonapartism *was* evident" already in that stage of the French crisis he was then witnessing, although hardly valid for the Third Republic and the France of 1935, suddenly seems to hold true for the France of 1958, for that Fourth Republic which is now dying under our own eyes. Right as he is in seeing the coming apocalypse, Trotsky seems, however, to be wrong in his expectation of the palingenesis that should accompany or follow it. Of his prophecy of the ultimate triumph of that Fourth International, this diary speaks surprisingly little except for saying: "The cause of the new International will move forward." Trotsky's International, the only one wholly composed of good Marxists, resembles a little that International wholly composed of decent people of which the meek old Jew Gedali dreams in Isaac Babel's *Red Cavalry*; and such a likeness may well reveal the messianic and utopian side of the thought of the man who was perhaps the last representative of scientific Marxism.

This, after all, is not so strange when we realize that Trotsky's mind was of the kind which sees the forest better than the trees. This holds particularly true in regard to his attitude toward Stalin and Stalinism. Trotsky perceives and apprehends the abstraction better than the concrete figure at the center of the phenomenon itself. If I say so, it is because it does honor to Trotsky rather than discredit. It is obvious that, if finally Trotsky yields to the belief that "the motive of *personal revenge* has always been a considerable factor in the repressive policies of Stalin," he does so reluctantly and against his best judgment. An all too direct experience prevents Trotsky from denying that Stalin is now running down not only the political associates but also the relatives whom his rival had been forced to leave within the tyrant's reach, and that their persecution cannot be fully explained on the grounds of political expediency alone. Yet as long as he can, Trotsky tries to interpret in pure Marxist terms the devious behavior of his adversary, what Trotsky himself calls Stalin's "mode of struggle," his habit of waging political warfare "on another plane" than the ideological one.

This does not mean that in his diary there is no *ad hominem* criticism of Stalin and his servants, but that such a criticism is found in only limited quantity. As far as Stalin is concerned, it varies from the statement, both indulgent and supercilious, that the latter "underestimated the danger of a struggle purely on the plane of ideas," to a lashing indictment of his intellectual cowardice and spiritual barbarism: "that savage fears ideas." Yet normally Trotsky prefers to affirm that, if Stalin behaves as he does, it is only because the economic and social reality he represents forces him to act in that, and no other, way. "The very possibility of such a mode of struggle," says Trotsky, "had been created by the formation and consolidation of an elaborate and self-sufficient social milieu — the Soviet bureaucracy." If Trotsky chooses such an explanation, it is because it is the one which, in the long run, does least violence to his most cherished intellectual beliefs. It is out of a deep loyalty to those beliefs that he compels himself to look at his own individual plight, even at the tragedy of his family, from a high, unimpassioned, and impersonal standpoint. It is only fair to say that, by transcending any private concern or human anguish, Trotsky succeeds in judging even his own personal enemy according to his own lights, and yet as objectively or, at least, as little subjectively as possible.

Although he fails to realize that the method he has chosen is perhaps ill suited to understanding the personality of Stalin, if not the social reality of Stalinism, Trotsky is well aware that the perspective he could not fail to adopt involves great risks on his part. He knows in advance that his attempt to judge Stalin objectively may well end by legitimizing Stalinism, by providing it with the august sanction of historical necessity. Yet Trotsky faces this danger squarely, and does not shirk the harsh intellectual duty of acknowledging that Stalin and Stalinism are something more than mere deviations or oddities in the march of socialism. He is even willing to admit that "in view of the prolonged decline in the international revolution the victory of the bureaucracy — and consequently of Stalinism — was foreordained." After all, if Trotsky had tried to explain Stalin differently, or to explain Stalinism away, he would have been left with only two alternatives, both unacceptable. The first would have been a purely moralistic rejection of the new Soviet order as an error and horror, as the wicked creation of a willful monster whom the whim of chance, rather than the dialectics of history, had unexpectedly placed at the revolution's helm. Trotsky does not lose any time in refuting such a hypothesis; he does so when he defines Stalin "as the half-conscious expression of the second chapter of the revolution, of its 'morning after.' "

By that significant adjective, Trotsky explicitly rejects the view that Stalin was the evil genius of the revolution, a view still held by so many disappointed party members, fellow travelers, and parlor pinks. Yet, in a sense, the man who is really "half-conscious" here is Trotsky himself. One may even claim that, while uttering that definition, Trotsky speaks unconsciously or subconsciously: beyond and behind the evident intention to refute the sentimental and pathetic view of the idealists of the revolution, who condemn Stalin as a monster, what inspires these words may well be the latent desire to refute the opposite view, held by all the cynics and the opportunists of the Left, which attribute Stalin's victory to the fact that, whether good or evil, he was a genius after all. It is obvious that Trotsky can accept this alternative hypothesis even less readily than the other one. His whole personality, or at least his most intimate being, reacts against it. This is why, almost in the same passage, he denies that very hypothesis again: this time not unconsciously or obliquely, but directly and deliberately, in a

straightforward statement and in clear-cut words. It is worth remarking that he does so by attacking all those who hold that hypothesis, not as cynical opportunists, as for the most part they were, but
rather as ignorant dolts: "The result which the idle observers and
fools attribute to the personal forcefulness of Stalin, or at least to
his exceptional cunning, stemmed from causes lying deep in the
dynamics of social forces."

Trotsky may grant Stalin and his henchmen everything except
a single blessing: what is for him the supreme endowment, that is,
intelligence. At the same time, while denying them any sense and
understanding as individual beings, he is willing to bestow a kind
of superior, if cynical, wisdom on the social group to which they
belong, although that group embodies all that Trotsky stands
against. That group, which Trotsky calls a caste, is identical with
what Milovan Djilas was later to label "the new class." Trotsky,
the first to indict the "new class," seems to have recognized in the
earliest manifestations of its class-consciousness so much self-awareness as to amount to a kind of insight. After evoking a meeting of
the Politboro where Molotov, Rudzutak, and others behaved toward
him as uncouth boors, Trotsky concludes: "But that, of course, was
not the main thing. Behind the ignorance, the narrowness, the ob-
stinacy and hostility of separate individuals, one could almost feel
with one's fingers the social features of a privileged caste, very
sensitive, very perceptive, very enterprising in everything that concerned *its own interests.*" Notwithstanding the closing words, inspired by the most orthodox historical materialism, and significantly
italicized in the original text, the writer's willingness to find a
meaningful and purposeful intelligence even in the forces which
represent a negative phase in the historical process, in the very
antithesis to the thesis he professes, seems to suggest that Trotsky
thinks here more like a Hegelian than like a Marxist.

Trotsky goes so far in his attempt to deny Stalin any intelligent
or independent policy, any freedom of action even in the most
restricted sense, as to claim that the very decision to deport Trotsky
had been suggested to Stalin by Trotsky himself. To this purpose
he tells a story which sounds both improbable and true. The story
refers to the visit a Soviet engineer paid to Trotsky during the latter's banishment to the Kazakh city of Alma-Ata. Despite all appearances to the contrary, Trotsky claims that the visitor was an

agent sent by Stalin "to feel my pulse." Trotsky sees the proof of this in the visitor's query whether his host thought that a reconciliation between him and Stalin was still possible. Trotsky quotes himself as replying that "at that moment there could be no question of reconciliation, not because I *did not want it*, but because Stalin *could not make peace with me*." Trotsky reports that he closed his reply with the prophecy that the matter could only "come to a sticky end," since "Stalin cannot settle it any other way." He maintains not only that his answer to that question was conveyed to Stalin, but that it determined, rather than precipitated, Stalin's decision to exile him.

The story itself could be viewed as a petulant anecdote that Trotsky tells merely to argue that he knew Stalin's mind even better than Stalin himself. I think, however, that it should be treated as a significant apologue, the moral of which is that Trotsky was a man who would rather be right than be president: in his own case, general secretary of the Russian Communist Party, rather than leader *ex officio* and *de facto* of the international revolutionary movement. What this telltale episode shows in effect is that Trotsky's *amour propre* led him to believe retrospectively that he had foretold, as well as accepted in advance, his own defeat. As such, it reveals a chink in Trotsky's armor; but the weakness so bared is a noble one. In a sense this story proves the moderation and the limits of Trotsky's *amour de soi*, and points out how impossible it would have been for him to yield for his own benefit to that "cult of personality" of which Stalin stood accused in the Khrushchev report. Trotsky was made of the stuff of the Robespierres rather than the Napoleons: he could not conceive of action as divorced from right, as long as it was the right of the revolution. Above all, Trotsky could not admit of power except as a weapon fashioned by intelligence to defend or uphold ideas, and to rule with them.

The lesson that the whole of this journal teaches us is that, although he rationalized defeat, Trotsky never sublimated it. It is this ability to accept political reality even when distasteful that explains why he prefers one image rather than another to suggest the role of the Marxist, of the revolutionary, of the Trotskyite himself. Here Trotsky rejects Max Eastman's metaphor of the revolutionary as an engineer, because it implies an all too mechanistic conception of both social reality and political action: and the scorn of such a rejection may be due to the fact that the same metaphor had wide currency even in Russia, where Stalin was then defining the Soviet writers as "engineers of the human soul." At least thrice in these pages Trotsky replaces that metaphor with his favorite image of the revolutionary as a doctor, which he develops so movingly in the passage where he likens the purge of his own followers in Soviet Russia to the killing of their medical helpers by ignorant peasants during the cholera epidemics which affected the Russia of the Tsars: "Distractedly the masses watch the brutal beating of the doctors, the only people who know both the disease and the cure."

The fitness of the image of the Marxist as doctor may be seen also in the ultimate indifference with which both look at the effects brought about by the laws of necessity — violence in history and death in the natural world. It is indeed with a sort of medical impassivity that Trotsky rehearses again in his mind the attitude he took once and for all when he learned for the first time of the slaughter of the Imperial family, which had been decided on in his absence, primarily by Lenin himself. Even in retrospect, Trotsky approves of that decision without reservation, justifying or, rather, explaining it with the following words: "The execution of the Tsar's family was needed not only in order to frighten, horrify, and dishearten the enemy, but also in order to shake up our own ranks, to show them that there was no turning back, that ahead lay either complete victory or complete ruin." Later he adds, as an afterthought, that judicial procedure would have made impossible the killing of the Tsar's children, which was, however, required by the terrorism of the act.

Up to this point Trotsky thinks and speaks like a practitioner willing to save his patient through the ordeal of surgery, at the cost of one of his organs or limbs. But at the end Trotsky acts more like the anatomist who has performed or watched an autopsy, and wants to forget all that bloody mess: "When I was abroad I read in *Poslednie Novosti* ["The Last News," a Russian emigré newspaper] a description of the shooting, the burning of the bodies, etc. How much of all this is true and how much is invented, I have not the least idea, since I was never curious about *how* the sentence was carried out and, frankly, do not understand such curiosity." Here Trotsky becomes inhuman. What makes him unable to understand such curiosity is his outright insensitivity to either one of the two psychological impulses which may motivate it: on one side, the pathological urge of morbidity; on the other, a moral or religious concern, a sense of piety and pity. Thus Trotsky fails not only to shed a single tear, but even to murmur a single word, on the grave of the Tsar's children, whom the revolution chose as guiltless sacrificial lambs. Unaware of any contradiction, blind to the tragic irony of his position, Trotsky refuses to pay such tribute of compassion at the very moment he is deeply worried about the destiny of his son Seryozha, the only member of his family who always avoided any political commitment or responsibility, and whom Stalin was then about to sacrifice as the scapegoat for his father, as the victim of both Stalinism and Trotskyism.

There is a striking contrast between Trotsky's reluctance to pay attention even to the negative side of Stalin's personality and the eagerness with which he emphasizes the most touching aspects of Lenin's psychology. He likes to catch Lenin in the moments he would "fall in love" with a fellow worker or any human being deserving his affection or respect; or while exhibiting a rare sensitivity, an exceptional delicacy of feeling, as he did when he sensed that Trotsky would feel uneasy entering the tragic Moscow of the fall of 1918 with the pots of flowers a bodyguard had ceremoniously put into his car. Yet, despite these tender touches, he paints a portrait of Lenin which tends to impress us with the heroic stature, with the monumental greatness, of its model. Nothing is more significant in this regard than the passage where he avows that Lenin was the only indispensable man for the triumph of October 1917. By doing so, Trotsky makes Lenin the peer of Marx, while putting himself only on a par with Engels. In an extraordinary passage he likens the task of the latter to the mission of Christ, who came to bring God the Father nearer to mortal men: "Alongside the Olympian Marx, Engels is more 'human,' more approachable." This comparison may well be read like an unconscious autobiographical allusion to the kind of role Trotsky liked to think he had played vis-à-vis Lenin himself.

At times, Trotsky's reminiscences of Lenin are almost hagiographic, in effect if not in intent. What is even more remarkable is that, in all his references to Madame Trotsky, of which this diary is so full, he employs the language of devotion and the imagery of mysticism. His wife is the only person seemingly endowed with what Trotsky unashamedly calls a soul: a soul which reveals itself through an enchanting voice, echoing the unique magic of its own "inner music." The noble and wild charm of her youth, which this journal recaptures in two splendid occasions, re-evoking Natasha while performing an acrobatic feat during a Parisian visit and while submitting with both humility and self-respect to the indignities attending an immigrant's landing in New York, seems to have survived unchanged through that old age which Trotsky defines as the worst of all vices. That charm endures because it is a spiritual gift, and if her husband is still able to see it, it is because he looks at her with the eyes of the spirit. Trotsky's affection for his wife is not a mere attachment, but a profound, genuine love. And the man experiencing it knows that love can utter only religious and sacramental words: it is nature, not convention, that makes love speak in such a holy and symbolic tongue, and no other.

It is both strange and wonderful that Trotsky finds it fit to compare the ordeal he and his wife are now undergoing to the tragic lot of the rebellious archpriest Avvakum and his faithful spouse. Avvakum was deported to Siberia for his refusal to accept the ecclesiastical and ritual reforms of Peter the Great. And it is with a grief so pure as to allow of neither self-pity nor self-irony that Trotsky quotes from Avvakum's autobiography the words which the old cleric once exchanged with the companion of his life, while marching together in the snows of the Siberian winter: "she, poor soul, began to reproach me, saying: 'How long, archpriest, is this suffering to be?' And I said, 'Markovna, unto our very death.' And she, with a sigh, answered: 'So be it, Petrovich, let us be getting on our way.' "

It is this courage and patience, the courage of Trotsky-Avvakum and the patience of Natasha-Markovana, which dictate the manifold testament that appears at the end of this book. In that document Trotsky reaffirms again with moving eloquence both his loyalty to the revolutionary ideal and his love for his wife. There he also faces unflinchingly the cruel vision of death. He knows that his end is near, although he expects it not from the hand of man, but from the hand of God. He even conceives the possibility of a violent death, which he however envisages as self-inflicted, in case he should be threatened "with a long-drawn-out invalidism" and with the loss of his mental powers. Yet, while thinking and writing thus, while staring in the very face of death, he can look at once with a loving eye at the green grass beneath, and at the blue sky above, the walls of that Mexican house which is both his fortress and his jail, and which will be his tomb. Yes, "life is beautiful," even then and there, despite present misery and imminent death.

Both testament and diary prove again that Trotsky is a first-rate author, one of the outstanding prose writers of his nation and time. He is not only this; he is also an excellent critic, as shown by his penetrating comments on the books he has been reading. No unfriendly judge of Soviet letters ever found anything better than his mocking definition of proletarian fiction, of the all too official and all too edifying products of "socialist realism," as "assembly-line romance." Although primarily interested in ideas, Trotsky shows himself in this diary also a shrewd observer of the human comedy, even of its most farcical side.

There is no doubt that his power as a writer rests on what one might call a sort of imaginative journalism: on his ability to be at once a vivid reporter and a visionary essayist. Those who will try to give a final assessment of Trotsky's contribution to literature will have to face the issue implied in such an attempt, which is the problematic and controversial question of the man of action as a writer. To make their task easier, they will do well to compare Trotsky with other leaders who wielded the pen no less successfully than the sword. The most obvious contemporary parallel is with a figure whom Trotsky would consider the strangest of all his possible bedfellows: Winston Churchill. The utility of such a juxtaposition would be to emphasize not so much their similarities as their differences. Besides many other differences, Trotsky is the one of the two who is an intellectual. Churchill is an aristocrat, even in the sense that he feels hardly at home among ideas: he prefers to dwell among traditions and values, among *beaux gestes* and high deeds. We can imagine Churchill painting a powerful, personal portrait of Clemenceau the Tiger; but we would hardly expect of him to draw from that portrait such a generalized inference as Trotsky does: "The main impediment that prevented Clemenceau — as well as many other French intellectuals — from advancing beyond radicalism was *rationalism*." This diagnosis, far from being merely ideological, is a highly philosophical one, revealing the cosmopolitan range and the cultivation of Trotsky's mind, his awareness of the famous antinomy which Kant bequeathed to Romantics and Hegelians, of the sharp distinction between classical Gallic intellect (*Verstand*) and modern Teutonic reason (*Vernunft*). In brief, all that Churchill has ever composed is monumental (even if the monuments so erected celebrate something higher than mere self), while everything Trotsky wrote, despite the conflicts of his nature and the contradictions of his temper, of which this diary is such an eloquent proof, is always *illuministic*, in the better sense of that term.

OTHER LITERARY PAPERS

THE DEATH OF THE SENSE
OF TRAGEDY

Nietzsche said in *Ecce Homo*, "I promise the advent of a tragic age: the highest art in the saying of yea to life, tragedy, will be born again when mankind has the knowledge of the hardest, but most necessary of wars behind it." And Leon Trotsky, apostle of permanent revolution (who announced that our age would be the classic age of revolution), unwittingly echoed Nietzsche's prophecy when he stated, in *Literature and Revolution*, that the poetry of the future will manifest itself by a rebirth of the ancient tragic spirit.

In contrast to this postulation of an imminent resurrection of tragedy, the salient characteristic of modern poetry is what might be termed a *death of the sense of tragedy*. As a matter of fact, tragedy has come to full flower in only two moments of Europe's intellectual life: in Greece during the century which began at Marathon and in Elizabethan England. The Spanish theater of the late Renaissance and the so-called classic tragedy of the great French century are not tragedy in the strict sense of the word. In Spain we have not tragedy, but drama: a poetic, picturesque, and popular drama, which the Spanish poets were well inspired to name *comedia*. In France the only masterpiece outside the theater of Racine and Molière is the *Cid*, which Corneille did not hesitate to define as tragicomedy, while Racine gave us an authentic tragedy only in the isolated miracle of *Phèdre*.

Even the Middle Ages which created the Christian drama were unaware of the tragic. It may not be inaccurate to suppose that Christianity, and particularly medieval and Roman Christianity, is incapable of conceiving life in tragic terms. In Christianity sin and the fall are canceled and transcended by the most universal of cosmic and metaphysical optimisms; and perhaps the greatest medieval Christian poet instinctively felt this when he gave his sacred poem the paradoxical title of *Commedia*.

The Christian spirit is incapable of producing tragedy, because tragedy is poetry of the consciousness of evil. It does not represent a struggle between God and the Devil, but a conflict between Man and God in which Man is fated to succumb. Tragedy conceives the Demoniac (which is only the myth-name for injustice) as an integral part of the Divine. For this reason the early Protestants were more disposed than other Christians to understand the nature of tragedy; but among both Lutherans and Calvinists the doctrine of grace proceeded to assume the extreme aspect of a modern *amor fati*. They were, in Aristotelian terms, unable to feel the moment of pity and felt only the moment of terror.

In recent times Protestant rigorism has been in a position to educate itself to a sense of tragedy in greater measure than has been the culture of the Catholic nations; at least the shadow, if not the substance, of tragedy has appeared, for example, in some of Ibsen's plays. In a Protestant atmosphere likewise was born the work which, with *Mourning Becomes Electra*, is the tragic masterpiece of the Catholic Eugene O'Neill: *Desire under the Elms* is inconceivable without the notion of the Puritan conscience. Moreover, the only great dramatic poet of modern France, and the Catholic poet par excellence, Paul Claudel, unable to resume the main direction of classical French tragedy, has returned to the medieval mystery or, as in the more recent *Le Soulier de satin*, to the Spanish *comedia*.

Shakespeare overcomes this religious dialectic of the spirit of tragedy. He is less of the Reformation than of the Renaissance, not the Renaissance of Catholic Italy but that other far-flung Renaissance which touches all times. Santayana's judgment, in the second volume of his memoirs, "I believe it was Protestantism which so completely stifled the Elizabethan genius," does not imply that Elizabethan tragedy was of Catholic inspiration; it simply condemns the Reformation's moralistic and classicizing rationalism that destroyed it.

The dramatic forms produced by Renaissance and Catholic Italy were the pastoral and, later, the melodrama. The latter began as an attempt to reconstruct, even to the musical accompaniment, the ancient Greek tragedy; but the spirit which dominated it from the beginning was that of the eclogue and the idyl. Nietzsche admirably understood this relationship among opera, Italian music, and pastoral poetry; he noted its duration to the epoch of Rousseau, and judged it a phenomenon antithetic to the tragic spirit.

The Italian pastoral merged on the one side into opera and, on the other, into an ideal neither Christian nor pagan: a dream of perfection which substituted for the retrospective nostalgia of a Paradise Lost or of an Age of Gold the vision of a future age in which a sacred and a profane love should triumph equally, a future wrought of bliss instead of passion. If the medieval spirit, which partially survived in the Renaissance, expressed itself dramatically in the Calderonian concept of *life as dream*, the Renaissance spirit, insofar as it reached the threshold of our age, expressed itself particularly in the dream of natural innocence and primitive felicity. The European cultural consciousness was never farther from the tragic spirit than in the eighteenth century, because tragedy is the opposite of utopia.

Nietzsche, who asserted that Greek tragedy was born of the *spirit of music*, never defined this spirit as heroic, but preferred to call it Dionysian. If at first he thought to see in Wagner the man who had revived ancient tragedy by means of music, one of the reasons for his later disappointment was precisely his recognition that the Wagnerian opera was rather epic than tragic. This, and many changes in his critical standards and aesthetic ideals, explain Nietzsche's return to Italian music and his later love for French classicism. Despite the poetic greatness of Racine, his drama (apart from *Phèdre*) does not succeed in reviving the tragic spirit. Although it remains among the loftiest artistic products of the state of mind which dominated European culture from the Renaissance to Rousseau, it is no more than eclogue in dramatic form. Hence the typical Racinean masterpiece is not the tragedy of *Phèdre* or the Christian drama of *Athalie*, but the perfect and delicate history of *Bérénice*, which Brunetière justly defined as an idyl.

It is therefore necessary to conclude that the European literary tradition from the Middle Ages on — with the single exception of Elizabethan England — knew no other form of dramatic poetry than comedy on the one side and Christian drama and pastoral or musical tale on the other. Shakespeare, who wrote histories, tragedies, and comedies, and who gave us one of the most sublime variations of the pastoral theme in *A Midsummer Night's Dream*, was never able to give us a poetic interpretation of the spirit and form of the Christian drama; he found no place for that genre in the immense gallery of his work. Everyman can be neither a comic character nor a tragic hero.

This is the fundamental reason that Goethe's *Faust* is not a tragedy. The intellectual and moral stature of the protagonist has made us forget that *Faust* is at bottom only a rare and elevated version of the type of Everyman. Faust is not only *homo humanus*, but also *homo sapiens*: he is only a humanistic and romantic sublimation of the Christian drama. The common test of the happy ending, the final redemption, sufficiently demonstrates that it is not a tragedy.

Among other causes, the example of *Faust* encouraged the first romantics to consider the mixed forms the supreme types of drama, thereby opposing themselves to what the neoclassic Napoleon termed, in his conversation with Goethe at Erfurt, *les genres tranchés*. And this despite the fact that the German romantics, especially the Schlegels, gave us the first sympathetic interpretation of Greek tragedy, whose greatness had remained inaccessible to the classical tradition from the Alexandrians to Seneca, and from the Renaissance theoreticians to Boileau and his school. One of the chief services of the romantics was opposing Greek *poetry* to Latin *literature*, Hellenistic genius to the classical tradition which considered itself the heir of that genius and the incorporator of its poetry.

Yet, although the Schlegels venerated Greek tragedy as the loftiest of poetry, they felt it was a form which the modern spirit could not revive. The modern master of tragedy could be only Shakespeare. This judgment was correct historically and critically, but on the theoretical side the romantics erred in basing it on two unessential factors, of which the first is the doctrine of the mixture of comic and tragic.

This mixture is the single element which Elizabethan tragedy has in common with the Spanish *comedia*, but only in the latter does the comic perform an essential function. *Don Quixote* admits the ultimate validity of the ridiculous, and even Sancho Panza bears a message. The most solemnly Catholic work of Castilian drama, Calderón's masterpiece, can be reduced to comedy but not translated into tragedy; the skeptic may reserve his right to smile at it, but the mystic has little reason to weep over *life* which is nothing but *dream*.

In the Spanish *comedia*, therefore, the comic element is an integral part of the drama itself, while in Elizabethan tragedy it is only a decorative element, a comedy of detail. It represents a moment of rest from the tragic tension, a pause in the peripateia, a contrast rendering more intense the surprise in the face of the imminent catastrophe. The comic episodes are only interludes; the characters, clownish, minor, or anonymous figures. Even Falstaff is only an enormous Thersites. In Shakespearean tragedy, the mission of the comic is secondary and subordinate; it is sufficient to cite the court jester who follows King Lear into misfortune, and who is — after the protagonist — perhaps the most tragic figure of Shakespeare's gloomiest tragedy.

The other error of the romantics was overvaluing (in accordance with Schiller's predilection rather than Goethe's) the importance of the historical element in Shakespeare's work, which is not properly divisible according to the traditional triple classification but exists in only two categories: tragedy and comedy. The histories are merely tragedies without the title. History is conceived by Shakespeare in the manner of classical and humanistic historiography, as monumental history. Such a monumentalism gives to history the character of fable and myth. The romantics could not understand the simultaneously primitive and humanistic character of Shakespeare's imagination, his lack of differentiation between chronicle and legend, between history and myth; and when they praised his historical tragedies as the example which modern drama should have followed, they felt the historicity of those plays only as a scene-painting and evocative particular, as temporal color and local color.

An historicity thus conceived has erudite, philological, and scientific roots, but certainly not poetic ones. It consists primarily in denying to anachronism the right of access to the field of literary fancy. The literary historicity of the romantics was only an anticipation wholly formal and external, picturesque and decorative, of the modern historical sense, or historism. Now historism does not mean merely a capacity for archeological reconstruction of the past; it means an intimate understanding of the spirit of the age and civilization and, what is more important, a dialectical reconciliation of all the contradictions, of all the antinomies of each epoch. It implies a legalizing and legitimizing attitude toward every usurpation which the human spirit commits in its history. In religious terms, historism might be defined as annulment or abolition of the sense of guilt, of sin, and of evil, within the historical consciousness.

But tragedy is nothing other than poetic consciousness of the sense of evil. Such a conception is, by itself, sufficient to demonstrate the incompatibility of the tragic spirit with the historical sense. Romantic drama was, therefore, destined to fail, because it showed itself almost entirely as historical tragedy. In this respect, the historical tragedies of Schiller and Manzoni were results no happier than the novels of Walter Scott.

The close relation between romanticism and realism is well known, or — to use cultural in place of literary terms — between historism and scientism. What Taine called the historical reason and the scientific reason are, as his work shows, only two aspects of the same phenomenon; and everyone knows the rapport which exists between the philosophic attitude of positivism and the artistic attitude of naturalism. The naturalistic experiment, like the romantic, showed itself incapable of rising to the sense of tragedy: the least tragic Ibsen is the one of *Ghosts*. The chronicle fact, the *tranche de vie*, turned out to be even less susceptible of tragic transcendence than the historic fact.

At the heart of the tragic sense there is, beyond doubt, a religious pulsation unattainable by any culture of skeptical or empirical disposition, which is to say, by any culture of historical and scientific disposition. Christianity failed to give us a tragedy, not because it was a religion, but because the myth of *Paradise Regained* exerted in it a greater force than that of *Paradise Lost*. If Christianity cannot admit the possibility of a long, and perhaps eternal, triumph of evil, so that in it faith kills terror, and hope, despite the practice of charity, makes pity an almost gratuitous sentiment, historism and scientism do not consider evil a reality, even relatively, but look upon it only as a myth or a metaphysical abstraction.

For the sense of tragedy to be reborn, modern culture must overcome scientism and historism, and must render more absolute, integral, and acute — one would almost say less Hebraic and Christian — our consciousness of evil. The traditional Occidental conception of man must be overthrown, particularly the form which it assumes in contemporary thought, because it is just this which prevents poetry from giving shape to an ideal or exemplary type of tragic hero.

Recent thought considers man only in the species *superman* or *mass-man*. Romantic titanism and decadent satanism recognized in the exceptional individual only an angel or a demon: for Nietzsche the true man is at once satyr and demigod, hero and centaur, an animal god or a divine animal. At the opposite extreme, political and social preachment, humanitarian or philanthropic thought, see in the common man the *type-man*, man through antonomasia, the only one which exists and which counts, independently of what he may be worth: an Everyman without God.

The tragic hero cannot be given to us from the superman; Aristotle was right in saying that he must be more elevated than the common man, but not too great or perfect, and unfortunate rather than wicked. The true tragic hero is Oedipus Rex, not Prometheus, as the heroine is Phaedra or Medea and not Madame Bovary or Hedda Gabler. The angelic, the demoniac, and the titanic have no place in tragedy. Dante obeyed this principle when he reduced Capaneus to a grotesque character; and it explains why Ibsen's only truly tragic figure is Brand, while Peer Gynt is but a lesser Faust.

On the other hand, the tragic hero cannot come from the mass-man. The type of person whom Andrew called *someone in gray* is a figure neither dramatic nor comic, but allegorical, abstract. For this reason works of peasant setting as powerful as Tolstoy's *Power of Darkness* and O'Neill's *Desire under the Elms* are dramas and not tragedies. They are, moreover, vitiated by the error of naturalism. The mass-man of modern thought cannot become a tragic hero; his nature fits him to be a voice in the chorus, and thus he was portrayed in T. S. Eliot's *Murder in the Cathedral*. This work comes close to being a modern tragedy, but it falls short because it is a too conscious and too literary work, a transcendent exercise in style, a tragedy constructed within the narrow limits of the English closet-drama.

As tragedy is always religious in a high if not literal sense, since the true antagonist is the soul of the hero, whose grief re-echoes in the collective conscience personified by the chorus, so, indeed, it is always historical in the ancient sense of the word, that is to say, capable of representing a military and political action. Its protagonist is nothing but the will of a hero who struggles against obscure and hostile forces and seeks escape for himself and his cause from a catastrophe which always assumes the form of a defeat. Such is the high poetic strategy of tragedy.

The history of recent years has shown us an infinite series of men forced to fight, and condemned to succumb, in a struggle not against their equals, but against an historic force which has assumed for millions of creatures the aspect of a fatality, of a destiny, of a cataclysm — against historical and metaphysical evil, even though it be incarnated in machine-men and materialized in machines constructed by man. As Nietzsche and Trotsky prophesied, it seems almost impossible that the classic age of war and of revolution should not sooner or later produce its own tragedy. The problem is to determine why this tragedy has not yet appeared.

It is certain that tragedy which is lived is not written; and later our capacity for pity and terror, always limited and human, may not be enough, even if multiplied a thousandfold, to re-evoke the historic crisis which we are not yet sure we have survived. How can the barbaric quality of this hecatomb, not of heroes and of armies, but of men and of peoples, be given within the real and ideal limits of dramatic poetry and the tragic stage? Tragedy is elevation, contemplation of human reality from a perspective which, though loftier, does not violate norm and proportion. The enormity of the historic tragedy which we have witnessed could perhaps be better rendered in the manner of the epic, the only poetic form which translates even the excessive and the extraordinary into fable and myth, and turns disproportion into measure.

In the course of the last years, the fate of life and death for millions of individuals has been reduced to a similarly chaotic and primordial relation; and from this point of view the crisis of our time is truly epic material, perhaps even theogonic. But the very fact that Simonne Weil should have turned back to the *Iliad* to be able to give us the sense of the omnipotence of death shows that she felt the peculiar circumstances of our age make it incapable of producing its own epic.

It seems probable that a present-day poet capable of expressing epically the historic tragedy of our time would be incapable of achieving the epic's spirit of serene impartiality and would be unable to concede dignity and honor to figures like Hitler and Quisling. Hitler is not a hero, but a *monstrum naturae*; Quisling, less monster than insect. The poet of the future will not be able to express the historic legend of our time save in the form of fairytale, in which the monstrous is only an aspect of the marvelous; certainly he cannot do it in the form of myth.

As usual, the task of humanizing the demoniacal characters and condoning the manifestations of recent history, impossible to poetry, will be assumed by that great leveler and justifier, written history, historistic historiography. It is even to be feared that, if it survives in the cultural consciousness of the future, this type of history will, as it has done before, perform that task only too well.

A similar work for narrative poetry, following the laws of poetic instead of historical justice, can be done only partially by the novel, which is the principal modern genre. Even though the historical novel is now generally recognized to be an invalid form, more than one mind continues to look upon the novel as a modern epic. Goethe, however, limited this definition in extraordinary fashion, modifying it with an adjective which reacts on the meaning contained in the noun; he called the novel a *subjective epic*. In fact, precisely because subjective, the modern novel is an ironic epic, a caricature of the epic. For this reason the most epic of modern novelists, Balzac, gave to his novel-cycle the title *Human Comedy*. For this reason *War and Peace*, conceived by Tolstoy as a new *Iliad*, is only a parody of the Homeric. In it, epic comparisons are used to place in relief elements which are prosaic and far from heroic; in it, peace and life triumph over war and death: the passiveness of Kutuzov overcomes the energy of Napoleon.

The Occidental novel of our century has made itself ever more lyric. As Ortega y Gasset justly noted (and he had in mind not only Joyce and Proust, but also Dostoevski), it has descended always more from the public world of heroic action toward the private world of emotion and dream, from the realm of the necessary to that of the arbitrary. In short, the modern novel has withdrawn not only from the epic, but even from the dramatic.

Paradoxically, in spite of the opinion expressed by Ortega, Dostoevski is the only modern novelist who possesses a sense of the tragic. The great scenes of his major novels are all tragic catastrophes, and assume the external form of drama also in expression, where passion becomes dialectic and dialogue. What is more important, the protagonists of his novels are all true tragic heroes. In the course of Dmitri's trial, the public official, in whom the author represents the type — odious to him — of the occidentalist, positivist, and liberal, opens in his argument a long digression. In it he condemns the secular obscurantism of the Russian spirit, and he concludes by saying, "There [in Europe] they have Hamlet, and we have only Karamazovs." Dostoevski here gives us a page of sublime and poetic irony; because, as Raskolnikov is our Macbeth, so, if not Dmitri, certainly Ivan Karamazov is the only figure worthy of Hamlet which the literature of modern Europe possesses.

As the works of Tolstoy and Dostoevski show, the epic and the tragic are — despite the contrary opinion of Aristotle — not correlative. The reasons which make it impossible to compose the tragedy of our time differ from, and are perhaps opposed to, those which prevent our writing its epic. One of these reasons is commonplace and simple: there have been too many corpses on the scene of history these last few years. Epic exaggeration, one of the forms assumed by love of the marvelous, makes possible and necessary — as in the *Iliad* and *Song of Roland* — the repeated, recurrent, and sometimes uninterrupted evocation of endless battles and innumerable duels, or — as in the episodes of Ulysses' vengeance or that of Crimilde — of inexorable slaughters and gigantic massacres.

In tragedy, however, from Aristotle on, the principle of limitation and concentration has dominated, not because of technical necessity, but because of definite exigencies of taste. It is the principle of verisimilitude, which was formulated in the first precepts of ancient poetics. By virtue of this principle, tragedy assumed a position opposed to that of the epic (in which the unlikely predominates in the form of exaggeration) and to that of fable and myth — of what was termed the marvelous.

Boileau affirmed that the true may sometimes seem improbable; or, as we would say, that reality, by being poetic, is sometimes excessively melodramatic, sensational, romantic. In spite of the narrowness of Boileau's interpretation, the principle has an undeniable aesthetic validity insofar as it fixes a just and clear distinction between truth and poetry. In the poetics of French tragedy, verisimilitude came to mean also decency, convention, propriety, manner; and this led not only to the reduction to least terms of instances of sudden and violent death, but forthwith to the banishment from the tragic stage of the spectacle of death and its relegation to the wings. But even at the opposite extreme from French tragedy, in the bloody tragedy of Seneca and his Renaissance imitators (especially those in Italy and England), similar theoretical and technical exigencies placed a limit to the frequency and enormity of tragic death. Without the shedding of blood, there is no tragedy; but even the modern spectator, to whom a romantic and naturalistic education has given a taste for the excessive, revolts from witnessing a performance whose inept repetition of the essential tragic bloodshed reduces the drama to slaughter.

From this results poetry's inability to give us the tragedy of recent history, to evoke on the stage that hecatomb of millions, cut down by an omnipresent and multiform death on battlefields and in devastated cities, in prisons and concentration camps, in hospitals and ghettos. The typical and concrete example can be selected only by a novel, a novel which retraces the lyric and subjective current and comes out again at its epic source. According to the traditional concept of Aristotelian and classical poetics, tragedy is a public world, and not a private world, like comedy. For such a tragedy there would remain only the allegorical and symbolic solution, and this would lead it back into the closed life of the medieval mystery and sacred representation. To such forms it would return also if it wished to evoke in spiritual fashion the calvary of mankind; for passion or sacrifice which is either more or less than heroic is not a tragic theme, but the prime subject — even without Christ — of the Christian drama.

The reasons that create the psychological impossibility of conceiving in epic terms the conflict of the two spiritual worlds which confront each other on every battlefield of our earth imply also the impossibility of interpreting that conflict in tragic terms. If tragedy is reborn and wishes to take as its material the history of our time, it neither can nor should choose as its precise subject the duel between the two parties; it should choose the various duels which have taken place within a single party.

Civil war is a worthier subject for tragedy than war between peoples and empires, which is the epic material par excellence. And by the laws of poetic sympathy, the future tragedy will not sing the monstrous conflict between Hitler and Roehm, but rather that between free France and enslaved France, between France fighting and France betrayed; that is, it will not treat the problem of evil alone, for that is a monstrous rather than a heroic subject, but the problem of good and evil, of the history of man. While an epic may spring even from the soil of recent barbarity, tragedy rises only from a high moral and civil conscience.

The loftiest tragic subject which the chronicles of our time offer the poet of the future is the struggle in Russia between the *enemy brothers*, between the left in power and the extreme left of the opposition — a struggle which reached a true and tragic catastrophe in the Moscow trials. And the tragic hero who perhaps will most attract the future Shakespeare or Sophocles is precisely that Leon Trotsky who was the prophet, not only of war and revolution, but also of a resurrection of the supreme and classic art of tragedy.

FOR A LITERARY HISTORIOGRAPHY
BASED ON PARETO'S SOCIOLOGY

1. *Literature and Society*

Antiquity and the Renaissance had considered literature and poetry as direct and almost exclusive expressions of *humanities*; that is, as activities almost identical with the very concept of culture. Such an attitude caused them to be recognized as independent, gratuitous manifestations which man would cultivate in the felicitous moment of *otium*. In this respect the moment of practical activity, called in fact by the derogatory negation, *negotium*, came to represent the inferior world of daily slavery, of suffering, and of toil: a sphere of material necessity in contrast to one of spiritual liberty.

The attempt to establish a contact between the realm of culture and the realm of practical life was accomplished for the first time by the Sophists, who were unable to conceive this relationship except as one of subordination. They replaced, therefore, the conception of the autonomous finality of culture with the idea of its practical instrumentality, of its mediate character. Culture came to be regarded as a means to worldly individual success, as eloquence and rhetoric, as technique. That such an innovation should be considered not only revolutionary, but subversive, is demonstrated by the energetic Socratic and Platonic reaction against the Sophist movement. Socrates was opposed to a cultural conception which no longer regarded spiritual and intellectual activity as a gratuitous search for truth and beauty, but rather as a means to attain ends of a particular and inferior order. Socrates was condemned to drink the hemlock, whereas none of the Sophists ran the risk of meeting the same fate. And yet it is not paradoxical to affirm that, from another point of view, the Sophists were more revolutionary than he. In a certain sense they were the first to affirm the concept of culture as propaganda, and it is precisely for this reason that they were in accord with the demagogues who condemned Socrates.

Thus, certain that we are committing no other anachronism than that of words, we could say that the concept of culture as propaganda became a part of the practice and theory of medieval civilization. In the scholastic period not only philosophy but literature, too, were the voluntary handmaids of theology. And the great Renaissance revolution was nothing more than a sudden powerful return to the classic concept of culture, a reaffirmation of its independence. The intellectual history of the last centuries, down to our own day, is largely reducible to a conflict between these two conceptions: of culture viewed, spiritually and practically, in a state of subjection or in a state of autonomy.

In modern culture, however, there comes to the fore a new current, which manifests itself in a third hypothesis, a hypothesis, that is, more historical, philosophical, and scientific than literary or political in character. According to this theory the relationship between literature and society is one neither of independence nor of subordination, but of reciprocal coordination. Society and literature would be different, but corresponding, manifestations of like causes. The first thinker to present this hypothesis was Vico. His *Scienza nuova* can, in the last analysis, be reduced to the assertion that, on different planes, the same force which creates political and social institutions generates the literature and culture of a nation and an epoch.

It is true that similar ideas seem to flourish later in that France whose philosophy was so vehemently opposed by Vico; but, on further observation, it is to be noted that the ideologists of the France of the Encyclopedia and the Enlightenment were revolutionaries, especially in the sense that they were the first to affirm in reverse form the old idea of subordination. For them culture and literature were, to be sure, propaganda and instruments of action, but of a future action: society and history itself were to subordinate their reality to the ideals of literature. The great discovery made by the movement which is called in so many languages by the same word, *Illuminismo* and *Siècle des lumières, Enlightenment* and *Aufklärung,* is essentially the certainty of the historical efficacy of education. The most important novelty of this viewpoint consists in the affirmation of the absolute validity of ideologies of utopias. It is in this sense that the statement made by Taine in *L'Ancien Régime,* according to which rationalism and classical poetry were the causes of the Revolution, continues to have a certain value. Poetic reason presumes, indeed, the right to subordinate political reason to itself.

Only the liberal reform and the conservative reaction to the ideas of the Revolution, along with the agitations of preromantic and romantic views, were capable of effecting in France the germination of concepts similar to those of Vico. The first to formulate them were, in fact, M. de Bonald and Mme. de Staël, who somewhat naively reduced the new rapport between literature and society to a relationship between literature and institutions. Michelet, a visionary but penetrating historical mind, felt the connection as something deeper, more vital, and more natural, while scientism and positivism, from Comte to Taine, were to bear the idea to its maximum development, to its most complete, and therefore excessive and material, expression.

The system of Taine. It is really with Taine that this relationship of coordination between different historical manifestations, juridical and cultural, social and political, reaches its utmost limit.[1] Like all Frenchmen of that time, Taine combines a systematic, abstract rationalism with a coarse and often metaphysical materialism. In fact, to the two vague, and yet genuinely historical, concepts of *milieu* and of *moment*, he adds for the first time the obscure, mystic, and hybrid concept of *race.*

What function and nature has the myth of race in the trinity of the methodological thinking of Taine? It is clearly the reduction to naturalistic and primitivistic absurdity of the romantic concept of people or nation. The historical relativism of the preromantics and the romantics, by way of reaction to the somewhat abstract universalism of the classical tradition and the academic cosmopolitanism of the Republic of Letters, had discovered, independently of the relation between literature and society, new ties between popular and national psychology and a given literary tradition. And while the history of culture and literature had remained in Vico typical and universal history, it becomes, first with the Germans, then with all the European romantics, the history of particular literatures, national literary history.

The step was one of progress, despite the infinite errors committed, despite the perilous mythologies it suggested; but it became a retrograde movement precisely with Taine's reduction of the factor "nation" to the factor "race." The factor "people," or nation, permitted the establishment of a relationship of coordination between literature and society in a concrete, particular sense, case by case. To state the same thing differently, one could say that national or popular tradition was nothing more than a synonym for civilization and culture; yet this implies a more vital concept of that civilization, a broader and less literary interpretation of that culture. But the myth of race was something new and irreducible, so untranslatable in corresponding intellectual and cultural terms as to become a cause rather than a factor or an effect — and not merely a concurring, but a determining, cause. Consequently, there came to be established once again (as with the Germans, especially in recent times) a relationship of subordination rather than of coordination. Instead of conceiving a people and a literature as products of a broader, common, historical condition, one came to consider race as a prime cause, and culture and literature a secondary cause, a result of the creative force of an entity which was presupposed rather than realized.

The system of Marx. The concept of race was the first rupture in the new equilibrium, and it was probably the precedent which facilitated the introduction of an analogous historical myth, the concept of class, in the doctrine of the relationship between society and literature.

Marx and Engels elaborated the doctrine of modern socialism and historical materialism in an epoch previous, and only in part contemporaneous, to the system of Taine. But it is not to be forgotten that in the work of Marx and Engels there are few references to the relationship between social history and literary and cultural history. The only important moment in the doctrine of Marx in this respect is the concept of ideology. Ideology is a cultural fact completely utilitarian and practical; it is, so to speak, the system of sophistry by which a class justifies the social institution constructed for its own advantage, which assures it the control of the machinery of state and the privileges that derive from it. The Marxian concept of ideology is, therefore, a return to the attitude of the Sophists, to the conception, that is, of the instrumentality rather than the finality of culture, of culture as propaganda. Only Marx, instead of examining the phenomenon from within, looks at it as an enemy, from without.

However, as we have already said, neither Marx nor Engels

establishes a series of precise, concrete relationships between society and literature; nor does either one of them attempt, even in a relative or approximate form, a class interpretation of culture and literature. Perhaps the problem seemed at that time secondary, but there is reason to believe that Marx felt that literature (considered as artistic, not ideological, expression) was by nature irreducible to a relationship of this kind. In private conversations and letters, for example, he showed more than once a noteworthy degree of understanding and indulgence toward poets and artists; and it was an attitude consciously based on the conviction of the irreconcilability of the purely aesthetic with the purely social, a point of view that reveals a breadth of vision of which the literary theoreticians of Marxism are usually incapable.

It fell, in fact, on Marx's pupils and followers to formulate for the first time a Marxian conception of literary and artistic history. And here they committed the same error as Taine. Instead of drawing a relationship between literary reality and social reality, the literature of a given society and the class structure of that society, they preferred, as usual, a solution not by means of coordination but, rather, subordination: and they submitted art, literature, and culture to their mythic idea, to their mystical or metaphysical hypostasis, to the concept of class. The history of literature, while claiming to be such, became nothing more than the literary history of the dominant social class, with the natural addition of a hostile, critical attitude, because the historian declared himself at the very outset an adversary of that class. This polemic position finally complicated itself with complementary, parallel attitudes of an apologetic, normative character, with the postulation, that is, of a culture or literature of the proletariat, a culture or literature of propaganda in the direct, full sense of the word.

The arbitrariness of Taine's position was at least caused by a theoretical error; in the case of the Marxists, metaphysical arbitrariness is conjoined with partisan prejudice and ideological bias. Yet in both cases the error is fundamentally the same: the relationship of coordination between a historic whole and a particular series of phenomena (between a society and its literature) is replaced by the subordination of literature to a cause more or less real or authentic, yet arbitrarily raised to the level of a single and absolute cause.

The system of Freud. The same function exercised by the concepts of race and class in the systems of Taine and the Marxists is attributed by the critics influenced by Freud and psychoanalysis to another arbitrary, monistic myth, to the idea of libido or, more generally, to that which they call the subconscious. The revolutionary character of this new hypothesis rests on the fact that the one factor it considers is no longer social, but psychological. Thus, the abolition of the rapport between society and literature is not so important as the implication, exceedingly important, that the decisive factors of artistic creation are outside the pale of history. Fortunately, for the very reason that such a conception is based on psychopathic diagnosis, the psychoanalytic interpretation of literature renounces the right of influencing literature, and reserves only the privilege of directing, a posteriori, its criticism.

The psychoanalytic interpretation of literary works derives from a conception as arbitrary as that of Taine and the Marxists; but the race of the former and the class of the latter, metaphysical concepts which can assume a certain reality only insofar as they are interpreted as factual historical data, have been replaced by a psychological entity, consequently stationary and eternal, which is that of the sex instinct. One can probably say that this instinct becomes a source of culture only insofar as it manifests itself in what are solely its deviations and repressions, and that these deviations and repressions are brought about predominantly by social causes. However, even if such is the case, we have to do with social forces which are, so to speak, of a permanent nature; and they are derived, in fact, from the common fount of traditional morality, to which the human spirit ever remained faithful in Greece and Rome and in the Christian Middle Ages, and which it observes, although in different forms, in primitive as well as advanced civilizations. This, of course, implies that morality is more a substratum than an element of history.

On the other hand, morality is for psychoanalysis only a negative element; the psyche does nothing but struggle eternally against it, and when it withdraws to avoid yielding, it always moves along different paths. It is in this way, under the guise of evasion or outlet, or, as the psychoanalysts say, of sublimation, that art and culture take root. With this idea, psychoanalysis succeeds in breaking the relationship between civilization (of which morality is only a part) and culture. The latter takes on the appearance of a product resulting from an interior crisis; and art is reduced therein to the transcendental hypocrisy of a sickly spirit. The important thing, however, is that art and culture become there not highly personal, but merely individual expressions, a creation, so to speak, of everyone and of no one.

In the hypothesis of the rapport between society and literature, in the supposition of their parallelism, one could at least find the sense of a natural or organic relationship, certainly not a mechanical one. Up to a certain point, the same thing occurred in Taine's subordination of literature to the myth of race because, if not in theory, at least in practice, this last concept had some of its own roots in the idea of people and nation. The connection between literature and the myth of class is, on the other hand, completely materialistic and practical, one of servitude and interest. Furthermore, in the reduction of the motivations of art to what Freud called the libido, the relationship is lowered to the level of reflex and of stimulus; or as Pareto would say, to a residue, nay, to the sole residue of sex.

11. *The Sociology of Pareto*

The system of Pareto. The reference to Pareto with which the preceding section concluded was not a casual allusion. The purpose of this article is to investigate whether, among the many modern sociological interpretations of literature, there be one, perhaps more valid and more profound, to be constructed on the basis of Pareto's sociology. In a certain sense, we aim at treating the sociology of Pareto in a manner analogous to that in which Marxian and Freudian critics have treated the doctrine of their masters, by completing it, that is, with a special interpretation of literary phenomena within the framework of a broader system of ideas.[2]

Contrary to the systems of Marx and Freud, the sociology and the psychology of Pareto are not reducible to single absolute values, to monads such as class and sex. Both represent only two of the many forms and forces that he studies and considers, some of which, if artificially consolidated in a whole composed of various factors, would give a resulting aggregate identifiable with Taine's concept of race. Not less than Taine, and probably more than any other literary or nonliterary sociologist, Pareto possesses a formidable literary culture; but unlike Taine he does not claim to be equipped with a doctrine or a historical-literary methodology. He uses literature as a document, and it is clear that if he had been reproved for having committed an error of omission in the *Trattato di sociologia generale*, in failing to formulate a sociological theory of literature, he would have replied that such a formulation, as in the case of so many other problems touched upon only incidentally in the *Trattato*, could only be the object of a special sociology.

As a matter of fact, his allusions to literature and culture (often theoretical and general) are innumerable; but, what is even more important, they are frequently contradictory. It is evident that we cannot begin our attempt to describe a special sociology of the Paretian type in the area of literature and its history except by examining those special references, and studying them on the basis of his system of ideas. Pareto, when treating literature not as a document, but per se, as an object of general theory, always speaks of it in relation to his doctrine of residues and derivations. We must, therefore, give a brief outline of this doctrine before beginning our investigation.

The concept of residue. Countless attempts have already been made to elucidate the two Paretian concepts of residue and of derivation, and these attempts by now constitute a small literature. Pareto often confuses residue with sentiment or instinct, but he always distinguishes it from interest. In the behavior of individuals and communities, the subordination of conduct to the principle of interest is considered by Pareto a logical, coherent act, while, on the other hand, the principal characteristic of residue is one of motivating directly an irrational conduct. Sometimes the residue is distinguished from sentiment and instinct to the degree that it is considered the manifestation of a general state of mind, of a complex psychic condition. Other times it is viewed as something less static and more dynamic than a condition or situation, like a goad to action. Elsewhere the residue is reduced to preconception, to prejudice; that is to say, to crystallization in pseudo-rational form of an unconscious force, inclination, or will. Often Pareto, with a term dear to the ancient moralists, speaks of a logic of sentiments, precisely as they used to speak of a logic of passions; and he speaks of it not only in regard to the derivations, which are pseudo-logic in character, but to the residues themselves.

In other words, the concept of residue is synonymous now with sentiment, now with symptom or expression of sentiment; sometimes it is considered a state, then again a psychic movement. Perhaps the most brilliant image possible is offered to us by the Paretian simile which compares residues to linguistic roots: a simile that makes one think of residues almost as psychic clusters or bonds, unconsciously generating or attracting other psychic manifestations. Probably the concept closest to that of residue is the psychoanalytic one of complex, with the difference that the sex instinct is regarded by Pareto as a single residue or complex, and that in psychic life are included infinite other complexes or residues which have nothing to do with sex.

The characteristic of a residue is its constancy, the extraordinary slowness of its metamorphoses, its resistance, almost invincible, to being uprooted or transplanted. In an individual being or in a society considered within very broad temporal limits, the residues may be considered immutable; only in the slow course of time, after a radical transformation of a personality or civilization, can one note perceptible changes, which consist in the relative proportion and importance that the various residues come to acquire in a new equilibrium, rather than in a radical transformation to which the residues in question have been separately subjected. Even in this, the concept of residue is analogous to the psychoanalytical one of complex, with the difference that psychoanalysis believes that the liberating intervention of the physician, consisting partly of suggestion and reasoning, is able to dissolve or dissipate, at least to control, a given complex. Pareto does not share such optimism in regard to residues. The residues may become for him an object of diagnosis and even of political treatment or exploitation by the statesman, provided he be content to use them and combine them, by renouncing the foolish, presumptuous, and, unfortunately, very frequent attempt to eradicate or destroy them.

The concept of derivation. The character of derivation is rather that of a superstructure which the mind of man imposes on the various residues. Each one of these superstructures both conceals and reveals the respective residue. Preferably, it hides and disguises them, because several derivations can be imposed at the same time on a single residue. Nor should we forget that the former, unlike the latter, change constantly with the ephemeral fickleness of fashion. In brief, derivation could be defined, not as the logical generalization (which is possible only when residue and derivation become the object of experimental examination and scientific investigation, in which case the result is the opposite of derivation), but as the rationalization of a residue. As is well known, in common parlance, to rationalize means to justify a posteriori, more sophistically than logically, the irrationalizable.

It is evident that with the word "derivation" Pareto intends precisely what Marx, on the trail of the Napoleonic use of that word, meant by the term "ideology." But there is a difference. The ideology of a society or a class is for Marx the series of sophisms with which that class or society sustains the validity, the absolute justice, of the political and social system that keeps it in power or defends its interests. In other words, an ideology is always hypocritical and, as such, conscious. The conscious liar acts rationally, subordinating the means of the lie to the end of interest. Ideology in this sense would deceive others, but not itself.

Just as from the point of view of the doctrine of residues the originality of Pareto consists in affirming that sentiments are often as strong or even stronger than instincts (the Freudian libido, for example) and interests (such as those of class, according to Marx), so in the doctrine of derivations the penetrating novelty of his thought lies in having given a more profound, authentic interpretation of the phenomenon of ideologies. The only real force of derivations is in proportion to the degree of approbation, more or less sincere, with which their inventors formulate them and their followers accept them. They are derivations exactly insofar as they are honest, frank attempts to rationalize the irrationalizable. The very stimulus of rationalization is a residue and is part of a system of residues which Pareto assembles under the name of "instinct of combinations." From the same root comes science itself, which is the opposite of derivations and whose object is, among other things, the study of residues and the criticism of derivations, but which in essence, continuing the parallel with psychoanalysis, is only the sublimation of that same residue of which derivations are the immediate, instinctive, and natural fruit.

This position reveals, so to speak, the vitalistic idealism of Pareto's system. On the one side he avoids the stumbling block of Freudian social pathology and, on the other, the contradictions of Marxism.

Marx reduced society to interests and founded a scientific socialism, which changed unexpectedly into political mysticism and revolutionary messianism. Now it is precisely this messianism (a residue) which creates the force of the socialist movement, not ideology or pseudo-science (a derivation). Pareto, on the other hand, being an observer rather than a maker, studies political and social reality without the intention of effecting any changes therein, and this permits him to understand that, even if socialism is an ideology, the ideology is not just a lie.

Precisely because of their character of instability and superficiality, derivations have no great importance in social life or in history. But, for obvious reasons, they have been treated till now as if they were not merely the principal but indeed the sole object of history, to the point of being considered almost identical with history itself. In reality they are only an intellectual parallel of fashion. Theories and ideologies change with every generation, and sometimes more than once in the course of a generation. A history which is a history of derivations is nothing more than a history of culture. On the other hand, real history is not so much a history of residues, which are rather the sociological and psychological data of history, as of the diverse proportion and importance they come to assume in a given society. Its most important task is perhaps to determine the relationship, the situation of equilibrium or lack of balance, which comes to be established between the residues that control the individuals of the subjected classes and the residues of a different order that prevail among the members of the governing class or elite.

Literature according to Pareto. Pareto hardly ever talks of art in his work, and only rarely of poetry; and when he uses this term, it is in the formal, traditional sense of rhythmic or metric discourse, of writing in verse rather than in prose. But he speaks very often of literature. And by literature he means very nearly what the humanists of every epoch, down to the eighteenth century, meant by that term: literature was for them not only lyrical poetry, drama, epos, or fiction; it was creative ideology, science and philosophy, history and criticism. Pareto's concept of literature is likewise composite, syncretic, eclectic, with the sole difference that unlike the humanist our sociologist attributes no judgment of value to the term.

Sometimes, on the other hand, Pareto uses such literature in a derogatory sense. The only two forms of literature according to the ancients to which Pareto as a modern man assigns the dignity of different disciplines are scientific and historical writing — when, however, they cease to be literature in order to become true science and authentic history. By science he means that science which partakes of the logico-experimental method; by history, that history which is something more than a derivation, however elegant or convincing it might be. The types of science and history he does not regard worthy of this name, he casts back, without further ado, to literature, which is what happens in the great majority of cases; but that does not prevent him from including in the literary sphere those kinds of history and science which are worthy of his ideal.

At first glance it appears evident that a literature so conceived is not only predominantly an expression, but an outright instrument, of derivations, and certainly the most perfect and complex one, if not, absolutely, the only one. In such a conception of literature there enters not only narrative, dramatic, and lyric poetry, but also eloquence and rhetoric. Eloquence is, by definition, polemic or apologetic — therefore, not only a derivation, in the sense of an ideological superstructure imposed upon the residues, but also a technique of persuasion, a means for stimulating the residues and exciting them to action. The only capacity for action on the part of derivations is precisely of this nature. And it is in such a faculty that Pareto sees a *raison d'être* for propaganda, nay, propaganda itself.

The more literature veers toward the extremes of propaganda and rhetoric, the more natural it seems to suppose that Pareto is inclined to consider it an expression or instrument of derivations. This, incidentally, would demonstrate once again the originality of his point of view, because by reducing rhetoric to derivation he seems to be able to solve, once and for all, the old argument about the nature of eloquence. The controversy about orator and oratory had been for centuries a conflict of opinions in regard to the ethical quality, or the lack of it, in eloquence and in rhetoric. Very few had perceived that it was a ridiculous argument, for eloquence by its very nature operates at a lower level than morality. That level was to be identified by Croce with the sphere of practical activity: and Pareto's solution is in this case the same. Just because it is an instrument of persuasion, eloquence is an instrument of action, a pragmatic act.

Paradoxically, Pareto denies the practical efficacy of derivations. Statesmen and political leaders move men to act in the desired sense, not by attempting to replace residues with derivations, but by manipulating the residues directly. Eloquence, in conclusion, if it does not turn immediately to the logic of passions, if it is a pure, simple derivation, is inefficient. But that does not indicate that it is naturally dishonest and fundamentally insincere. If it consciously manipulates residues, it is not only rational and scientific, but effective and utilitarian. But to act on residues means not to share them, just as it implies disbelief in the effectiveness of derivations. There can be therefore an eloquence which, although being derivation, unconsciously sets in motion certain residues.

Analogously, can there be a literature which unconsciously expresses residues, just as we have seen that there exists one which expresses derivations more or less consciously? A literature of this kind must exist, not only as a logical hypothesis, but also for the simple reason that Pareto uses literary proofs to confirm his doctrine of residues as well as that of derivations. On the other hand, there are partial, often contradictory, references in his work, which seem to identify literature now with derivations, now with residues, now with both. Perhaps the best way to clear up this problem is to study all these partial and incidental assertions, one by one, and classify them in accordance with the special direction toward which they seem to incline in each case.

III. *The Cultural Sociology of Pareto*

Derivations and residues in literature. It seems a strange thing to say, but the Paretian passages in which literature is reduced to simple, pure derivation are of little importance and scant in number. Paragraph 1084 of the *Trattato,* for example, leads one to suppose that literature, if not an outright instrument or expression of derivation, is at least a means, more voluntary than involuntary, for masking or concealing residues: this is generally the typical function of derivations. Paragraph 1415 seems to go even further in this direction, as well as the numerous passages in which Pareto criticizes political economy as science. In fact, his criticism consists in leveling at that discipline the accusation of not having elevated itself to the rank of science, but of continuing to function as a branch of literature, with which, he says, it is to be judged in accordance with the doctrine of derivations.

Much more frequent are the passages in which literature is viewed as an expression of residues. In paragraph 1017, while speaking incidentally of the institution of family and its origins, Pareto asserts that there is no reason to believe that the patriarchal system on which the ancient family was based, and on which ours continues to be based, is the only one historically existent or possible from a practical point of view. The opinion that supports the universality of the system is due to the fact, he claims, that we possess no other proof in this respect except what is offered by the literature of peoples whose domestic society is based on that system. In other words, Pareto maintains that the only known residues relative to the institution of family, which we have come to know by means of literature, are the residues which correspond to the patriarchal system. The passage is important because it implies the concept of literature as an expression of residues.

More than once, and especially in paragraph 1445ff, Pareto affirms that the residue of sex figures actively in the major portion of literature; and in this regard he is no less penetrating than Freud. In fact, for Pareto, not only erotic and obscene literature but also rigoristic or edifying writing is an expression of the residue of sex, of which asceticism is only one aspect. Thus our author advances unawares an hypothesis similar to the Freudian theory of the repression of the sexual instinct as a part of the instinct itself. But Pareto, broader and more universal in his thinking than Freud, does not believe that psychic life is monopolized by a sole residue, that is, by the libido.

Pareto has demonstrated extraordinary acumen in the examination of the residues of religion and superstition, in the study of the paradoxical relations which exist among certain individual and collective psychic states and the forms assumed by human behavior in regard to the objects of worship. Thus paragraph 1321 maintains that some motives of the *Iliad* — and, first among all of them, the one, incomprehensible to us moderns, of the feelings of hostility and rivalry manifested by mortals toward the divinities of Olympus — are a direct expression of powerful, diffuse sentiments in the Greek soul; that is, of residues of which the Homeric poem would be an expression.

We have already said that the most suggestive image with which Pareto has attempted to give us the intuition of his concept of residue is the similitude with linguistic roots. Pareto devotes many incidental, but profound, pages to the phenomenon of speech; linguistics and philology are for him the only disciplines applied to the study of man and of society that have become sciences. And he accepts enthusiastically the modern linguistic doctrines which support the hypothesis of the irrationality of speech. Sometimes he uses linguistic facts as symptoms or examples of broader or more diverse phenomena, as when what he calls the slowness of linguistic metamorphoses is cited as proof of the stability of sentiments, of the constancy of residues. It is evident that Pareto has exaggerated this slowness to the advantage of his own argument. We, instead, are led to underline in speech the opposite nature, the fluid state, the condition of continual change. It is paradoxical but natural that in order to demonstrate the same principle he has also made use, ad absurdum, of the phenomenon inverse to that of the spontaneous development of speech. He maintains, in fact, that archaizing pedantry and linguistic purism, which are a cultural, academic attitude — therefore conscious, artificial, and conventional — also converge to prove what could be called the traditionalism or conservatism of residues.

Even if we do not approve or consider the example appropriate, it is, nevertheless, quite true that this affirmation of speech as an expression of residues is extremely important. In this respect Pareto approaches the aesthetic and philosophic linguistics which Croce had been preaching in Italy for about ten years, more than he does the scientific linguistics of recent German creation. The residue, in such a case, may be nearer than is apparent to what Croce calls intuition. However, from the point of view of scientific discourse, which ideally is mathematical, one is not to forget the Paretian polemic against the language of pseudo-science, which to him seems completely composed of derivations.

It is well known that the identification of language and poetry is at the base of Crocean aesthetics. Such a problem was not pertinent or interesting to the sociology of Pareto, who, at any rate, would have cast aside that interpretation or relationship as a metaphysical abstraction. Nevertheless, even to him, the relations existing between language and literature were, in a more or less evident or conscious manner, well known. How many times he says, albeit in the manner of a methodological and theoretical reproof, that spoken language (and even written language) is vague; that is, intuitive, sentimental, and poetic rather than mathematical or scientific. It is evident that even in Pareto's case the assertion about the irrationality of speech broadens to include the irrationality (or the pseudo-rationality) of a large portion of what we call literature.

Just as the concept of intuition, understood as the expression of the particular, which becomes universal through that very expression, leads Croce to affirm the universality of art, to such a point as to render it irreducible to history, so, likewise, the opinion that residues are among the sources of literary inspiration causes Pareto to support the idea that the glory, permanency, or the so-called immortality of great works of art is also due, among other things, to the survival in time, within the consciousness of mankind, of some of the more important residues. In paragraph 1719 he asserts that our capacity to understand and admire the masterpieces of classic literatures is due to the fact that they express residues of which we still partake; and in a footnote he quotes the opinion of an obscure French critic of Racine to prove that the classical quality of this poet does not consist in a literary classicism but, rather, in a psychological one, to be recognized in his treatment of nonephemeral sentiments, of valid, solid residues. The same idea appears in paragraph 1937, where Pareto places on the same plane Greek epic poetry, the modern novel, and the psychological literature of the French moralistes (from the "Characters" of Theophrastus to those of La Bruyère), as kinds of writing expressing permanent traits of the collective and individual psyche; that is to say, residues.

Literature and culture. Correspondingly numerous, nevertheless, are the pages of the *Trattato* where literature seems to be, at one and the same time, an expression of deviations and residues. In paragraph 1074 the allegorical or metaphorical device of personification is regarded as a means of transforming sentiments or residues into objective realities. It is not clear whether the stimulus which leads to the use of that device is just any residue whatsoever, or that instinct of combinations which is in itself a residue. On the other hand, in many places in the *Trattato* the personification thus obtained is considered a derivation. Finally, in the passage already cited, Pareto adds that these objectivations can, in turn, themselves become objects of merely literary admiration; this places literature on a plane where neither residues nor derivations operate any longer.

Paragraphs 1450ff are intended to prove that a tradition (cultural or religious) is a perfect ground for the study of derivations. In the book which creates that tradition one can find what one wills, so says Pareto; and he quotes the case of Homer among the Greeks, of Virgil among the Latins, and of the Bible among the Christians. But, shortly after, he also says that tradition is strongly affected by residues; and so true is this, from the viewpoint of the sentiments of those who treat it as an object of faith, that a traditional belief remains unassailable before the attempts of destruction or negation by hostile or scientific criticism. Accordingly, Pareto cites the case of the Scriptures and of Biblical criticism. Thus, he would seem to indicate that those books express residues and are an object of derivations. While the latter change, the former persist and continue to give validity and consistency to that tradition.

Evidently, faith in a book has nothing to do with the book itself; the residue resides in that very faith, and not in the object or motive of the belief. But it is likewise true that the work must be capable of giving sustenance to those sentiments and, therefore, of containing them and expressing them. In this passage, as well as in others of the same kind, literature is treated as an object of study, without any attention paid to what might be called its subject. And this is certainly one of the reasons for which it is difficult to construct, inside or outside Pareto's system, yet with the leaven of his ideas, a nonmediate conception of literature.

A special point of view is offered by those passages where literature is not only considered as a means of expression (it does not matter whether what it expresses be residues or derivations), but also as a means of persuasion. This faculty now seems to partake even more of the nature of derivations. In paragraph 1624 Pareto affirms that poetry, literature, and eloquence may function as means to the end of stimulating and exciting sentiments; but here the stimulus is considered pseudo-logical and pseudo-sentimental at the same time, which reduces it to a superstructure imposed upon residues, therefore to derivation. In paragraph 1892, on the other hand, he alludes directly to those frequent literary productions whose aim is persuasion, and asserts that their convincing power resides, not in the derivations, but in the residues and the interests which they put in operation. It follows, therefore, as Pareto indicates earlier, that only those literary works which associate ideas with potent residues and important interests are capable of surviving.

In the same paragraph there appear some new and significant elements. The first is the factor of interest, which would render consciously pragmatic the function of literature and which would reduce it in part, at least, to eloquence in the traditional and legal sense of the word, thus contradicting the normal conception of eloquence as derivation. The other element is the definition of the work of literature as an association of ideas, interests, and residues; from this it seems to proceed that literature is not expression or creation, but an interpretation and elaboration of data which precede it, a heterogeneous complex, rather than a simple, single whole.

Opposing this concept of literature as a composite entity is the one which views it also as a composing force, fully delineated in paragraph 971. Here Pareto asserts that literature satisfies the completely human need of combining residues. It would even satisfy the human demand for logic, which ideally ought to be satisfied by science but which, except for rare individuals, is generally satisfied by literature, by pseudo-logic of literary composition. This passage is very important, and it lets us understand what Pareto perceived with the word "ideas," which we found in the preceding reference. The ideas expressed by literature are logical myths, therefore irrational in substance and rational only in appearance. Looking at this conception from the point of view of a Croce or a Bergson, those ideas could be defined as intuitions. From the point of view of a thinker dear to both Croce and Pareto, Sorel, those ideas could be called myths, in a sense broader than the purely social one of the term. By adding to the thought of Pareto something which it does not contain, one could say, then, that for him literature oscillates between the extreme limits of mythology and ideology.

According to Pareto, it is really these pseudo-logical demands which draw literature near to, and separate it from, science. They draw it near insofar as science satisfies the logical demand exactly and rationally, which it tries to put in agreement with experience, while literature tries putting the pseudo-logical demand in agreement with sentiments. Analogies of the same kind put literature on the same plane with the most frequent object of Pareto's hatred and scorn, metaphysics, a name under which he assembles every kind of philosophy, not only gnoseological but also ethical, every scholastic or dogmatic theology, every pseudo-science of the universal, from the philosophy of law to the philosophy of history, and, finally, every utopia and ideology. Metaphysics is the triumph, par excellence, of derivations. We could say that it is, at one and the same time, their hypostasis and their idolatry.

Pareto's interest in literary works, although relative, is nevertheless authentic; and it is due to the fact that literature is a complete cultural body, a thesaurus, where derivations and residues find expression at the same time, thus giving direct and indirect evidence of psychic states. In the case of the social sciences, he is inclined to a greater indulgence when he sees them affected by the literary rather than by the metaphysical contagion. In the first alternative, when they are cultivated by practical, keen intelligences, by a Machiavelli or a Polybius, they become sciences of man analogous to that which is the only science truly worthy of the name, the science of nature. In the second alternative, historiography and sociology always decline to the level of moralistic allegories; as a matter of fact, Pareto thinks that he is the first to attempt to reduce social anthropology to an exact science.

It can be said that Pareto the scientist reveals toward literature a saner attitude than that of the practical man, who scorns it because he recognizes in it no truth or utility, but only derivations; and also a saner attitude than the moralist, the puritan, and the rigorist, who condemn it because they believe it expresses only sentiments, instincts, and residues. The fact is that none of these three entities, science, literature, and metaphysics, operates in a psychic vacuum; they correspond, rather, to an exigency so elementary and essential that, thanks to it, they can be reduced to a single, natural principle. For Pareto, they all proceed from a single powerful residue, the instinct of combinations. These three types of activity, says Pareto, are probably manifestations of a single psychic state, the hypothetical extinction of which would necessarily and simultaneously lead to their own disappearance.

Croce and Pareto. A conception so constituted could, perhaps, serve as a basis for a new interpretation of the nature and the function of culture. The philosophic system of one of Pareto's great contemporaries, Bendetto Croce, has been justly defined as a methodology of culture. That system is limited to the contemplation of activities of the spirit; to that speculation about universal concepts which gives us logic, science, and philosophy; to that speculation about intuitions and images which gives us language and art, literature and poetry, aesthetics and criticism; to that construction of an ideal of action which gives us ethics if contemplated from the viewpoint of the universal; and to that study of the concrete behavior, individual and collective, of man exemplified by the practical sciences of economics and politics. Just as all these activities are expressed in that history which is lived and acted, as they are documented and interpreted in that history which is reflected and written, so all of life comes to be reduced to culture, and philosophy, to the theory of history, to historiography. The human, in the thought of Croce, is identical with the humanistic; the spirit, with intelligence alone. There is nothing more humanistic, in the full sense of the word, than the Crocean reduction of theoretical error to practical error; than his negation of the validity of the principles of good and evil, of pleasure and pain, in other terms, of sentiment; finally, than his very idea that religion is only an inferior philosophy.

The greatest contrast between the thought of Croce and the thought of Pareto lies right here, in the immense importance which the latter gives to sentiments, a word which he himself used often as a synonym for residues. Pareto considers sentiments as authentic psychic energies, capable of acting and reacting on what Croce, with a term well agreeing with his romantic humanism, calls activities of the spirit. It is clear that on the basis of this principle, just as Pareto has constructed a philosophy of history different from that of Croce (nor does it matter much that both violently cast aside, though for different reasons, the hypothesis that a philosophy of history is necessary and possible), so there could be constructed a conception of culture distinct from that of Croce, or rather, opposed to that entirely humanistic one of his great contemporary. Perhaps some future scholar may draw forth naturally from Pareto's thought a conception of culture not so much sociological as anthropological. In reality, Pareto's thought suggests the idea that culture is not, as for Croce, a structure but, on the contrary, a superstructure; in Freudian terms, a sublimation of residues, a brilliant and unconscious fiction.

Be that as it may, the time has now come for a philosophy of culture constructed on a system of thought which is humanistic and scientific at one and the same time, transcending in a synthesis the limitations of the two points of view. The intellectual, the humanist, is bound on the one hand to view culture as an autonomous value, absolute and supreme; and on the other hand, to recognize everywhere the presence of spirit, to reduce the history of humanity to the history of intelligence and of culture. This historical overvaluation of the influence of culture is an error. Few thinkers have noticed it. Very seldom does one encounter a mind like that of Ortega y Gasset, who has postulated, among other things, the necessity of a study on the nature and influence of stupidity. We have now reached the opposite extreme of the illuministic conception, which in past history saw only a history of error. Historicism only sees in history truths which are realized. On the other hand, scientism and abstract rationalism are led to see outside themselves only the absurd, the irrational, the erroneous.

That which we are inclined to call the cynical idealism of Pareto may offer us, perhaps, an agreement and a solution. History is made, in a large part, by residues, and among the residues are those which represent stupidity, like those which represent intelligence. Culture is largely composed of derivations; therefore, the influence in the history of an intelligence more or less conscious of itself is always limited. Derivation is neither truth nor science, but neither is it error or falsehood. On the contrary, it is an attempt, though difficult and weak, to conciliate the needs of thought with those of sentiment. As residue is energy or resistance, an active or passive force, a mechanism of defense and offense, so derivation is an attempt to give a certain order to the chaos of existence. Alongside the powerful, almost animal naturalness of residue, then, there is in history, even if futile and ephemeral, the humanity of derivation. It may be theology or ideology, but more generally it expresses itself in genuine culture.

The literary sociology of Pareto. The digression was necessary, but now it is time to return to our theme, which is that of the possibility of constructing a methodology of literary history on the basis of Pareto's sociological system. As we have already seen, according to Pareto, a matter of this kind can only be the object of a specialized sociology, in view of the generality of his doctrine; this implies that, from now on, the help we have been directly receiving from the work of our author will be scarce or nil. While Pareto treats literature as an extrinsic sociological document, we must treat it as an intrinsic document.

Yet, even in this regard, the *Trattato* is still useful reading: we think especially of the pages where Pareto studies literature as a manifestation of broader and more complex phenomena. On the other hand, it is only relative to the study of such a connection that we can find passages which fit our case. He puts us on guard, for example, against the traditional emphasis in the sociological interpretation of literature; in other terms, against the too common inclination to consider the history of society and of culture as absolutely parallel phenomena. Into this error the romanticists, the positivists, and even the humanists and the idealists of the Crocean type often fell, being too easily inclined to find nonexistent similarities between political history and literary history. Pareto says in paragraph 1734 that literature undoubtedly gives us a direct documentation of residues, but of residues reducible to states of mind, sentiments and customs, dominating not the entire society of a given time, but only the elite of which the writer is, or aspires to be, a part and whose refinement and taste it is his aim to express.

Analogously, the humanistic, the idealistic, or more generally the cultural historians are often inclined not only to identify social history with history of culture but, when they do distinguish between them, to subordinate the former to the latter. They claim, for example, that the triumph in a given society of a new sentiment or a new idea is the effect of the sudden appearance of that sentiment or that idea within literature, which comes thus to assume a causative function. Instead, they have been sentiments and ideas already confusedly present in the minds of the men of that society and that epoch, which have inspired that literature and have determined its success. In this sense Rousseauism is not only more important than the work of Rousseau, surpassing it in influence and duration, but, what is more important, it plainly precedes it in time.

The enormous historiographic and methodological importance

of such a point of view is evident, as well as its revolutionary implications in regard to a further reappraisal of concepts, such as that one of source and influence, and similar terms so frequently used in the writing of literary history. Pareto is aware of the novelty and the significance of this idea, because he mentions and discusses at least twice the case of the diversity of success accorded two writers of like inspiration, such as Lucian and Voltaire. While in the ancient world Lucian's success was only literary, because of a difference of conditions and circumstances, Voltaire succeeded instead in becoming a catalyzer of ideas, an instrument of history.

IV. *Hypotheses*

Literature of residues and literature of derivations. At the end of the preceding section we saw Pareto touch upon exact, even if typical or general, phenomena of literary and cultural history; and yet, in spite of this, his concept of literature remains approximative and empirical. As we have already seen, he indicates with that term all activities, often heterogeneous, which are readily assembled under that word. That is why literature seems to him principally an expression now of residues, now of derivations, but sometimes also of interests and ideas. In some cases, as we have already remarked, "literary" is an epithet used to designate creative literature, no matter from what it may spring, from observation or from fantasy; in others, as when he speaks of political economy as a pseudo-science, the accusation of being literary seems to imply a conception of literature as defective or erring theory. We have also already noted that Pareto never speaks of art, and rarely of poetry, a term which he always uses in the ordinary sense of being the antithesis of prose. In conclusion, one could say that the Paretian concept of literature unites under the same name two essentially different entities: poetry and literature, the former regarded as literature of art and creation; the latter, as literature of ideas and deeds. There is missing, consequently, in the Paretian concept of literature an equivalent of the Crocean distinction (which is Aristotelian) of poetry and prose, in which the first is not merely writing in verse and the second merely writing in *sermo solutus*, but in which one is literature as creation and the other is literature as reflection or praxis (that is, history and rhetoric, science and criticism).

To have neglected such a distinction cannot be considered an error; Pareto never intended to use empirically the concept of literature, in order to study it, but as a document of phenomena other than literature itself. Yet the distinction he omitted to make will enable us to formulate the only hypothesis on which one can base the attempt to apply Pareto's sociology to the writing of literary history. This hypothesis is that literature is a manifestation of derivations and residues, the residues being the substratum of creative literature, of poetry; and the derivations, of the literature of ideas, of prose. Poetry (even when not written in verse) is therefore the literary expression of residues; prose (even if composed in rhythmic form) is the literary expression of derivations.

This hypothesis has no absolute value, but a relative one — relative even when referred to an important page of the *Trattato*. In paragraph 545 Pareto asserts that purely literary compositions (here literary signifies poetic and creative, fantastic and inventive, as is demonstrated by the subsequent allusion to legends and imaginative works) are very often valid sources for a knowledge of sentiments; and he adds that testimonials of this kind are frequently more significant sociologically than more technical texts, or even concrete historic documents. The allusion to legends and imaginative works, the very preference, on the part of Pareto, to quote old, primitive texts, gives us the right to develop our hypothesis and to suppose that indigenous, original, and archaic literatures are those which express the greatest possible quantity of residues in comparison to the least possible quantity of derivations. The ratio will change according to a series of different gradations, according to the greater or lesser self-knowledge of a given civilization, and consequently to the greater or lesser awareness of its literary tradition, until reaching those epochs where literature is predominantly literature and, in a lesser (at times least) degree, poetry. In such periods or ages, literature would instead express the greatest possible quantity of derivations in comparison to the least possible quantity of residues. The most typical and the most extreme example of this last case is that of the ideological, encyclopedistic, and illuministic literature of eighteenth-century France; in fact, that literature is precisely the source from which Pareto draws his greatest number of proofs for documenting this theory of derivations. In that culture

Pareto sees the minimum of residues; Croce, the maximum of nonpoetry.[3]

Historiographic hypothesis. Thus there is set forth a theoretical hypothesis on the nature of literary phenomena on the basis of Pareto's sociology: a hypothesis which has been suggested both by our examination of his work and by the application of a modern conception of literary activity (distinguishing it in the two diverse moments of art and culture) to the doctrine of residues and of derivations. Now we wish to see if that hypothesis can be developed in a dynamic, concrete sense, if it can be applied also to the history of literature; in other words, if from theory it can become a historical method. In spite of his irony directed against the *corse* and *ricorse* of Vico, against Ferrari's theory of political periods, against the Hegelian historiographical metaphysics of thesis, antithesis, and synthesis, Pareto accepts, in practice if not in principle, their concept of history as an unfolding, as a development, as a series of ascending and descending phases, as an alternation of crisis and progress, or, as he says, of undulations and fluctuations. Precisely on this conception of his, one could base a theory of the history of literature according to the relative predominance of poetry in a broad sense over literature in a narrow sense, or the reverse; that is to say, a literary history that would study and point out the succession and alternation of periods in which literature is at times an expression of residues and at times an expression of derivations.

It is worth remarking that, in addition to the interest that he frequently shows in the Homeric poems, Pareto devotes a considerable number of pages to the study of Greek tragedy as a document of the ancient, Hellenic psyche. In this case, naturally, he is interested especially in the study of residues: as a matter of fact, he draws almost all his documents from the work of Aeschylus, a few from Sophocles, none from Euripides. Implicitly, and without any aesthetic theory to impose, his attitude postulates a judgment which intellectually (not morally) seems to coincide with that of Nietzsche. For Nietzsche, Euripides is the Socrates of tragedy; the one who rationalizes it, who renders it bourgeois and decadent just because he introduces philosophy. If the spirit of music, the Dionysian afflatus of ancient tragedy, could correspond to what Pareto calls the force of ancient residues, the "philosophy" of Euripides could evidently be seen as a system of derivations. In Greek culture after Euripides, derivation assumes the level of metaphysics with Plato, and sometimes, in rare instances or flashes, is transcended into science in the work of Aristotle. Even these hypotheses are not arbitrary; this is what Pareto himself says of the work of Plato and Aristotle. Severe toward all that remains of the metaphysical in Aristotle, he recognizes in him, however, the merit of a partial, scientific anticipation; but, like few moderns, he has always been an inflexible denier of all validity to the thought of Plato.

An analogous examination of Latin literature would be difficult because it is in large part, like the Alexandrine, a literature, so to speak, exclusively literary, academically interested in the business of writing, recasting, and imitating. But one could easily submit medieval literature to a similar examination. Always on the authority of Pareto (who sees the expression of residues in legends and imaginative works and, on the other hand, considers theology and religious writing a manifestation of derivations), it is divided neatly into what we have called poetry and literature, poetry and prose: the first is popular, primitive, a literature of residues which culminates in the pagan and Christian epics of modern nations, in ingenuous mythologies; and the second reaches its zenith in apologetics and scholasticism, expressing predominantly or exclusively derivations. In the great artistic literature of the late Middle Ages, in Dante, for example, one would have, as happens in large, mature literary civilizations, a balance between residues and derivations. This balance would be maintained approximately in the culture of the Renaissance, where, however, residues begin relatively to lose their vigor and derivations to increase in theirs. An analogous balance, always with some oscillation in favor of derivations, is repeated in the golden age of French literature. On the other hand, the great literatures of the English and Spanish seventeenth century, especially the drama, would show a noteworthy predominance of residues. As we have already said, French eighteenth-century writing, and its various European equivalents, would instead illustrate the extreme case of a literature composed almost entirely of derivations.

Consequently, a reaction in which residues should regain the upper hand was only natural; and such was the case with early romanticism. But, with the flowering of idealistic philosophy in

Germany, of scienticism and positivism in France and elsewhere, of ideologies everywhere, romanticism was followed by a literature in which there seemed to be a reawakening of derivations. Perhaps the most important literary phenomenon of last century was the advent of Russian literature, which, though largely ideological, triumphed in Europe chiefly by reason of the residues to which it gave expression.

It can perhaps be said that, for a national literature to raise itself to the level of universal literature, it is necessary, if the other conditions are favorable, that it represent one of the two extreme cases. Only in periods of special balance does there flourish and triumph a literature in which one can find a proper ratio of derivations and residues; and these periods are the ones to which is generally given the attribute of classic. The literature of our times, paradoxically, instead of establishing an external balance between residues and derivations, seems to keep the two elements within each work in a state of confusion, conflict, and disorder, which perhaps suffices to define it as the literature of an age of decadence.

Aesthetic hypothesis. As we have seen, in Pareto the ultimate source of what one can call the cultural instinct (even when its products are only derivations) is identified in a residue or a complex of residues. But in the social psychology of Pareto, which keeps logical exigency in mind to the point of viewing it as the fruit of special residues, there does not exist that which one could call the aesthetic residue. Why not suppose the existence of an aesthetic residue, to which we could give an old-fashioned name, such as "cult of form" or "sense of the beautiful"? Why could not man, in addition to being the "political animal" of Aristotle and the "sociological animal" of Pareto, also be, as Hazlitt calls him, the "poetic animal"? "Homo nascitur poeta," says Croce with a term that could be Vico's, and which is an original variant of the old maxim *poetae nascuntur, non fiunt.* Now then, just as science is a sublimation of derivations, would it not be possible for art to be a transfiguration of residues? Evidently, a conception of this kind would lead to a consideration of literature as subordinate (as a sociological document) and, at the same time, autonomous (as a fruit of its own residue); but all this would lead us once again to the traditional distinction of form and content.

A few vague references to the independence of art (to the autonomy of its residue) are also found in the *Trattato*. In the important pages Pareto devotes to the methodology to be followed in textual and exegetical criticism, he distinguishes between the literal significance according to the author and the interpretation which is derived from it by other authors and readers, especially by the contemporaries of the author. As a sociologist, Pareto is interested only in the second of these two facts; but nevertheless he affirms the second's independence of the first, and this distinction is significant, although irrelevant from the sociological point of view. In the same instance, as elsewhere, Pareto asserts that the ideas of an author have a direct relation to the sentiments of his time, but more so in the case of mediocre ones than in that of outstanding ones. This qualifies the assertion that a literary work is more effect than cause; even without admitting the possibility of the reverse, even considering it a historical, social cause, this leads to viewing literature as an activity capable of freeing itself from its own causes and effects, transcending them by means of its *raison d'être*, its own specific function.

Pareto himself seems to suggest, although not too clearly, that there is an aesthetic residue, or an aesthetic manifestation of one or several residues. In paragraph 2049, for instance, he draws a parallel between the decadence of literature in the period that extends from the decline of the Roman Empire to the late Middle Ages and the predominance in the society of that period of residues which are hostile to manifestations of culture. With this hypothesis so implied we can, for the present, satisfy ourselves. By way of conclusion we shall add that Pareto offers, informally and incidentally, several sound bits of advice to the literary historian, who could draw more than one useful lesson in method from the *Trattato*. Perhaps the pseudo-scientific habits of the literary historians of our time have never found judges more severe than this lucid observer, this fanatical scientist. His attacks against sentimental, anecdotal, biographical psychologism are amusing and always to the point (see, for instance, paragraphs 859 and 505); in almost every passage, there is cutting and scornful judgment on the cultivators of bibliographical research, on the idolators of supposedly complete bibliographies. But perhaps the wisest recommendation is to be found on the page where he places scholars on guard against the illusion that an author presents a thought — that is, a complete, perfect, coherent system of ideas — an illusion that often leads too many scholars to the vain, ridiculous, antihistoric, and antiscientific attempt to reconstruct and to expound arbitrarily a logical system that does not exist.

As we know, Pareto's sociology attempts to be, as he says, logico-experimental; and it is, exactly like the work of so many metaphysicians whom he ridicules, "ordine mathematico et more geometrico demonstrata." For Pareto science is not qualitative, but quantitative; this, however, does not prevent him, although accumulating enormous documentary materials (which also have a great qualitative value), from making fun of those who believe in the necessity of collecting all possible data before formulating any kind of theory. At any rate, Croce was right in mocking that quantitative method which leads directly to the opposite error: that of the abstraction of arbitrary principles from a mass of particulars. The section in the *Filosofia della pratica* where Croce derides the method of Pareto the economist still remains the most valid criticism even for the truer, greater Pareto, for the social theorist and the author of the *Trattato*. Because, in a sense which is neither mystic nor metaphysical, it can be said that not only philosophy but true science also, especially if it be the science of man rather than that of nature, is *scientia qualitatum, non quantitatum.*

It is clear, therefore, that in Pareto's sociology there could be no place for aesthetics, which is the affirmation of an autonomous value, to be called art or poetry, and which in its practical and reflected activity must always imply a judgment of value. This would seem to suggest that every attempt to put a theory of literature in relationship with Paretian sociology is destined to failure: and it would be true if Pareto were only a scientist. In reality, the great Pareto is a historian or a philosopher. The very doctrine of residues and derivations is not a postulate, but a hypothesis based on observation; hence its great value. Like Croce, he admires Polybius and Machiavelli; and he is, in all truth, a thinker of their stock. Unlike them he is an ideal, that is, a typical or general, historian. In the main what he has given us is really a philosophy of history — a paradoxical result because, like Croce, he denies the validity of that discipline with fervor and singular animosity. As a matter of fact, he denies the validity of every kind of philosophy, which for him is but metaphysics. Yet, in a second paradox, Pareto is after all the modern Italian who stands nearest Vico, but not the metaphysical Vico, whom he scornfully condemns, and even less the Vico of the idealistic interpretation of Croce and his school, by now conventional and traditional. He is a new, minor Vico, who has given us a *scienza nuova*, whose value lies not in the fact that its science is new, but exactly in the fact that it is a theory: a theory in the etymological sense of the word, that is to say, a synthetic vision of the real.

It is necessary to recognize that a theory thus understood is a phenomenon which has not yet taken place in that field of studies called history of culture. The cultural historian of positivistic temperament has no conception of what culture itself is. The cultural historian of humanistic tendency starts from a religious attitude toward culture; and this attitude is for him an initial, psychological presupposition. What is needed in this field is the appearance of a thinker of Pareto's temper to give us a special sociology, a philosophy of culture which transcends culture itself without denying it. The time has come for the formulation of a theory of culture capable of understanding its essence and function, of expounding its phenomenology. To such an end it is necessary to avoid two dangers. The first is the danger of positivism, or of a judgment determined only by material functions and quantitative elements, which leads to a negative conception of the action of culture in history: and this is especially the case of Marxist historiography, which reduces all culture to ideology. The second is the danger of humanism, which consists in the overvaluation of cultural factors in the historical evolution of mankind, a frequent error with thinkers whose training is more literary and philosophic than sociological or scientific.

A new sociology of culture will be capable of throwing light on such diverse problems as the action or the efficacy of education and propaganda, two activities for which extraordinary illusions are nurtured, on the one hand, and excessive fears on the other. With its help one will be able to study on new bases the most important problem of our time, which is the historical function of ideologies and utopias. In this respect, Pareto has given us more than one bit of enlightenment. Perhaps in line with his thought, we could say that education and ideologies operate as derivations, and propaganda and utopias as residues. The important thing is that we learn to look at these problems without allowing ourselves to be seduced by idealistic desires or ethical myths. The shining intellectual honesty of Pareto teaches us that there is no science where Hypocrisy persists.

NOTES

1. A careful examination of the contribution of Taine (and of other thinkers to whom we allude in these pages) to the formulation by contemporary culture of the problem of the relationship between literature and society, is found in the essay by Harry Levin, "Literature as an Institution," *Accent*, VI (1946), 159–168. The final position which, by way of hypothesis or theoretical proposition, the author takes in this study is that literature is to be considered, among other things, as a civil and social institution in itself. This concept would certainly have met with the approval of Pareto, always intent upon discovering institutional characteristics and sociological functions, even in those cultural activities which may seem purer and freer.

2. The English translation of the *Trattato di sociologia generale*, which is the only work of Vilfredo Pareto to which the present study refers, has been reprinted several times since 1935 as *Mind and Society*, by Harcourt, Brace and Company of New York. This American edition, in which Andrew Bongiorno also collaborated as the translator, is due above all to the patience and skill of the late Professor Arthur Livingston, of Columbia University. To him we owe what can be definitely called a new edition, an intelligent and practical reorganization of the original text. It is not incorrect to assert that the reading of the American edition not only is useful but necessary to the Italian scholar. Precisely for this reason, the numerical references of the paragraphs in this article direct the reader not to the original edition, but to the translation and American edition prepared by Arthur Livingston. It is to his memory that this essay is respectfully dedicated.

3. Analogous theoretical hypotheses could be formulated for the aesthetic doctrine of Marxism and for that kind of literary criticism which is based on psychoanalysis. In the first case one could speak of a literature that would be the unconscious expression of a given social condition, which instinctively expressed a historical datum, a factual state; and, on the other hand, of a literature that would be consciously intent, like the new philosophy presaged by Marx, not to interpret the world but to transform it: in other terms, a literature that would be not only passively but even actively ideological. Marxian critics, however, would not be ready to accept without protests the idea that, while what we have properly called literature may be able to serve their political ideal (without excluding that it may also serve the opposite one), poetry in a narrow sense ought, in the light of their theology, to exercise only the function of *advocatus diaboli*.

A dichotomy of this kind would be, on the other hand, easy to transplant to the soil of psychoanalysis, whose literary theoreticians are still undecided about the doctrine of literature and art as a psychological document or as its opposite, on the basis of that phenomenon which psychoanalysis itself calls sublimation. It could be supposed that these theoretical alternatives admit the possibility of the coexistence of a classical hypothesis and a romantic hypothesis within the aesthetic doctrine of psychoanalysis. In this sense, poetry would come to be interpreted as an expression of the conscious or of the unconscious according to the two opposite points of view, while literature could not be viewed except as an individual and personalistic ideology, as a mechanism for psychic defense. In other words, psychoanalytic criticism still must decide if the literary work is a direct expression of the man or of the poet, and if literary psychology is to be judged from the standpoint of the creator or of the character created.

THE ARTIST IN THE MODERN
WORLD

1. *Art and Society*

In a democratic society, as Baudelaire wrote in discussing Poe, the tyranny of public opinion prevails morally as well as culturally; but since this is a tyranny incapable of exercising authority or of establishing absolute conformity, such a society ends by tolerating — within a limited area — manifestations of eccentricity and nonconformity affected by individuals and groups operating in a direction opposed to the norms of society. Even in the field of culture, democratic society is forced to admit — in addition to conventional and official art — what is called *art d'exception.* In the very act of transgressing the norms of society by proclaiming itself to be antidemocratic and antibourgeois, avant-garde art does not realize that it pays involuntary homage to democratic middle-class society. It is not aware that it is expressing the evolutionary and progressive principle of this social order even as it abandons itself to the opposing illusions of inversion and revolution.

The avant-garde artist, like the romantic artist, often accuses modern society of killing him, and Antonin Artaud, in his knowledgeable biography of Van Gogh, does not hesitate to describe the Dutch painter as "a suicide of society." It is interesting to note that these words echo Vigny's where, in a letter on Chatterton, he described that poet as a "suicide of society." Such an accusation would make no sense, however, if it did not presuppose that the historical and psychological type of the avant-garde artist — a phenomenon typical of our social system — would be inconceivable except in a society and culture like our present one. Even if one admits that this social order condemns him to die, a different social order would simply have made it impossible for the avant-garde artist to be born. Perhaps the relationship between the artist and contemporary society was best expressed by Mallarmé, when, in an interview with newspapermen which permitted him to borrow a political image, he declared that in a period and culture like ours the artist finds himself "on strike against society." A strike cannot take place except where there are labor relations which give rise to conflicts of interest.

As we have already said, the complex series of links between avant-garde art and the society to which it belongs willy-nilly are also considered from the specific and distinct perspective of cultural reality. In terms of historical necessity, the relationship cannot help being a positive one: it is the relation of parent to child. On a deeper level, however, and in the less comprehensive sphere which is that of culture in the narrower sense of the word, this same relationship can also become consciously, deliberately, and freely negative. In this sense, avant-garde art assumes the functions and aspects of a cultural opposition to its own society and especially to the conventional, official culture.

In this connection, we may recall that this formula was first used by the critic von Sydow to define the special characteristic of European decadence. It can also be applied, with even greater validity, to modern art as a general phenomenon, without any qualifications or exceptions. The concept of a negative culture cannot mean the absolute negation of the prevailing culture, which would be a contradiction in terms, except in a metaphorical sense. It means rather the radical negation of a general culture by a specific one. In other words, decadence and avant-garde art appear only when a conflict arises between two parallel cultures in a given historical situation and in a given society. The wider and more inclusive culture can sometimes — although not always — ignore the exclusive and particular culture, but the latter has no alternative but to assume a hostile attitude toward the former.

Avant-garde art, as a minority culture, must attack and deny the majority culture to which it is opposed, that is, the mass culture which has recently appeared in the modern world because of the growth of mass communication, information, and education. Mass culture has reached the highest point of its development in American society, the most typically liberal-democratic, middle-class capitalistic, and technical-industrial of all modern societies.

At least in theory, the avant-garde artist means to react not so much against society itself as against the civilization created by society. To him the mass culture looms as a pseudo-culture, against whose specious values he directs his revolt. Faithful to a qualitative system of values, the modern artist, faced with the quantitative values of modern society, feels both left out and rebellious. This state of mind has practical social consequences, but above all it arouses in the modern artist a particular anguish: a consciousness that artists of other times and civilizations never felt so rejected or isolated, even if they were infinitely less free. From this feeling of isolation emerge dreams of revolution or reaction, of past and future utopias, and other equally impossible visions of new orders to come or old ones revived.

This social and psychological condition, characteristic of the cultural anarchy of our times, has been called *alienation*. It will be my task in the coming pages to diagnose and outline its principal features. Reversing the usual process for the moment, let us look at the prognosis, which is easily summed up in saying that the disease is chronic and destined to continue. In fact, it can only end with the death of the patient, that is, with the disappearance of the avant-garde type of artist from the historical and cultural scene, which in turn could only take place if there were to be a radical change in the social and political system. One of the reasons we presumed to deny the validity of certain statements by artists and contemporary critics predicting the imminent disappearance of the avant-garde movement — statements based on its alleged decline — was that we have not yet reached the point of believing in the imminent or fated decline of the society and civilization in which we live. To make a hypothetical and somewhat negative equation, we could say that avant-garde art is condemned to perish if our civilization is condemned to perish, that is, if the world we know is destined to decline in a future, different social order, where mass culture would be the only possible and recognized one. If an undifferentiated series of totalitarian societies were to be established, which would not permit the survival of a single intellectual minority, they would be unable to conceive, let alone recognize, the value — or even the existence — of the exceptional and individual. If, on the other hand, a change of this sort is neither imminent nor fated, avant-garde art is destined or condemned to last, blessed in its freedom and cursed in its alienation.

11. *Psychological and Social Alienation*

The state of alienation will first be considered from the viewpoint of psychological alienation. Even Marx, who first used the term, borrowing it from Hegel and from the lexicon of law (although he found the causes of what he called *Entfremdung* in progressive social degeneration, in the irreparable crises of a society incapable either of renewing itself or of dying), nevertheless traced its features in terms of individual psychology with some ethical and religious implications. He described the course of social degeneration as a process of demoralization. In short, he defined it as the feeling of futility and isolation which the individual experiences when he realizes that he is completely estranged from a society which has lost awareness of the human condition and of its own historical mission. It was above all in a psychological sense that the concept of alienation was later stretched or made narrower. At its broadest it has been applied to the situation of modern man in general, and to the plight of the modern artist in particular.

Even at the start of an analysis of the psychological phenomenon of alienation, we can see that it is not merely a painful state of mind, but a pain capable of being felt as a positive reality, as a source of enthusiasm and exaltation. In fact, there have been many romantic artists, and other eager pioneers of successive artistic generations, who have regarded this state of mind as a source of pride, and therefore as a pretext to hurl a defiant, gigantic, or Promethean challenge to the world of man, of history, and of God.

Forced to live in the desert of his abandonment or on the mountain tops of his own solitude, the artist comes to find the consolation of heroic destiny in what Baudelaire has called his "curse." In Nietzsche's terms, the artist thus thinks he can sublimate his fatal and prophetic illness in the almost superhuman creative activity which the German philosopher presupposed to be the condition of all spiritual and mental health. The artist thus hopes to fulfill himself and his own work by following the path of sin and transgression. He hopes to taste the fruit of knowledge by means of disobedience and rebellion. The artist then becomes, in Rimbaud's words, *le grand malade, le grand criminel, le grand maudit, et le supreme savant!*

Such euphoria was short-lived, however, and was found to be only a morbid illusion. Later, the state of alienation came to be considered a pathetic and tragic rather than a heroic and Dionysian experience. Because of this feeling, the artist was driven to turn the weapons of his antagonism and nihilism against himself, instead, as formerly, against society and the external world.

Baudelaire already approached this attitude in his myth of the *heautontimoroumenos*, the self-tormentor. Sometimes the artist ends by considering the state of alienation as a disgrace or as a moral ghetto. When he tries to react against such a fate, he finds no other escape than self-caricature or self-mockery. Aware that bourgeois society looks at him only as a charlatan, the artist deliberately and ostentatiously assumes the role of comic actor. From this stems the myth of the artist as Pagliaccio and mountebank. Between the alternating extremes of self-criticism and self-pity, the artist comes to see himself sometimes as a comic victim and sometimes as a tragic victim, although the latter seems to predominate. In recent years, in the milieux of avant-garde artists and critics, under the influence of psychological and anthropological theory, the artist has consequently been conceived as a sort of *agnus dei*, or sacrificial lamb, an innocent creature on whom society turns its own sense of error and sin. The artist is sacrificed so that the blood thus spilled will redeem the sins of the whole tribe. In this way the poet or artist, having fallen from the position of the elect to that of the rejected (one has only to think of the themes of exile on earth, of curses, of disappointment, in the well-known words of Nerval, Baudelaire, and Mallarmé), assumes in turn the new role of saint and martyr. He may even assert that he has a quasi-religious vocation rather than emphasize the satanic impulse of revolt, evoked by Baudelaire in his dictum, "the man of letters is the enemy of the world."

Sometimes the state of alienation is conceived not only in ethical and psychical terms, in the "science of the mind," to use Toynbee's phrase, but also in purely pathological terms. We have already mentioned the exaltation of illness and of the accursed condition by Baudelaire and Nietzsche; but now the exaltation gives way to submission and piety, precisely because these states are no longer treated as metaphysical realities — in the mystical and figurative sense — but as objective, physical phenomena, as illnesses in the literal sense of the word.

This approach has established a fatal identity between *art* and *neurosis*, as an obvious consequence of the theories of Freud and psychoanalysis. It has, in fact, equated the concept of alienation with the occupational illness of the artist and the writer. Edmund Wilson, for instance, in his collection of essays *The Wound and the Bow*, revives the myth of Philoctetes, abandoned with the shame of his wound on the island of Lemnos, with no other support than that of his own bow, to suggest that the vocation of the artist is linked to an innate pathological tendency, to a rift between body and mind and to evil in the body, no less than in the mind. Sometimes that most terrible illness, which corrodes the brain and the intelligence, insanity, is considered to be almost an occupational hazard of the artist, just because the state of alienation, with the fatal dualism that accompanies it, might contribute to the development of that split in the mind of the patient which is called schizophrenia. In this connection, it is perhaps worth noting that many psychoanalysts who have studied the alienation of the artist are naturally inclined to interpret the concept in a sense analogous to the psychiatric sense of the term.

The historical origin of the term alienation — the significant fact that it was coined and first applied by Marx — as well as the internal logic of the concept, which presupposes the existence of a larger body to which the individual must first belong before he can be alienated, suffice in themselves to show that the psychological definition of alienation is inseparable from the sociological definition. We have already said something about what we may call the *social alienation* of the modern artist elsewhere, speaking of the unpopularity of avant-garde art and its relation to politics. We shall return to this problem from a different point of view. Here it is sufficient to repeat again what we said about the relation of the avant-garde to its public, that is, to deny again that this public is identical with the cultural and social group known as the intelligentsia, and to deny that the state of alienation can justifiably be considered in purely classical terms. For other reasons, however, this does not prevent us from examining the state of alienation in the particular perspective of the economic conditions of modern art, and the relations between the artist and society which are affected by work. There is no doubt that an important aspect of the social alienation of the artist takes the form of *economic alienation*.

III. *Economic and Cultural Alienation*

It might be maintained that the development of the alienated state of mind, like the appearance of avant-gardism, is a phenomenon, if not wholly determined, at least partly conditioned by the economic situation of the artist and the writer, notably by the practical, ideological, and psychic effects of sudden economic changes in relatively recent times. In other words, the modern artist or writer has not yet succeeded in reconciling himself wholly to the fact that capitalist, bourgeois society tends to treat him on the one hand as a parasite and consumer and, on the other, as a worker or producer rather than as a creator. The society which gives him the opportunity to earn his living directly by the public sale of his own work, and by selling his time and labor, has subjected him to the dangers of alternating economic independence and dependence. By putting him on a level with the industrial worker, society has subjected the artist to the hazards of unemployment and overproduction, thus creating what the English critic Christopher Caudwell described as "the false position of the poet as a producer for the market." Courtier or artisan, the writer or artist of other times could count on the relative security offered him by the protection of a sponsor or the responsibility of a patron. Reduced to the status of an industrial worker, the modern artist is deprived of any guarantee that the fruits of his labor — under the market law of supply and demand — can fill certain needs which, if not urgent, are at least fairly extensive and regular.

Given the fact that bourgeois society, with its cult of respectability and its tendency to distinguish clearly between intellectual work and manual labor, prefers to consider the fruit of artistic and literary endeavor as a service rather than as a product, the modern artist or writer is naturally led to assume the attitude that he is a free professional; but in most cases he lacks the fixed clientele that the doctor, the lawyer, and the engineer can count on. Bourgeois society and government are naturally (and fortunately, we think) not inclined to regularize and set norms for the artist's work as a necessary, although unproductive, social service, as they do for the clergyman, the judge, and the teacher. Thus when a tendency of this sort appears to any considerable or lasting degree, it is recognized as a symbol of radical change in the social structure. In totalitarian or nonliberal societies, or in exceptional circumstances such as temporary dictatorship during a major war, there occurs the fairly recent phenomenon of bureaucratization of intellectuals, writers, and artists.

For different but equally important reasons, it is interesting to observe the rare examples of contemporary patronage of the arts, which cannot help operating in a bourgeois way. While the patrons of the past operated with individual initiative even if they had access to public funds, in our day even private patrons tend to operate in a public and civic sense.

Despite the dangers and difficulties of the situation, the modern artist and writer have opened the door to financial success to a point simply unthinkable in earlier times or societies. It is certainly not pure coincidence that our era, in which — to take an example from the field of literature — the important book is one written for a selected public, in a small edition for a limited number of collectors and literary persons, should also be the era of bestsellers, which are sometimes sold by the million. In other words, the age of modern art and *littérature d'exception* is also the era of commercial literature and industrial art.

This gives rise to the frequent and usually sincere refusal, on the part of the real artist in our day, to give in to the lure of material success. Furthermore, even if he allows himself to be tempted, the artist can only put his trust in chance or luck because the public he wishes to reach is not reducible to a definite entity or to a series of classifiable groups — thanks to its great numbers, the complexity of its needs, and the variations in its structure. Nothing is more significant than the American tendency to classify the public in the three categories of "high-brow," "middle-brow," and "low-brow." It is still true, however, that neither the critic and the sociologist, who operate with hindsight and judgment *a posteriori*, nor, even less, the writer and the artist, who must act intuitively and *a priori*, are in a position to determine even approximately the structure and the particular standards of taste of any of these categories at a given moment.

We repeat that the modern artist tends to reject the temptation of material success and, if it is an undefined public to which he addresses himself, it is necessarily limited in number, socially incoherent, and perpetually subject to capricious changes of fashion. It must, perforce, be the group known by the ridiculous and mocking epithet, "high-brow." This tendency might seem to be a quasi-traditional and classical return to the judgment of an intelligent, elite public, appealed to by a creative aristocracy, but this would be only a surface judgment. This public has no clearly defined existence as a social group or distinct entity. The very concept of "high-brow" presupposes the coexisting groups of "middle-brow" and "low-brow"; the boundaries are often blurred or distinguished only by degree. What is more important in this alleged return to an older pattern is a very new phenomenon, directly determined — by way of an extreme unyielding reaction — by the historical attitude which prevailed in the immediate past and which operated in the opposite way.

As a psychological phenomenon avant-garde art — at least in its most recent and extreme forms — may seem to have arisen as a reaction provoked by the failure to establish a different and contrary type of social order. In the hundred years from the last quarter of the eighteenth century to the last quarter of the nineteenth century, many writers, and to a lesser degree some artists, conceived the ambitious notion of transforming the pen or the brush, the fiddler's bow or the conductor's baton, into a marshal's baton. In other words, they hoped to acquire with their own tools intellectual power, moral prestige, and social authority comparable to conquests which were being made with the scepter, the miter, and the sword. The same degree of commercial success was not sought except as a symbol of the triumph, a laurel won with the victory.

This was the dream of Balzac, who chose as his mission "to complete with the pen what Napoleon had begun with the sword." The dream was shared, with greater or less intensity, by the greatest artists and writers of the period, from Voltaire and Rousseau to Dostoevski and Tolstoy. This ambition was often conceived in terms of religious preaching and moral conversion, rather than as an armed conquest of new realms of the mind. No one represented this dream or embodied this ambition with greater audacity and magnificence than Balzac himself. He did not succeed, however, in gaining the power he sought; even less did he gain the economic authority of that power. For this very reason Pedro Salinas describes this dream — "the power of the writer" — and the failure of this ambition, by a phrase which is also the title of one of Balzac's famous novels, *Lost Illusions*. By a highly significant coincidence, the role of historic symbol, identical to Salinas', had already been attributed to the same novel of Balzac's by a very different critic, the Marxist Georg Lukács. Lukács, in fact, considered Balzac's masterpiece to be the first conscious revelation on the part of any modern artist that he had fallen permanently to the level of a pure and simple "producer for the market," in Caudwell's phrase. Lukács' opinion is that in *Illusions perdues* Balzac focuses the story not only on Lucien de Rubempré but also on the transformation of literary production into merchandise.

Although the modern artist may be conscious that those illusions are forever lost, he has not yet succeeded in ignoring or in forgetting completely the very dream in which he is no longer able to believe. This psychological ambivalence, caused by disappointment and nostalgia, justifies the artist's paradoxical lament, which is both antihistorical and illogical, about the scarcity — or the outright lack — of a contemporary public for his work. In fact, this lament was voiced in a period when for the first time that public potentially coincided with the majority of the population. It was voiced by the type of artist who, by definition, addressed himself to a restricted or specific public, which is differentiated from an unlimited, general public by means of a deliberate act of opposition. This lament makes sense only insofar as the contemporary artist — despite his disdain and affectation — continues to nurse an unspoken yearning for happier and safer times when the creator could count on an attentive, faithful, and unified public, however small it might be, to which he was linked by a set of identical presuppositions and by the same artistic and aesthetic values. One might say that the modern artist, who worships genius, does not at all resign himself, at least in his inner mind, to the permanent loss of the advantages inherent in cultural environments which are dominated by the principle of genius rather than by that of taste.

In the optimistic atmosphere of early romanticism, Wordsworth, while recognizing the difficulty of the situation, accepted it as an inevitable and natural circumstance when he stated that "every poet must create the taste by which he is to be enjoyed." In postromantic culture, however, this particularly arduous task of the modern genius becomes an enormous undertaking, futile and also impossible. The pathos of this vain and titanic effort, symbolized by many modern artists in the myths of Tantalus and Sisyphus, leads the poet of our time to choose as the supreme theme of art the tragic, problematic nature of his own work, the labor of poetry itself. A culture which is dominated by such a dichotomy between culture and taste, rather than coordinating them or subordinating one to the other, is destined at first not to be able to count on the existence of an elite capable of accepting, appreciating, and judging works of art, because it is not only the artist but also the elite which finds itself perpetually in the state T. S. Eliot suggestively describes as "disassociation of sensibility." In any case, the artist must continually search for this elite without the certainty of finding it either at the beginning or at the end of his career. He may spend all his life aimlessly plodding on in his desolate no-man's land. This futile pilgrimage makes him consider the act of creation itself as a game of chance, a toss of the dice on the table of fate, as Mallarmé did. Whereas the classical artist, who looked only to the remote past and the distant future, succeeded in finding himself in harmony with his own contemporaries, the modern artist, so conscious of the task assigned to him by the *Zeitgeist* itself, ends by considering even a work in progress as a sort of posthumous work. Mallarmé himself showed awareness of this particular situation when he declared in a little-known interview, "for me, the case of the poet in this society, which does not allow him to live, is the case of a man who isolates himself to carve his own tomb."

Such considerations, which bring into paradoxical relief what we might call the contemporary artist's feeling of *historical alienation*, lead us to the purely sociological interpretation of the concept of alienation. A cultural sociology of our times can only be constructed on the hypothesis of a pluralism of intellectual levels, which are distinct and contradictory. This pluralism blocks crystallization or formalization. What occurs is really the opposite of the clearly hierarchical stratification of medieval society, or of primitive, archaic civilizations. The cultural and social situation of our time is in a state of continual flux, a never-ending process of agitation and metamorphosis.

From the political point of view, this situation produces a phenomenon opposite to what Pareto called "the circulation of the elites," which really means circulation within the elites. Instead, what happens is a continual rise and fall from one elite to another, and between elite and nonelite. For this very reason, the artist and the intellectual are naturally led to form their own group and to assume a distinct position, detached from the traditional culture of the society to which they belong, at least by origin. It is a continuous process of disintegration, because society and various social groups react in their turn in an equally strong, but contrary, direction. It can be said that this relationship of reciprocal destruction is, on the surface at least, the only real link which connects avant-garde art to its own social environment. This reduction of the relations between art and society to a purely negative function, which from the artist's point of view is alienation both in name and in form, is a new historical fact of incalculable importance and profound significance. When critics and observers praise or blame avant-garde art for its refusal not only to serve but even to express contemporary society, they fail to realize that avant-garde art is not only the direct expression of a negative cultural relationship, but also the indirect expression of the human and social condition which has created this schism in the structure of the culture.

Sometimes the negative nature of this relation takes the form of reciprocal inertia, creating the illusion that a given aesthetic experience occurred virtually without any contact with its setting. In this case, social alienation takes the form of isolation from history and isolation in time. To describe manifestations of this kind, or, rather, to locate them on the map which represents the battlefield of modern culture, Caudwell, a Marxist, coined the idea of the "poetic pocket," using an image from the art of the past, seeing them in those aesthetic expressions that seem to unfold by a purely internal logic for which it would be impossible to find analogous or parallel lines of development in contemporary social and political life. There are even more examples in modern art, in my opinion, especially in the movement of aestheticism, and in the groups which are partially distinct from the movement as a whole and become what are called "sects." Caudwell knows better than we do that no human activity, even the freest, can function in a void, in a condition of absolute ignorance of its own historical context. For this reason, the term "poetic pocket" describes a situation which is more apparent than real. If it is applied with discrimination to the theme of this study, however, the term is useful and suggestive, just because it puts into clear relief — to the point of absurdity — the state of opposition in which avant-garde art has found itself when faced with present social reality.

It is really the fanatical supporters of the absolute value of aesthetic isolation who are most disposed to accuse society of failing in its alleged duty to give practical aid and moral support to the activities of *art d'exception*. Forgetting that such activity is often characterized by social inertia, they do not seem to realize that society cannot respond to this inertia except by a similar inactivity. Need we repeat that avant-garde art is short-sighted in accusing, from its own isolation, the only type of society in which this isolation has become both necessary and possible? Avant-garde art has no right to protest that it is not treated like a wildflower when it is a hot-house flower. Like the metaphor of the poetic pocket, this image of the hot-house flower may perhaps serve to emphasize a truth already mentioned, that is, that the alienation of modern art from its society, and vice versa, not only manifests itself in psychological and sociological, economic and practical forms, but also in cultural and aesthetic forms. And although we have not heretofore had occasion to examine purely formal values, alienation in cultural and aesthetic forms is the most significant and striking of all. Turning now to the formal aspects of the question, let us consider the more intimate aesthetic criterion of style from the viewpoint of stylistic alienation.

IV. *Stylistic and Aesthetic Alienation*

Malraux observed that the origins of modern art coincided with the repudiation of bourgeois culture on the part of the artist. In contemporary aesthetic ideology, he said, "it is not the proletariat or the aristocracy which is the object of antagonism, but the artist." The antagonism between the bourgeois mind and the artistic mind, which, like all antagonisms, implies an interdependent relationship between the two forces, has become the theme par excellence of Thomas Mann's work, in which the antagonism is reduced from a social controversy, a public and external conflict, to a private question, a psychic crisis. If at times the drama falls to the level of comedy, describing the artist as bourgeois and ironically invoking the ambivalence created by that situation, at other times it borders on tragedy, when the writer describes the bourgeois as artist, representing him as the victim of an alter ego in his innermost self, and as the creator of work which is the artistic nemesis of bourgeois culture. If, on the sociological plane, the problem of the relations between the artistic mind and the bourgeois mind ends, in spite of everything, in a synthesis, on the historical plane the problem remains unresolved and in a state of antithesis. In the latter perspective, that of culture, which underlines the separation as well as the reciprocal nature of the two opposites, it must of course be asserted as an absolute principle that the real art of bourgeois society must be antibourgeois. It is more important to note that such a principle operates not only in the realm of content but also in that of form. Modern art, therefore, opposes the stylistic theory and practice which dominate the society and civilization it belongs to. Its chief function is to react against bourgeois taste. We say taste, rather than style, because, to quote Malraux again, "there are styles of the bourgeois era but there is not a single bourgeois style." What matters here, therefore, is not so much the denial of the existence of a bourgeois style as the affirmation — a paradox only in appearance — of the coexistence of many styles within the culture of the middle class. The postulate that interests us is, then, that a pluralism of styles is one of the defining characteristics of the contemporary artistic situation, or, if you will, of bourgeois culture.

It is really by way of reaction against the pluralism of bourgeois taste that avant-garde art takes the path of stylistic dissent. According to Malraux, the modern artist ventured into the field of deformation and abstractionism with the intention of escaping from that "imaginary museum" or "museum without walls" in which he had found himself enclosed since the invention, perfection, and diffusion of photographic reproduction, which has made even the most archaic and esoteric artistic creations of all schools, all styles, all times, and all countries accessible and familiar to the most inexperienced artist and to the most provincial and remote public. *Art d'exception*, in this case painting, might thus appear as an act of protest against the cosmopolitanism and universalism of contemporary taste. These, incidentally, are the most obvious, external characteristics of a phenomenon as ambiguous and complex as contemporary aesthetic pluralism. If the preservation of such pluralism is also the fruit of negative factors, such as eclectic tolerance or skeptical indifference, its initial appearance was made possible by a series of conflicts and crises. The first of these conflicts was, naturally, that which divides once and for all the art and culture of the avant-garde from popular art and culture in the traditional sense. One becomes conscious of the separation provoked by such a conflict only after the failure of romantic "populism" or exaltation of "the people." The separation itself, seen as an unbridgeable chasm, came later, when scientific sociology established rather too neat a distinction between culture in the humanist sense and culture in the anthropological sense. Since then, purely ethnic cultures have almost completely disappeared from Western civilization, and this disappearance is only one of many nemeses in a democratic, technological, and industrial civilization like ours. Many artists of our time, those, so to speak, less extremely and typically futuristic, have realized that the very nature of our civilization leads to loss or annihilation of the values represented by more deeply rooted traditions, which are less self-conscious and more spontaneous. They have imagined that they could alter the process by postulating unattainable restorations or expecting impossible solutions.

The first of these illusions deceived a man of the Right, T. S. Eliot, who dreamed of a new medievalism in the future, with a hierarchical society and a stratified culture. The other illusion was cherished by a man of the Left, Herbert Read, who recommended the reconstitution of a popular culture and a craftsman's art in the setting of a progressive society. Unfortunately, modern society, through specialization and technology, has broken all ties between craftsmanship and artistic endeavor and has destroyed every form of folklore and ethnic culture, transforming the very concept of the people, which today is synonymous with the quite different concept of the masses. Thus Read's program, like Eliot's nostalgia, is easily recognized for what it is, a retrospective utopia. In reality, there has been only one modern poet who has penetrated the sources of national folklore, the Spaniard García Lorca, who belonged to a society which was still static and crystallized. Despite the similarity of the situation, the modern Irish poets, from Yeats on, were not in a position to achieve equally successful results, because they were constrained to use English — the language of a modern culture — as their instrument.

In the figurative arts, the ethnic element operates at present only on the lower level of applied arts and decoration. Modern painting and sculpture, as shown by abstractionism, immediately produce a rigid, mechanical effect, rather than the effect of the ingenious arabesques of popular art. Despite its modernism, recent art has allowed itself to be more easily seduced by esoteric and archaic styles, preferring to follow the pattern of archeology rather than the example of ethnology. An intermingling of popular and modern styles is very rare, since the art of our time — just because it flourishes in a state of stylistic pluralism — tends to take on the pure form of any style, unless, as in the special case of Decadence, it hates eclectic styles and syncretic forms. The same principle applies to the great "chameleon-like" artists of our time, such as Picasso and Stravinsky, who, in passing with facility from one stylistic phase to another, finally attain a unique style which pervades every one of their works.

The more important conflict is not between avant-garde art and ethnical culture, but between avant-garde art and mass culture. The latter, which is absolutely different from culture in the anthropological sense, is nevertheless called in English "popular" art and culture. This does not mean popular in the romantic sense — culture or art created by the people — but popular in the empirical and practical sense of art and culture produced *for* the masses. From this point of view, such popular art is the most genuine aspect assumed by bourgeois cultures in countries of great technical and industrial potentiality. In such countries, furthermore, the very concept of "the people" today has no other function than to distinguish the group of manual laborers from the vast class called *petite bourgeoisie*, which also includes farmers, artisans, and others. It seems almost inevitable that in this society, which has seen the assimilation of the proletariat by the bourgeoisie, there arises immediately also the proletarianization of culture. The second of these phenomena does not appear by itself; it appears exclusively in capitalist society. The mass culture which dominates in Communist Russia is imposed from above; it is not the natural result of public consensus, according to the law of supply and demand, but an artificial political production, following the authoritarian formula of the "social mandate." In other words, what has taken place in Russia is not so much a proletarianization as a "bureaucratization" of culture, which has made the artist a functionary rather than a producer. The immediate effect of this special change is that it has destroyed avant-garde art and produced a state of alienation. Meanwhile, from our particular point of view, this new fact suffices to prove that Trotsky was right when, toward the end of the first phase of the Communist experiment, he denied that a proletarian art or culture could — or should — continue to exist under the domination of the "dictatorship of the proletariat."

The only genuine form of proletarian art and culture is that which is prefabricated at the lowest intellectual level of the bourgeoisie itself. As to literature, this phenomenon has already been noted by Christopher Caudwell, on one of the most suggestive pages of his *Illusion and Reality*: "The authentic proletarian literature of every day consists of the thrillers, the love-stories, the cowboy stories, the popular movies, jazz and the yellow press." Essentially, it is this culture of the mass and proletarian art (the only types of popular art and culture possible in a society like ours) that avant-garde art opposes, an opposition supporting the fact, already noted, that the task of avant-gardism is to fight against articulate public opinion, against tradition and academic culture, against the bourgeois intelligentsia.

The tragic and unique predicament of avant-garde art lies in its necessity to fight on two fronts, that is, to fight against two types of artistic or pseudo-artistic production which are in a state of opposition and mutual negation. Edmund Wilson has given these two types the paradoxically contrasting names, "classics" and "commercials." Bourgeois culture is certainly incapable of discriminating between the value of the first and the worthlessness of the second, just as the bourgeois critic is incapable of setting up criteria of taste which would distinguish between the various levels of the contemporary public. Avant-gardism instinctively opposes them both, however. It fulfills a function no less genuine and primary than its protest against the culture of the dominating class when it opposes its minor by-products in the art and culture of the masses (in Caudwell's sense of the word).

This double reaction, against bourgeois taste and against proletarian taste, can definitively explain the statements — contradictory only in appearance — that the psychology of the avant-garde is dominated by an aristocratic or antiproletarian tendency and by an anarchical or antibourgeois tendency. On the sociological level as well as on the aesthetic level, there is no conflict between the two tendencies. The parallel oppositions to bourgeois taste and to proletarian taste converge in the single opposition to the criterion they hold in common, that which unites them. This can be identified as a common cult of the cliché. Thus reappears on a higher level the relationship already established between avant-gardism and the banal, a relation of interdependence, precisely because it is determined by a reciprocal resistance of equal strength on both sides. As we have already said, banality is only the modern form of ugliness. If the criterion of beauty is as indefinable as it is unique, the category of ugliness — even if considered as a series of historical variants — is, on the other hand, infinite and thus susceptible of innumerable definitions. This proves again, to the point of absurdity, the complex and irreducible aesthetic pluralism of our time.

The recognition of pluralism, very important in the sociology of taste, loses all meaning or value on the level of artistic creativity, where it has only a negative function, if any. An epoch which has many styles has none. This truth holds also in the case where multiplicity is reducible to a simpler dualistic relation. By-passing for a moment the basic antithesis of modern art — between avant-garde style and all opposing styles — and limiting ourselves to a partial and provisional antithesis, it is easy to recognize that, where no bourgeois style exists, no proletarian style can exist. In other words, proletariat and bourgeoisie, in relation to mass culture, take their styles where they find them, that is, from cultures and societies different from their own. In short, the absence of a style of its own is a phenomenon not confined to capitalism or socialism, but is characteristic of all democratic societies, in the liberal sense or otherwise, of all quantitative, technical, and industrial civilizations.

Just because it is deprived of a style of its own, a civilization of this type prefers an eclectic style, in which technical ability in the aesthetic sense is combined with technical ability in the practical sense. Such a style is formed by means of a synthesis, or rather a syncretization of traditional forms, academic and realistic, regulated by the wholly modern taste for photography and stereotype. The artist of our time, just because he can easily imitate all techniques, ancient or modern, scientific or artistic, since he has at hand the means to realize perfectly the effects of *trompe l'oeil*, refuses to accept as his own a style which becomes a purely mechanical product and is thus the negation of style in the real sense of the word. This refusal becomes an act or gesture impossible for the artist who operates in a technical civilization or in a mass culture when it is at the same time a totalitarian society. The point is, again, proved by the case of Soviet Russia, where the formula of "socialist realism" is not only an ideological dogma which determines the content of art but also a stylistic canon, so that in the graphic arts as well as in literature, the point is reached where any divergence from official style is regarded not only as an aesthetic heresy but also as a political deviation, and is condemned specifically as "formalism." The refusal to follow a prescribed style or mass taste sanctioned by public consensus, whether active or passive, remains both positive and necessary within a really bourgeois society, which is obliged to admit the existence of minorities and exceptional individuals. Naturally, this tolerance is only a negative reality and as such provokes in turn the intolerance of the artist. Jean-Paul Sartre went so far as to say that, thanks to the unification of the public (he might more accurately have said the confusion), a phenomenon resulting from the diffusion of mass culture from the lowest social levels to the highest, the modern writer has no alternative but to assume a position of absolute intransigence, undifferentiated antagonism, to the often numerous and always indistinct mass of his own readers. The quotation is worth including, for it closes with a just recognition of the historical uniqueness of this negative relationship: "To tell the truth, the drastic blurring of levels in the public since 1848 has caused the author initially to write against all readers . . . this fundamental conflict between the writer and the public is an unprecedented phenomenon in the history of literature."

The affirmation of the existence of such discord and the attempt to define its essence appears in almost the same words in Georg Lukács' preface to his book, *Studies in European Realism*, in which the Hungarian critic traces the origins of the phenomenon to the French Revolution and romanticism, once more situating the turning point in Balzac's work: "From the French Revolution on, social evolution has proceeded in one direction, which makes for an inevitable conflict between the aspirations of men of letters and their contemporary public. In this entire period the writer could achieve greatness only insofar as he reacted against the everyday currents. Since Balzac, the resistance of everyday life to the basic trends of literature and art has grown constantly stronger." Sartre's judgment, confirmed by Lukács, leads us to conclude that in the course of the last century, and perhaps for more than a century and a half, the state of alienation has changed from an exceptional condition to the regular norm for the modern artist and writer.

In this condition we find one more reaffirmation that the principle of bourgeois art is to be antibourgeois. It is again to Sartre that we turn for the expression of this general truth from the particular perspective of the artist: "The bourgeois writer and the accursed writer work on the same level." This means that the bourgeois writer or artist is in a constant state of social protest; it does not mean that he becomes a real revolutionary in the political sense. Similarly, even when the artist is driven to embrace — sometimes for purely aesthetic motives — a reactionary ideal, he is not necessarily transformed into a conservative. It should not be forgotten that his social protest manifests itself mainly on the level of form, and thus alienation from society becomes also *alienation from tradition*. In contrast to the classical artist, who could draw on tradition as a stable and recurrent series of public expressions, the modern artist works in chaos and in darkness and is overcome by the feeling of impending upheaval in language and style.

Avant-garde art seems destined, therefore, to oscillate forever between opposing poles of alienation, psychological and social, economic and historical, aesthetic and stylistic. There is no doubt that all forms of alienation lead ultimately to ethical alienation, and it is certainly to the latter that Sartre refers in the passage quoted above. This alienation expressed itself, even before the advent of existentialism, in the art and literature of revolt that has been so conspicuous in culture and thought from romanticism onward, and which, in the case of avant-gardism in the narrow sense, shows itself with the greatest intensity in German expressionism. The investigation of this revolt would carry us too far and go beyond the limits of the present study, whose task is to examine avant-gardism and alienation as historical norms and as intellectual expressions. Here we would say only that, even when it refuses to yield to the siren-song of aestheticism and renounces the temptation of self-worship, avant-gardism is nonetheless condemned to a liberty which is slavery, and to serve too often the negative and destructive principle of art for art's sake.

POETICS AND METRICS

Students of literature have insufficiently taken into account that complex relationship between poetics and versification which takes place within the framework of each national literature, and which changes within each of its several periods. Such a relationship should be first established theoretically, and then studied in its concrete historical details. What must be avoided in either phase of research are wrong critical generalizations or false aesthetic presuppositions. Since such generalizations and presuppositions derive in most cases from mistaken interpretations of linguistic peculiarities, or from national preconceptions and prejudices, raising into universal standards the special values or the peculiar bias of a given tradition, it is evident that the relationship itself may be fully understood only if it is viewed and assessed from the standpoint of comparative literature.

In its functional sense, poetics may be properly defined as a set of empirical rules or precepts seeking to direct, or at least to affect, literature in the making. Ideally, and even actually, poetics is then a very different discipline from aesthetics; and we should sharply differentiate between the two. Such a differentiation failed, however, to take place in Western culture before the modern age: the distinction or separation of their respective methods and outlooks is a feat that must be credited to romantic thought. It is symptomatic that from romanticism on there have been numberless thinkers and artists producing aesthetic treatises, either for their or for our own benefit, while practically no one has ever again presented his fellow workers or the public with one of those handbooks of poetics which once were held the most permanent feature or fixture of the classical tradition.

This does not mean that the classical tradition was indifferent to the philosophical principles of art; it rather means that practical and pedagogical concerns were more important for that tradition than thinking or teaching about art in the abstract. Now it appears that the situation has been reversed, or even that it has radically changed. Modern writers about artistic and literary problems either subordinate poetics to aesthetics or, more often, ignore poetics entirely. Naturally enough, poetics seems to be no longer a live issue for the modern literary mind, which is intolerant of any didacticism in the domain of the arts. This is particularly evident in practical criticism, where at present no one judges a literary work from the viewpoint of its failure or success in realizing the ideals of the genre to which it belongs. A poem, a novel, a play are no longer appraised *qua* poem, novel, or play. In other words, the rules of traditional poetics have ceased to act as critical standards.

It would be wrong to infer from this that the normative function of poetics is wholly inoperative in modern literature. On the contrary, even in our time every author accepts and follows a given set of presuppositions, determining and conditioning his writing at least in the realm of what is now being called "conventional form." The very truth which leads contemporary literary thought to condemn "the intentional fallacy" prevents that thought from acknowledging another truth: from recognizing the existence, as well as the effectiveness, of a modern poetics, fulfilling the outstanding task of all poetics, which is to influence the conception and creation of a work in progress as related to the traditional model or conventional pattern after which it molds itself. After all, like its ancient counterpart, modern poetics is but a system of literary genres.

On the theoretical plane, we may accept or reject Croce's denial of the validity of aesthetic categories, his paradoxical belief that literary and artistic genres do not exist, or that they exist only as fictitious classification devices. The partial aesthetic truth contained in this extreme negation prevails in modern critical practice: as already noted, almost all the critics of our time may well begin by describing or explaining a literary work within the frame of reference of the pertinent genre, only to discard or transcend that frame of reference as soon as they are faced with the task of evaluation. Yet, all this notwithstanding, the empirical and historical existence of genres can hardly be denied. What counts more, however, is that genre concepts are still very much alive in the consciousness of the creative writer of our time.

Before writing *À la recherche du temps perdu, Der Zauberberg,* and *Ulysses,* Marcel Proust, Thomas Mann, and James Joyce had in mind an idea, both general and unique, of the novel they wanted to write. In other words, those writers worked within a vague, vast, and yet definite circle of literary possibilities: a circle constituting by itself a modern poetics of the novel. By the very novels so produced they outlined, enlarged, and even opened that circle, which now may well look like a spiral, with Proust's novel at its center, Mann's at its closed end, and Joyce's at its open and shifting one. Since Proust, Mann, and Joyce could not rely, as the writers of other ages could, on an Aristotle or a Boileau who would codify for them and their readers their own principles, one must conclude that they worked not after a written poetics, but after an unwritten one. Such was certainly the case: and from this fact we must deduce that the poet or the playwright of our epoch also works like the novelist after an unwritten poetics of the genre he has chosen to cultivate.

This discovery helps us to recognize that the existence of an unwritten poetics is not a phenomenon peculiar to our time. Although this fact has escaped the conscious attention of most literary scholars, unwritten poetics have existed in every age, either alone or alongside written ones, the last alternative being characteristic of all neoclassical periods. In primitive ages, we have only unwritten poetics; in eclectic, composite, and decadent epochs, they predominate over the written ones; in classical or neoclassical periods they are less influential than the written ones, affecting preferably those special or minor currents which flow apart from the main stream. Sometimes a writer feels the need to fix one of those unwritten poetics: it was against the authority of Aristotle and his disciples that Lope de Vega wrote his *Arte nuevo de hacer comedias*, where he justified and codified the practice of himself and other popular playwrights. By doing so, Lope showed his double awareness of the existence of the written poetics of classical tragedy, on one side, and of the unwritten poetics of the popular drama on the other. Paradoxically, he wrote down the rules of the latter while claiming that the writer of *comedias* should lock "with seven keys" the book of classical rules.

There is another fact literary scholars have failed to notice or to examine with the attention it deserves. All handbooks of poetics, and with them the literary praxis of all classicism, concern themselves exclusively with compositions in verse. This is another of the meanings of the term "poetics," which must thus be traditionally defined as a set of precepts referring to poetic genres, where the adjective stands for "couched in metered speech." From Aristotle to Horace, from Vida to Scaliger, from Boileau to Pope, all *artes poeticae* deal at least with the epic poem and the drama, both as tragedy and comedy; or also with the ode and the hymn, with satire and the elegy, with the eclogue and the idyll. In brief, whatever their range, all those *artes poeticae* concern themselves only and always with versified structures. Their authors fail to discuss any nonpoetic genre: so, for instance, Boileau and Pope refuse to treat or even mention the romance and the novel, since the latter cannot qualify as legitimate, "regular," or "classical" forms for being written in prose. In conclusion, what a traditional *ars poetica* offers us is only and always a stylistics of verse writing, and this is why it handles not only the problem of genres, but also the question of "poetic diction," while leaving the stylistics of prose writing, along with the theory of tropes, to the handbooks of rhetorics.

From this two consequences derive. One concerns modern poetics, which is generally unwritten; the other concerns the silent poetics existing within traditional poetics, which is vocal par excellence. The first consequence is that modern poetics deals also with prose forms, not only with the novel, which is one of the chief genres of modern literature, but also with the drama, now rarely written in verse, and even with those lyrical forms which admit of nonrhythmical media, such as the prose poem. The other consequence is that, while dealing at length with all genres written in the medium of verse, traditional poetics neglects almost regularly to prescribe the metrical vehicle best suited to a given genre or sub-genre.

Such a neglect may well be due to the fact that in many cases writers and readers act on the unvoiced postulate that a certain kind of literature can be written only in a certain kind of meter: but this is another way of saying that within or alongside the written or articulate poetics there exists another, inarticulate or unwritten. At least for our purpose, what seems even more significant is that one of the main tasks of the latter is to interconnect a historical system of literary genres with a parallel system of verse forms. It is through the sanction of unwritten poetics that a given meter comes to be generally viewed as the most characteristic technical and formal instrument of a given genre. In conclusion, it is predominantly through tacit agreement that poetics legislates the exchanges taking place between metrics and itself.

Even here legislation comes after, rather than before, the fact. Many specialized literary historians, particularly Hellenists and medievalists, are aware of this truth, as well as of a literary law which has hardly attracted the interest and speculation of students cultivating such broader disciplines as literary theory or general literature. That law can be stated by saying that the apparition of a new literary genre is always accompanied by the invention or the exclusive adoption by that genre of a definite verse form. In a primitive age a definite verse form seems to be uniquely apt for a given genre, so as to become almost identical with it. For a primitive as well as for a popular poet, it is practically impossible to conceive the possibility of employing a different metrical medium for the genre of his choice, or of employing the same medium for a different one.

We consider still valid Friedrich Schlegel's statement that, though the dogmas of classical literary thought are no longer acceptable for the modern mind, the natural development of Greek poetry from Homer to Euripides remains canonical and exemplary. As Schlegel and most romanticists found, we also find the same canonical and exemplary quality in the development of medieval poetry, at least within the period which opens with the emergence of vernacular writing and ends with the rise of humanism. In order to prove the point made above, we shall use these two cases as perfect historical archetypes, neglecting to seek other samples in more distant and remote traditions, of which we are totally ignorant. To those who know we shall leave the task of inquiring whether the same conclusions we are about to draw from our chosen examples may be inferred from the literatures of the ancient and modern East, whether Far or Near: from the poetry of Iran and the Arabic world, as well as from the poetry of India and China.

Examining first the earlier of our two archetypes, we immediately see that the epos and the hexameter are born together; that the iamb rises originally with the passionate lyricism of Archilochus; that the further evolution of melic poetry coincides with the successive apparition, in monodic and choral variants, of more and more complicated strophic forms; and that finally the creation of the elegy is accompanied by the coupling together of the hexameter and the pentameter into the distich, which for this very reason is called elegiac. Passing to tragedy and comedy, which reflect a richer and more varied literary culture, we suddenly discover that they are polymetric: a phenomenon which should not unduly surprise us, since drama is a complex genre by nature and definition. At any rate, that polymetrism follows other norms than those of chance; even in tragedy or comedy the use of a particular verse form is subordinated to a particular genre effect. So for those "episodes" which now we prefer to call "scenes," the great Greek playwrights employed exclusively the iambic trimeter, which thus was made into the unique vehicle of dramatic dialogue, while for the lyrical interludes sung by the chorus they adopted the metrical medium of choral poetry, or the strophic structure of the Pindaric ode.

Before passing to our second archetype, we may, by way of digression and contrast, cast a glance at the special case of Roman literature. In its highest and most perfect phase, the latter may be simply defined as a Hellenistic literature written in Latin. Because of their own cultural lag, the Romans took at once the whole of Greek poetry for their province. According to the "law of combined development," they imitated at random, without following the pattern after which their model had originally unfolded. Yet at the very beginnings of Roman literature, before the Greek influence was effectively felt, there must have obtained a similar relationship between native meters and native genres. A sign of this might be seen in identical etymology of two literary terms: the word *saturnium*, indicating an indigenous verse form, which was to be superseded as soon as Latin poetry adapted Greek versification and prosody to itself; and the word *satura*, or satire, indicating the only literary genre which was a genuine Roman creation and which had been unknown to the Greeks.

Later Roman literature, following the example of the Alexandrians, took the observance of the established code for granted, not on the authority of history, which admits of development and change, but on the authority of an academic tradition received from outside, which was bound to remain fixed through the theory and practice of literary imitation. Only in the closing phase of Latin literature, as it had already happened at the decline of Hellenism, did all the rigid bonds joining together the verse (and the genre) system first relax, and then break down. A wave of experimentation, almost an anticipation of the modern vogue for endless technical and stylistic change, along with a constant shifting of taste between the opposite extremes of barbarism and decadence, ultimately led to the establishment of an eclectic poetics and a syncretic formalism.

If we now return to our archetypes, we shall see that the pattern repeats itself in the medieval poetry of the Romance world. We shall take our examples from the literatures of France and Spain, neglecting the literature of Italy, which remained for too long under the thumb of the Latin tradition, both scholastic and classical. In both French and Spanish medieval poetry we witness again the steady identification of a given meter with a given genre. So, for instance, the oldest variant of the French decasyllable is still called *épique* for being the invariable vehicle of the epic inspiration, as it manifested itself in the *chansons de geste*, and especially in the *Chanson de Roland*. As for the oldest variant of the alexandrine, it served only and always another kind of narrative, which was termed *roman* and which only in later times was bound first to replace the alexandrine with the octosyllable, and then to exchange verse for prose. Despite a curious coincidence (the author of the very early *Roman d'Alexandre* was also called Alexandre), it is both evident and significant that the alexandrine was so named not after that poet, but after the hero or title of his romance. This is the best proof that the alexandrine was practically born with the *genre romanesque*.

In Spain, the long and irregular double line in which the *Poema de Mio Cid* was couched cannot be found outside of the *cantares*, which correspond to the French *chansons de geste* and equally express the medieval epic genius in its most forthright manner. For another and shorter kind of poetic narrative, at once epic and lyrical, the poets of ancient Spain preferred instead a series of double eight-syllable lines, tied together by a single assonance. Such a series took the name of *romance*, a term designating, with significant equivocation, a metrical structure as well as a literary genre or sub-genre, both considered as popular or vernacular in character, as the name clearly suggests. As for *octosílabo*, created by the separation of the two hemistichs forming the original unit of the romance, it became later the vehicle of a more personal kind of lyricism and was then designated as *verso de arte menor*, in contrast with the irregular double six-syllable line, generally employed for religious and gnomic themes and therefore labeled *verso de arte mayor*. Such a terminology obviously implies an awareness of the correspondence of given metrical means with definite literary purposes or poetic pursuits, thus tending to prove that between poetics and metrics there is some sort of connecting link.

If now we briefly shift our attention to more learned and self-conscious poetic ages, or to more conventional and artificial literary cultures, we shall again discover the presence of such a link. This is certainly the case with a tradition of lyrical poetry opening with the Middle Ages and closing with the Renaissance. That tradition, which began with the Provençals' *gai saber*, unfolded into the Italian *dolce stil nuovo*, culminated in Petrarch, and ran its course after it had ruled for two centuries over the whole of Renaissance poetry under the name of Petrarchism. Its task, which it achieved in full, was to introduce at once a novel conception of lyricism and a corresponding set of verse forms.

The student of that tradition will note, for instance, that the Provençal *ensenhamens* were almost exclusively versification handbooks, treating in detail such stanzaic structures as the *balada* and the *chanso*, but neglecting to indicate the poetics of the new lyrical genre which those structures were supposed to serve, and which the authors of those handbooks merely subsumed. That part of *De vulgari eloquentia* where Dante chose to deal with the poetry in the vernacular was also meant as a versification treatise, developing at length the theory of the *canzone*, but failing to suggest what the literary aim of that medium was or was to be. Here we face again another example of the implicit existence of an unexpressed poetics within the detailed exposition of a metrical system interconnected with it.

Dante, like the Provençal theorists before him, took it for granted that the technical vehicle he was about to describe could not be aptly employed but for that poetry of spiritual love which was the exclusive concern of the *gai saber* and *dolce stil nuovo* schools. In the *Vita nuova* he once referred, with a passing stricture, to "coloro che rimano sopra altra materia che amorosa," showing by this critical allusion that what he found both remarkable and blameworthy was not the steady observance of the norm, but its casual breach. Along with this, one could not offer better proofs of the rigidity of the link between metrics and poetics within the same tradition than the refusal by most poets of the Italian Renaissance to use sonnets and *canzoni* for other kinds of lyrical inspiration than the one exemplified by Petrarchism, as well as the adoption of the Latin language and its meters on the part of other poets who felt the urge to express a less Platonic and more earthy *eros*, or a naturalistic world view. It is evident also that in the second of these two cases we witness the reciprocal subordination of an established rhetorical and formal code and of an unstated poetics chiefly related to subject matter and content.

A similar situation took place in a kind of narrative poem which triumphed in the Italian Renaissance, an aristocratic genre brought about by refining a popular precedent and by reshaping it into a more classical mold. After taking the *ottava* of his popular predecessors and employing it in a half-comic and half-heroic poem of his own, Pulci bequeathed it to Boiardo and Ariosto, who made of that stanza the distinctive seal of the chivalric romance, marking its difference from the epic poem written to imitate Homer and Virgil, which found its vehicle in the newly created blank verse. It is well known that Tasso tried to merge the two genres in his masterpiece, but the very fact that he wrote the *Gerusalemme* in *ottava rima* rather than in blank verse proves by itself that that work was primarily conceived, and was more successful, as a chivalric romance than as an epic poem.

There is no reason to examine in detail such an obvious link as that between the alexandrine couplet and the classical tragedy of France, or the far more complex bond tying the Elizabethan drama and the Spanish *comedia* to their respective repertories of verse forms. The Spanish *comedia* is polymetric in a far more extreme way than the tragedy or comedy of the Greeks; yet even there, to give a single example, serious personages and solemn scenes use different meters from those employed in ridiculous situations, or by such a comic stock character as the *gracioso*. As for the Elizabethan drama, everybody is acquainted with the special function performed within that genre by a nonmetrical medium, by those passages in prose which are the chosen vehicle of clowns and other plebeian characters, or the proper means to convey the absurd and formless language of madness or mental disease.

From all this we may expect that the organic relation between given genres and given meters which we have recognized in our two archetypal examples, or in the poetry of ancient Greece and of the early Romance world, repeats itself in the primitive literatures of the Germanic and Slavic peoples, and perhaps of the non-Western nations as well. We may further presume that in all learned, academic, and neoclassical periods similar norms are observed, and that they are fixed by the doctrine of convention and by the praxis of imitation. We may finally guess that in all cultivated, sophisticated, and decadent epochs (as we have already remarked in the case of Hellenistic and late Roman literature), the relation becomes confused and complicated, and that the search for novelty and the urge of technical experimentation lead to the triumph of eclecticism and syncretism even in this respect. Without facing the issue whether our age is indeed a decadent one, we must acknowledge that the condition just described seems to dominate the present literary picture.

The culture of which we are part is so self-conscious that it believes posterity will truly term our time "the age of criticism." It is therefore surprising that the main body of our poetics remains still unwritten. Truly enough, modern poetics seems to find an exuberant vocal expression in the manifestoes of our numberless movements. Such proclamations are, however, generally discredited since they produce only confusions and divisions, as is the case with all kinds of propaganda and advertisement. As for their positive assertions, they tend to be far less effective than the subtle prohibitions which even an unwritten poetics is often able to enforce, so to say, with a mute gesture. Precisely for being speechless, poetics frequently acts as a purely negative code: hence its tendency to proscribe, rather than prescribe, or to sanction a new distaste in lieu of a new taste. So, for instance, the surfeit provoked by centuries of sonneteering has brought about a tacit and yet rigid veto which prevents any contemporary Italian poet worthy of the name from trying his hand at sonnet writing.

The literary culture of our time is characterized by a paradoxical situation: on one side, by the prevalence of a very abstract kind of aesthetic thinking; on the other, by the almost invisible presence of a poetics which does not dare to spell out its name. The didactic function once accomplished by the great *artes poeticae* of the past is thus primarily performed by the all too concrete and unique revelations of the works of art themselves. Modern poetics reacts against such an usurpation apologetically, and seems content to reappear, disguised and compromised, in those prefaces by which the writers of our times plead their individual or special case, rather than the ideal and general cause of the genre which they both use and serve.

Yet, this state of things notwithstanding, during the last quarter century we have been witnessing a reawakening of interest in questions of poetics; and those who have been watching the literary scene with a sharper eye may have noticed a few signs indicating that modern poetics is already seeking to find written expressions, as well as unwritten ones. It is, for instance, noteworthy that Benedetto Croce, the philosopher of art who had debunked all aesthetic categories, wrote in later years an essay entitled *Per una poetica moderna*, where he recommended the rethinking of such notions as "classical," "romantic," and the like, or of the labels indicating trends and movements, rather than a redefinition of the concept of genre or a reformation of our system of genres. It is even more noteworthy that a creator like Igor Stravinsky chose the name "Poetics of Music" for a famous series of lectures where he exposed the private and public secrets of the craft of which he is the greatest living practitioner.

Yet the best pledge of a lasting and effective revival of poetics within the cultural consciousness of our age is to be seen not in these and other contributions by aestheticians and artists, but in the considerable spadework already done by a circle of critics and linguists. Such a circle, which unfortunately is no longer active, was the so-called Formalist school, which flourished in Russia for a span of twenty years, from just before the First World War to the early thirties. The Russian Formalists placed poetics at the very head of their vast and ambitious program of literary research. The modernity of their position is to be viewed not in their subject matter, since they studied genre systems other than the one prevailing in contemporary writing, but rather in the attention they paid to the tie between poetics and metrics, and in their pioneering attempts to determine the inner laws of meter and rhythm.

By doing so, they opened a new path, leading into different and even opposite directions from those toward which poetics had marched before. One must say that, despite all appearances to the contrary, classical poetics was primarily concerned not with literary effects per se but with psychological factors, ethical standards, and social values: a fact which may be easily proved by the decisive role played in the classical doctrine of tragedy by Aristotle's conception of the tragic hero, or by such notions as catharsis and decorum. It is not a paradox to maintain that classical poetics was substantially a poetics of content, and that it treated formalism only as a vague and general ideal. But modern poetics is, and should be first of all, a poetics of form, or rather of forms.

The plural is important, since our literary culture, like the whole of our civilization, is pluralistic and relativistic. Such a relativism affects more than anything else our literary and artistic standards, which are manifold and ever changing; and this is why the Russian Formalist school, despite and beyond its name, pursued a new literary morphology rather than a novel literary formalism. It is only by following their precedent and example that modern literary scholarship may soon be able to realize that historical poetics which another Russian philologist and literary historian, Alexander Veselovski, postulated more than half a century ago.

As for us Americans, we could make a good start toward such a goal by distinguishing in thought two things which our language fails to distinguish for us. In current American usage, the noun "criticism" confuses critical procedure and practice, which are what that word means in all continental languages, with critical theory and literary thought. If one wants to avoid that confusion in word as well as in concept, one could do worse than reserve the term "criticism" for the first, and to adopt the term "poetics" for the second, of these two tasks. There is no doubt in my mind that these two activities or disciplines are equally necessary for the growth of a vital literary culture.

THE ADDED ARTIFICER

One may very well wonder about the psychic urge, or cast of mind, that turns a writer into a translator, or makes him behave like one. Is that urge more or less identical with the one leading a painter or sculptor to make a copy? Even if the motive were the same, the outcome would still be different, since a translation is more than a mere study or unpretentious formal exercise. Would it be more correct to assume that the operation of translating does not differ too radically from interpretive performances such as playacting or, to adopt a more fitting simile, such as the public reading of a poem? In theory the difference may seem slight, but it is far from negligible in practice. The intent in playacting and poetry reading is to give voice and gesture to a verbal composition which, though physically mute and inert on the written or printed page, may speak and "act" eloquently by itself for the inner ear, and imaginary vision, of the "lonely crowd" of its readers. Translating, however, endeavors to give the verbal composition a strange clothing, a changed body, and a novel spirit. Should we then extend the previous analogy to another set of interpretive crafts, and suggest that translating is the literary equivalent of musical direction and execution? After all, like the performing musician, the translator goes to work only when he has another artist's creation before his eyes. The parallel may seem less misleading if we keep in mind that the complex technique of musical execution demands of its practitioners the deciphering and retranscribing of the whole score.

That translation is an interpretive art is a self-evident truth. Yet it is a paradox peculiar to the translator that he is the only interpretive artist working in a medium which is both identical with and different from that of the original he sets out to render in his own terms. Except for him, all artistic interpreters may be said to belong to one of the following categories. The first is that of the performing artist, who, whether he is an actor, singer, or instrumentalist, employs as his own vehicle the expressive material forming the aesthetic substance of the original work he is interpreting. The second is made up of all those artists I would like to call decorative, in the figurative sense of that epithet, and is exemplified by the scene designer, by the composer writing music to accompany a play or a ballet, by the mime or dancer reshaping words and tunes into facial gestures, bodily acts, and choreographic figures. Obviously the mime and the dancer who manipulate the pure stuff of their art, and treat their literary script or musical score as servants rather than as masters, are not interpreters, but creators in their own right. Otherwise, the artists of the decorative class are equivalents of the book illustrator, who is their archetype, and who, like them, uses a medium other than that which is specific to the work he is supposed to decorate or illustrate.

Giving the term a restricted and derogatory connotation, one might designate the artists of the first category as mere "interpreters," while the members of the second deserve to be called "translators" in a general or ideal sense. As for the artist whom we name translator in the normal and restricted meaning of that term, he is in a class by himself, since he works in a dual mode, and follows both methods at once. If we look at him from an abstract and generic perspective, we see that he molds the same aesthetic material as that of his model, namely, language. But if we replace that perspective with a more concrete and specific one, we discover that he elaborates a linguistic and literary material alien to, or estranged from, that of the text he translates. In scholastic terms, both original and translation deal with a single substance, differentiated into two unique, and incommensurable, accidents. It is this oddity, or quiddity, that changes the translator from a decorator into a re-creator, that turns him into an author or a poet, a lesser author or a minor poet, to be sure, but still a genuine one. From this viewpoint he stands at the opposite pole from the performing artist, whether musician, singer, or actor: especially from the last two, since the one dresses himself all too often in the peacock's feathers, and the other conceals his menial task under the cover of his professional "hypocrisy," to use a term that originally alluded to the hiding of the actor's face under the mask of his role.

Thus the translator is the only interpretive artist who reveals his modest calling and precious craft under the honest trademark of his name. By reducing all other interpretive artists to a common denominator, one can see that when compared to the translator most members of the second group are hardly more than simple transliterators, while those of the first descend to the level of mere scribes. The truth of this must not allow us to forget that the nature of the translator's task denies him an opportunity that lies within the grasp of his more fortunate rivals. A few of them, like the illustrator who takes his text as a pretext, may become original creators by transcending rather than by transposing their model. What enables them to achieve this feat is the absolute estrangement of their technical modes from those of the original work. The translator cannot be original in the same degree because he works with images and words which, like a grafted branch or even a transplanted tree, still owe their life to a seed planted elsewhere by other hands. This is the reason that the translator cannot share with any one of his fellow adapters or remakers the classical definition of *artifex additus artifici*, which suits him alone, even though originally it was not coined for his exclusive benefit.

As in the case of every interpretive artist, the chief task of the translator seems to be the transposing of an alien aesthetic personality into the key of his own. If this is true, then the most relevant question one can ask is whether, when he feels his way toward the foreign text — close contact with which will finally ignite the vital spark — the translator looks at that text in a mirror reflecting the other or the self. It is my contention that, like the original poet, the translator is a Narcissus who in this case chooses to contemplate his own likeness not in the spring of nature but in the pool of art. This may not apply to those translators who flourished in other more traditional cultures, and who took upon themselves the single task of rendering into the living speech of their own nation or people the sacred books of divine revelation and of ancient wisdom. If the translators of the Holy Writ worked only in teams of scholar-priest, searching through the babel of tongues for no other mirror than that reflecting the Word of God, the individual authors of those pre-Renaissance vernacular versions of the classics, which took in Italian the significant name of *volgarizzamenti* (a word containing already, at least potentially, the very meaning it would acquire only in our time), acted primarily as servants of culture, as transmitters of a beauty or truth which would be lost without them. Using the dichotomy by which Schiller divided the poetic world of the ancients from that of the moderns, one could define the trans-

lators of that old-fashioned type as "naive" and those of the type
we now know as "sentimental." This is another way of saying that
the translator of our time is, like all moderns, a highly subjective
artist. It seems evident to me that the modern translator, like the
modern artist, strives after self-expression, although the self-expression may well be a not too literal expression of the self. The
experience he tries to fix within an alien framework may be either
psychological or cultural, or both: it may be rooted in history, or
even in biography. In brief, the translator, no less than the literary
creator, tries to reshape within his work an *Erlebnis* in the Diltheyan
sense of the term.

In reality, what Dilthey named *Erlebnis* does not differ too
greatly from what more traditional thinkers or more conventional
critics are wont to name with the old-fashioned designation of content. Yet, if such a conception is applied to the translator, it seems
at first sight that he works without a content of his own. This is the
generally accepted hypothesis, so well conveyed by the images describing translating as the decanting of a liquid from one vessel into
another, or as the pouring of an old wine into a new bottle. Both
metaphors obviously suggest that there is a single content, the original one, supplying the one thing or substance that remains unchanged, or hardly changed in the translating process. Both similes,
within the limits of the hypothesis they express, are apt and proper
in more ways than one. Their greatest merit lies in the dialectical
complexity of their very images, which thus qualify and modify the
hypothesis itself. So the first metaphor implies that, during the
operation of decanting or pouring, the liquid may be spilled, or
more than a negligible part of the original content may be lost. As
for the second metaphor, it may suggest the altogether paradoxical
case of an *old* wine breaking a *new* bottle. All this notwithstanding,
both metaphors are dangerously misleading: the student of translation can no longer be satisfied with the conventional supposition
that what takes place during the operation is but a change of containers, affecting only slightly the decanted content.

It may well be an error to believe that the translator has nothing
to offer but an empty vessel which he fills with a liquor he could
not distill by himself. One should play, at least tentatively, with
the contrary hypothesis; one should even suppose, using a related if
opposite image, that the translator himself is a living vessel satu-

rated with a formless fluid or sparkling spirit, which he cannot hold any longer in check; that when the spirit is about to fizzle, or the liquid to overflow, he pours it into the most suitable of all the containers available to him, although he neither owns the container nor has he molded it with his own hands. Were this true, one could even claim that translating is like pouring a new wine into an old bottle; and that if the wine fails to burst the bottle, it is only because the new wine required the old bottle as the only form or frame within which it could rest. To accept such a hypothesis one must believe, with the protagonist of *Dr. Zhivago*, the novel by the great Russian poet Boris Pasternak (who, by the way, is also a great translator of Shakespeare), that art is not "an object or aspect of form, but rather a mysterious and hidden component of content." According to such a view, the translator is a literary artist looking outside himself for the form suited to the experience he wishes to express.

This seems to run against the usual presupposition that the translator is not a creator or a poet but merely an artisan or a craftsman of words, by which one means that he himself has nothing to say. Yet one must reject the notion that the translator's is a voice singing tunes that others have composed for him. The view that he is a shallow virtuoso or an empty formalist is fundamentally wrong. There are, to be sure, translators of this sort, but they are not exemplary ones: even among so-called original authors there are also artists of the same breed. The translator who aims solely at reproducing the web or shell of an alien poem through his own technical skill should be considered an imitator, and treated as if he were an unconscious parodist (not a plagiarist, because to plagiarize means to copy, and the very necessity of re-creating a foreign original into another set of verbal norms prevents the translator from copying, even if he wants to). At any rate what moves the genuine translator is not a mimetic urge, but an elective affinity: the attraction of a content so appealing that he can identify it with a content of his own, thus enabling him to control the latter through a form which, though not inborn, is at least congenial to it.

Such a hypothesis turns translation into a kind of *Gelegenheitsdichtung*, in a sense which is not at too great variance with the Goethean use of that term. Through the shock of a recognition primarily psychic in quality, the translator suddenly finds that a poem newly discovered, or discovered anew, offers him an exemplary solution for his own formal problems, as well as an expressive outlet for his subjective *Erlebnis*. The foreign poem becomes for him a "model," in the sense that this word has recently acquired in the field of scientific theory and inquiry. It is in such a context that we can define translation as a form of literary mimesis, and in such a context alone. If this is true, then translation is, both formally and psychologically, a process of inscape rather than of escape; and this is why, of all available aesthetic concepts, the best suited to define the activity and the experience of the translator is that of *Einfühlung* or "empathy," which must not be understood merely as the transference of an emotional content. The foreign poem is not merely an object, but an archetype, which provokes an active spiritual impact. The translator is peculiarly *disponible*, to use an epithet which was very dear to André Gide, a man of letters who paid tribute to translation in words and deeds, and who publicly praised literary influence and the writer's willingness to submit to it.

The *disponibilité* of the translator is primarily formal, precisely because an external formal sanction is the main object of his quest. There is no paradox in maintaining that this leads us to a psychological theory of translation, and even in claiming that such a theory must be a Freudian one. Yet the translator is not an inhibited person; he is rather an inhibited artist, satisfied only when he is able to lay the burning ashes of his heart in a well-wrought urn outside of himself. Or one can say that he succeeds in overcoming his repressions only in his tête-à-tête with a foreign poet; and that he ends by sublimating his inhibitions through the catharsis of an alien form. Translation is up to a point an exorcism or, if we prefer, the conjuration, through another spirit, of one's Self. Using for our own purpose the title of the famous play by Pirandello, one may say that the translator is a "character in search of an author," in whom he can identify, or at least transpose, a part of himself. Such identification is not an impersonation; it is rather a transference, in the psychoanalytic meaning of the term. The translator is not a masquerader who deceives others as well as himself by acting an alien role or by aping somebody else: the ultimate mimesis for which he is striving is after all an aesthetic one. He is a character who, in finding an author without, finds also the author within himself.

There may be some sense in the claim that the translator even more than the critic is a poet *manqué*, but this applies not to the translator's achievement, but rather to his pursuit or quest. Nor must we forget that such a quest or pursuit may intermittently attract the original writer also, when he too must search anew for the author in himself.

The process by which an artistic personality is "transposed" into the key of another takes place on such a mysterious plane that critical evaluation must content itself with inarticulate acknowledgments — a nod of approval, an outburst of applause, or some graphic sign of enthusiasm such as the exclamation point the reader traces on the margin of his text. When looking at the raw material which the translator molds and reshapes into a work of his own, however, the critic finds a set of concrete problems that may and must be submitted to detailed analysis and elaborate judgment. Here the terms of comparison are not only the language of the original work and the language of the translated one, but even more the two literary traditions involved. It is difficult, but possible, to establish a critical bridge between them. To a foreign reader any literary composition, even if relatively near in spirit and time, always looks in part or in degree like an exotic product. This impression of exoticism is often due to the very traits that make the work intimate and familiar to the native reader. How should the translator deal with such traits? Should he reduce them to a maximum, or a minimum, degree? Should he attenuate or accentuate the effects implied in details like these? In simple terms, should the translator's diction tend toward under- or overstatement? Or, in a broader literary context, should he lean toward the splendid anonymity, toward the glorious commonplaceness of classical taste, or toward that picturesque emphasis, that sense of local color, that predilection for the characteristic and the unique, which distinguish the romantic outlook? These are some of the questions which the critic of translation must ask of the translator and his work. The translator addresses the same questions to himself, and answers them, both in theory and practice, through a written or unwritten *ars poetica* of his own.

If these are the most pertinent questions, the only ones really worth asking, I wonder whether we can still consider unavoidable the double alternative suggested by the well-known French saying

that translations are like women, homely when faithful and unfaithful when lovely. After all, in every artistic pursuit beauty is
the highest kind of fidelity, and ugliness is only another name for
disloyalty: there is no literary genre where immorality is less
frowned on than translation itself. Its immorality is to be seen only
in transgressing the precept of Dante Gabriel Rossetti, according to
which no good poem should ever be turned into a bad one. A famous
aesthetician maintains that the modes of the ugly are many, and
yet easy to classify, while the beautiful has in each case a mode
that is at once universal and unique. If this is true, then Novalis
was right in claiming that successful translations can be only
verändernde, or "metamorphic," not literal. The gifted translator is
an alchemist who changes a piece of gold into another piece of
gold, thus obeying Rossetti's rule in full.

Those who repeat approvingly the old Italian pun making a *tradi-
tore* of every *traduttore* forget that the translator becomes the traitor
only out of necessity and against his will. The good translator errs
almost always in good faith; his greatest vice is not falsity, but ignorance, which is one of the blessings of innocence as well as one
of its frailties. Ignorance leads primarily to sins of omission, which
are venial ones. Outrageous as the mistakes of a translator may
appear, they are faults, not wrongdoings, a fact all too often over-
looked by his critics, who in this seem still to follow the old-fashioned practice of pointing out failings and failures, rather than
merits and *réussites*. The reviewer of a translation in print, who,
before recognizing its worth with faint, final praise that sounds like
a supercilious dismissal, yields for too long to the nasty self-indul-
gence of *Schadenfreude*, endlessly and sneeringly listing all the
occasions on which the poor translator fumbled and stumbled, is a
worse sinner than he. There is no other literary situation where a
plea for critical fairness is equally overdue.

The mythology of translation all too often compares the plight
of the translator to that of Tantalus and Sisiphus, thus emphasizing
the helplessness of his role. Heine made the same point when with
a quaint image he defined the translator's attempt to recapture the
ravishing and vanishing beauty of his model as "straw-plaiting sun-
beams." Heine seemingly forgot that the poet tries to achieve the
same miracle, and that he succeeds only rarely in doing so. How
many mystics or symbolists have claimed that even original poetry

is a form of translation, an attempt to rephrase the heavenly music that many can no longer hear in the noisy chaos of this world! Yet the fact that the translator tries to reproduce at once two pre-established harmonies, one of which has already been shaped into literary form, does not necessarily mean that he must accept the latter as his absolute aesthetic norm. He may well break the pattern he has chosen, before rebuilding it anew. Many critics think otherwise, and this is why they make too much of the difference between translating into verse and translating into prose. (If I use the preposition *into* rather than *from*, it is because the distinction so suggested is the more significant of the two.) Yet translation is not a composition, as the Italians say, on a set of *rime obbligate*; its measure is never given beforehand. The challenge of the original predetermines an infinite number of responses: and one may easily mention numberless instances of the rendering of poetic works into non-metered speech. Even such a master of versecraft as Mallarmé, who believed that verse was the whole of literature, chose to translate Poe's poems into prose. One could also list a few of the rarer occasions when a work originally composed in *sermo solutus* was subjected by some of its translators to the yoke of rhyme or to the rule of rhythm. To cite a single case, which is also a famous example, Melchiorre Cesarotti transformed the leaden prose of Macpherson's Ossian, through the alchemy of his Italian translation, into a golden blank verse. At any rate the miracle of translating may differ in degree, but not in kind, when its medium is prose rather than verse. The only differentiation worth making is between a translation undertaken with an artistic intent, provided it achieves the intent it strives for, and a translation which aims at being nothing more than a pedagogical tool: a type that does not exclude the far less educational intent of helping the lazy student unable to translate Horace, Virgil, or Cicero by himself. Functional and utilitarian as this type of translation is, it is effective only in a constant reference to the original, without which it has no independent existence. Artistic translation presupposes, however, both the ideal presence of the original and its physical absence. This is the reason the Abbé Galiani recommended that a good translation be read for itself, without comparing it to the original work.

Ars est celare artem: if this principle is but a matter of tactics for any creative artist, it becomes a matter of strategy for the man of letters who cannot call himself an author precisely because he gives his voice to another one. The aesthetic inhibition that leads a littérateur to become a translator (either permanently or intermittently) does not easily transform itself into its own opposite, even in the most successful, or unsuccessful, cases. The ethos of the translator is a perfect blend of humility and pride. His two greatest virtues or assets are the reverence he feels toward the author or work he translates, and the sense of his own integrity as an interpreter, which is based on both modesty and self-respect. It is this alliance of independence and honesty that saves him from the temptation of peddling under his own trademark wares manufactured by others, even though he often remolds them after a design that is at least in part his own. There is no literary worker more respectful of the property of his fellow artist, none less willing to infringe on what takes the legal name of copyright. The translator always gives full credit, sometimes even more credit than is due, to the maker of a blueprint that he could not use without considerably changing and adapting it. All these characteristics indicate that the translator is perhaps the only modern artist who acts and behaves as if he were only an artisan, "pure in heart" and "poor in spirit," serving with simple and single-minded devotion a beauty to which he cannot give his name, and yet not unaware of the nobility of his calling, of the dignity of his task.

The critic must never forget that translation is an art in the old sense of the term, a sense which has disappeared in the word "artist," but which is still preserved in the word "artisan." In brief, translation must still be considered a craft. Thus the practical criticism of translation must deal, even more than in the case of original literary creation, with what the French call *questions de métier*. While the total judgment of the value of a translation (which, like all values, is a value per se) must be a synthetic judgment, a judgment *a priori*, thus involving no parallel with the original text, the analysis of the technical problems that the translation has faced and solved cannot be made without comparisons and contrasts. The comparisons and contrasts need not turn exclusively on the relation of the translation to the original work. They should extend to its relations with the particular literary traditions to which the original and the translation belong. If we cannot relate a uniquely personal style to another style equally personal and unique, we can and must relate two historical styles, as well as all possible historical variations within each of them. Perhaps there is no literary genre where the comparative method is an apter tool of critical investigation than translation itself. The literary equivalent of the stylistic tendency which in the field of painting takes the name of "mannerism" is after all never so frequent as in the field of translation: and the latter should perhaps be considered as the most typical and perfect manifestation of what Friedrich Schlegel once called *Poesie der Poesie* (although its author wanted to define by that formula the attempt to translate the poetry of the world into the poetry of the word).

Yet, when all is said, the translator is something more than a "mannerist," than a "poet of poetry," than an artisan or juggler of words. Even when he seems attracted only by the novel and the strange, by the foreign and the exotic, by the innovations or experimentations of an alien advance-guard of which he wants to become the representative *in partibus infidelium*, the translator is always a humanist, a worshiper of tradition, a believer in the eternal values of arts and letters. In every translation there is always, even if it is hidden or buried, a vein of classicism. The whole poetics of translation could be reduced to a single tenet, that of *la difficulté vaincue*, which implies on one side the free acceptance, or better the deliberate choice, of a resistant, even refractory material and, on the other, the hard-won triumph of the worker, who by the will of his mind and the skill of his hand succeeds in remolding and reshaping that material into the orderly pattern of art. Yet the translator is classical also in a less formal sense: as I have already said, he is a kind of humanist. Like the humanist, he is at once a learner and a teacher, or a cultivator of *humanitas*, which involves both appraisal and learning, and which nobody has defined so pointedly as Aulus Gellius in a celebrated passage of *The Attic Nights*: "Those who created the Latin tongue and spoke it well never gave *humanitas* the notion inherent in the Greek word *philanthropia*. They gave that word the meaning of what the Greeks call *paideia*, i.e., knowledge of the fine arts." The noble paradox of his craft allows the translator, however, to transcend even this distinction: far from being a mere humanistic pedagogue, he may often become a humanitarian *Aufklärer*, serving even higher causes than "the aesthetic education of the human kind."

All this simply means that the translator's total function cannot be defined except through each one of his manifold tasks. Let us not forget that he often willingly pays the tribute which the human mind owes to science by contributing to learning and knowledge as well as to beauty and art. Sometimes the translator must take erudition as his province; often, like Martianus Capella's Mercury, he must marry Philology, who is not always a lovely maid. The variety and multiplicity of the gifts required of him make the great translator as infrequent an apparition as the great critic, who, as everybody knows, is an even rarer bird than the great poet. Yet literature cannot afford to do without good translators; in given situations, it may well need them even more than good authors. Translators are after all the most cosmopolitan among the citizens of the Republic of Letters; their absence from the scene, or their presence in a too limited number, may mean that the literary tradition will rest all too easily within the Chinese wall it has erected around itself. By denying itself a look beyond that wall, a literature is bound to die of slow exhaustion or, as Goethe said, of self-boredom. Especially in modern times, a national literature reveals its power of renewal and revival through the quality and number of its translators. Sometimes it is able to survive only because of their efforts. We know all too well that a culture survives only by a proper response to the challenge of change, and by its timely refusal to go on aping itself.

PUBLISHER'S NOTE
INDEX

PUBLISHER'S NOTE

Renato Poggioli had written a bibliographical postscript for this volume, but it was not quite complete. We present a summarized version of his draft here, together with certain necessary additions. The essays, with their publishing histories, are listed according to their arrangement in this volume. At the outset we should like to say that all essays are included here with the generous permission of the original publishers. Only minor changes have been made, most of them by Mr. Poggioli.

"The Igor Tale." English version of the introduction to *Cantare della gesta di Igor: Epopea russa del XII secolo*, introduction, translation, and commentary by Renato Poggioli; annotated critical text by Roman Jakobson (Turin: Einaudi, 1954). Permission granted by Franz J. Horch Associates, New York, and Agenzia Letteraria Internazionale, Milan. Translation by Patricia Arant, as revised by R. P. English text published here for the first time.

"Tragedy or Romance? A Reading of the Paolo and Francesca Episode in Dante's *Inferno*." From *Publications of the Modern Language Association*, LXXV (June 1957).

"Pascal's Classicism: Psychological, Aesthetic, and Scriptural." First version in Italian published in *Letteratura*, May–June 1947. Rewritten for *Harvard Library Bulletin*, Autumn 1960. [In his original draft of his bibliographical postscript, Mr. Poggioli had this sentence: "I cannot mention the title of the latter without mentioning the name of its former editor, George W. Cottrell, Jr., one of the many American friends who have helped my literary work with their wise counsel and useful advice."]

"Tolstoy as Man and Artist." From *Oxford Slavonic Papers*, X (1962).

"Pirandello in Retrospect." First drafted in 1939. Written originally as a lecture and given at Brown University in 1940. Published in *Italian Quarterly*, I (Winter 1958).

"A Note on Italo Svevo." Preface to Svevo's *Confessions of Zeno*, translated by Beryl de Zoete (New York: New Directions, 1948).

"Leo Ferrero's *Angelica*." First drafted in 1939. Published after the war as the preface to the first Italian edition: *Leo Ferrero: Angelica*, satiric drama with commentary by Renato Poggioli and a note by Guglielmo Ferrero (Florence: Fratelli Parenti, 1946). English text, translated by Frances Keene, published here for the first time.

"The Italian Success Story." From the final issue of *Wake*, XII (Winter 1953–54).

"The Poetry of St.-J. Perse." Written in Italian and translated by Lowry Nelson for *Yale French Studies*, I (Fall–Winter 1948). Italian version appeared later in *Inventario*, III (1951).

"Mythology of Franz Kafka." Reworking of essay in Italian published in
    Solaria, March 1938. English text, translated by John G. Conley, was
    included, under the title "Kafka and Dostoyevsky," in *The Kafka
    Problem*, a critical miscellany edited by Angel Flores (New York: New
    Directions, 1946).
"Trotsky's Diary in Exile." From *The Yale Review*, Winter 1959 (copy-
    right Yale University Press).
"The Death of the Sense of Tragedy." First published in Italian in *Inventario*,
    II (1946). Condensed English translation in *Voices*, Summer 1947.
"For a Literary Historiography Based on Pareto's Sociology." First published
    in Italian in *Inventario*, Winter 1949. Translated by Frederic T.
    Jackson, as revised by R. P., and published in *Symposium*, I (May
    1949).
"The Artist in the Modern World." From *The Graduate Journal*, VI (Winter
    1964).
"Poetics and Metrics." Paper delivered at the Second Congress of the In-
    ternational Comparative Literature Association; included in the first
    volume of the *Proceedings* of the congress (Chapel Hill: University of
    North Carolina Press, 1959).
"The Added Artificer." From *On Translation*, edited by Reuben A. Brower
    (Cambridge: Harvard University Press, 1959).

Harvard University Press would like to thank all those who have helped
in preparing this volume for publication, especially Harry Levin and Renata
Poggioli.

INDEX